Religion, Race, and the Making of Confederate Kentucky, 1830–1880

This book sheds new light on the role of religion in the nineteenth-century slavery debates. In it, Luke E. Harlow argues that ongoing conflict over the meaning of Christian "orthodoxy" constrained the political and cultural horizons available for defenders and opponents of American slavery. The central locus of these debates was Kentucky, a border slave state with a long-standing antislavery presence. Although white Kentuckians famously cast themselves as moderates in the period and remained with the Union during the Civil War, their religious values showed no moderation on the slavery question. When the war ultimately brought emancipation, white Kentuckians found themselves in lockstep with the rest of the Confederate South. Racist religion thus paved the way for the making of Kentucky's Confederate memory of the war, as well as a deeply entrenched white Democratic Party in the state.

Luke E. Harlow is Assistant Professor of History at the University of Tennessee, Knoxville. His published work has appeared in *Slavery and Abolition*, *Ohio Valley History*, and the *Register of the Kentucky Historical Society*. He is the co-editor of *Religion and American Politics: From the Colonial Period to the Present*.

Cambridge Studies on the American South

Series Editors:

Mark M. Smith, *University of South Carolina, Columbia*
David Moltke-Hansen, *Center for the Study of the American South, University of North Carolina at Chapel Hill*

Interdisciplinary in its scope and intent, this series builds upon and extends Cambridge University Press's long-standing commitment to studies on the American South. The series not only will offer the best new work on the South's distinctive institutional, social, economic, and cultural history but will also feature works in national, comparative, and transnational perspectives.

Titles in the Series

Religion, Race, and the Making of Confederate Kentucky, 1830–1880

LUKE E. HARLOW

University of Tennessee, Knoxville

CAMBRIDGE
UNIVERSITY PRESS

CAMBRIDGE
UNIVERSITY PRESS

University Printing House, Cambridge CB2 8BS, United Kingdom

Cambridge University Press is part of the University of Cambridge.

It furthers the University's mission by disseminating knowledge in the pursuit of education, learning and research at the highest international levels of excellence.

www.cambridge.org
Information on this title: www.cambridge.org/9781316620649

First published 2014
First paperback edition 2016

A catalogue record for this publication is available from the British Library

Library of Congress Cataloguing in Publication data
Harlow, Luke E.
Religion, race, and the making of Confederate Kentucky, 1830–1880 / Luke E. Harlow.
    pages   cm. – (Cambridge studies on the American South)
Includes bibliographical references and index.
ISBN 978-1-107-00089-6 (hardback)
1. Antislavery movements – Kentucky.   2. Abolitionists – Kentucky.   3. Kentucky – History –
Civil War, 1861–1865.   4. Christianity and politics – Kentucky – History – 19th century.
I. Title.
E445.K5H37   2014
976.9′03–dc23   2013044709

ISBN 978-1-107-00089-6 Hardback
ISBN 978-1-316-62064-9 Paperback

Cambridge University Press has no responsibility for the persistence or accuracy of URLs for external or third-party internet websites referred to in this publication, and does not guarantee that any content on such websites is, or will remain, accurate or appropriate.

for Amber

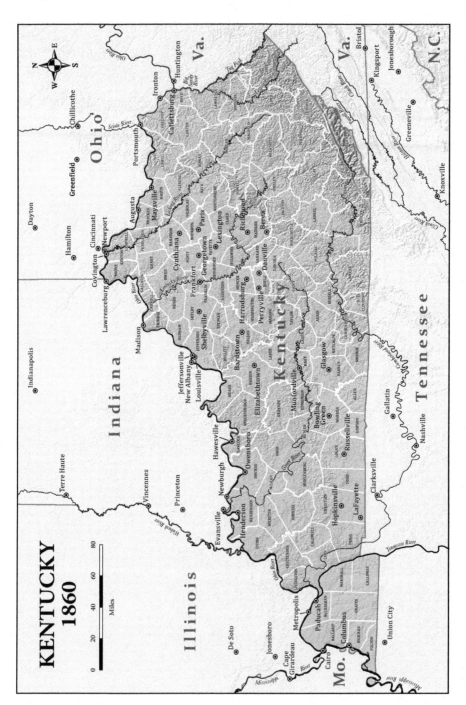

Kentucky, 1860

Contents

Acknowledgments

This book began as a doctoral dissertation at Rice University under the direction of John Boles. As much as in this project's earliest stages, the finished work is indebted to John's advice and care. His students are familiar with his palpable enthusiasm for their projects, which is inspiring. Specifically for the range of questions that animate this book, there was no better mentor. Yet more broadly, for the range of questions that animate academic life, John's wisdom has always proven sage.

Mark Noll's influence on this project has also been profound. When I was his MA student, he first pointed me to the multiplicity of religious perspectives on American slavery, and his direction originally led me to think about Kentucky as the locus of the religious struggle over the slavery question. Having read most of what I have written on that subject for more than a decade, Mark has been a faithful guide.

I also owe much to Vernon Burton, who encouraged me early on to pursue answers to complicated moral questions in American history. His support for this book was often sustaining. Becky Goetz's keen insights about race and Christianity gave shape to the project in an early phase, and she has been a major source of encouragement throughout the process. I owe many of my central interpretive insights about the slavery debates to ongoing exchanges with Caleb McDaniel. His meticulous analysis helped transform the dissertation into a book. Michael Emerson has taught me as much as any scholar about race and American religion, and Randal Hall's advice has been indispensable. Bethany Johnson read the final manuscript of this book with her renowned editorial judgment. That task alone deserves many thanks, but she was a mentoring and reassuring voice well before that effort.

As a student at Western Kentucky University, I had no interest in Kentucky's history, but that had little to do with my professors, who were some of the finest teachers any undergraduate could hope for. I was first drawn to the histories of slavery and emancipation, the Civil War era, and American religion in the classrooms of Marion Lucas and Larry Snyder, and their counsel did not end when I graduated. At Wheaton College, Kathryn Long provided first-rate advice. At Rice University, I learned much about framing the ideas in this book from Carl Caldwell, Ira Gruber, Thomas Haskell, Alex Lichtenstein, Allen Matusow, Carol Quillen, and Martin Wiener. At Oakland University, I thank Dan Clark, Todd Estes, Derek Hastings, Craig Martin, and Karen Miller for their collegiality and good cheer. The University of Tennessee, Knoxville, has been an ideal intellectual home. My colleagues in the history department are engaging and dynamic, and it has been a pleasure to complete this book on the sixth floor of Dunford Hall. I especially thank department heads Tom Burman and Ernie Freeberg for their support and mentorship, as well as Chad Black, Monica Black, Dan Feller, and Tore Olsson for their perspectives on the ideas in this book.

Two friends have helped me think about this project since the beginning. Karl Gunther deserves much praise for his unending willingness to read and critique my arguments. His knowledge of the world of sixteenth-century radical English Protestants has always helped clarify my own thinking about religious polemics three centuries later; on the other side of the Atlantic. Rusty Hawkins has also added much to this work, first as a classmate in graduate seminars and later as a measured voice whose work on twentieth-century evangelicals and massive resistance to civil rights has pointed to a latter-day version of the struggle described in this book. In general, my colleagues at Rice were the most vibrant and supportive a developing historian might imagine. This book is the product of many influential conversations with Drew Bledsoe, Andrew Canady, Greg Eow, Gale Kenny, Allison Madar, Scott Marler, Carl Paulus, Wes Phelps, Jim Wainwright, Marty Wauck, Ben Wise, and Ann Ziker.

Heath Carter and Charles Irons patiently helped me work through many complex interpretive issues. But more than that, I thank them for their friendship. Greg Downs has also been an invaluable interlocutor and friend; this book is the better for his intellectual generosity. I am grateful to Joseph Moore and Laura Porter for their ongoing engagement with my ideas and their willingness to push against my moments of sloppy thinking. I also thank Aaron Astor, Ed Blum, Darren Grem, Paul Harvey, Jacob Lee, Anne Marshall, Ethan Schrum, John David Smith, and Mitchell Snay, who each provided crucial insights throughout the project.

Mark Smith and David Moltke-Hansen exercised a wonderful balance of criticism and enthusiasm as series editors, which greatly improved the book from its earliest forms. At Cambridge University Press, Eric Crahan, Lewis Bateman, and Shaun Vigil provided key guidance through the publishing process. I am pleased to recognize the efforts of Will Fontanez and the University of Tennessee Cartographic Laboratory in creating the map of Kentucky in 1860. I thank as well Anne Barrington for her work on the index. Generous financial support came from the Filson Historical Society, the Kentucky Historical

Society, Rice University's History Department and the Office of Graduate and Postdoctoral Studies, the University Research Committee at Oakland University, and the University of Tennessee, Knoxville. The Summer Seminar program at Calvin College enabled me to work through part of this book with a remarkable group of colleagues in a 2010 interdisciplinary symposium on "The Power of Race in American Religion." Administrative personnel in the various history departments that I have been affiliated with have been essential in facilitating the work that went into this book: Paula Platt and Rachel Zepeda at Rice University; Janet Chandler and Joanna McReynolds at Oakland University; and Mary Beckley, Kim Harrison, and Bernie Koprince at the University of Tennessee.

Support staffs at many libraries and archives made it much easier for me to complete the necessary research for this book. At the Filson Historical Society, I thank Glenn Crothers, Jim Holmberg, Jacob Lee, Mike Veach, and Mark Wetherington. At the Kentucky Historical Society, I am pleased to acknowledge Nelson Dawson, Darrell Meadows, and Beth Van Allen. Shannon Wilson and Jaime Bradley at Berea College went above and beyond any normal expectations. At the University of Tennessee, Knoxville, Anne Bridges has been indispensable. Maggie Yancey provided useful research assistance in the project's final stages. I also thank the library and archival staffs at Baylor University, Centre College, Eastern Kentucky University, JKM Library, the University of Kentucky, the University of Louisville, Louisville Presbyterian Theological Seminary, the University of Michigan, Rice University's Fondren Library and Kelley Center for Government Information and Microforms, Southern Baptist Theological Seminary, Wayne State University, and Western Kentucky University. During visits to various archives and during the writing process, Heath and Thais Carter, Tommy and Ruby Kidd, Keith and Christen Morgan, Brian and Lee Ann Payne, Bruce and Sara Williams, and Larry and Sheila Witten helpfully provided lodging and meals.

Different, and earlier, versions of the work here appeared as "Religion, Race, and Robert J. Breckinridge: The Ideology of an Antislavery Slaveholder, 1830–1860," *Ohio Valley History* 6.3 (Fall 2006): 1–24; "Neither Slavery Nor Abolitionism: James M. Pendleton and the Problem of Christian Conservative Antislavery in 1840s Kentucky," *Slavery and Abolition* 27.3 (December 2006): 367–89; "Slavery, Race, and Political Ideology in the White Christian South Before and After the Civil War," in *Religion and American Politics: From the Colonial Period to the Present*, 2nd ed., ed. Mark A. Noll and Luke E. Harlow (New York: Oxford University Press, 2007), 203–24; and "The Religion of Proslavery Unionism: Kentucky Whites on the Eve of Civil War," *Register of the Kentucky Historical Society* 110.3–4 (Summer/Autumn 2012): 265–91. I am grateful for the permission to republish this material, and I thank the many editors, anonymous reviewers, commentators, and audiences who have helped shape the ideas that appear in the pages that follow. Comments from Fitzhugh Brundage, Charles Israel, Jim Klotter, Elizabeth Leonard, John

Quist, George Rable, and Clarence Taylor greatly refined my thinking on the project.

I have drawn significant support from my extended family. Mike and Betty Miller have long shown much interest in the subjects of my work. I also thank Seth, Ashley, and Waylon Miller; Ian and Danielle Miller; and Zach Miller for their love. I am not a Kentuckian, but my father, Gary, is. Kentucky is also the state where he met my mother, Bette. This acknowledgment is inadequate reciprocation for the love they have always shown me, but this book would not exist – in ways literal and figurative – without the two of them. Somehow two mathematical minds managed to produce a historian, and they always found ways to encourage the curiosities and questions of a son who was more taken with the written word than formulas and equations. My sister, Emily Davis, and brother, Grant Harlow, are the most wonderful siblings – and friends – I can imagine. The additions that have joined them in the family, Kyle and Madilyn, and Nicole, have added much to the joy of being their brother.

My immediate family is the exceptional and overwhelming wellspring of all good things that I know in this life. My daughter, Hope, was born toward the end of the research and writing of this book. Although she knows little about the shape of my work, her life is more of an inspiration than she can possibly imagine. Her presence is a daily invocation of the significance of her namesake. My wife, Amber, has lived with this project from the start. There are times when it is a cliché to claim that "no words exist" to express one's gratitude and affection – but this is not one of those times. To document the ways that Amber has been my source of strength and vitality would require a book of its own. I have devoted much effort to the study of humanity's darkness, but Amber's love is an ongoing reminder that there is light that illumines even the deepest of shadows. This work's dedication is only a small acknowledgment of my own love for her.

Introduction

This book tells the story of Kentucky in the era of the American Civil War. It explains how a slaveholding state that remained with the Union during the conflict, which claimed a long-standing and variegated antislavery tradition before the war, came to see itself as part of the Confederate project after the fact. This book is about the role of conservative evangelical Protestant theology in driving the course of American political and cultural history in nineteenth-century America. It is also a book about the great slavery debates of that century: it tracks the fate of gradual emancipationism and the vitality of proslavery belief from 1830 to 1880. But because of the centrality of white Kentucky believers in defining the contours of argument about slavery in the United States, this book's purview and argument address a great deal more than what happened within the boundaries of one state. The argument is straightforward: to fail to understand the significance of conservative evangelical theology or Kentucky is to fail to understand the American struggle over slavery and abolition more broadly.

After the American Revolution, the Northwest Ordinance of 1787 defined the territory north of the Ohio River as free soil, whereas lands to the south retained slavery. That division would profoundly shape the region up to the Civil War. Early American migrants into the Ohio Valley came from a variety of ideological persuasions, and they held conflicting views about the place slavery should occupy in the American nation. That conflict never waned: the region remained contested ground throughout the nineteenth century. Six hundred sixty-four miles of the Ohio River touched both the slave soil of Kentucky and the free soil of Ohio, Indiana, and Illinois – the longest of any slave state/free state border. The river's physical fluidity highlighted the range of ideological positions on slavery that marked the region – it was as much the Lower North as it was the Upper South. Given the close proximity of slavery to freedom, the Ohio Valley became a key locus of the contest over the slavery question.[1]

In Kentucky – a slave state on the border – religious believers on each side of the debate came into direct contact with one another as nowhere else. They constructed arguments designed to provoke responses from their opponents and, in turn, shaped the arguments of the other side. The Ohio Valley, more broadly, fostered a rhetorical environment on the slavery question that allowed for a considerable degree of nuance in the antebellum era. But the close contact between pro- and antislavery forces did not make the Bluegrass State any more moderate on the most contentious issue of the day. Antebellum Kentucky was not a "middle ground" that produced an idealized and fantastical version of liberal toleration. Rather, it was a battleground where the drama of the American struggle over slavery and freedom played out in sharp relief.

Kentucky was not simply the ideological middle, nor was it merely the geographical middle of the antebellum United States: it stood at the center of the nineteenth-century American debate over race, slavery, and abolition. In Kentucky, deeply held opinions about slavery's future met one another head on; they were challenged, sharpened, and refined by this collision. In this way, proslavery thought and abolitionism were mutually constitutive. Conservative white Kentuckians' dialogue with black and white abolitionists in their midst – or nearby on the other side of the Ohio River – over the merits of slavery, which took place against a shared backdrop of evangelical religion, thus frequently defined the debate over race and abolition narrowly in terms of "orthodoxy." And that theological move constrained each side's visions of slavery's future.

Abolitionism and proslavery thought were by no means rigid polarities, but rather were ideological constructs created as the result of back-and-forth argumentation over time. As antislavery and proslavery actors came to understand one another, they did not reach social harmony. Rather, they created further discord. Because of the rhetorical and discursive confines in which it took place, the debate over slavery strengthened the theologies of both slavery and white supremacy. Kentucky thus shows both the potentialities and limitations of public discourse on race and slavery. Placing both sides of that discourse together in a single study clarifies why abolitionism was so contested and why even those who sympathized with it did not go further than they did.

One of the more vexing problems in American history has been explicating the nineteenth-century relationship between slavery and Christianity. Although the literature on this problem is vast, it is really only in the last several decades that the most important advances have been made toward understanding the role of religion before the Civil War in shaping ideas about slavery. A growing number of scholars have demonstrated in different ways the centrality of

---

[1] For a perceptive book that reaches a different conclusion about the significance of the Ohio River in shaping the slavery debates, see Matthew Salafia, *Slavery's Borderland: Freedom and Bondage along the Ohio River* (Philadelphia: University of Pennsylvania Press, 2013).

theological considerations in political and economic debates about slavery. Much of the public argument over the nature of slavery that occurred from 1830 to 1860 was evangelical in nature and stemmed from a debate over the authority and role of the Bible. Proslavery Protestants in the antebellum South, the literature suggests, affirmed a commonsense, literalist biblical sanction for slaveholding, which approved, in their language, "slavery in the abstract." Combined with a relatively pessimistic outlook about the abilities of humans to effect social change on their own apart from divine action, an idea that drew from a thoroughgoing conception of humanity's innate sinfulness, proslavery believers embraced a fundamentally conservative worldview. Abolitionists, by contrast, adopted a broader interpretive scheme – anathema to the literalists – and concluded that the "spirit" of Scripture denounced slavery, in spite of its literal word. This version of "Bible politics," as historian James Brewer Stewart has called it, led abolitionists to emphasize a postmillennial view of their faith, where the earthly millennial reign of Christ might be ushered into the here-and-now through determined human work to destroy all forms of sin in this life – of which slavery was a major constitutive element. Slavery, in other words, presented a theological impasse by the late antebellum period. Both sides held deeply religious views on the issue, and both sides claimed a Christian mandate – but they believed different things. Because of differing core interpretive principles, both proslavery and abolitionist believers saw their opponents as fundamentally and hopelessly lost.[2]

---

[2] William Sumner Jenkins' foundational chapter, "Moral Philosophy of Slavery" in *Pro-Slavery Thought in the Old South* (Chapel Hill: University of North Carolina Press, 1935), 200–41, in many ways set the agenda for future scholars looking at the debate over slavery as a debate about the nature of Christianity and the role Christian doctrine should play in shaping society. More recent historians have extended Jenkins' work much further. Some of the most significant examples include, but are certainly not limited to, Mitchell Snay, *Gospel of Disunion: Religion and Separatism in the Antebellum South* (1993; Chapel Hill: University of North Carolina Press, 1997); the collected essays in John R. McKivigan and Snay, eds., *Religion and the Antebellum Debate over Slavery* (Athens: University of Georgia Press, 1998); Mark A. Noll, *America's God, From Jonathan Edwards to Abraham Lincoln* (New York: Oxford University Press, 2002), 367–401; Eugene D. Genovese, *"Slavery Ordained of God": The Southern Slaveholders' View of Biblical History and Modern Politics* (Gettysburg, PA: Gettysburg College, 1985); Elizabeth Fox-Genovese and Eugene D. Genovese, "The Divine Sanction of Social Order: Religious Foundations of the Southern Slaveholders' World View," *Journal of the American Academy of Religion* 55 (Summer 1987), 211–33; Fox-Genovese and Genovese, *The Mind of the Master Class: History and Faith in the Southern Slaveholders' Worldview* (New York: Cambridge University Press, 2005), 505–65; Fox-Genovese and Genovese, *Slavery in White in Black: Class and Race in the Southern Slaveholders' New World Order* (Cambridge: Cambridge University Press, 2008); Fox-Genovese and Genovese, *Fatal Self-Deception: Slaveholding Paternalism in the Old South* (Cambridge: Cambridge University Press, 2011); E. Brooks Holifield, *Theology in America: Christian Thought from the Age of the Puritans to the Civil War* (New Haven: Yale University Press, 2003), 494–504; John Patrick Daly, *When Slavery Was Called Freedom: Evangelicalism, Proslavery, and the Causes of the Civil War* (Lexington: University Press of Kentucky, 2002); Charles F. Irons, *The Origins of Proslavery Christianity: White and Black Evangelicals in Colonial and Antebellum Virginia* (Chapel Hill: University of North Carolina Press, 2008);

Much debate turned, in other words, not simply on contrasting accounts
of how to read the Bible but also on competing visions of what the Bible said
about how Christians should engage the political and social order. For more
conservative believers, their political theology led them to argue that the affairs
of church and state were to be kept entirely separate. And because slavery
was a spiritual institution as much as a political one, it meant that antislavery
believers erred grievously in agitating that question. Certainly James Henley
Thornwell (1812–62), the South's leading proslavery cleric before the Civil
War, spoke for many religious southerners – and even many in the North –
when he described the debate as a fight between "Christianity and Atheism,"
with "the progress of humanity the stake."[3]

Such heated rhetoric, however, masked a much more complicated relationship between slavery and Christianity in the United States. Southern proslavery
divines made much of the biblical warrant for slavery, but many notable and
otherwise antislavery ministers in the North – such as Presbyterian Charles
Hodge (1797–1878), Baptist Francis Wayland (1796–1865), and Congrega-
tionalist Moses Stuart (1780–1852) – also conceded the biblical imprimatur
for slavery. Such concessions did not mean that antislavery clergy rejected
the narrow proslavery biblical argument, but rather that they distinguished
between ancient and American slavery. Although some antislavery activists,
such as Boston's William Lloyd Garrison (1805–79), argued from a radical
perspective that a higher human law demanded the Bible be rejected for its
endorsement of slavery, more moderate antislavery religious voices held to
biblical authority yet attempted to show how the slavery in Scripture differed
greatly from American slavery. Not only did the American system refuse to
recognize such biblical concepts as the Jubilee year – in Mosaic Law, when all
slaves were set free every seven years – or allow for marriage between slaves
but also, most significantly, biblical slavery also was not based on racist power
relations. American slavery clearly was.[4]

Certainly the southern religious proslavery elite did their part to defend
the peculiar institution. They maintained a commonsense understanding of
their own racial superiority. When applied to a commonsense reading of Holy

and Molly Oshatz, *Slavery and Sin: The Fight against Slavery and the Rise of Liberal Protes-
tantism* (New York: Oxford University Press, 2011). On "Bible politics" in abolitionism, see
James Brewer Stewart, "Reconsidering the Abolitionists in an Age of Fundamentalist Politics,"
Journal of the Early Republic 26 (Spring 2006): 1–23.
[3] James Henley Thornwell, "The Christian Doctrine of Slavery," in *The Collected Writings of
James Henley Thornwell*, eds. John B. Adger and John L. Girardeau, 4 vols. (1873; Carlisle, PA:
Banner of Truth, 1974), 4:406.
[4] Noll, *The Civil War as a Theological Crisis*, 31–50; and Noll, *America's God*, 386–401. See also
J. Albert Harrill, "The Use of the New Testament in the American Slave Controversy: A Case
History in the Hermeneutical Tension between Biblical Criticism and Christian Moral Debate,"
Religion and American Culture 10 (Summer 2000): 149–86; and Holifield, *Theology in America*,
494–504.

Scripture, the Bible affirmed what southern white Christians already wanted to believe it said about American race-based slavery.[5]

Yet the proslavery argument held the capacity to question American slavery. Even in the years after 1830, where historians have traditionally pointed to a shift in southern attitudes from ambivalence about slaveholding to decisive support for the practice, southern theologians wrote that slavery as it was practiced in America needed reformation. They did not doubt that God had established the master–slave relationship as foundational for Christian society. But the holy sanction of "slavery in the abstract" did not suggest to southern divines that slavery as practiced below the Mason and Dixon line or the Ohio River was necessarily beyond reproach. The proslavery clergy frequently lamented what they saw as slavery's abuses and excesses – whether to decry the domestic slave trade that destroyed families, to denounce the prohibition against slave marriage, or to disparage a system that made slave literacy illegal – though never its racist foundation. If they were opposed to antislavery measures, if they were unwilling to say that slavery itself was sinful, the proslavery clergy remained hopeful that American slavery could become more equitable and more just – more Christian. Southern divines saw American slavery as a flawed system that needed to be brought into conformity with an identifiably Christian standard.[6]

That southern ministers recognized weaknesses in the American slave system suggests that the traditional historical emphasis on a hardened, rigid religious proslavery ideology has been exaggerated. Among much of the southern evangelical population, there was no clean shift from a "necessary evil" to a "positive good" view of the peculiar institution. That process was hard-fought and long in development.[7]

---

[5] Stephen R. Haynes, *Noah's Curse: The Biblical Justification of American Slavery* (New York: Oxford University Press, 2002), 126. On the creation of a distinctive southern evangelicalism centered around slavery, see Donald G. Mathews, *Religion in the Old South* (Chicago: University Press of Chicago, 1977), 136–84; John B. Boles, "Evangelical Protestantism in the Old South: From Religious Dissent to Cultural Dominance," in *Religion in the South*, ed. Charles Reagan Wilson (Jackson: University Press of Mississippi, 1985), 13–34; and Boles, *The Irony of Southern Religion* (New York: Peter Lang, 1994), 3–36.

[6] See Kenneth Moore Startup, *The Root of All Evil: The Protestant Clergy and the Economic Mind of the Old South* (Athens: University of Georgia Press, 1997), 67–77; and Eugene D. Genovese, *A Consuming Fire: The Fall of the Confederacy in the Mind of the White Christian South* (Athens: University of Georgia Press, 1998), 3–33. For a classic statement that posits 1830 as a stark period divide on southern attitudes toward slavery, see Anne C. Loveland, *Southern Evangelicals and the Social Order, 1800–1860* (Baton Rouge: Louisiana State University Press, 1980).

[7] As Charles Irons has put it in his study on Virginia evangelicals, "Post-Revolutionary evangelical leaders did not arrest any religious momentum for abolition because no real momentum ever existed." See Irons, *Origins of Proslavery Christianity*, 57. For a detailed description of how evangelical proslavery was neither situated in language of "necessary evil" nor "positive good," see Daly, *When Slavery Was Called Freedom*, 30–56.

The American South, moreover, held no monolithic opinion on slavery's merits. Although the Confederate States of America would appear in 1861 dedicated to the proposition that African American slaves should be held in perpetuity, that political project was no inevitability – and some of the South's most dedicated slaveholders refused to join when it came together. To be sure, regional location played a role in shaping clergy attitudes toward slavery. Especially outside the Lower South, public sentiment never completely crystallized in favor of slavery. The Middle South – including states such as Virginia, Tennessee, and North Carolina – retained pockets of antislavery dissent up to the Civil War. And in the Border South, where geography dictated forms of agriculture that were not conducive to large chattel labor forces and where long state borders touched free soil, the discomfort with slavery was magnified. In Delaware, Maryland, Kentucky, and Missouri, a degree of antislavery sentiment persisted throughout the antebellum period.[8]

Slavery had existed in Kentucky since its earliest days, and more Kentuckians per capita owned slaves by 1850 than did whites in any other slaveholding state except Georgia or Virginia. But instead of the dominant planter class that would mark most other southern states, Kentucky possessed a widespread middle class of slaveholders who owned five slaves or fewer. On the eve of the Civil War in 1860, Kentucky's population was more than 1.1 million, with just more than 225,000 slaves – slightly less than 20 percent of the total population. The state sat too far north to grow cotton, sugar, or other crops that were traditionally grown using large numbers of enslaved laborers. Even the state's largest hemp and tobacco farms were not comparable in size to the giant plantations farther south, and just over fifty Kentucky farms claimed more than fifty slaves.[9] Although these factors did not serve to make slavery more "mild" in Kentucky compared with the rest of the South, as historians once thought, they did make the Commonwealth both a more volatile and a more receptive

[8] For a cogent description of the differences between these "Souths" and regional attitudes toward slavery, see William W. Freehling, *The Road To Disunion*, vol. 1: *Secessionists at Bay, 1776–1854* (New York: Oxford University Press, 1990), 17–19. For a dated, but incredibly valuable study of the persistence of antislavery views in Virginia churches, see Patricia Hickin, "'Situation Ethics' and Antislavery Attitudes in the Virginia Churches," in *America: The Middle Period: Essays in Honor of Bernard Mayo*, ed. John B. Boles (Charlottesville: University Press of Virginia, 1973), 188–215.

[9] On the nature of the Kentucky slave economy and agriculture, see Ivan E. McDougle, *Slavery in Kentucky, 1792–1865* (1918; New York: Arno Press, 1970), 26–9; J. Winston Coleman, *Slavery Times in Kentucky* (Chapel Hill: University of North Carolina Press, 1940), 41–7; James C. Klotter, *The Breckinridges of Kentucky* (Lexington: University Press of Kentucky, 1986), 63–5; Lowell H. Harrison and Klotter, *A New History of Kentucky* (Lexington: University Press of Kentucky, 1997), 133–8, 168–9; Marion B. Lucas, *A History of Blacks in Kentucky*, vol. 1, *From Slavery to Segregation* (Frankfort: Kentucky Historical Society, 1992); and Gary R. Matthews, "Beleaguered Loyalties: Kentucky Unionism," in *Sister States, Enemy States: The Civil War in Kentucky and Tennessee*, eds. Kent T. Dollar, Larry H. Whiteaker, and W. Calvin Dickinson (Lexington: University Press of Kentucky, 2009), 16–18.

arena for antislavery thought. It meant that controversial opinions would be heard, measured, and judged.[10]

As time went on and debate grew more constrained, conservative antislavery activists in Kentucky came to make common cause with their proslavery opponents. Though one side rejected slavery and the other endorsed it, the two groups both affirmed a threefold, profoundly religious, conservative argument on slavery that remained a fixture in the thought of white Kentuckians through the antebellum era and, indeed, persisted throughout the Civil War and Reconstruction. First, the Commonwealth's religious whites, overwhelmingly evangelical in affiliation, affirmed slavery as a divinely mandated, biblically sanctioned institution for the ordering of society – at least as an abstract social formulation. Second, Kentucky's religiously conservative whites drew on the broad cultural belief in white supremacy, which they also saw as ordained by the Christian God. Third, they collectively rejected abolitionism for its ostensible radicalism, which Kentucky whites believed challenged divine dictums and threatened the racial order. Emancipationism suggested a gradual end to slavery, whereas abolitionism meant an immediate end. Taken as a whole, this tripartite argument ultimately led Kentucky's conservative white believers to one obvious conclusion: abolitionists were heretics.

That understanding shaped the world of ecclesiastical politics in the 1830s and 1840s, where white Kentucky's gradual emancipationists played central roles in the founding of theologically conservative, proslavery evangelical

---

[10] Ivan McDougle, *Slavery in Kentucky*, 73, 77, 78, wrote in 1918 that most Kentucky slaves "seem to have been content in their condition" and that "personal interest in a slave and his welfare took precedence over merely his economic value to the owner." McDougle partially qualified his assessment by acknowledging, "life among the slaves of Kentucky was not by any means a path of roses." J. Winston Coleman, *Slavery Times in Kentucky*, vii, claimed in 1940 that Kentucky had the "mildest form" of slavery, "better than in any other state, with the possible exception of Maryland or Virginia," and certainly a more mitigated form than the Deep South's "proverbially harder" chattel version. Lowell Harrison and James Klotter accept a qualified version of Coleman's view. They highlight the racist dimension of slavery but state nonetheless, "Relative mildness was no excuse for the existence of slavery, but a slave in Kentucky probably received somewhat better treatment than a slave in Mississippi or Alabama." See Harrison and Klotter, *New History of Kentucky*, 174. For a challenge to this line of reasoning, see Lucas, *History of Blacks in Kentucky*, 42–50. More recently, Harold Tallant has argued contrary to Coleman that Kentucky slavery was in fact harsher than slavery farther south. Although the types of labor may have differentiated Kentucky slavery from its practice elsewhere, the Commonwealth's many small farms and widespread middle class of slaveholders meant that the enslaved operated in close proximity to their masters, which meant constant contact with whites and a high degree of unfreedom. See Harold D. Tallant, *Evil Necessity: Slavery and Political Culture in Antebellum Kentucky* (Lexington: University Press of Kentucky, 2003), 62–5. For a reappraisal of Coleman that remains critical of the "mildness" thesis but that also emphasizes the historiographical importance of *Slavery Times in Kentucky* for its description of the "darker side" of slavery, see John David Smith, "'To hue the line and let the chips fall where they may': J. Winston Coleman's *Slavery Times in Kentucky* Reconsidered," *Register of the Kentucky Historical Society* 103 (Autumn 2005): 691–726.

denominations in the South. Whether in the 1837 division of the Presbyterian Church into Old and New Schools or the 1845 creations of the Southern Baptist Convention and Methodist Episcopal Church, South, white Kentuckians were critical figures. Yet many of these same southern denominational leaders in Kentucky who sided theologically with proslavery Christians continued to cling to their gradual emancipationism.

What had been accomplished in the churches by 1845 – the emergence of sectional bodies hinging on the slavery question – remained contested in broader political affairs. White Kentuckians may have roundly avowed slavery for their churches, but civic life was another matter, still up for debate. By the middle decades of the nineteenth century, public support in Kentucky for slavery was on the rise, and the political power of the slaveholding class was increasing. Some evangelical whites in the Commonwealth agitated in the late 1840s for a revised state constitution that would slowly kill off slavery. But when that new state constitution was overwhelmingly approved by popular vote in 1850, it strengthened the rights of slaveholders and guaranteed slavery's survival well into the future. Still, even though the influence of conservative antislavery advocates waned in the state after 1850, a small minority continued to work against slavery through the years until the beginning of the Civil War.[11]

This complex approach to the slavery question did not necessarily make the Bluegrass State unusual in the antebellum United States. Instead, Kentucky's nineteenth-century history can be read as representing a series of critical issues concerning the nation. Overwhelmingly, the dominant religious tradition in nineteenth-century Kentucky, as in the United States as a whole, was evangelical Protestantism. Evangelical churches were the most significant voluntary organizations in Civil War–era America, both in terms of popular adherence and political clout. Roughly 40 percent of the national population held some sort of evangelical affiliation by the mid-1850s. Connected by networks of faith and facilitated by its ability to harness a burgeoning print culture, nineteenth-century evangelicalism became a powerful national presence. Moreover, if evangelicalism's nineteenth-century national hegemony has not been lost on historians, south of the Mason-Dixon line and the Ohio River the evangelical presence was even more pronounced, visible, and culturally powerful. As the table below enumerates, in mid-nineteenth-century Kentucky, white evangelicals accounted for nearly 60 percent of the state's total population, but more than 70 percent of its white population.[12]

[11] On Kentucky's constitutional debates of 1849–50, see Harrison and Klotter, *New History of Kentucky*, 117–19; and Tallant, *Evil Necessity*, 151–60.
[12] See Richard Carwardine, *Evangelicals and Politics in Antebellum America* (New Haven: Yale University Press, 1993), 44, who has memorably called evangelicalism the "largest, and most formidable, subculture" in antebellum America. See also C. C. Goen, *Broken Churches, Broken Nation: The Coming of the American Civil War* (Macon, GA: Mercer University Press, 1985), 55–6; and Candy Gunther Brown, *The Word in the World: Evangelical Writing, Publishing, and Reading in America, 1789–1880* (Chapel Hill: University of North Carolina Press, 2004).

For the estimated percentages in Kentucky for the purposes of this study, Christian Churches (followers of the Campbellite/Restorationist movement), Baptists, Methodists, and Presbyterians counted as evangelical: these were the largest and most prominent denominations in the state. In 1860, Kentucky's Baptists claimed nearly 95,000 members, Methodists numbered nearly 57,000, and Presbyterians counted roughly 10,000 on their rolls. Membership figures for the Christian Churches are harder to determine for 1860, but they claimed more than 41,000 members in 1846 and it is plausible to estimate that there were more than 50,000 members by 1860. By no means, however, did these four ecclesiastical traditions represent all – or the only – evangelicals in nineteenth-century America. Outside of Kentucky and the South, Congregationalists, Reformed Christians, Lutherans, and Episcopalians exhibited evangelical traits.[13]

Membership numbers are suggestive, but they vastly undercount the number of religious adherents in nineteenth-century America. Due to relatively restrictive membership standards, most churches saw many more regular church attendees – perhaps double or triple the number – than actual members. As a result, ascertaining the actual number of Christian adherents in the period is highly imprecise. Most careful historians of American religion tend to rely on the U.S. Census's tally of church seating capacity (called "accommodations" in the Census), but currently lack effective ways of determining just how many people considered themselves active faith practitioners in the period.[14]

Understanding these statistical problems, it is nevertheless possible to make a few comparative points that suggest the popular influence of Christianity in Kentucky. In 1860 the Masons had only slightly more members (10,319 by an 1858 count) than there were seats in Kentucky's twenty-five – statistically insignificant – Episcopal churches (9,940). The same year, all the Masons in Kentucky could not have filled the Methodist pews of Louisville's Jefferson County, in whose twenty-two churches sat 11,700 parishioners. If every man in the Bluegrass State who voted for governor in 1871 (215,172) or 1875 (224,262) – or president in 1872 (191,552) or 1876 (259,614) – had proceeded to sit down in a local Baptist church, there would have been seats to spare. Meanwhile, every Methodist, Christian, Presbyterian, Episcopal, Lutheran, and Roman Catholic church would have sat empty. Using church membership numbers alone, in 1870 there were more Baptists (121,728) and Methodists (77,517) than there were people attending school (181,225). The

---

[13] See J. H. Spencer, *A History of Kentucky Baptists: From 1769 to 1885*, 2 vols. (Cincinnati: J. R. Baumes, 1885), 1:722; and Lewis Collins and Richard H. Collins, *History of Kentucky*, 2 vols. (Covington, KY: Collins, 1874), 1:425–6, 456, 459.

[14] See George C. Rable, *God's Almost Chosen Peoples: A Religious History of the American Civil War* (Chapel Hill: University of North Carolina Press, 2010), 11–12. For an elucidation of this problem as it applies to antebellum Virginia, see Irons, *Origins of Proslavery Christianity*, 3–10.

Kentucky Church Accommodations and General Population Statistics,
1850–1870[15]

	1850	1860	1870
Baptist	291,855	267,860	288,936
Christian Churches	46,340	104,980	141,585
Cumberland Presbyterian*	n/a	31,335	n/a
Episcopal	7,050	9,940	15,800
Jewish	600	n/a	n/a
Lutheran	2,850	5,400	1,650
Methodist	169,060	228,100	244,918
Presbyterian	99,106	67,440	100,750
Roman Catholic	24,240	44,820	72,550
United Presbyterian*	n/a	400	n/a
Total Evangelical Accommodations	606,361	700,115	776,189
Total Church Accommodations	671,053	778,025	876,439
Total Slave Population	210,981	225,483	n/a
Total Free Colored Population	10,011	10,684	n/a
Total African American Population[†]	220,992	236,167	222,210
Total White Population	761,413	919,484	1,098,692
Total Free Population	771,424	930,201	n/a
Total Population	982,405	1,155,684	1,321,011
Total Church Accommodations as Percentage of Total Population	68.3	67.3	66.3
Total Evangelical Church Accommodations as Percentage of Total Population	61.7	60.6	58.8
Total Church Accommodations as Percentage of White Population	88.1	84.6	79.8
Total Evangelical Church Accommodations as Percentage of White Population	79.6	76.1	70.6

* Cumberland and United Presbyterians only appear in the 1860 U.S. Census. They were included in the general "Presbyterian" category in 1850 and 1870.

† Total African American population for 1850 and 1860 represents the sum of the "slave" and "free colored" populations given by the U.S. Census.

[15] Population and church accommodation (termed "sittings" in the 1870 census) figures taken from the 1850, 1860, and 1870 U.S. Census reports. These are the only decades in the period considered by this study – 1830 to 1880 – when the U.S. Census recorded data on religious adherence. See *Seventh Census of the United States, 1850*; *Eighth Census of the United States, 1860*; *Ninth Census of the United States, 1870*; all accessed at Historical Census Browser, University of Virginia, Geospatial and Statistical Data Center: http://fisher.lib.virginia.edu/collections/stats/histcensus/index.html.

state's population was just over 1.3 million that year, meaning, in essence, that one of every ten Kentuckians had formally joined a Baptist church.[16]

In explicating the interface between religion and political culture in Kentucky, this book downplays denominational distinctiveness and analyzes arguments that emerged from the state's – and country's – three most powerful denominations: Baptists, Methodists, and Presbyterians. It is nevertheless important to acknowledge that for questions of ecclesiological identity and authority, the theological particulars of denominationalism always counted for much more in Kentucky – and elsewhere – than broader evangelical allegiances. Baptists, for example, devoted much more space in their denominational press to debates about, and defenses of, the proper mode of baptism (for the willful believer, by full bodily immersion in water) than to issues of race, slavery, or national loyalty. Methodists spoke more overtly on the broad religio-political questions of slavery and sectionalism, especially after the Civil War, in the context of denominational reunification debates. Yet Methodists too devoted much intellectual energy to the particulars of denominational belief. As just one example, in 1873 the *Central Methodist,* the official newspaper of the Kentucky Conference of the Methodist Episcopal Church, South, published a debate on the most appropriate biblical form of baptism (it approved of baptizing children), which included ten "arguments" and "replies" and spanned more than twenty issues – more than half of the year's catalog.[17]

Kentucky's Christian Churches, moreover, are an even clearer example of the robust nature of denominational commitment compared to purely political alignments. Birthed by the early-nineteenth-century Restorationist movement led by Alexander Campbell (1788–1866) and Barton W. Stone (1772–1844), by 1860 Christian Churches constituted the third largest denomination in the Commonwealth and the fourth largest overall in the United States. In 1849, in the midst of the political drive to amend Kentucky's state constitution with an emancipationist clause, Alexander Campbell did publish an essay in his theological journal, *Millennial Harbinger,* that advocated gradually ending slavery in Kentucky. Although that article drew ire from proslavery Restorationists, it

[16] *Eighth Census of the United States, 1860; Ninth Census of the United States, 1870;* Rob Morris, *The History of Freemasonry in Kentucky, in its Relation to the Symbolic Degrees* (Louisville: Rob Morris, 1859), 431; Lowell H. Harrison, ed., *Kentucky's Governors,* updated ed. (Lexington: University Press of Kentucky, 2004), 102, 105; American Presidency Project, University of California, Santa Barbara, http://www.presidency.ucsb.edu/showelection.php?year=1872; http://www.presidency.ucsb.edu/showelection.php?year=1876; and Spencer, *History of Kentucky Baptists,* 1:750.

[17] See "A Discussion on the Mode of Baptism: Gospel Baptism is the immersion of a believer in water in the name of the Trinity. The *Record* affirms; the *Methodist* denies," *Central Methodist,* January 11–July 5, 1873. The best argument for emphasizing denominational distinctions over a pan-denominational "evangelical" rubric is Beth Barton Schweiger, *The Gospel Working Up: Progress and the Pulpit in Nineteenth-Century Virginia* (New York: Oxford University Press, 1999), 8–9.

also represented something of an aberration among Kentucky Christian Church members. By and large, they steered a moderate course, which – as was the case among other conservative white believers in the state – meant their commonsense biblical literalism led them to reject radical abolitionism and maintain proslavery convictions. However, it also meant that Restorationists tacitly agreed to make the slavery question and other political matters secondary to those of denominational theology and polity.[18]

Indeed, the notable Civil War–era Restorationist journal, *Lard's Quarterly*, published in Georgetown, Kentucky, from 1863 to 1868 by Campbell associate Moses Lard (1818–80), had little to say about contemporaneous political debates. As Lard explained in his inaugural issue, the journal existed to promote "the claims of *Primitive Christianity*." The publication "aspire[d]," in short, "to contain a clear, true statement, and just defense of Christianity as taught in God's holy word." Over its five-year run, the journal did contain religious reflections on the "Union of Church and State" and Christian views of warfare, but those essays avoided making extreme partisan statements and represented only a small fraction of the quarterly's printed output. In fact, Lard warned readers in 1863 that taking too extreme a position on the sectional crisis represented nothing less than a "deep strategy of Satan" to undermine the work of the true faith. Acknowledging that individual believers could hold differing political opinions, Lard wanted Restorationists to remain committed to one of their core doctrinal principles: Christian unity.[19]

Lard's contention said more about his theology than it did about his fellow Christians. Kentucky's Christian Churches contained much division during the Civil War era, even if they avoided the massive church splits on slavery and the war that shattered Baptists, Methodists, and Presbyterians. Restorationists' more muted approach to the key matters at stake in the Civil War era spoke more to their social and theological conservatism than it did to their professed apoliticism. In Kentucky, there can be no doubt that they followed the trajectory of white evangelicals more broadly, and there can be no doubt that slavery and the war were divisive problems – even if Restorationists did not fulminate about them publicly to the extent that Baptists, Methodists, and Presbyterians did.[20]

---

[18] Alexander Campbell, "Tracts for the People – No. XXXIII. A Tract for the People of Kentucky," *Millennial Harbinger*, 3rd Ser., 6 (May 1849): 241–52. On the slavery question among Restorationists, see David Edwin Harrell Jr., *Quest for a Christian America: The Disciples of Christ and American Society to 1866* (Nashville: Disciples of Christ Historical Society, 1966), 91–138. According to Harrell, p. 121, Campbell's 1849 essay to Kentuckians "marked the last real conflict between Campbell and Southern slavery apologists."

[19] Quotes from Moses Lard, "Preface," *Lard's Quarterly* 1 (September 1863): 1; and Lard, "The Cause and the Work it Needs," *Lard's Quarterly* 1 (December 1863): 223. See also L. B. Wilkes, "Union of Church and State," *Lard's Quarterly* 4 (April 1867): 125–8; and G. W. Able, "War," *Lard's Quarterly* 4 (April 1867): 139–48. Throughout this book, all quotes contain the emphasis of the original sources. Any italicized or boldfaced text is from the quoted material.

[20] For an account of fissures over slavery among Restorationists, which argues that after Barton Warren Stone's 1844 death an earlier abolitionist tradition was supplanted by a more

In analyzing the institutional machinations of nineteenth-century denominations, it is appropriate to downplay the significance of a more expansive, more ecumenical notion of evangelicalism. Baptists, Methodists, Presbyterians, and Restorationists all maintained strident and robust denominational differences. Yet in the hands of such conservative evangelicals, those differences did not lead to markedly different viewpoints on slavery, race, or the nation. As a result, the technical particulars of denominational identification – though recognized as central to the lives of historical actors and analyzed significantly throughout this book – are emphasized to a lesser degree than generic affinities between evangelical belief and social, cultural, and political opinion. For that reason, this study does not probe the activities of Restorationists or explore debates between pedobaptists and adult immersionists.[21]

As an examination of public and, to a lesser extent, private discourse among clergy and politically connected actors, this book closely analyzes an extensive range of evangelical newspapers, tracts and treatises, sermons, and ministers' correspondence. It is largely – though by no means exclusively – engaged in the study of social elites. Although it was not the most popular denomination, because of their high standards for education among the clergy, Presbyterianism exercised influence among Kentucky's white believers disproportionate to its numbers. Baptist and Methodist ministers generally came from much more humble backgrounds than Presbyterians and had few educational requirements for ordination, but their careers often elevated their status in communities.

That acknowledgment, however, should not suggest a massive disjunction between pulpit and pew. The history of Christianity in nineteenth-century America is the history of the democratization of church polity. Clergy were obliged to carry themselves as representatives of the congregations they served. If nineteenth-century evangelical clergy ceased to speak to the interests of the people, the offending clergy would quickly lose followers, and often their congregations. Not only is it fair to claim that Civil War–era clergy approximated the opinions of people in the pew, but to take cues from historical work on religion and the white South a century later during the era of civil rights, parishioners were also likely more conservative on the key issues in this book – race, slavery, and the nation – than their clergy.[22]

accommodationist gradual emancipationism, see Matthew D. Smith, "Barton Warren Stone: Revisiting Revival in the Early Republic," *Register of the Kentucky Historical Society* 111 (Spring 2013): 161–97. On general politicization among the Disciples of Christ in America over the Civil War, see Darin A. Tuck, "The Battle Cry of Peace: The Leadership of the Disciples of Christ Movement during the American Civil War, 1861–1865" (M.A. thesis, Kansas State University, 2010).

[21] As historian John Boles once wrote in a foundational essay on the topic, "The [southern] evangelical hegemony ... was less a sense of religious community than a religious culture." See Boles, "Evangelical Protestantism in the Old South," 27.

[22] See Nathan O. Hatch, *The Democratization of American Christianity* (New Haven: Yale University Press, 1989); David L. Chappell, *A Stone of Hope: Prophetic Religion and the Death*

Yet in the slaveholding state of Kentucky, many clergy retained a conspicuous antislavery presence into the 1860s. Kentucky's antislavery populace never gained a majority in the Commonwealth, but did generate enough support to make political waves. As such, the long life of antislavery agitation in nineteenth-century Kentucky has been a subject of much historical reflection.[23] Not only have historians been interested in the persistence of southern dissent against slavery in the decades immediately preceding the Civil War but they have also highlighted the varieties of opinion among antislavery advocates. Although the Bluegrass State did feature abolitionists on its religious and political margins who hoped for the immediate eradication of slavery – such as the pacifist evangelical John G. Fee (1816–1901) and James G. Birney (1792–1857), who left the state in 1835 – Kentucky's late antebellum antislavery movement remained dominated by emancipationists who sought to end the institution gradually, with compensation given to the owners of freed slaves. These gradualists favored black expatriation through West African colonization schemes, forthrightly invoked the language of white supremacy, and unapologetically rejected the ideas of "radical" abolitionists who sought slavery's immediate end.

Kentucky thus fostered the fiction that it held a "neutral" middle-ground stance toward slavery, navigating between abolitionist and proslavery polarities, before the Civil War. Indeed, it was that belief in neutrality – which meant that when white Kentuckians had to choose sides, for or against slavery, they often chose neither – that fostered Unionism in the state. To remain on the middle ground, however, was not benign, nor was it morally or politically neutral. Moderation was an ethical stance that sought every possible avenue to avoid confronting directly the most pressing dilemma of the nineteenth century. It was thus symptomatic of a conservative stance toward slavery. In 1860 and 1861, when no threat to slavery appeared imminent, there was no reason to leave the Union. The United States had fostered both slaveholding and evangelical Protestantism. In that sense, to reject the Union was to reject Christian America.

of Jim Crow (Chapel Hill: University of North Carolina Press, 2004); Carolyn Renée Dupont, *Mississippi Praying: Southern White Evangelicals and the Civil Rights Movement, 1945–1975* (New York: New York University Press, 2013); and Paul Harvey, *Freedom's Coming: Religious Culture and the Shaping of the South From the Civil War through the Civil Rights Era* (Chapel Hill: University of North Carolina Press, 2005).

[23] In addition to a great number of journal articles, several important monographs have surveyed late antebellum Kentucky's antislavery activism. See Asa Earl Martin, *The Anti-Slavery Movement in Kentucky prior to 1850* (Louisville: Standard Printing, 1918); McDougle, *Slavery in Kentucky*, 93–118; Coleman, *Slavery Times in Kentucky*, 290–325; Lowell H. Harrison, *The Antislavery Movement in Kentucky* (Lexington: University Press of Kentucky, 1978); and Tallant, *Evil Necessity*. Kentucky antislavery has also been of some interest in more general histories of antebellum America. See, for example, Clement Eaton, *Freedom of Thought in the Old South* (1940; New York: Peter Smith, 1951), 247–79; Freehling, *Secessionists at Bay*, 462–74; and Stanley Harrold, *Border War: Fighting over Slavery before the Civil War* (Chapel Hill: University of North Carolina Press, 2010).

The Civil War, however, closed off any alternate paths that moderates might follow on the slavery question. Emancipation changed the meaning of the Union. In turn, it changed the way white Kentuckians felt about the Union. At the war's end, Kentucky still held some 65,000 souls in bondage – even though many African Americans had moved toward freedom, especially through Union military service. When the Thirteenth Amendment finally sealed American slavery's fate in December 1865 – against Kentucky's vociferous opposition – white Kentuckians embraced a decidedly pro-Confederate stance. Racist religion accomplished after the Civil War what was impossible before: it created cultural and political solidarity with the white South.

It was a move that could not have happened without theological solidarity among whites. And that solidarity was in place before the war itself. Thus nineteenth-century Kentucky demonstrates the strength and vitality of proslavery religion as well as the more general tendency of ideologies to outlive the institutions they were first intended to justify. Though proslavery religion would not have existed without slavery, it eventually became an independent intellectual system that was more than merely ideological. As an unquestioned truth in much of nineteenth-century America – not only in the South but also in the North – theological proslavery remained after emancipation. In the absence of legal slavery, however, old arguments came to be deployed in new ways.[24]

White religious understandings of slavery and racial difference were key to the forging of Confederate identity in the postbellum Bluegrass State. When slavery was legally abolished, and when victorious Union armies ended the slavery debates that religious interlocutors refused to concede, Kentucky's prewar antislavery conservatives changed to make common cause with those who had exhibited a more stridently proslavery approach before the war. In other words, when slavery disappeared, so too did the conceit of an ideological middle ground. The result was a racist unity legitimated by postbellum clergy and laity who rejected civil rights for African Americans, embraced a Confederate memory of the war, and paved the way for the emergence of a dominant white Democratic political bloc in the state. In short, the political reality of emancipation and its religious implications moved Kentucky's religiously conservative whites from their avowedly neutral antebellum ideological position as a Border South state to a postwar affinity with an emerging Solid South, comprising the former Confederacy and starkly racist.

---

[24] Historians have long known that many of the ideas associated with proslavery arguments persisted well beyond the immediate years surrounding emancipation and Confederate defeat. See John David Smith, *An Old Creed for the New South: Proslavery Ideology and Historiography, 1865–1918* (Westport, CT: Greenwood Press, 1985).

I

The Challenge of Immediate Emancipationism

The Origins of Abolitionist Heresy, 1829–1835

[Abolitionists] have pondered over the horrors of slavery, until their imaginations have become fevered, and they have mistaken the visions of fancy for the realities of existence. On this principle only, can I account for good men mistaking gradualists for perpetualists – on this principle only, can I account for a highly intelligent man's asserting that a gradualist is "a transgressor, who is determined to hold on in his sin, and in the mean time wishes to quiet his conscience and retain his standing in the church, by seeming to repent."

> – Presbyterian minister John C. Young (1803–57),
> "The Doctrine of Immediate Emancipation Unsound" (1835)[1]

On March 1, 1836, Kentucky's state legislature passed a resolution condemning the work of "abolition societies." Issued in the heat of a national political discussion over whether slavery's opponents had the right to fill southern mailboxes with abolitionist literature, the resolution argued that any individuals who called immediately for "an entire abolition of slavery in the United States" were motivated by a "wild and fanatical spirit." The profile of these northern antislavery immediatists had increased drastically in recent years, thanks to a widespread campaign of printed "tracts, pamphlets, almanacks, and pictorial representations." Although Kentucky's white officials claimed no quarrel with the freedom of the press – "secured to the citizen by the constitution of the country" – they did have a problem with those who would "prostitut[e]" that freedom "to such unhallowed purposes" as the total abolition of slavery. Abolitionists strove, as the Kentucky legislature saw it, "to produce a spirit of discontent, insubordination, and perhaps insurrection within the slave population of the country." No one could claim a right "to excite a portion of

---

[1] John C. Young, "The Doctrine of Immediate Emancipation Unsound," in A Committee of the Synod of Kentucky, *An Address to the Presbyterians of Kentucky, Proposing a Plan for the Instruction and Emancipation of their Slaves* (Cincinnati: Taylor and Tracy, 1835), 33.

the population of a sister [slave] state to rapine and murder." As a result, the legislature resolutely denounced "the effort of the abolitionists to stir up a portion of the population of eleven states of this Union to rebellion and bloodshed." The point was made: abolitionists were "fanatics." They would resort to a "radical" program of achieving their aims through violence – particularly by inciting slave insurrection. For Kentucky whites, such an agenda was unconscionable.[2]

The possibility of slave violence and race war, however, was not the only reason Kentucky lawmakers rejected abolitionism. In their view, northern anti-slavery immediatists also worked actively to undermine the laws of racial order the Christian God had clearly given to human society. As the legislature put it, "the people of Kentucky hold themselves responsible to no earthly tribunal, but will refer their cause to Him alone, through the mysterious dispensations of whose Providence, dominion has been given to the white man over the black." It was God "alone" who would "judge of [slavery's] compatibility with his will," and Kentucky's white political leaders believed they were upholding a divine institution, mandated for the racial ordering of American society.[3]

Just a year earlier, however, a group of Kentucky Presbyterians seemed to offer a rival interpretation of the divine will for American slavery. In 1835, after a request from their denomination, ten leading Bluegrass Presbyterians, including both laity and clergy, published *An Address to the Presbyterians of Kentucky* that offered a "plan for the instruction and emancipation" of the state's enslaved population. They were led by minister John C. Young, president of Centre College in Danville, located roughly thirty-five miles southwest of Lexington, and later moderator of the General Assembly of the Presbyterian Church USA in 1853. Following Young, these white religious Kentuckians argued "that the system of slavery, which exists among us, is not right." Employing biblical language, they implored their audience: "May He 'who hears the cry of the poor and needy,' and who has commanded to let the 'oppressed go free,' give to each one of us wisdom to know our duty and strength to fulfill it." Against the common proslavery claim that "the Bible sanctioned slavery," these Kentuckians contended that the biblical imprimatur did not extend to American slavery but only to ancient "*Greek and Roman slavery*" – in other words, "the kind of slavery" common to "the countries where the apostles preached and wrote their epistles." American slavery was "a system which exhibits power without responsibility, toil without recompense,

---

[2] *Acts Passed at the First Session of the Forty-Fourth General Assembly of the Commonwealth of Kentucky* (Frankfort, KY: J. H. Holeman, 1836), 683–6. For further elucidation of this particular legislative decision, see William Elsey Connelley and E. M. Coulter, *History of Kentucky*, ed. Charles Kerr, 5 vols. (Chicago: American Historical Society), 2:802–4; for broader national context, see William W. Freehling, *The Road to Disunion*, vol. 1: *Secessionists at Bay, 1776–1854* (New York: Oxford University Press, 1990), 308–52; and James Brewer Stewart, *Holy Warriors: The Abolitionists and American Slavery* (New York: Hill and Wang, 1976), 68–71.

[3] *Acts of the Kentucky General Assembly, 1836*, 683–4.

life without liberty, law without justice, wrongs without redress, punishment without guilt, and families without marriage." These blatantly sinful features of the southern system compelled Young and his cohort to argue that "THE NEW TESTAMENT DOES CONDEMN SLAVERY, AS PRACTICED AMONG US, IN THE MOST EXPLICIT TERMS, FURNISHED BY THE LANGUAGE IN WHICH THE INSPIRED PENMAN WROTE." In short, the Bible did give warrant to a form of slaveholding, but the time for that type of slavery – the slavery of biblical antiquity – had long since passed. As these white Kentucky Presbyterians asserted in 1835, their fellow southern believers needed to move toward ending the institution as it existed in the present day.[4]

The Presbyterian proposal gained little traction within the Kentucky Synod – the state-level denominational ruling body – but it was not as stark an antislavery platform as its authors suggested. The proposal was, in its essentials, conservative, advocating a plan of gradual emancipation. As the authors viewed the matter, African Americans were not yet ready to participate in free white society: "At present, an emancipated black among us is placed in peculiarly unpropitious circumstances." Furthermore, although the Presbyterians devoted most of their space to concern for the enslaved, they also wanted their white readers to understand their own particular racial stake in the matter, contending that slavery "*demoralizes the whites as well as the blacks.*" In short, while condemning American slavery as it existed, these ministers offered no *immediate* abolitionist program to their white coreligionists in Kentucky.[5]

To be sure, elsewhere Young and his colleagues connected their gradual emancipation plan with colonization schemes – the removal of the African American population to the colony of Liberia in western Africa – and distanced themselves from abolitionist activism.[6] In fact, to clarify and press his anti-abolitionist position, and with the blessing of his fellow emancipationist Presbyterians, Young appended a treatise to an early edition of their published

[4] Committee of the Synod of Kentucky, *An Address to the Presbyterians of Kentucky* (1835; Newburyport, MA: Charles Whipple, 1836), 3, 20, 21, 23.

[5] Ibid., 17, 30. On the Synod of Kentucky's negative response to Young and his colleagues' proposal, see Mark Hardin, *Action of the General Assembly on Slavery* (Louisville: Hanna & Duncan, 1865), 18–19; and Peter J. Wallace, "'The Bond of Union': The Old School Presbyterian Church and the American Nation, 1837–1861," 3 vols. (Ph.D. diss., University of Notre Dame, 2004), 2:400–2.

[6] See "President Young on Slavery," *African Repository* 11 (April 1835): 119–23. Charles C. Jones, *The Religious Instruction of the Negroes* (Savannah, GA: Thomas Purse, 1842), 78–9, documents John C. Young's leadership in the gradualist "Kentucky Union, for the moral and religious improvement of the colored race," comprised of a "union of the several denominations of christians, in the State." See also "Kentucky Union," *African Repository* 11 (November 1835): 333–4. In reality, Young leaned much closer to a more radical antislavery platform and was fairly realistic about the practicality of colonization schemes, believing black expatriation all but impossible to implement on a wide scale and acknowledging the widespread lack of support for such efforts, especially within the African American community. See Harold D. Tallant, *Evil Necessity: Slavery and Political Culture in Antebellum Kentucky* (Lexington: University Press of Kentucky, 2003), 38–9, 60–1.

Address. Two abolitionist clergy – one of whom, Samuel Crothers of Greenfield, Ohio, had spent much of his youth in Kentucky – had attacked Young's proposal as too short-sighted and tepid a solution to the problem of slavery in America. In a bluntly titled series of two letters, Young made his view even plainer. Although he certainly endorsed a gradual end to the evil institution, he saw "The Doctrine of Immediate Emancipation Unsound" (1835).[7]

The statements of the Kentucky legislature and the state's Presbyterians were manifestly different in their views on slavery, but they were also deeply similar: they held a shared conservative religious approach to the slavery question, they affirmed white supremacy, and they denounced abolitionism. Historians have spilled much ink showing the multitudinous ways that abolitionism failed to cohere as a movement on American soil. Especially given the fracture of the American Anti-Slavery Society in 1840, interpreters have found manifest divisions among immediatists over a host of competing interests and goals, for both pragmatic and idealistic reasons.[8] Without a doubt, the sources of dissension were real among abolitionists, even if at times overstated by historians.[9] Yet from the perspective of conservative evangelical whites, especially in slaveholding states such as Kentucky, those sorts of distinctions counted for little.

[7] Young, "The Doctrine of Immediate Emancipation Unsound."

[8] Among the most noted and glaring, moral suasionists broke with those interested in directly engaging with the political process; some pressed for nonviolence, whereas others advocated armed resistance. Some evangelical Protestant believers sought to work through established churches and religious institutions, even as others rejected such approaches because of their skepticism and anticlericalism; more radical voices called for the equal inclusion of women and blacks in the movement – or white women over African Americans, and vice versa – whereas more conservative abolitionists thought such egalitarianism would stir up common social prejudices and undermine attempts to first end slavery. For representative discussions that deal with these issues in differing ways, see Stewart, *Holy Warriors*, 89–95; David Brion Davis, *Inhuman Bondage: The Rise and Fall of Slavery in the New World* (New York: Oxford University Press, 2006), 259–67; Julie Roy Jeffrey, *The Great Silent Army of Abolitionism: Ordinary Women in the Antislavery Movement* (Chapel Hill: University of North Carolina Press, 1998); Stacey M. Robertson, *Hearts Beating for Liberty: Women Abolitionists in the Old Northwest* (Chapel Hill: University of North Carolina Press, 2010); Bertram Wyatt-Brown, *Lewis Tappan and the Evangelical War against Slavery* (1969; Baton Rouge: Louisiana State University Press, 1997), 185–204; John R. McKivigan, *The War against Proslavery Religion: Abolitionism and the Northern Churches, 1830–1865* (Ithaca: Cornell University Press, 1984), 13–17; Hugh Davis, *Joshua Leavitt: Evangelical Abolitionist* (Baton Rouge: Louisiana State University Press, 1990), 134–63; and Bruce Laurie, *Beyond Garrison: Antislavery and Social Reform* (Cambridge: Cambridge University Press, 2005).

[9] For a classic critique of scholarship emphasizing abolitionist division after 1840, see Ronald G. Walters, *The Antislavery Appeal: American Abolitionism after 1830* (Baltimore: Johns Hopkins University Press, 1976). See also James Brewer Stewart, *Abolitionist Politics and the Coming of the Civil War* (Amherst: University of Massachusetts Press, 2008), esp. pp. 3–31; as well as work that challenges the binary between moral suasion and political activism or between violence and nonviolence: W. Caleb McDaniel, "Repealing Unions: American Abolitionists, Irish Repeal, and the Origins of Garrisonian Disunionism," *Journal of the Early Republic* 28 (Summer 2008): 243–69; and Stanley Harrold, "Violence and Nonviolence in Kentucky Abolitionism," *Journal of Southern History* 57 (February 1991): 15–38.

All that mattered was one line of demarcation among antislavery activists: the line between immediatism and gradualism. One was heresy; the other was not. This chapter examines how that sharp line came to be drawn.

That Manichean realization did not enter the minds of religiously conservative whites in the Commonwealth, or elsewhere in the South, overnight. In making this argument, this chapter follows closely the careers of three Kentuckians – John C. Young, James G. Birney, and Robert J. Breckinridge (1800–71) – in the early 1830s, as well as those of several close associates, to illustrate how a shared antislavery position splintered into competing factions regarding immediatism. It took white Kentuckians many years to view immediatists as unequivocal heretics, and along the way such a view did not obviously lend itself to a univocal proslavery consensus in the antebellum Bluegrass State.

Rather, white Kentucky's religious mind, like its political mind, always remained conflicted about slavery. Even before statehood in 1792, antislavery activists maintained a modest presence in Kentucky. By the early nineteenth century, all the major denominations in the state – the Methodists, Baptists, and Presbyterians – had vocal antislavery constituencies. Even though these believers would argue for what in a later period would become staples of conservative emancipationism – they emphasized gradualism, the use of legal and constitutional means, and, in differing degrees, white supremacy – their views challenged the larger populace of white Kentuckians who supported slavery's longevity. In one hallmark example, David Barrow (1753–1819), a Baptist minister from Montgomery County, on the eastern outskirts of central Kentucky's Bluegrass region, was forced out of his local association of Baptist churches in 1807 for espousing antislavery views. Barrow was followed by several sympathetic ministers and lay elders, as well as nine churches, who decided to form a dissenting, antislavery association of their own. Called the "Baptized Licking-Locust Association, Friends of Humanity," its foundational principles stated that those who "appear[ed] friendly to perpetual slavery" would remain outside its fellowship. Although there were some exceptions to the rule, slaveholders were not permitted as members.[10]

The Baptist "Friends of Humanity" never claimed more than a dozen churches and three hundred members, and the organization did not survive long beyond Barrow's death in 1819, but its platform was paralleled and succeeded by the nonsectarian Kentucky Abolition Society (KAS). Barrow and his fellow antislavery Baptists established the KAS in 1808, but members of other denominations also populated the society and the Kentucky Methodist Conference sanctioned its efforts. Its membership ranks were also small, with no

[10] Lowell H. Harrison, *The Antislavery Movement in Kentucky* (Lexington: University Press of Kentucky, 1978), 18–27; Asa Earl Martin, *The Antislavery Movement in Kentucky prior to 1850* (Louisville: Standard Printing, 1918), 11–40; Carter Tarrant, *History of the Baptised Ministers and Churches in Kentucky, &c. Friends to Humanity* (Frankfort, KY: William Hunter, 1808), 37–40; Donald G. Mathews, *Slavery and Methodism: A Chapter in American Morality, 1780–1845* (Princeton: Princeton University Press, 1965), 53.

more than two hundred members on the rolls at any one time, but the society did provide a noticeable critique of slavery. In 1822 the KAS began publishing a journal, the *Abolition Intelligencer and Missionary Magazine*. From the start, the operation was hampered by financial difficulties; it published only twelve issues and never circulated to more than five hundred people. The Kentucky Abolition Society's aims were conservative and sought to effect the gradual end of slavery through legal processes. Yet at the time of the journal's founding – aside from Quaker abolitionist Benjamin Lundy's *Genius of Universal Emancipation* published in Jonesborough, Tennessee, and Baltimore, Maryland, from 1821 to 1836 – the *Abolition Intelligencer* was the only antislavery periodical in the United States.[11]

Historians have long debated the relationship between southern antislavery movements before 1831 and the mostly northern "radical" abolitionist movement that pushed for immediate emancipation after that time. Before then, much national antislavery work was like that in Kentucky: conservative in approach and gradual in its application. But 1831 was a turning point. In January of that year, William Lloyd Garrison began publishing his weekly newspaper, *The Liberator*, in Boston, which focused the energies of abolitionists around the cause of immediatism. Then in August, Nat Turner led the largest slave insurrection in American history in Southampton, Virginia, which – in leaving nearly sixty whites dead – reminded white Americans of their horror in the wake of the Haitian Revolt of 1791, sent shockwaves through the nation, galvanized much proslavery opinion, and all but silenced antislavery dissent in the South. Finally, in late December, hundreds of enslaved blacks in Jamaica rose up against a planter class hostile to the idea of emancipation. The "Baptist War" – so called because many of the enslaved leaders were Baptists – spilled into the early weeks of 1832 and was harshly suppressed. As a result of the insurrection and the "trials" of conspirators that followed, well over five hundred blacks were killed. On the heels of the news of Turner's rebellion, word of events in Jamaica traveled to the United States and quickened the resolve of slavery's defenders, but it also did the same for abolitionists in the North who saw an unwarranted religious persecution of Jamaican missionaries and believers who had been accused of fomenting rebellion. Thus, historians have perceived 1831 as a fork that split the road traveled by antislavery activists: immediatists took one path and gradualist-colonizationists another.[12]

---

[11] For examples see "The Curse of Noah," *Abolition Intelligencer and Missionary Magazine* 1.10 (February 1823): 145–7; Appellant, "The Appeal. No. I. To the Citizens of the United States," *Abolition Intelligencer and Missionary Magazine* 1.10 (February 1823): 147–50; and Appellant, "The Appeal. No. II. To Christians in the United States," *Abolition Intelligencer and Missionary Magazine* 1.11 (March 1823): 167–70. See also Harrison, *Antislavery Movement in Kentucky*, 18–29.

[12] The classic statements on the southern roots of national antislavery, which also strongly emphasize its evangelical character, include Dwight L. Dumond, *Antislavery Origins of the Civil War in the United States* (1939; Ann Arbor: University of Michigan Press, 1959), esp. pp. 21–36;

Yet things were never that clean and easy. The harsh distinction between gradualists and abolitionists is a fissure that appears more clearly in the light of historical distance and with the knowledge that the two camps would become increasingly hostile toward one another. As deep as the divisions appear in hindsight, there was much debate between the two groups to follow. That abolitionists especially felt the need to reject colonization as viscerally as they did – as well as the converse, that colonizationists pilloried immediatists – suggests an intellectual interplay between the factions. It is simply false to assume that immediatist antislavery advocacy rapidly disproved and then eclipsed the colonization movement. Instead, it is more accurate to describe a dialogical relationship between the two antislavery positions. Although an irreparable breach later occurred between gradualists and abolitionists, the debate between the camps continued well beyond 1831. Afterward, conservative emancipationists in the Commonwealth may not have accepted the radicalism of immediate abolition, but they all the same continued to deny that they supported the cause of slavery.

Broadly considered, Kentucky's collection of gradual emancipationists – including John C. Young and his like-minded Presbyterian colleagues – believed that sending the state's black population to the Liberia colony was the best way to end slavery. When the Kentucky Colonization Society (KCS) began in 1829 as an extension of the American Colonization Society (ACS; founded in 1816), it became the primary forum for the expression of antislavery sentiment in the Commonwealth. Yet, it never achieved much success. From 1829 to 1859, the KCS sent only 658 blacks to Liberia. Despite some leaders' claims that thousands of African Americans per year would be deported, such wishful thinking failed to account for limited financial resources and an overwhelmingly unwilling black population. Furthermore, colonizationists themselves tended not to agree about their own reasons for supporting the scheme. Colonizationists came from a variety of ideological casts; they were not a monolithic group. As careful historians have shown, colonization was invoked for proslavery, antislavery, and "separationist" – not dealing with slavery per se, but seeking a means of removing blacks from American soil – ends. Still, the primary

Merton L. Dillon, *Benjamin Lundy and the Struggle for Negro Freedom* (Urbana: University of Illinois Press, 1966); and James Brewer Stewart, "Evangelicalism and the Radical Strain in Southern Antislavery Thought during the 1820s," *Journal of Southern History* 39 (August 1973): 379–96. Historians who followed, including Stewart and Dillon themselves, found this argument less persuasive – especially as it concerned southern antislavery's influence on radical abolitionism in New England and its lack of attention to African American voices and actions. However, there can be no question that the Upper South – particularly Kentucky and the Ohio Valley more generally – was a major site of contest over the slavery question. For a clear delineation of the terms of historiographic debate on this issue, see Stanley Harrold, *The Abolitionists and the South, 1831–1861* (Lexington: University Press of Kentucky, 1995), 9–25. For the significance of Jamaica and the Caribbean context, especially its link to Turner's insurrection, see Edward Bartlett Rugemer, *The Problem of Emancipation: The Caribbean Roots of the American Civil War* (Baton Rouge: Louisiana State University Press, 2008), 96–142.

impulse behind colonization was racist: supporters held a paternalistic view of African Americans and believed that free blacks could not thrive among the Commonwealth's white population. Black freedom would be best experienced apart from whites. Slavery may have been wrong, but so too was an interracial society.[13]

Many of the state's chief gradual colonizationists were also some of Kentucky's most prominent slaveholders. Their ranks included such noted politicians as Henry Clay (1777–1852) and Joseph R. Underwood (1791–1876), the long-time U.S. congressman from Bowling Green. Among white Kentucky's religious adherents, no one embodied this antebellum gradualist emancipationist position more clearly than Robert J. Breckinridge, a politician from a prominent Kentucky family who, by 1832, had accepted a call to the Presbyterian ministry, becoming one of the state's most vocal religio-political activists into the 1860s. Breckinridge rose to prominence within national Presbyterian circles – he was elected moderator of the Presbyterian Church USA's General Assembly in 1845 – and maintained an active and domineering presence within the Bluegrass State, helping to found Danville Theological Seminary, which was affiliated with Centre College, in 1853. Like much of white Kentucky's antislavery elite, Breckinridge was a slaveholder himself, owning nine slaves in 1825, seventeen in 1830, and thirty-seven in 1860. If this actuality suggests a contradiction to modern observers between values and action, no such conflict existed in Breckinridge's mind. In the memorable phrase of historian James C. Klotter, slavery in nineteenth-century Kentucky was "ingrained and convenient" for its whites. The inertia perpetuating slavery trumped the forces opposed to the institution.[14]

Breckinridge published his first important antislavery work, *Hints on Slavery*, in 1830, as a series of seven weekly articles in Lexington's *Kentucky*

---

[13] On the varieties of colonizationism, racist motivations, and the denunciation of abolitionism by Kentucky's antislavery mainstream, see Jennifer Cole, "'For the Sake of the Songs of the Men Made Free': James Speed and the Emancipationists' Dilemma in Nineteenth-Century Kentucky," *Ohio Valley History* 4.4 (Winter 2004): 27–48; Tallant, *Evil Necessity*, esp. pp. 27–57; and Harrison, *Antislavery Movement in Kentucky*, 30–7. On colonization as a legitimate form of antislavery expression, see Jeffrey Brooke Allen, "Did Southern Colonizationists Oppose Slavery? Kentucky 1816–1850 as a Test Case," *Register of the Kentucky Historical Society* 75 (April 1977): 92–111; Carl N. Degler, *The Other South: Southern Dissenters in the Nineteenth Century* (New York: Harper & Row, 1974), 22–5; and Beverly C. Tomek, *Colonization and Its Discontents: Emancipation, Emigration, and Antislavery in Antebellum Pennsylvania* (New York: New York University Press, 2011), which emphasizes prominently the role of African American colonizationists. In her work on Rufus W. Bailey, the leading agent of the American Colonization Society in Virginia, Ellen Eslinger concludes that colonizationists may have held sincere antislavery views, but the ACS nonetheless also affirmed the "basic premise that the United States was a society for white people." See Eslinger, "The Brief Career of Rufus W. Bailey, American Colonization Society Agent in Virginia," *Journal of Southern History* 71 (February 2005): 74.

[14] James C. Klotter, *The Breckinridges of Kentucky* (Lexington: University Press of Kentucky, 1986), 63.

Reporter. At the time, Breckinridge – not yet an ordained minister – was serving in the Kentucky legislature. The essays were part of his contribution to an emancipationist movement to amend the state's constitution so as to ban the importation of slaves into the state. According to Breckinridge, state governments needed to handle the slavery question because "the national government has not the smallest power over the subject of slavery within the limits of any state." Breckinridge's emphasis on the sovereignty of states to regulate institutions within their borders would mark many of his arguments in the years that followed.[15]

As he affirmed state sovereignty, Breckinridge also made clear his belief that slavery undermined moral law and needed to be ended in Kentucky. Slavery, he claimed, was a scourge on the land. "[O]ne unborn cannot be a slave," he argued. "You may take a man at his birth, and by an adequate system make him a slave – a brute – a demon. This is man's work." Appealing to his readership's religiosity and common sense, he continued: "The light of reason, history and philosophy – the voice of nature and religion – the spirit of God himself proclaims that the being he created in his own image he must have created free." Consequently, Breckinridge proposed a system of gradual emancipation whereby slaves born after a certain date would become free at a certain age. The young politician proposed that those born to slave women in Kentucky after 1835 be freed at age twenty-one, those born after 1840 should be freed at age sixteen, and those born after 1856 should be free at birth. Thus, he wrote, hereditary slavery would cease to exist.[16]

Once free, he argued, slaves ought to be sent to Liberia. In his support of colonization, Breckinridge demonstrated his commitment to the racial ideology of the ACS, arguing that the races should govern their own kind. If this principle were followed, he asserted, free blacks would have much better opportunities. Ignoring Liberia's ongoing difficulties with both finances and native discontent toward the colonial presence – along with a brutally fatal disease environment – Breckinridge saw the colony as "a model of good order" as a result of its racially homogeneous populace. In America, "[f]ree negroes are very seldom good citizens," he continued, because "they are not citizens at all. The law views them with constant jealousy, and barely tolerates their existence in the country.... The end proposed should be to get rid of both classes, or if that is not practicable, then of the worst." Like many of his fellow advocates of colonization, Breckinridge saw the movement as a Christian endeavor. According to the future Presbyterian minister, in a twist of "presiding Providen[tial]" irony God had allowed "the wretched African"

15 The original articles were later republished as a pamphlet in 1843. Robert J. Breckinridge, *Hints on Slavery* (Lexington: n.p., 1843), 9.
16 Ibid., 16, 23. This plan followed earlier gradualist approaches to ending slavery in the North. For a brief summary, see Steven Hahn, *The Political Worlds of Slavery and Freedom* (Cambridge, MA: Harvard University Press, 2009), 7–10.

to be enslaved, yet "now demands his restoration that he may Christianise his brethren."[17]

Lest anyone think that Breckinridge primarily cared for the welfare of blacks, he was sure to let the readers of *Hints on Slavery* know where he stood. Breckinridge did not advocate immediate abolition. "Slavery itself was preferable to the general residence among us of manumitted slaves," he wrote. Yet a gradual emancipation that sent the African American population abroad would greatly benefit Kentucky's white working class. Which would be "better," he asked – a slave population with "no motive for toil but the rod" or a "hardy, happy, and laborious yeomanry," the future white population of the state? For Breckinridge, in the question lay the answer.[18]

Breckinridge was neither the first nor the only Kentuckian to place white concerns at the center of his antislavery argumentation, and the strategy proved a successful one in *Hints on Slavery*. The state's immediately contentious Nonimportation Act passed in February 1833, due in large part to the activities of antislavery conservatives such as Breckinridge. The "Law of 1833" legally blocked Kentuckians from bringing more slaves into the Commonwealth and placed restrictions on slave trading. Opponents disdained the 1833 nonimportation law almost from the moment it passed, and proslavery Kentuckians spent the greater part of the next two decades seeking its repeal.[19]

In the three years between *Hints on Slavery* and the passage of the Nonimportation Act, Breckinridge left professional politics for a career in the Presbyterian ministry. Though sparked by a religious conversion, Breckinridge's career move did not mean that he gave up political activity. No longer in Kentucky to relish firsthand the success of the Nonimportation Law of 1833 – he had accepted the pastorate of Baltimore's Second Presbyterian Church in 1832 – Breckinridge continued to write publicly against slavery and in support of conservative emancipation. In June 1833, just a few months after Kentucky codified nonimportation, he published "Hints on Colonization and Abolition,"

[17] Breckinridge, *Hints on Slavery*, 6, 11. Breckinridge's arguments about colonization as a Christianizing endeavor follow closely those made by some of colonization's earliest advocates. For an example, see the writings of Robert Finley, a Presbyterian minister from Baskingridge, New Jersey, and an early member of the American Colonization Society, in Isaac V. Brown, *Biography of the Rev. Robert Finley*, 2nd ed. (1857; New York: Arno Press, 1969), 99.

[18] Breckinridge, *Hints on Slavery*, 5–8.

[19] The argument that slavery was wrong because it ultimately undermined the interests of Kentucky's white population featured prominently in writings and speeches by Henry Clay, Joseph Underwood, and Cassius Clay, among others. To quote historian Lowell Harrison at length: "In whatever lowly economic status a poor white found himself, he had the psychological assurance that he was superior to all blacks, no matter how much better off they might be in material terms. This racial distinction helped forge a bond between poor whites and wealthy planters that often baffled and infuriated opponents of slavery." On the white-over-black antislavery arguments, see Tallant, *Evil Necessity*, 11–14, 80–2; Harrison, *Antislavery Movement in Kentucky*, 48–9 (quote); Cole, "James Speed and the Emancipationists' Dilemma," 31–4; and Stanley Harrold, "Cassius Clay on Slavery and Race: A Reinterpretation," *Slavery and Abolition* 9.1 (May 1988): 42–56.

an article designed to answer charges brought by Boston's most noted radical abolitionist, William Lloyd Garrison (1805–79), against the colonization movement.[20]

In his influential and hard-hitting *Thoughts on African Colonization* (1832), the Bostonian built on arguments he had been making in his immediatist antislavery newspaper, *The Liberator*, since its founding in 1831. The Yankee abolitionist had supported colonization in the late 1820s, but had recently abandoned that scheme, decrying it as a ploy that merely served the goals of slaveholders. Garrison was especially influenced by a group of leading African American antislavery activists in Boston, including Methodist minister Samuel Snowden and a member of Snowden's congregation, David Walker.[21]

In 1829, Walker (1785–1830), a free black originally from North Carolina, published arguably the most damning attack on slavery in the period, *Appeal to the Colored Citizens of the World*. Drawing from a deep well of evangelical moral reasoning and biblical textual analysis, Walker excoriated the *"white Christians of America"* for their endorsement of slavery and – especially relevant for free blacks north of slavery – blind acceptance of white supremacy. As Walker had argued, even the biblical Hebrews, enslaved "by the Egyptians" and "under *heathen Pharoah*," were treated better than nineteenth-century African Americans "under the *enlightened Christians of America*." Moreover, no white American Christian could make honest claim to the title of that faith when, in Walker's analysis, there had not been a single pagan civilization in the world history that "ever treated a set of human beings, as the white Christians of America do us, the blacks, or Africans."[22]

In striking at the heart of American racism, as well as slavery, Walker did not make the distinction that so many conservative emancipationists made: that ending slavery was one thing, but ending racism was another. To this end, Walker blistered colonization as "a plan got up, by a gang of slave-holders to select the free people of colour from among the slaves, that our more miserable brethren may be the better secured in ignorance and wretchedness, to work their farms and dig their mines, and thus go on enriching the Christians with their blood and groans."[23]

A particular target of Walker's anger was Kentucky's most famous citizen and a foremost proponent of colonization, Henry Clay. Clay had presided over

---

[20] Vivien Sandlund, "Robert Breckinridge, Presbyterian Antislavery Conservative," *Journal of Presbyterian History* 78 (Summer 2000): 148–50.

[21] On Garrison and colonization, see Stewart, *Holy Warriors*, 30–31, 55. On Walker's influence on Garrison, see Peter P. Hinks, "Introduction," in David Walker, *Appeal to the Colored Citizens of the World*, ed. Hinks (University Park: Pennsylvania State University Press, 2000), xi–xliv, esp. pp. xviii, xli–xliv. On the larger free black community of Boston, and especially Walker and Garrison, see Stephen Kantrowitz, *More than Freedom: Fighting for Black Citizenship in a White Republic, 1829–1889* (New York: Penguin, 2012), 13–83.

[22] Walker, *Appeal*, 11, 16, 76.

[23] Ibid., 58.

the December 1816 meeting in Washington, DC, that led to the founding of the American Colonization Society and he championed the cause for the next several decades. Not long after his term as secretary of state in President John Quincy Adams' administration (1825–9), Clay gave a speech to the Kentucky Colonization Society that presaged arguments to come from Robert J. Breckinridge. In December 1829 Clay endorsed free labor and expressed concern about slavery because, given "the cruelty of the origin of negro slavery... it is impossible not to anticipate frequent insurrections among the blacks in the United States." Because enslaved peoples "are rational beings like ourselves," Clay claimed, they would not long accept the condition of bondage. Yet once freed from slavery, according to the Kentuckian, there would be manifest difficulty for African Americans. As he contended, "the free people of colour are by far, as a class, the most corrupt, depraved and abandoned." Though there may have been a few "honorable exceptions" to this blanket assertion, Clay believed that it was "not so much their fault, as the consequence" of allowing free African Americans to persist in what was by all accounts a white man's country: "The laws, it is true, proclaim them free; but prejudices, more powerful than any laws, deny them the privileges of freemen." As the politician contended, free blacks "occupy a middle station between the free white population, and the slaves of the United States," but "the tendency of their habits is to corrupt both." The solution for Clay was therefore to support the American Colonization Society's program of black expatriation. Not only would the United States be divested of a troublesome populace but also Africa would benefit from receiving "Missionaries, of the descendants of Africa itself, with the same interests, sympathies, and constitutions of the natives, to communicate the benefits of our religion" to "untutored savages." Africa was "destitute of the blessings both of Christianity and civilization," but helpfully, according to Clay, the ACS was "an instrument which, under the guidance of providence," was prepared to convert the African continent to faith and bring it within "the pale of civilization."[24]

David Walker found abominable such a perspective on American slavery and racial inequality. Noting especially that Clay had claimed a Christian mandate for the work of racial exclusion, Walker offered the following: "Here I ask Mr. Clay, what kind of Christianity? Did he mean such as they have among the Americans – distinction, whip, blood and oppression? I pray the Lord Jesus Christ to forbid it." In Walker's prophetic interpretation, the slaveholder Clay had risen to his position of power thanks in no small part to divine blessings. "But what," Walker asked, "has this gentleman done for the Lord, after having done so much for him? The Lord has a suffering people, whose moans and groans at his feet for deliverance from oppression and wretchedness, pierce the very throne of Heaven, and call loudly on the God of Justice, to be

---

[24] Henry Clay, *An Address Delivered to the Colonization Society of Kentucky, at Frankfort, December 17, 1829* (Frankfort, Ky.: J. H. Holeman, 1830), quotes 12, 24.

revenged." As far as Walker was concerned the answers to these questions were obvious:

> Do you believe that Mr. Henry Clay, late Secretary of State, and now in Kentucky, is a friend to the blacks, further, than his personal interest extends? Is it not his greatest object and glory upon earth, to sink us into miseries and wretchedness by making slaves of us, to work his plantation to enrich him and his family? Does he care a pinch of snuff about Africa – whether it remains a land of Pagans and of blood, or of Christians, so long as he gets enough of her sons and daughters to dig up gold and silver for him? If he had no slaves, and could obtain them in no other way if it were not, repugnant to the laws of his country, which prohibit the importation of slaves (which act was, indeed, more through apprehension than humanity) would he not try to import a few from Africa, to work his farm? Would he work in the hot sun to earn his bread, if he could make an African work for nothing, particularly, if he could keep him in ignorance and make him believe that God made him for nothing else but to work for him? Is not Mr. Clay a white man, and too delicate to work in the hot sun!! Was he not made by his Creator to sit in the shade, and make the blacks work without remuneration for their services, to support him and his family!!!

For Walker, colonization was nothing more than a ruse designed to keep African Americans, free or enslaved, in a subservient position. By proposing that blacks should be removed from American soil, colonizationists never had to come to terms with their false notions of racial superiority. Colonization perpetuated, rather than solved, America's race problem.[25]

It was precisely this sort of critique that found its way to William Lloyd Garrison, and he put it to use in *Thoughts on African Colonization.* Lending support to colonization offered the white populace a means of easing its conscience about slavery without, as the Bostonian put it, "giving offence to those slaveholders with whom they associate...nor denounc[ing] the crime of holding human beings in bondage." He allowed that many colonizationists thought they were serving antislavery ends and were unaware of these consequences. Yet such individuals, he asserted, "are laboring under the same delusion as that which swayed Saul of Tarsus – persecuting the blacks even unto a strange country, and verily believing that they are doing God service." Garrison's interpretation of colonization represented a watershed in the American antislavery movement, becoming the foremost articulation of the radical antislavery critique of colonization.[26]

In response, Robert J. Breckinridge argued, following Henry Clay, that colonization was rooted in the desire both to end slavery and to spread the gospel

---

[25] Walker, *Appeal*, 49–53.

[26] Ibid., 150; William Lloyd Garrison, *Thoughts on African Colonization* (1832; New York: Arno Press, 1968), 3, 2, 19. On the growing division between colonizationists and abolitionists, see Stewart, *Holy Warriors*, 55–6; Harrold, *Abolitionists and the South*, 18–19; Tallant, *Evil Necessity*, 38–9, and Degler, *The Other South*, 22–5.

to the African continent. The minister's "Hints on Colonization and Abolition" elaborated the argument he first raised in 1830. "We hazard nothing in
asserting," he wrote, that the relationship between black and white "cannot
remain as it" is. Moreover, the health and stability of the United States did
not permit "a nation of idle, profligate, and ignorant persons." Like other ACS
members, Breckinridge claimed that white Americans had a responsibility to
ameliorate the condition of the nation's black population. "They are victims
to our fathers and now us," he wrote. "[H]ow, we pause not to ask. But they
are victims: and every sentiment of religion impels us to regard their case with
an eye of pity."[27]

According to Breckinridge, there were two possible solutions to the race
problem. Free blacks could be "admit[ted] all the privileges of whites," or
Americans could "divide the two races totally, by colonizing the free blacks."
The Presbyterian minister favored the latter approach. Outright egalitarianism,
he argued, could never be achieved without racial "amalgamation," and he
could not "see what good was to be effected, by reducing all races of men to
one homogeneous mass; mixing the white, the red, the tawny, the brown, the
black, all together and thus reproducing throughout the world, or in any single
State, a race different in some physical appearance from all that now exist."
To maintain racial autonomy, he wrote, free blacks should be sent to a climate
"perfectly fitted to [them], and to nobody else on earth." "[I]n Liberia," he
wrote, "the moral and intellectual condition" of American blacks would be
"immediately and greatly improved," and they would "retain in an equal or
higher degree" any "advantage" they possessed in the United States.[28]

In "Hints on Colonization and Abolition," Breckinridge also denounced the
slave system as a whole. "Slavery," he wrote, "cannot be made perpetual,"
because it was "ruinous to the community that tolerates it" and "most cruel
and unjust to its victims." He decried "instant abolition," but asserted that
God "will, in his own good time and way, break the rod of the oppressor,
and let all the oppressed go free." Unlike his evangelical counterparts farther
south who found biblical sanction for slavery, Breckinridge saw an inherent
conflict between slavery as described in the Bible and as it existed in the United
States. Masters in the Scriptures, he noted, were commanded to "give unto their
servants that which is just and equal." "[T]o what feature of [American] slavery
may that description apply! Just and equal!" he exclaimed. Such a system did
not exist in the United States where slaves could not marry or raise families
unmolested. Anyone who tried to deny this fact, he argued, "has simply no
moral sense." Furthermore, "he who presumes that God will approve, and
reward habitual injustice and wrong, is ignorant alike of God, and of his own
heart." Shaped by Kentucky's conservative antislavery heritage and evangelical

[27] Breckinridge, "Hints on Colonization and Abolition; with Reference to the Black Race," *Biblical
Repertory and Princeton Review* 5 (July 1833): 283–4.
[28] Ibid., 284–5, 287–9.

Protestantism's emphasis on biblical authority, Breckinridge in 1833 concluded
that U.S. slavery was "undeniably ... contrary to the revealed will of God."[29]

Breckinridge followed "Hints on Colonization" with a public speaking
appearance on behalf of the scheme in Boston in June 1834. As he hoped, he
succeeded in attracting Garrison's attention. The Boston abolitionist quickly
denounced Breckinridge as an enemy of American black equality, accused him
of "fostering 'a spirit of Negro hatred,'" and even suggested that Breckinridge
was, in truth, proslavery. Breckinridge condemned Garrison in kind. With the
paths of colonization and abolition diverging at the national level, Breckinridge
became a bitter enemy of abolitionism. The rise of militant antislavery thought
pushed Breckinridge, like colonizationists around the United States, to assert
more forcefully a conservative position on race. In this way, Breckinridge's
trajectory serves as a model for the larger population of white religious conservative emancipationists. He came to despise abolitionists and later in his career
often turned to proslavery circles for support rather than look for aid among
the Garrisonians.[30]

Race was not the only point of contention between Breckinridge and more
radical abolitionists. Breckinridge also disapproved of what he saw as their
more cavalier approach to conservative Christian doctrines. "We do not pretend to justify slavery," Breckinridge argued in 1833, but "abolitionists err in
principle." "Instant abolition," he concluded, "is not more sound in morals,
than it is hurtful if impossible in practice." After his exchange with Garrison,
in September 1835 he argued that abolitionist "principles" were "false, pernicious, and immoral. They are not true in morals, they are not the principles of
the gospel, they are not good for the human race, they are impracticable, they
are unreasonable, and some of them stupid and shocking." In short, Breckinridge believed that gradualism and colonization rested on firmer Christian foot-
ing than did immediate abolitionism. In making this contention, Breckinridge
revealed how closely his religious understanding of gradualist emancipationism
aligned with proslavery ideas.[31]

Abolitionism – and its integrationist implications – was a threat that
nineteenth-century whites in the Commonwealth knew much about, perhaps
more so than many of their southern neighbors after 1830, because lands just
to the north of Kentucky hosted many debates about the merits of radical
abolition. In many ways, most religious whites on the Lower North's free soil
differed little from their counterparts on the slave soil of the Upper South
regarding matters of race and slavery: insofar as they wanted to end slavery, they predominantly were committed to paradigms that emphasized white

---

[29] Ibid., 294–7.
[30] Klotter, *Breckinridges of Kentucky*, 68–9; Sandlund, "Breckinridge, Antislavery Conservative,"
    150–1; Garrison and Breckinridge quoted 151.
[31] Breckinridge, "Hints on Colonization and Abolition," 300, 302 (quotes); Robert J.
    Breckinridge, "Abolitionism," *Baltimore Literary and Religious Magazine* 1 (September 1835):
    285.

over black and pushed for gradual emancipation connected to colonization. As recently as 1829, several hundred whites rioted in Cincinnati and called for the enforcement of Ohio's "Black Laws" (passed in 1804 and 1807). The moment compelled some 1,100 to 2,200 African Americans to leave the Queen City for a settlement in Upper Canada, where the provincial governor welcomed them. It was precisely because of such views, so hostile to black freedom, that by the 1830s many abolitionist northerners interested in immediately eradicating the curse of slavery from American soil saw the Ohio Valley as a chief site in the contest for the future of the institution.[32]

At the same time that Breckinridge was sparring with Garrison, a fellow Presbyterian minister in southern Ohio, Samuel Crothers (1783–1855) – who a few years later would antagonize John C. Young and his gradualist colleagues – published a pamphlet, *Strictures on African Slavery* (1833), celebrating immediatism and denouncing slavery. Two years earlier, Crothers announced his support for abolition in a series of fifteen articles in the *Cincinnati Journal* and then served as chair of a committee for the Cincinnati Presbytery in August 1831 to investigate the slavery question in the churches. In this succession of activity, Crothers argued that slavery was a sin that could only be dealt with by breaking fellowship with slaveholders. By 1833 Crothers' opinions had sharpened. Writing to a Protestant audience steeped in anti-Catholic prejudices, he argued in *Strictures on African Slavery* that the evil practice of slavery had been introduced to the western world by the Roman Catholic Church as a part of fifteenth- and sixteenth-century Spain's imperial project. Over time, slaveholding came more broadly to the Christian world, and Protestant European nations found their "lusts . . . blinding their understandings, and stupefying their consciences" as they engaged in the slave trade. Here was a complex historical irony, and Crothers aimed to answer the question it raised: "how did it happen, that while Protestants professed to reject, in mass, the abominations of Popery, they retained the sin of slaveholding?" The fact was, as Crothers explained, that Protestants in Europe had made an "unhallowed alliance of *Church and State.*" Because Protestants in Europe all lived in nations with established religions – unlike the American arrangement – "they might have cleansed themselves from this sin [of slavery]," but instead they had "become harlots, by leaning, in imitation of the 'mother of harlots'" – the Catholic Church – "on the arm of kings and emperors, instead of the arm of their husband," Jesus Christ. Because, as Crothers argued, "African slavery in the Christian church, is the child of the 'Mother of Abominations,'" it was as if

[32] See Robert H. Abzug, *Passionate Liberator: Theodore Dwight Weld and the Dilemma of Reform* (New York: Oxford University Press, 1980), 74–97; Leon F. Litwack, *North of Slavery: The Negro in the Free States, 1790–1860* (Chicago: University of Chicago Press, 1961), 72–4; Joe William Trotter Jr., *River Jordan: African American Urban Life in the Ohio Valley* (Lexington: University Press of Kentucky, 1998), 35. On the fate of the Canadian colony, see Patrick Rael, *Black Identity and Black Protest in the Antebellum North* (Chapel Hill: University of North Carolina Press, 2002), 120–4.

Protestants had given up their post-Reformation liberalizing doctrinal legacy and instead taken on a bastard progeny.[33]

Like Walker and Garrison before him, Crothers blasted colonization as a mask for proslavery interests. Continuing to draw on anti-Catholic rhetoric, Crothers made his case: "The name of penances and indulgences, is odious among Protestants. But it is only the name that is universally hated." To be sure, Crothers claimed, "Many a slave holder has cleared scores with his conscience, both for the past and future, by a contribution to a Colonization society." Yet this was not nearly enough, according to Crothers. Any church that tolerated slaveholders was "defiled," "polluted," and "leprous." The only way to avoid having one's soul implicated in such a "church's defilement" was to repent with more than mere words: "The abandonment of gross sin from selfish motives, accompanied with refusal to repent, will not avert the judgments of heaven from a nation, much less cleanse and save a guilty church." An immediate end to slavery was the only way to demonstrate that one had fully repented of such destructive behavior.[34]

Crothers' arguments were radical by Kentucky standards, but even in southeast Ohio, where he ministered, they were not popular. That much became clear the year after his abolitionist essay appeared in print. One of the most formal and widely influential debates on a related set of questions took place in early 1834 just across the Ohio River from Kentucky, outside Cincinnati, at Lane Theological Seminary, where Crothers served on the board of trustees. The fledgling seminary had been founded by Presbyterians in 1829 to prepare ministers for the task of missionizing the new American West and – consistent with Crothers' manifest anti-Catholicism – making sure that the United States remained a Protestant nation. Within a few years Lane made its mark as a serious ministerial and intellectual training ground, securing in 1832 one of the most famous ministers in the country as a professor of theology and its president, Lyman Beecher (1775–1863) of Boston. With Beecher's arrival, the seminary's profile rapidly expanded: by 1833 it began to attract more funds for its endowment, and it also recruited students from diverse geographical backgrounds, though they were almost entirely from the North.[35]

Several of these new students, including Theodore Dwight Weld (1803–95), as well as brothers Henry B. Stanton (1805–87) and Robert L. Stanton (1810–85), had already developed reputations as influential speakers and religious leaders, but they were relatively recent evangelical converts thanks to the ministry of the revivalist minister Charles G. Finney (1792–1875). Finney was a

---

[33] Lawrence Thomas Lesick, *The Lane Rebels: Evangelicalism and Antislavery in Antebellum America* (Metuchen, NJ: Scarecrow Press, 1980), 75–6; Samuel Crothers, *Strictures on African Slavery* (Rossville, OH: Taylor Webster, 1833), quotes 4, 7.

[34] Crothers, *Strictures on African Slavery*, 26–7.

[35] For the classic Protestant argument for missionizing the American West in this period, see Lyman Beecher, *A Plea for the West* (Cincinnati: Truman and Smith, 1835). On early Lane and its students, see Lesick, *Lane Rebels*, 20–51, 70–1, 76. Of the one hundred students enrolled by January 1834, only eight were from the South.

wildly popular – and wildly controversial – preacher from Presbyterian circles who had risen to prominence in the 1820s in upstate New York. A former lawyer, Finney was known for using what he called the "new measures": his teaching drew from the early republic's democratic evangelical ethos, rejected traditional sources of religious authority in favor of the individual's own sensibilities, and emphasized an individualized faith that centered on the personal conversion experience. Many evangelical groups in the period taught some version of this Christian gospel – especially Methodists, who served as models for Finney's ministry – but for Presbyterians, much of Finney's teaching undermined their core principles. He directly attacked Calvinist verities that emphasized divine sovereignty over human free will in matters of salvation. Humans, in Finney's teaching, were "free moral agents" who could choose for themselves if they would reject sin and follow the call of Jesus Christ. Thus, Finney was famous for his "anxious bench," special seating reserved at the front of the congregation for those in the crowd who seemed most ripe for conversion.[36]

Yet it was not just Finney's theology and soteriology that proved beyond the pale to many more conservative believers. They also chafed at what Finney saw as the logical conclusion of his version of Christianity, which compelled disciples to aim for nothing less than the total transformation of the world they found themselves in so that sin might be removed and greater access to salvation would be offered to humanity. Finneyite belief was particularly demanding of its adherents. It required complete moral change and a disciplined life. Though the teaching would not fully cohere until the late 1830s, Finney and his cohort argued that believers could become – and should strive to be – entirely sanctified within their lifetimes. This "evangelical perfectionist doctrine" called for a rejection of all forms of sin as part of the converted Christian life, including those sins that were broadly pervasive in society and inhibited individuals' abilities to live free from social, intellectual, and spiritual constraints. Such teaching led its followers to embrace causes such as broad moral reform, temperance, and – particularly bracing for conservative believers – antislavery.[37]

Theodore Dwight Weld was one of the earliest spokesmen for this Finneyite antislavery application of the gospel. When he arrived at Lane in 1833, Weld had recently conjoined Finney's theology with a Garrisonian emphasis on immediate abolition, and he seemed particularly keen to sway the student

[36] Abzug, *Passionate Liberator*, 47–50; Nathan O. Hatch, *The Democratization of American Christianity* (New Haven: Yale University Press, 1989), 196–9; Lesick, *Lane Rebels*, 72–6, 82–8; James H. Moorhead, "The 'Restless Spirit of Radicalism': Old School Fears and the Schism of 1837," *Journal of Presbyterian History* 78:1 (Spring 2000): 26.

[37] For a discussion of the multivalent meanings and applications of perfectionism in the 1830s North, see Douglas M. Strong, *Perfectionist Politics: Abolitionism and the Religious Tensions of American Democracy* (Syracuse: Syracuse University Press, 1999), 12–43, esp. pp. 28–33; Abzug, *Passionate Liberator*, 82–97; Lesick, *Lane Rebels*, 82–8. For an early and representative argument by Finney against slavery that was linked expressly to temperance, see Charles G. Finney, *Lectures on Revivals of Religion* (New York: Leavitt, Lord, and Co., 1835), 265–6, 274–80.

body to an embrace of abolitionism. Several members of the faculty, including Beecher and Calvin Stowe, were vocal gradual emancipationists and members of the Cincinnati Colonization Society, and many students shared their views. For Weld, however, gradualism was not enough. The year before Weld enrolled at Lane, in the summer of 1832, the seminary's students had formally debated whether the North should, as an abstract principle, support the suppression of slave rebellions in the American South. In the wake of Nat Turner's rebellion, the only person who dared to argue that enslaved peoples should be allowed the right to violently throw off their chains without interference was Henry B. Stanton. Not only was the opinion unpopular at Lane but also such a notion – which most whites saw as fomenting race war – was unthinkable to most Cincinnati whites. Gradual emancipation, with attendant black expatriation from American soil, made sense in this locale. Abolition certainly did not.[38]

Within a year of Weld's arrival, however, he began pushing his fellow students to see the limitations of their views. Mostly, this effort took place in the form of individual conversations, but in February 1834, Weld led a group of students to press the faculty for the opportunity to debate the merits of abolition publicly. For Beecher and the faculty, a discussion of such a controversial set of issues – held in a region that was not friendly to antislavery in general – risked sowing seeds of dissension at the new seminary and threatened to undermine its reputation. In an official statement, Beecher informed the students that the faculty hoped to support such a debate one day, but they could not do so at that moment.[39]

Although the faculty argued that a student debate over antislavery would be "inexpedient," they also refused to prohibit free speech among the students. As a result, the students ignored the faculty's counsel and, beginning February 5, 1834, argued over the course of nine evenings about answers to two separate but related questions: first, whether "the people of the Slaveholding States" should "abolish Slavery immediately"; and second, whether "the doctrines, tendencies, and measures of the American Colonization Society" were "worthy of the patronage of the Christian public." In the course of the debate, the students explored key colonizationist arguments in official literature produced by the ACS, especially from its flagship publication, the *African Repository*. The students then contrasted it with leading abolitionist writings, including the founding document of the newly formed American Anti-Slavery Society, "Declaration of Sentiments" (1833), which called for immediate abolition with "no compensation" for "planters emancipating the slaves" and, in Garrisonian language, flatly denounced colonization: "We regard as delusive,

---

[38] Abzug, *Passionate Liberator*, 82–8; Lesick, *Lane Rebels*, 72–6; Henry B. Stanton, *Random Recollections*, 3rd ed. (New York: Harper Brothers, 1887), 46–7. On Lane's colonizationist faculty, see Lesick, *Lane Rebels*, 75; and "Cincinnati Colonization Society," *African Repository* 10 (July 1834): 148–9.

[39] Lesick, *Lane Rebels*, 76–8.

cruel, and dangerous, any scheme of expatriation which pretends to aid either directly or indirectly, in the emancipation of the slaves, or to be a substitute for the immediate and total abolition of slavery." Several students had entered the debates committed to colonizationist principles, and the more visceral writings of William Lloyd Garrison had been prohibited from consideration because – in addition to his religious skepticism – they did not want to unfairly prejudice the discussion against colonization. Yet, if the students had hoped initially for a balanced discussion, the results were anything but: at the end of the debates the overwhelming majority of the student body concluded, by vote, that true believers must reject colonization and push for the immediate abolition of American slavery. One week after the debates, most of the students formed an antislavery society and committed themselves to immediatism. A substantial number of students also began relief work among Cincinnati's African American community, which included giving talks, teaching literacy and religious knowledge, and establishing a library.[40]

The results especially impressed Henry Stanton, who in the aftermath of the debate wrote a letter that was later reprinted and widely circulated by William Lloyd Garrison. In it, Stanton argued that the Lane debates proved "that prejudice is vincible, that colonization is vulnerable, and that immediate emancipation is not only right, and practicable, but is '*expedient*.'" Noting that there were some southern-born students who became abolitionists in the midst of the debates, Stanton went on to assert his belief "that southern minds, trained and educated amidst all the prejudices of a slaveholding community, can, with the blessing of God, be reached and influenced by *facts and arguments, as easy as any other class of our citizens.*"[41]

No doubt much of Stanton's opinion was abolitionist fantasy, but as evidence for his claims, Stanton did not have to look much further than his colleague James A. Thome (1813–73) of Augusta, Kentucky. The son of a slaveholder, Thome was among the students converted from a colonizationist to an abolitionist paradigm. Just over two months after the debates, in May 1834, Thome appeared at the annual meeting of the American Anti-Slavery Society in New York City as the delegate from Lane Seminary. There, Thome told an attentive audience that he had been practically raised by the institution of slavery – "suckled at its breast and dandled on its knee" – and absorbed its "oft-taught lessons of the coloured man's inferiority." Like many white religious Kentuckians, Thome argued that he "was for several years a member of the Colonization Society" and in his past he had financially supported and "eulogized its measures." Yet now as an abolitionist, Thome could see that the

---

[40] Henry B. Stanton, "Great Debate at Lane Seminary," in *Debate at the Lane Seminary, Cincinnati* (Boston: Garrison & Knapp, 1834), 3; *Declaration of Sentiments and Constitution of the American Anti-Slavery Society* (Philadelphia: Pennsylvania Anti-Slavery Society, 1861), 9–10; Lesick, *Lane Rebels*, 79–89, 106 n94; Abzug, *Passionate Liberator*, 94–5.

[41] Stanton, "Great Debate at Lane Seminary," 5.

actual "direct influence [of colonization] upon my mind was to lessen my conviction of the evil of slavery, and to deepen and sanctify my prejudice against
the coloured race." This was the truly "mournful" aspect of colonization's
"work in Kentucky." The evil scheme, Thome contended, "like the Hindoo
goddess, with smiling face and winning air, grasps in her wide embrace, the
zeal of the church and the benevolence of the world, and, pressing them to
her bosom, thrusts them through with the hidden steel." Still, if colonization's
results in his home state were seductive, deceitful, and ultimately murderous,
Thome held out hope. Even if most Kentucky whites were beholden to colonizationism, he thought that some in the state were "rising above this influence."
Yes, Thome maintained, "the tendencies of the system *I know* to be pernicious
in the extreme," but he also believed that "Kentucky was rapidly awakening"
to the fact that "[s]lavery stands in opposition to the spirit of the age."[42]

Thome's confidence rested on the belief that some "[c]onscientious citizens"
in Kentucky appeared to be organizing themselves into abolitionist "associations." It was not an unfounded assumption. Weld and several other Lane
students had been corresponding for some time with an agent of the American
Colonization Society in central Kentucky named James G. Birney. Shortly after
the Lane debates, Birney – an attorney by training and a former slaveholder
turned colonizationist-emancipationist – found himself persuaded by abolitionist logic. Birney had been born into a slaveholding family from Danville and,
after training for law at Princeton, became a slave owner through marriage
in 1816. Following a brief stint in the Kentucky legislature shortly thereafter,
Birney moved in 1817 to northern Alabama to seek his fortune as a cotton
planter. By 1821 he owned forty-three slaves – a number that indicated significant wealth and financial commitment – but by 1823 a reversal of fortune due
to heavy gambling debts, crop failure, and fallout from the Panic of 1819 convinced Birney to quit planting, sell most of his slaves, and open a law practice
in Huntsville.[43]

After giving up most of his slaves and the planter life, Birney became a fast
success in the legal profession, and he also emerged as an active participant in
local and national politics. At that time, though he believed in a Jeffersonian sort
of way that slavery was a problematic institution, and although he claimed that
he wanted his slaves to be treated well, Birney was no antislavery activist. Like
several of the students at Lane Seminary, however, Birney's opinion about the
evils of the institution began to change because of an 1826 religious conversion
through Finneyite revivalism; he subsequently joined the Presbyterian Church
because of an affinity for Finney's theology. By the summer of 1826, after
reading the American Colonization Society's *African Repository*, Birney began
financially supporting the ACS and persuaded his church in Huntsville to also

[42] James A. Thome, "Speech of James A. Thome, of Kentucky, Delivered at the Annual Meeting
of the American Anti-Slavery Society, May 6, 1834," in *Debate at the Lane Seminary*, 7, 10.
[43] Betty Fladeland, *James Gillespie Birney: Slaveholder to Abolitionist* (Ithaca: Cornell University
Press, 1955), 1–24.

take up collections on behalf of the society. He pressed successfully for an 1827 Alabama law that barred the importation of slaves into the state, and even though it was repealed two years later in 1829, Birney continued to work against slavery's expansion in the state.[44]

Birney's connection to Weld began when the younger orator passed through Huntsville in June 1832. Although Weld himself was not yet fully committed to immediate abolitionism, he was a forceful critic of the slavery system. Even if Weld would shortly thereafter condemn colonization in a letter to Birney, it was probably because of Weld's influence that Birney became convinced that he needed to work more directly, in a full-time capacity, for the advancement of colonization. He subsequently accepted a position with the American Colonization Society as an agent over a five-state territory in the South. However, when he continually found his efforts frustrated in Alabama, Birney opted in late 1833 to move back to his home state of Kentucky and return to his native Danville to advance the cause.[45]

Birney had good reason to think his work would be well received in Danville. In late 1830 and early 1831, several Kentucky slaveholders with Danville connections, including Robert J. Breckinridge, John C. Young, and Birney's cousin John Green, had publicly endorsed a platform calling for "gradual and safe emancipation," but their efforts short-circuited before work began in earnest. Soon after his return to the state, in December 1833, Birney reconnected with some of those same emancipationists, including Green and Young, to establish the "Kentucky Society for the Gradual Relief of the State from Slavery." As the group's name stated, its approach was gradualist, but in a widely circulated statement on the society's goals, Birney wrote that its "object" was nothing less than *the total abolition of slavery throughout the Commonwealth.*" The Kentucky gradualists rejected "simultaneous emancipation," which tended to present itself "only under the pressure of *revolution*" and thus conjured up fears of the Haitian revolution as well as the recent events in Southampton and Jamaica; however, they pushed for "*immediate* preparation for *future* emancipation." The plan included an apprenticeship system for enslaved peoples as well as a pledge from society members to emancipate their own slaves when they reached the age of twenty-five. Unlike previous gradualist programs, however, the Birney-led Kentucky Society took a more pessimistic approach to colonization. Even though "most of us [are] members of the Colonization Society," they contended, "we would not . . . make colonization on the coast of Africa, the certain consequence of emancipation."[46]

---

[44] Ibid., 25–50.

[45] Ibid., 51–74; Abzug, *Passionate Liberator*, 85; Theodore D. Weld, letter to James G. Birney, September 27, 1832, in *The Letters of James Gillespie Birney, 1831–1857*, ed. Dwight L. Dumond, 2 vols. (Gloucester, MA: Peter Smith, 1966), 1:27.

[46] William Birney, *James G. Birney and His Times* (New York: Appleton and Company, 1890), 98–101; Fladeland, *Birney*, 77–9; "Constitution and Address of the Kentucky Society for the Gradual Relief of the State from Slavery," *Letters of Birney*, 1:100, 103–4, 106.

Here was a substantial deviation from earlier gradualist paradigms. The American public had not yet provided the kind of financial "aid which is necessary to ensure success," and state budgets were strapped for cash. Colonization might have thus been desirable to these Kentucky gradualists, but it increasingly appeared "that the friends of perpetual slavery are, year after year, and generation after generation, amusing the friends of emancipation and drawing them off from the main question" – ending slavery – "and engaging them in discussions upon incidental points. They agree in the necessity of preparation; but they are never ready to begin to prepare."[47]

Privately, Birney put his opinion even more succinctly. Writing to Ralph R. Gurley, the secretary of the American Colonization Society, he thought colonization was "impracticable" as "the means of ridding us of *Slavery*," although he still thought that "[i]t will be the mode under Divine providence of enlightening and Christianizing robbed and spoiled AFRICA." While he remained a colonizationist, seeing the scheme as "a valuable auxiliary to the cause of gradual emancipation," Birney's private correspondence reflected a growing pessimism. He was elected a vice president of the Kentucky Colonization Society in January 1834 – at a meeting he did not attend – but it was clear that he was distancing himself from much of the movement. A few months later, Birney read of the results of the Lane debates and felt compelled to go visit his friend Theodore Weld in Cincinnati. Impressed by the moral resolve of the students as well as their arguments, Birney resolved to give up gradualism. In May 1834 he resigned from his posts both with the KCS and the Kentucky Society for the Gradual Relief of the State from Slavery. Then in early June he manumitted the six slaves he still owned.[48]

With the help of Weld, Henry Stanton, Lane board member and abolitionist minister Asa Mahan, and several other seminary students, Birney made public his resignation from the KCS, preparing and publishing an open letter of resignation to Thornton Mills, the secretary of the KCS. The letter appeared in mid-July 1834 – shortly thereafter circulating in pamphlet form and as a reprint in abolitionist newspapers – and placed Birney squarely in the immediatist camp. It argued that colonizationists drew from "a strange mixture of true principles, with others that are utterly false." He maintained that colonization, far from a program that would ultimately serve the interests of the African American community, actually kept blacks in a second-class status and caused whites to "excite a malignant and persecuting spirit against the free colored people." Contrary to the claims of some voices within the movement,

[47] "Constitution and Address of the Kentucky Society for the Gradual Relief of the State from Slavery," 105–6.
[48] James G. Birney, letter to Ralph R. Gurley, December 11, 1833, *Letters of Birney*, 1:98–9; "Prospective Gradual Emancipation: Speech of Mr. Birney," *African Repository* 10 (April 1834): 45; Fladeland, *Birney*, 78–83; Abzug, *Passionate Liberator*, 95. See also Theodore D. Weld, letter to James G. Birney, May 28, 1834, *Letters of Birney*, 1:112–14.

the "impulse" of colonizationism was "opposed to emancipation" outright in Birney's view. The drift of colonization, he argued, was to resist the golden rule. Colonization allowed slaveholders to ignore the broad biblical teaching that God "*has made of one blood all nations of men.*" The Christian mandate, Birney contended, was "*to do justice and love mercy*; and, in the history of the good Samaritan, has taught us that *all men are our neighbors.*" Moreover, even though there was clear scriptural precedent of divine "judgments desolating and awful" for "all nations who have persisted" in enslaving the "poor and oppressed," colonization suggested that "we are not under obligation, now, to do unto others as we would they should do unto us." Instead, a different notion of justice was in play, and the argument seemed to be "that all men are *not* created equal."[49]

Apparently, Birney deduced, "*some* are authorized, nay required, *under existing circumstances*, to withhold from others their liberty, to block up every avenue to their happiness, to abridge their lives by reducing them to slavery." There was no real charity in the colonization movement, Birney claimed, because at the very moment an emancipation plan would be proposed, the following series of questions would emerge from gradualists to shoot it down: "what shall we do with our slaves, if we manumit them? Where shall we send them? It will never do, in the world, for them to remain among us – it is better to retain them as they are, indefinitely in slavery, than to liberate them here." It was thus obvious to Birney "that under the colonization regimen, slavery, *as a system*, remains unshaken." Slavery was clearly the greatest evil of his time. And the fact that colonizationists would rather perpetuate a system of racial inequality than end slavery exposed the scheme for the "opiate" it really was.[50]

The reaction to Birney's letter was pronounced. Late in 1834, the ACS's *African Repository* devoted a lead article to an attack on Birney's *Letter on Colonization*. Although it dealt little with the substantive aspects of Birney's critique and reasserted ACS platforms, the *African Repository* claimed that Birney misconstrued colonization's aims. The world was not a perfect one, the journal argued, and "[t]he Society proposes to provide a remedy for an existing state of things; and not to diverge into controversies about the justice or injustice belonging to that state of things." Still, there was no proof that colonization supported "perpetual slavery," because no colonizationist had ever made "such an argument." Moreover, in providing an opportunity for "safe manumission" – presumably meaning the avoidance of insurrection and

---

[49] See Theodore D. Weld, letters to James G. Birney, June 17 and 19, and July 8 and 14, 1834, *Letters of Birney*, 1:115–25, 127; Lesick, *Lane Rebels*, 90; Fladeland, *Birney*, 84–6; "Letter of Hon. J. G. Birney," *The Liberator*, August 16, 1834; Birney, *Letter on Colonization, Addressed to the Rev. Thornton J. Mills, Corresponding Secretary of the Kentucky Colonization Society* (New York: Anti-Slavery Reporter, 1834), 10, 11, 16.

[50] Birney, *Letter on Colonization*, 11, 13, 18, 19, 20.

then subsequently separating the races – the *African Repository* was confident that the work of the ACS had "undoubtedly shaken slavery as a system" and would likely "continue to do so."[51]

The response of colonizationists notwithstanding, Weld, William Lloyd Garrison, and several leaders of national abolitionism considered Birney's *Letter on Colonization* a major success for the immediatist movement. Thousands of copies had been distributed, and Lane Seminary students had played a prominent role in that effort. July 1834 had seen New York City consumed with anti-abolitionist and anti-black rioting. Lewis Tappan, a Finneyite abolitionist and founding member of the American Anti-Slavery Society, fled his home before it was sacked, and several other leading abolitionists were targeted by proslavery and colonizationist forces. In this moment, having a prominent southerner – especially a recent slaveholder and colonizationist – recant in such a public way gave much energy to abolitionists. Later that summer, Weld and other Lane students published a second pamphlet from Birney, *Letter to Ministers and Elders, on the Sin of Holding Slaves, and the Duty of Immediate Emancipation*, which he addressed to the clergy and lay leadership of his home denomination, the Presbyterian Church, in his home state. He rejected white fears of "amalgamation" – arguing that even if prejudice against interracial unions might persist in the nineteenth century that "one of our great-great-great-grand-children" might "overcome it" – and repudiated the notion that emancipation would lead to race war. Birney seemed a living example that, as Henry B. Stanton and fellow Kentuckian James Thome believed, the logic of abolition proved too morally convicting to resist.[52]

Colonizationists in the Ohio Valley were not so moved. If the students at Lane Seminary had come to overwhelmingly endorse abolition, the faculty and trustees saw matters differently. Of the board's twenty-five members, most were colonizationists; only four, including Samuel Crothers and Asa Mahan, supported immediatism. For his part, President Lyman Beecher hoped to preserve the peace and long-term viability of the new seminary. He believed that "slavery is wrong, and a great national sin and national calamity, and that as soon as possible it should be brought to an end." However, he was a gradualist, and although Beecher respected his abolitionist students, he did not support extremism – in either pro- or antislavery form. In short, Beecher believed in the

[51] "Review. *A Letter from* James G. Birney, Esq. *to the* Rev. Thornton J. Mills, *Corresponding Secretary of the Kentucky Colonization Society, dated Mercer County, Ky. July* 15, 1834," *African Repository* 10 (November 1834): 257–79, quotes 264, 266–7.

[52] Lesick, *Lane Rebels*, 118; Wyatt-Brown, *Lewis Tappan*, 115–20; Davis, *Joshua Leavitt*, 109–12; Theodore D. Weld, letter to James G. Birney, August 7, 1834, *Letters of Birney*, 1:127–9; "African Repository vs. James G. Birney," *The Liberator*, November 29, 1834; "African Repository versus James G. Birney. No. III," *The Liberator*, December 13, 1834; James G. Birney, *Letter to Ministers and Elders, on the Sin of Holding Slaves, and the Duty of Immediate Emancipation* (n.p., 1834), quote 16.

kind of antislavery movement that hearkened back a decade, where immediatists and colonizationists were ostensibly unified.[53]

The day for such unity had passed. Convinced that a discussion of slavery politicized, and thus threatened, the spiritual and academic environment
around the school, Lane's board passed a series of harsh measures to suppress
student discussion. In practice, the board had the recent slavery debates in
mind, but in theory the new regulations all but made it impossible for the
students to have a free discussion of any issue without first consulting the faculty. The board also planned to expel the most vocal abolitionist students, and
because Weld was clearly the leader of the immediatists, he was among the first
targeted as "the main stirrer up of sedition." Speculation suggested that Thome
and Henry Stanton were also on their way out. Beecher likewise thought that
Weld undermined the school's learning environment, but he had no desire to
make a spectacle of the situation. Still, as Weld wrote to Birney, after Beecher
"succeeded in '*Quashing*' the indictment against me," Weld applied for and
was granted leave.[54]

Most of his colleagues soon followed him out the door. By January 1835,
only 8 out of 103 students remained enrolled at Lane. Some left for personal
reasons, but at least seventy-five dropped out because of the school's quelling
of abolitionist speech – and of the students who remained, most were colonizationists. Fifty-one of the so-called Lane Rebels, including Weld, Stanton, and
Thome, signed the widely read *Statement of the Reasons Which Induced the
Students of Lane Seminary to Dissolve Their Connection with that Institution*
(1834). Steeped in a Finneyite evangelical moral sensibility whose robust confidence in innate human character would have seemed like doctrinal laxity to
conservatives, the document asserted emphatically their right to free discussion
of controversial issues. There existed a "duty" placed on every human to search
"after immutable truth, whether embodied in the word, or hid in the works of
God, or branching out through the relations and duties of man." As the rebels
explained, "whereas, the single object of ascertaining truth is to learn *how to
act*, we are bound to do at once, whatever truth dictates to be done." Those
trustees who sought to limit the abolitionist conversation at Lane needed to
know what the departed students believed: "This duty of discussion and action
is not confered by human authority, and we have no *license* to resign it upon
entering into any association, literary or political. Free discussion being a duty
is consequently a right, and as such, is inherent and inalienable. It is *our* right.

---

[53] Lesick, *Lane Rebels*, 116–23; "Dr. Beecher's Address," *African Repository* 10 (November
1834): 279–83, quote 281. Calvin Stowe also shared much in the way of Beecher's moderate
approach, both to running the seminary and the slavery question. See Stowe's colonizationist
views in this period articulated in "Professor Stowe on Colonization," *African Repository* 10
(December 1834): 300–4.

[54] Lesick, *Lane Rebels*, 116–31; Theodore D. Weld, letters to James G. Birney, October 6 and 20,
1834, *Letters of Birney*, 136–40, 145–7.

It *was* before we entered Lane Seminary." It was a *"right* the institution 'could neither give nor take away.'"[55]

In the end, most of the Lane Rebels would find an institution more willing to support such a view of education at the Oberlin Collegiate Institute in northern Ohio. The school, founded in 1833, had broad and ambitious academic goals but little financial support. The former Lane students could secure financial backing from Arthur Tappan in New York, as well as other abolition-friendly financiers. Although many at Oberlin objected to an influx of such noted immediatists, the prospect of financial viability proved impossible to resist. The school recruited Asa Mahan to serve as president and, on Weld's recommendation, Charles Finney as a professor of theology. Then, on the final condition that African American students would be admitted on an equal basis, the Lane Rebels enrolled at Oberlin in 1835.[56]

On the other side of the Ohio River, Birney would likewise end up an exile, though for a short time he experienced a different degree of success than that of the abolitionists at Lane Seminary. In August 1834 he lost a debate at Centre College with John C. Young over the merits of abolition against gradualism, but the results were close. Students voted 22–20 in favor of Young's position, which indicated that there was at least some significant sympathy for immediatism. The following October, Birney's *Letter to Ministers and Elders* in Kentucky produced quite a discussion among the state's Presbyterians at their annual meeting. On its heels, the synod voted 56–8, with 7 abstentions, to support a scheme of gradual emancipation connected to colonization. It then commissioned a committee of ten Presbyterians, led by Young, to produce a statement for the denomination to consider in the state. Encouraged by this action, and thinking the immediatist approach might have secured modest traction in the Bluegrass State, Birney formed the Kentucky Anti-Slavery Society as an auxiliary of the American Anti-Slavery Society in March 1835.[57]

Birney's optimism was misplaced. The Kentucky Anti-Slavery Society's forthright statement of its immediatist goals and open alignment with national abolitionism proved too much for white Kentucky. Birney spent the spring and part of the summer of 1835 touring the North and meeting leading Yankee abolitionists to raise funds to begin publishing an abolitionist paper called *The Philanthropist* in Danville. All the while, local whites grew more agitated. A group of thirty gradualists "who would [not] see slavery perpetuated" wrote to Birney that he was making a grave mistake. "*You do good to none,*" his opponents argued. "You injure yourself. You injure the society at large. You injure the slaves themselves." Framing the letter in ominous language, these men were

[55] *Statement of the Reasons Which Induced the Students of Lane Seminary to Dissolve Their Connection with that Institution* (Cincinnati: n.p., 1834), 5. Lesick, *Lane Rebels*, 132–7.

[56] Lesick, *Lane Rebels*, 169–70.

[57] See *Proceedings of the Kentucky Anti-Slavery Society, Auxiliary to the American Anti-slavery Society at its first meeting in Danville, Ky., March 19, 1835* (n.p., 1835). Harrison, *Antislavery Movement in Kentucky*, 43; Fladeland, *Birney*, 98–9; William Birney, *Birney and His Times*, 145–6.

"willing to avoid violence," but also wanted to "advise" Birney "of the peril that must and inevitably will attend the execution of your paper." As the anti-abolitionists contended, the line between them and Birney was clear: "Many of us have been members and warm supporters of the Colonization Society. All of us believe slavery moral and political evil. But whilst they [slaves] are amongst us... we would see them so kept and treated as to make them most happy and contented and society at large most quiet." Although Birney defended himself and the freedom of the press to his critics, when he was unable to secure a printer willing to publish *The Philanthropist*, the writing was on the wall. Birney's vocal abolitionism was not welcome in his hometown.[58]

By the end of the summer of 1835, Birney felt it unwise to stay in the state any longer. John C. Young had interviewed him in 1834 for a post at Centre College, but his *"abolition views"* led the trustees of the school to reject Birney's candidacy. A year later, he no longer even considered prominent emancipationist-colonizationist positions worth engaging, writing that work by leading lights of the movement such as Robert J. Breckinridge on the question were "a farrago of incongruities. He thinks slavery a sin, but when it should cease is questionable." Realizing that the time he could "remain in Kentucky" was short, Birney opted to leave slave soil and relocate to Cincinnati, where he hoped to find a more charitable and receptive audience.[59]

A few months before leaving the state, Birney debated John C. Young in Danville over the merits of immediatism. The precipitant event was the publication of Young's essay denouncing immediate abolition – the same essay that would later be appended to the Kentucky Presbyterian's gradual emancipation treatise – which first appeared in the *Cincinnati Journal*. The gradualist Young contended that "every unprejudiced mind will recognize the cause I have espoused, to be the cause of truth." Abolitionists, including Samuel Crothers, had "clothed" Young's emancipationism in "false and ridiculous garb" that had "mistak[en] gradualists for perpetualists." Not only did Young reject such an association but he also argued that abolitionists operated from false theological principles: "This redoubtable argument – this Achilles, on which abolitionists so securely rely, runs thus: – Slaveholding is a sin; every sin ought to be immediately repented of and abandoned." Yet, that view misunderstood the nature of true Christian repentance. As Young saw the matter, *"the abolitionist and not the gradualist is the one who fails in the duty of repentance*. Repentance has not done its perfect work, when we merely cease from further infliction of evil, without taking the measures, which reason and the circumstances of the case show to be best for correcting the mischief we have

---

[58] F. T. Taylor and others, letter to James G. Birney, July 12, 1835, *Letters of Birney*, 1:197–200 (quotes); Birney, letter to Taylor and others, July 22, 1835, *Letters of Birney*, 1:204–12; Thomas Ayers, letter to Birney, August 1835, *Letters of Birney*, 1:212–22; Fladeland, *Birney*, 100–24.

[59] Harrison, *Antislavery Movement in Kentucky*, 44–5; Fladeland, *Birney*, 100–24; James G. Birney, letter to Theodore D. Weld, n.d., in William Birney, *Birney and His Times*, 144.

already perpetrated." In short, gradualism was the most Christian solution to the slavery question because it allowed for white society and African Americans themselves to slowly adjust to new conditions of freedom.[60]

Even though Young and Birney had been friends and collaborators in the antislavery movement in Kentucky, their differences were becoming manifest. As far as Birney was concerned, Young's gradualism showed an intellectual "weakness"; "as an argument it was grossly sophistical and unworthy of his mind." In March 1835 Birney gave a public lecture in favor of abolition at the Danville Lyceum, and Young showed up to hear Birney directly scrutinize his gradualist language. As Birney later reported privately, Young was "so stung" by Birney that he asked for an opportunity to give his own response the following evening. There, according to Birney, Young "greatly abused abolitionism" and made an uncharacteristically dualistic argument: "in speaking of Mr. Garrison, he out-Garrisoned G. himself." Birney was shocked that Young went so far as to claim that "he would not be an abolitionist" for the simple reason that "Mr. Garrison was one." Such opinions had been building for the last several years, but no careful gradualist had stated this opposition so bluntly. In Young's mind, the taint of immediatism shut down antislavery cooperation.[61]

In this way, John C. Young and James G. Birney's 1830s careers in Kentucky were symbolic of the larger transformation in the state's antislavery movement. Where Young might have expressed an antislavery position out of step with the general populace, his denunciation of immediatism signaled his disdain for radicalism and made him tolerable to white Kentucky's conservative populace. Birney, in contrast, received no such favor because he endorsed immediatism. Although he would not be the last abolitionist to grace the Commonwealth's soil in the antebellum era, his decision to exile himself from his home state signaled that immediatism would have no popular salience within its boundaries. Yet this sensibility did not mean that gradualists such as Young and Robert J. Breckinridge were proslavery, even though Birney and Garrison characterized the split that way. They were more correct in seeing the basic distinction as being about race.

In the decade that followed 1835, the three largest evangelical denominations in the United States would all fracture for reasons directly or tangentially connected to the slavery question. Those splits would have major ramifications for the shape of religious life in Kentucky, especially as it concerned race and slavery. And they were schisms that could not have happened without first recognizing that the gradualist–immediatist divide was actually a yawning religious chasm that no honest faith could bridge.

[60] Young, "The Doctrine of Immediate Emancipation Unsound," 32, 33, 39.
[61] James G. Birney, letter to Theodore D. Weld, January 23, 1835, *Letters of Birney*, 1:172; Birney, letters to Gerrit Smith, January 31 and March 21, 1835, *Letters of Birney*, 1:174, 189; Fladeland, *Birney*, 104–5.

2

Heresy and Schism

The Uneasy Gradualist-Proslavery Ecclesiastical Alliance, 1836–1845

> I was charged with being an "Abolitionist." . . . [My critics] made no distinction between an "Abolitionist" and an "Emancipationist." The latter was in favor of doing away with slavery *gradually*, according to State Constitution and law; the former believed slavery to be a sin *in itself*, calling for immediate abolition without regard to consequences. I was an Emancipationist . . . but I was never for a moment an Abolitionist.
>
> – Baptist minister James M. Pendleton (1811–91),
> Reminiscences of a Long Life (1891)[1]

The seeds of dissension sown between gradualists and immediatists bore much bitter fruit in the years between 1836 and 1845. Those dates bracket a series of schisms that rocked the national polities of American Presbyterians, Methodists, and Baptists. Each denomination suffered a split in which debates over slavery and abolition played a prominent role. By 1845, there would be northern and southern versions of the Baptist and Methodist faith; Presbyterianism would be divided into Old and New Schools that reflected, though somewhat imprecisely, division on the slavery question. This chapter not only explores the place of these divides in shaping the political attitudes of white Kentuckians but it also shows how important Kentuckians were in the development of sectional tension in the United States. Though gradualists and proslavery believers alike had recognized abolitionists as heretics for many years, the ecclesiastical convulsions of the 1830s and 1840s brought conservative believers together like never before. Central to the debates of this period were questions about race, colonization, and America's national manifest destiny.

---

[1] James M. Pendleton, *Reminiscences of a Long Life* (Louisville: Press Baptist Book Concern, 1891), 112–13.

On each of these matters there was strong agreement between gradualist and proslavery Protestants. When it came to the church splits, abolitionists were on one side and conservatives were on the other. And because Kentucky was home to so many gradualists, the state's white believers played crucial roles in the efforts to construct a conservative front against abolitionism. In that sense gradualist theology was proslavery theology: southern proslavery denominations emerged in the 1830s and 1840s thanks to the work of gradual emancipationists, especially from Kentucky. This union would not be a perfect one outside ecclesiastical circles, where much contention exposed the distance between proslavery and gradualist political ideology. However, within the churches, the two groups built an uneasy alliance that served to minimize abolitionist influence in the South.

The process was well underway by 1836, but it came into direct consideration when the Methodist Episcopal Church's quadrennial national meeting, the General Conference, convened in Cincinnati in May of that year. April 1836 had seen a major race riot in the Queen City that resulted in a number of African American deaths and the destruction of several black homes. Moreover, the shadow of abolitionism hung ominously over the proceedings of the Methodist conference. Two New England immediatists, both Methodists, had recently "lectured" in the city. Holding ecclesiastical jurisdiction in the area just south of Cincinnati, the Kentucky Methodist Conference passed a series of resolutions condemning abolitionism before the 1836 General Conference. An august committee that included two future bishops of the Methodist Episcopal Church, South – Henry B. Bascom (1796–1850) and Hubbard H. Kavanaugh (1802–84) – authored the resolutions. In the committee's view, the American Colonization Society remained "worthy [of] their approval and patronage," but "any minister or member of the Methodist Episcopal Church" who called for "extra-judicial means" of "interfering with the question of slavery" via abolition was not "allowable."[2]

These Methodist Kentuckians did not hold an extremist position. Their views were echoed by the 1836 General Conference, which argued that promotion of the "agitating topic" was "unjustifiable" and "calculated to bring upon [the General Conference] the suspicion and distrust of the community, and misrepresent its sentiments in regard" to the slavery question. A number of abolitionists attended the Cincinnati meeting, including James G. Birney, who began publishing *The Philanthropist* in the city that April as the official newspaper of the Ohio Anti-Slavery Society. Birney's presence, as well as his coverage of the proceedings, proved a disruptive presence to many at the General Conference – as well as to many in the host city.[3]

---

[2] A. H. Redford, *Life and Times of H. H. Kavanaugh, D.D., One of the Bishops of the Methodist Episcopal Church, South* (Nashville: n.p., 1884), 171–2. On the April 1836 Cincinnati race riot, see Joe William Trotter Jr., *River Jordan: African American Urban Life in the Ohio Valley* (Lexington: University Press of Kentucky, 1998), 35.

[3] *Debate on "Modern Abolitionism," in the General Methodist Conference of the Episcopal Church. Held in Cincinnati, May, 1836* (Cincinnati: Ohio Anti-Slavery Society, 1836), 5; Betty

Within a few months of the Methodist meeting, Birney received a number of threats, some of which came from Kentuckians across the river. July 1836 proved particularly violent. That month, whites in Cincinnati rioted against African Americans celebrating Independence Day, and Birney's newspaper office was sacked twice by angry mobs. In mid-July a handbill from "OLD KENTUCKY" offered one hundred dollars for Birney's apprehension, declaring "Birney in all his associations and feelings is *black*; although his external appearance is white." Then, on July 30, part of Birney's printing press was thrown into the Ohio River, and the mob set its sights on apprehending Birney. The abolitionist was out of town on a speaking engagement, so the rioters instead turned their attention to Cincinnati's African American district and set loose on what one historian has called "an orgy of destruction." For Birney, such mob action was a temporary setback. He quickly resumed publishing *The Philanthropist*; not long after he added Gamaliel Bailey, a local physician converted to abolitionism by the Lane debates, as his assistant editor; Bailey then took over the paper in 1837.[4]

Despite Birney's paper's quick recovery, these incidents show that Birney's mere presence provoked hostility from anti-abolitionists, who saw his program as a call to disorder. In the context of the 1836 Methodist General Conference, leading theologian Nathan Bangs of New York called Birney's *Philanthropist* "incendiary" and accused it of "pursuing the same unjustifiable and ungentlemanly course" that characterized American abolitionism more broadly. As a result, the gathered Methodists in Cincinnati – from both North and South – responded unequivocally: "they are decidedly opposed to modern abolitionism, and wholly disclaim any right, wish or intention, to interfere in the civil and political relation between master and slave, as it exists in the slaveholding states of the Union." Antislavery immediatism was for national Methodism what it was for Kentucky Methodists: a nonstarter in 1836.[5]

That sort of ecclesiastical rejection of abolitionism compelled James G. Birney to write one of the period's most famous denunciations of slaveholding Christianity, *The American Churches, The Bulwarks of American Slavery*. Just before it first appeared in print, in 1840, Birney and several evangelical abolitionists – Gerrit Smith, Joshua Leavitt, and Henry B. Stanton among them – had broken with William Lloyd Garrison and the American Anti-Slavery Society.

Fladeland, *James Gillespie Birney: Slaveholder to Abolitionist* (Ithaca: Cornell University Press, 1955), 133–44.

[4] See Birney's compiled *Narrative of the Late Riotous Proceedings Against the Liberty of the Press, in Cincinnati* (Cincinnati: Ohio Anti-Slavery Society, 1836), quotes 17; Fladeland, *Birney*, 133–44, quote 141; and Stanley Harrold, *Border War: Fighting over Slavery before the Civil War* (Chapel Hill: University of North Carolina Press, 2010), 67–8.

[5] Fladeland, *Birney*, 133–5; Lawrence Thomas Lesick, *The Lane Rebels: Evangelicalism and Antislavery in Antebellum America* (Metuchen, NJ: Scarecrow Press, 1980), 132; *Debate on "Modern Abolitionism," in the General Conference*, 5, 79. See also C. C. Goen, *Broken Churches, Broken Nation: Denominational Schisms and the Coming of the Civil War* (Macon, GA: Mercer University Press, 1985), 80.

Part of their discontent, as historians have traditionally explained, stemmed from the Garrisonians' religious skepticism, but it also had to do with the role of political action. Because Garrisonians traditionally argued for moral suasion, they did not see the political arena – fraught as it was with the necessity of compromise – as proper for abolitionist activism. Birney and his allies disagreed and founded the Liberty Party to offer voters legitimate abolitionist choices. In the 1840 election, despite fully understanding that his campaign was no real challenge to either the Democratic or Whig candidates, Martin Van Buren and William Henry Harrison, Birney ran for the U.S. presidency.[6]

The fracture of the American Anti-Slavery Society and the creation of the Liberty Party have received no shortage of attention from historians. Yet overemphasizing the very real discord among competing abolitionist factions obscures the fact that Birney and Garrison were not so far apart in their negative assessment of the established churches and traditional orthodoxy. Although Lewis Tappan and his evangelical associates – including Theodore Dwight Weld, Amos Phelps, George Cheever, and George Whipple – also rejected Garrisonianism in 1840, they refused to endorse the political approaches of the Liberty Party. Instead they founded the American and Foreign Anti-Slavery Society. Yet that apolitical stance was relatively short-lived. By 1843 Tappanites had made their peace with the Liberty Party, mostly because of the large number of other evangelicals affiliated with it. Although Tappanites remained invested in evangelical churches, their later efforts in the American Missionary Association (founded in 1846) rejected fellowship with slaveholding bodies, which included most major American denominations.[7]

Thus, the abolitionist schism of 1840 quite obviously revealed a collective dissatisfaction among all abolitionists with the established Christian denominations. The thesis of Birney's *The American Churches, The Bulwarks of American Slavery* was no mystery: the title made it plain. In the slim volume, Birney compiled evidence from every major American Protestant denomination – Methodists, Baptists, Presbyterians, and Episcopalians all came under fire – to show how they were de facto proslavery organizations. Because Birney spent time developing the volume during his trip to London in 1840 as a delegate to the World Anti-Slavery Convention, he wrote with a transatlantic audience in mind: he had "the single view to make the British Christian public acquainted with the real state of the case" so that it "might persuade [American churches] to purify themselves from a sin that has greatly debased them, and that threatens in the end wholly to destroy them." Indeed, Birney's judgment

---

[6] James Brewer Stewart, *Holy Warriors: The Abolitionists and American Slavery* (New York: Hill and Wang, 1976), 89–98; Fladeland, *Birney*, 175–89.

[7] Ibid.; Lawrence J. Friedman, "Confidence and Pertinacity in Evangelical Abolitionism: Lewis Tappan's Circle," *American Quarterly* 31 (Spring 1979): 87–106; and John R. McKivigan, *The War against Proslavery Religion: Abolitionism and the Northern Churches, 1830–1865* (Ithaca: Cornell University Press, 1984), 113–17.

that American churches could not be persuaded to change from within led him to pursue direct political action. Perhaps some day the churches might change, but Birney and many of his colleagues held little hope for that in the short term.[8]

As it turned out, Birney was not the first believer with Kentucky ties to consider questions before a British audience about the culpability of American churches in perpetuating slavery. In June 1836, just a few years before the publication of Birney's *American Churches*, there was a major debate in Glasgow between British abolitionist George Thompson (1804–78) and Robert J. Breckinridge, who at that date was pastor of Baltimore's Second Presbyterian Church and was visiting Britain as a delegate from the Presbyterian Church USA to the Congregational Union of Scotland and Wales. Thompson, an English friend of Garrison, was well known by the early 1830s in the British Isles as an advocate for immediate, universal emancipation in the Empire. An agent of the British and Foreign Society for the Abolition of Slavery throughout the World, Thompson set sail for America in 1834, the year after Parliament ended the institution in all the British colonies but India, and embarked on an antislavery tour with Garrison. He ended up delivering more than 130 speeches during his time in the United States, but his presence proved a constant provocation – because of both his English nationality and his abolitionism. Garrison and Thompson frequently found themselves threatened with mob violence and, after determining that the ongoing promotion of immediatism imperiled his life, Thompson left America in November 1835 and returned to Britain.[9]

As was the case with Birney, Thompson found much blame to place on America's leading Protestant churches for the nation's conservative stance on slavery, as well as its racial inequality. On his return to Britain, Thompson issued a challenge in the British press to any minister interested in debating the nature of American slavery before a public audience. Agitated and emboldened by his earlier disputes with Garrison, in which he had also seen fit to criticize Thompson, Breckinridge agreed to face the British abolitionist in June 1836. As Breckinridge explained, his "chief reason" for accepting Thompson's challenge "was to defend the Churches, Ministers and Christians of America" on the slavery question, and thus "to prevent the total alienation of British and American christians from each other." He proposed that they debate for "three or four hours a-day, for as many days as consecutively may be necessary." The arrangement suited Thompson, and the two argued their positions from June

---

[8] James G. Birney, *The American Churches, The Bulwarks of American Slavery*, 3rd ed. (Newburyport, MA: Charles Whipple, 1842), 3; McKivigan, *War against Proslavery Religion*, 74–6; Ronald G. Walters, *The Antislavery Appeal: American Abolitionism after 1830* (Baltimore: Johns Hopkins University Press, 1976), 40–2; Fladeland, *Birney*, 190–206.

[9] See Ronald M. Gifford II, "George Thompson and Trans-Atlantic Antislavery" (Ph.D. diss., Indiana University, 1999), 101–63; and Edward Bartlett Rugemer, *The Problem of Emancipation: The Caribbean Roots of the American Civil War* (Baton Rouge: Louisiana State University Press, 2008), 181–2.

13 through 17. An anonymous third-person narrator documented the debate, and the account was circulated throughout Britain and the United States.[10]

In his letter accepting Thompson's challenge, Breckinridge claimed that slavery was "contrary to the spirit of the gospel, and the natural rights of men," but he nonetheless remained concerned that "some may consider me defending the institution of slavery." Given the rancor between Breckinridge and his gradualist colleagues and their immediatist opponents, his concern was not misplaced. It probably was the case that many abolitionists' minds were made up about the American minister's arguments – even if the moderator, Scottish Presbyterian Ralph Wardlaw, promised Breckinridge a fair hearing at the outset – but Breckinridge did more than enough on his own to turn the Glasgow audience against him. He argued that "the American nation was divided into two parties" on the slavery question: pro- and antislavery. In his view, far more people were anti- than proslavery in the United States, and much progress had been made toward ending slavery. However, within the broad antislavery movement there were divisions; the recent rise of radical abolitionism – "that small party with which Mr. Thompson had identified himself" – "had ruined" the general "cause of emancipation" because it promoted ending slavery through violence. Throughout the debate Breckinridge denounced abolitionism as the harbinger of social chaos and specifically accused Garrison of writing "placards" and using his *Liberator* to raise "a mob stirred up against" the gradualist during his 1834 visit to Boston. Although Breckinridge "had never obtained direct proof" of this charge, he nonetheless believed abolitionist radicals gave as good as they got when it came to civil disorder.[11]

According to Thompson's summation of Breckinridge's argument, Breckinridge flatly asserted that abolitionists were "the chief promoters of all the riots that had taken place in America on this question" because they "[made] inflammatory appeals to the passions of the people." It was a shocking charge, and because of these opinions, the American minister never convinced the Scottish audience that his antislavery beliefs were sincere. Still, Breckinridge proved more of a challenging interlocutor than Thompson expected. Both

---

[10] *Discussion on American Slavery between George Thompson, Esq., and Rev. Robert J. Breckinridge, Holden in the Rev. Dr. Wardlaw's Chapel, Glasgow, Scotland*, 2nd American ed., annotated by William Lloyd Garrison (Boston: Isaac Knapp, 1836), 3, 54, and see pp. 69–77 for Thompson's rebuke of American churches. All subsequent quotes and citations from this debate are taken from the abolitionist-circulated American edition. For the British edition, see *Discussion on American Slavery, in Dr. Wardlaw's Chapel, between Mr. George Thompson and the Rev. R. J. Breckinridge of Baltimore, United States, on the Evenings of the 13th, 14th, 15th, 16th, and 17th June, 1836*, 2nd ed. (Glasgow: George Gallie, 1836). For Breckinridge's criticisms of Thompson, see Robert J. Breckinridge, "Abolitionism," *Baltimore Literary and Religious Magazine* 1 (September 1835): 284–5. See also Viven Sandlund, "Robert Breckinridge, Presbyterian Antislavery Conservative," *Journal of Presbyterian History* 78 (Summer 2000): 145; and James C. Klotter, *The Breckinridges of Kentucky* (Lexington: University Press of Kentucky, 1986), 69.

[11] *Discussion on American Slavery*, 3, 6, 7, 17, 19–20.

abolitionists and gradualists claimed victory on behalf of their spokesman – although Breckinridge found virtually no British supporters. A version of the debate later published by New England abolitionists and heavily annotated by Garrison himself called Breckinridge an "apologist for the slave system" whose "professions of hostility to slavery are insincere or delusive." That judgment may not have been entirely accurate, but it was clear all the same that abolitionists saw gradualists as no different from those who would never work toward slavery's end.[12]

Much in the debate turned on Thompson and Breckinridge's opposed understandings of the problem of race. For Thompson, racism was "the peculiar sin of America." As he contended, "Slavery might be found in many countries, but it was in America alone that there existed an aristocracy, founded on the color of the skin." American society was dominated by a "race of pale-skinned patricians" who wanted to keep their "claims to peculiar ranks and privileges." That, in Thompson's view, was the real aim of the colonization project, not "the improvement of the black man's condition." It may have been the case that many colonizationists were devout, "pious and excellent men." He did not doubt the sincerity of their motives. But colonization "had grown out of prejudice; was based upon prejudice; made its appeal to prejudice; and could not exist were the prejudice against the colored man conquered." Colonizationists argued that American "prejudice against color was *invincible.*" Abolitionists such as Thompson disagreed. Theirs was a project to destroy not only slavery but also the caste of race that sustained the evil institution.[13]

The difference with Breckinridge could not have been more obvious. Against Thompson and his abolitionist associates, who contended that "prejudice against color was the national sin of America," Breckinridge maintained that racism was only a mere "symptom" of a larger ill. By contrast, the "disease" was "the relation of slavery." As Breckinridge saw it, "If there were no black slaves on earth there would no longer be any aversion against that color." Abolitionists erred because they diagnosed the wrong social sickness.[14]

In addition, Breckinridge argued, racial difference was part of the divine order: it was not to be meddled with. As a serious student of the Holy Writ, the American minister followed the account of the book of Genesis, which showed how humanity came from a single, common progenitor. However, even if humankind "were all once of one complexion," the truth was that the Christian God had seen fit to allow "diversities" to emerge over time between peoples. The same Genesis record showed that "the three [racial] families of

---

[12] Ibid., 3, 6, 7, 21. Gifford, "George Thompson," 176–82; Thomas F. Harwood, "British Evangelical Abolitionism and American Churches in the 1830s," *Journal of Southern History* 28 (August 1962): 301–2; and Sandlund, "Breckinridge, Antislavery Conservative," 153n7.

[13] *Discussion on American Slavery*, 36, 37. See also Garrison's arguments against "the cord of caste," Ibid., 8.

[14] Ibid., 55–6.

mankind" had "descended from the three sons of Noah." The result, according to Breckinridge, was that racial difference would always remain "upon the earth's surface." It was the providential design for all human societies in all times.[15]

In rejecting this truth, Breckinridge argued, abolitionists reached completely misguided conclusions. Accordingly, the "advocacy of amalgamation" was a core "doctrine of abolitionism," which could only be described as "utter folly" and "wickedness." To promote race mixing meant actively working against the Christian God's will. It meant fundamentally changing the structure of human society and attempting to remake the racial order by destroying those racial groups that currently existed. What had transpired in the natural world of human societies – the creation of race – came about because God actively shaped human affairs. Thus, even though Breckinridge found abolitionism abhorrent, he argued that its integrationist designs would come to nothing. Immediatists called for "universal levelling and mixing the world," and Breckinridge imagined that, even if abolitionists got their way, they "would soon find that they had done a work which nature did not permit to stand." The inescapable fact was that there was "something in the structure of nature that would effectually prevent the obliteration of either race."[16]

Taken together, this religious framework led Breckinridge to conclude that abolitionists "who attempted to promote amalgamation are fighting equally against the purposes of Providence, the convictions of reason, and the best impulses of nature." True believers were thus required to "receive with suspicion, as an undoubted and fundamental rule of Christian morals – a dogma which requires us to contend against the clear leadings of providence, and the good and merciful intentions of our Creator." Race mixing was what conservatives had long said it was: "pernicious heresy."[17]

The maintenance of white racial purity was thus a sacred cause – and colonization was part of the plan. Because "God had kept several races of men distinct," providential design dictated that the separate races ought to rule themselves. In all times, from the offspring of Noah "down to the present day," Breckinridge contended, "wherever the descendants of Shem had colonized a country, occupied by the descendants of Japhet or Ham, they had extirpated those who were before them," as did Noah's other children when they took lands occupied by a different people. This biblical evidence led Breckinridge to conclude that "the only means in our power to prevent the ultimate colonization of central Africa by some strange race, and the consequent extirpation of its race of blacks, is to colonize it with blacks." Race determined a people's ability to achieve "civilization." Despite his initial affirmation that blacks were entitled to "natural rights" as human beings, he clearly believed

[15] Ibid., 57.
[16] Ibid.
[17] Ibid.

them to be less capable than white people. No one, he argued, ever thought of enslaving an Englishman or a German because they had established ordered societies. In contrast, Breckinridge saw Africans as a people "sitting in darkness and drinking blood," and colonization was the only realistic way such a people might be saved – by being both Christianized and civilized. Once Africans were colonized and westernized, however, no one would ever again consider enslaving them.[18]

In response, Thompson proved he could argue theological principles just as well as the American minister. As the abolitionist contended, "We are told that, in attempting to bring about amalgamation, and in preventing colonization, we are interfering with the *purposes* of God – fighting against his ordinances and exposing Africa to the horrors of extermination, should the descendants of Shem or Japhet colonize her shores, and not the black man who has sprung from her tribes." As Thompson argued, this was an unusual formulation for a minister in the Presbyterian and Reformed tradition:

> I confess I am somewhat surprised, when told by a Presbyterian clergyman of Calvinistic sentiments, that I am to regulate my conduct towards my fellow-men by the *purposes* of God, rather than by the *law* of God. This is surely a new doctrine! What, I ask, have I to do with the decrees of the Almighty? Has he not given me a law by which to walk? Has he not told me to love my neighbor as myself – to "honor all men?" Am I not told that God hath made of *one* blood all nations of men for to dwell on all the face of the earth? Where is the prohibition to marry with Shem or with Ham? I know of no directions in the Old Testament respecting marriages, save such as were founded on religious differences, and I have yet to learn that there are any in the New Testament.[19]

Furthermore, Thompson contended, Breckinridge was altogether wrong that abolitionists "were directly aiming to accomplish the amalgamation of the races." No, abolitionists worked only so that the "colored man should now be delivered from the condition of a beast; that he should cease to be regarded as the property of his fellow-man; and that" African Americans might achieve full citizenship. That, however, was not "the doctrine of amalgamation." Thompson fully admitted that race mixing was well under way, but abolitionists had nothing to do with it. Instead, the blame fell at the feet of the master class. The truth was that "[t]he slaveholders are the amalgamatists, whose licentiousness has gone far to put an end to the existence of the black race in the South." Sexually predatory masters "carr[ied] on, to use their own expression, 'a bleaching system,' whitening the population of the South, so that you may now discover all the shades of colored persons; from those who are so fair that they are scarcely distinguishable from the whites, to the pure black of the unmixed negro." If Breckinridge was really so concerned about interracial sex, Thompson asked, how did he explain away what was the patently obvious reality of

[18] Ibid., 34–5.
[19] Ibid., 69.

American slavery to all who bothered to look? In Thompson's reading, this obvious hypocrisy exposed Breckinridge's arguments for what he knew they were: an apology for the American slave system.[20]

Breckinridge did not reply to this list of charges, but he later wrote a widely circulated letter to Ralph Wardlaw that denounced British citizens for "the universal ignorance which prevails in regard to America" and "the almost universal prejudice against us." As he claimed succinctly, "You do not know us. You have little sympathy with us. You do us wrong in all your thoughts." Although Breckinridge chose to engage Thompson in an attempt to maintain healthy relations between American and British Christians, he now felt that the two groups shared no mutual understanding of the faith. He expressed "gratitude to God, that he permitted your ancestors to persecute ours out of" England. His valediction was just as acerbic: "If I may not call myself your fellow-christian, without offence, I can at least sign myself your fellow-sinner." The debate with Thompson had clarified many points of distinction between gradualists and immediatists, leading to greater understanding between the antislavery factions. Yet that understanding did not lead to greater affinity, but instead polarization.[21]

In reality, there could be no denying that Breckinridge's gradual emancipationism shared much more in common with proslavery viewpoints than with abolitionism. Breckinridge's arguments in Glasgow revealed quite a lot about the way he understood the American national project. In arguing for colonization, he claimed that Europe became Christianized via the scheme, as did North America. Of course, while Breckinridge advocated that African Americans be sent to Africa because that continent was filled with the same race, white Europeans had colonized a continent filled with Native Americans and taken control of the land by force. Moreover, the Europeans who traveled to America were already Christians and did relatively little to convert indigenous peoples. Still, Breckinridge's comments reflected the dominant white American sense of the nation's "manifest" destiny: Arkansas (1835) and Michigan (1836) "had recently been added to the Union; and God speed the day when others would be added, till the whole continent from the Atlantic to the Pacific was included in the Union, carrying with the Union, Liberty and Independence." For Breckinridge, naturally, this vision applied only to the United States' white population. African Americans would have to experience their own providential destiny in another location.[22]

---

[20] Ibid., 68–9.

[21] "Rev. R. J. Breckinridge's Letter. To the Rev. Ralph Wardlaw," in appendix to *Discussion of American Slavery*, 12.

[22] *Discussion of American Slavery*, 34–5, 10. For his part, Garrison thought that the fact that Breckinridge could celebrate the expansion of slavery, through the admittance of Arkansas to the Union, proved his antislavery stance was insincere. See Ibid., 10.

Breckinridge was not the only contemporary commentator to connect ideas about American expansion and black racial inferiority. If he differed from his fellow southerners in his evaluation of slavery, he shared their thinking about the place of whites in the North American continent. Between 1815 and the mid-1850s white Americans frequently invoked the primacy of their Anglo-Saxon heritage to justify expansion. The philosophy justified the forced expulsion of Native Americans from the eastern half of the United States and fed support for the Mexican-American War (1846–8). For many whites, the perceived inferiority of African Americans relegated them to chattel status, and the future growth of the American republic depended on white leadership. Although Breckinridge publicly sought to have blacks removed from the United States ostensibly for their own good and the good of Africa, his emancipationist language always reflected his concern for white interests. Breckinridge may have believed all people possessed certain natural rights, but that did not preclude him from affirming hierarchies based on race.[23]

In the next year, 1837, Breckinridge showed how comfortably that outlook fit with that of the white South when his denomination, the Presbyterian Church, split into two factions. Here the slavery question was not the primary issue at stake, although it played an important secondary role. In 1837 an "Old School" majority of the Presbyterian General Assembly – including Robert J. Breckinridge, who was a major voice of conservatism at the meeting – voted to remove four "New School" synods located in New York and Ohio. The New School was accused of deviating from the denomination's stricter Calvinist roots, embracing more liberal revivalist doctrines in the mode of Charles Finney and advocating forms of interdenominational cooperation – especially with Congregationalists – that modified the traditional church polity. In 1838 a newly formed New School General Assembly claimed roughly 100,000 members, 85 presbyteries, and 1,200 churches. It had slightly less than the Old School's approximately 127,000 members, 1,763 churches, and 96 presbyteries.[24]

The Old School's action did not reflect a direct attempt to squelch abolitionist agitation. Yet conservative theological stances also generally meant conservative stances on race and abolition, so it was no surprise that the Presbyterian abolitionists came from New School ranks. There was little doubt that the South's presbyteries, overwhelmingly populated with conservatives, supported

---

[23] See Reginald Horsman, *Race and Manifest Destiny: The Origins of American Racial Anglo-Saxonism* (Cambridge, MA: Harvard University Press, 1981). See especially the sections, "American Destiny" and "An Anglo-Saxon Political Identity," 81–297.

[24] Goen, *Broken Churches*, 68–9; James H. Moorhead, "The 'Restless Spirit of Radicalism': Old School Fears and the Schism of 1837," *Journal of Presbyterian History* 78 (Summer 2000): 19–33; Edmund A. Moore, "Robert J. Breckinridge and the Slavery Aspect of the Presbyterian Schism of 1837," *Church History* 4 (December 1935): 282–94.

the Old School on theological grounds. And because much of the Presbyterian North remained theologically conservative and thus also anti-abolitionist, there is no reason to assume they had much difficulty seeing spiritual common ground with their southern coreligionists.[25]

In 1837 Nathan L. Rice was pastor of a church in Bardstown, Kentucky. A gradualist-colonizationist, Rice later served as the Old School Presbyterian Church's moderator (1855) and famously debated the righteousness of slavery with evangelical abolitionist Jonathan Blanchard – a Lane Seminary graduate and New School Presbyterian – for four days in Cincinnati in 1845. As Rice reflected on the Presbyterian schism years later in 1853, the split had ensured a kind of conservative unity among Old School Presbyterians: "It is a fact that ours is the most united, homogeneous Church in the world; whilst Abolitionism, Congregationalism and errors in Theology continue to agitate the New School." In short, schism was a "course" marked by "wisdom and justice."[26]

The Presbyterian cleavage of 1837–8 could not have happened without southern support for the Old School, but the divisions were not clearly sectional – nor were all New School Presbyterians radicals or abolitionists. For the Old School, its ecclesiastical cooperation across the slave-free line was made possible by the recognition that, although proslavery and gradualist Christians did not agree on slavery, they agreed on enough in the way of baseline orthodoxies – racial and theological – to preserve Christian unity. Theology thus drove the Presbyterian politics of slavery. Until the Civil War, it allowed an uneasy peace to prevail between northern and southern adherents.[27]

For other evangelical denominations in America, slavery played far more of a central role in bringing about sectional division. As the largest denomination in the state, Kentucky Baptists were not aloof from the controversies that caught up the Methodists and Presbyterians. Baptist minister James M. Pendleton, a gradual emancipationist who spent most of his antebellum ministry laboring in south central Kentucky, provides a clear demonstration of how theological commitment often trumped particular views on slavery among Kentucky's white evangelicals, collectively unifying the populace against abolitionists. Pendleton's posthumous memoirs, *Reminiscences of a Long Life* (1891),

---

[25] George M. Marsden, *The Evangelical Mind and the New School Presbyterian Experience: A Case Study of Thought and Theology in Nineteenth-Century America* (New Haven: Yale University Press, 1970), 93–103; Moorhead, "Restless Spirit of Radicalism," 28–9.

[26] N. L. Rice, *The Old and New Schools: An Exhibit of the Most Important Differences in their Doctrines and Church Polity*, 2nd ed. (1837; Cincinnati: John D. Thorpe, 1853), vi. On the debate between Rice and Blanchard, see *Debate on Slavery: Held in the City of Cincinnati, on the First, Second, Third, and Sixth Days of October, 1845, upon the Question: Is Slave-holding in Itself Sinful, and the Relation between Master and Slave, a Sinful Relation?* (Cincinnati: William H. Moore, 1846). See also Laura Rominger, "The Bible, Commonsense, and Interpretive Context: A Case Study in the Antebellum Debate over Slavery," *Fides et Historia* 38 (Summer/Fall 2006): 35–54; and Mark A. Noll, *The Civil War as a Theological Crisis* (Chapel Hill: University of North Carolina Press, 2006), 41–2.

[27] Goen, *Broken Churches*, 68–78; McKivigan, *War against Proslavery Religion*, 81–4.

provide several critical insights regarding why the Baptist minister rejected abolitionism and slavery at the same time. Published decades after the "overthrow of slavery" at the end of the Civil War, Pendleton argued that the development "was God's work." Yet the Baptist minister did not mean to suggest that he considered all antislavery activity worthwhile. Pendleton argued that, even though he sought slavery's end, he "was never for a moment an Abolitionist." If Pendleton's contemporary or future readers did not inherently understand the problem with abolitionism, he made it plain: there was a "distinction between an 'Abolitionist' and an 'Emancipationist.' The latter was in favor of doing away with slavery *gradually*, according to State Constitution and law; the former believed slavery to be a sin *in itself*, calling for immediate abolition, without regard to consequences." There is no simple way to conclude what Pendleton might have meant when he said he was "never an abolitionist," but in the context of Kentucky emancipationism, it is not difficult to infer. Pendleton, who saw "consequences" for his actions, placed himself on the same ideological plane as most of Kentucky's evangelical antislavery activists. They were theological and racial conservatives, not radicals.[28]

Pendleton from the start of his ministry must have known of all the religious problems posed by slavery. Perhaps that is why he worked so hard in the early stages of his career to avoid the question as much as possible. As a young minister of growing renown, Pendleton lacked a formal education, but that was not a requirement for ministry. His terms of call for the pastorate of Bowling Green's First Baptist Church in 1836 reveal much about popular evangelicalism in the region at that time: according to Pendleton, he was the first Baptist pastor "in all of Southern Kentucky" to take a salary sizable enough to ensure a pastorate as his primary and only vocation.[29]

From the beginning of his tenure in Bowling Green, Pendleton endeavored to ensure that locally enslaved African Americans would have access to the gospel. His church voted in 1838 to admit slaves into the congregation, and the next year they voted to create a separate "Negro congregation" that was allowed to gather for worship at the First Baptist Church. Other than these measures, however, Pendleton relegated the slavery matter to a secondary status. Several

[28] Pendleton, *Reminiscences*, 112–13, 124. Published just months after his death, Pendleton wrote his memoirs over the course of a few months in the winter of 1890–1. At seventy-nine years of age and in declining health, Pendleton wanted to tell his life's story in his own words. For the most part *Reminiscences* dealt with the minister's ecclesiastical affairs, but the book also provided many interesting anecdotes pertinent to his role as an antislavery activist.

[29] Pendleton was baptized in April 1829 at age 17 and joined the local Baptist congregation in Christian County, Bethel Church. Though Pendleton lacked educational credentials, he worked for a short time as a teacher, and his church called him to preach in 1830. By 1833, Pendleton was ordained and leading both the Bethel Church and a congregation in Hopkinsville. Then, in 1836, the First Baptist Church of Bowling Green offered Pendleton its pastorate at the rate of four hundred dollars per year. See Pendleton, *Reminiscences*, 23–9, 48–9; and Bob Compton, "J. M. Pendleton: A Nineteenth-Century Baptist Statesman (1811–1891)," *Baptist History and Heritage* 10 (1975): 28–30.

members of his church held slaves, and slaveholding was not a concern in determining who could become church members. The issue rarely made its way into sermons except to affirm that Christian slaveholders had the moral obligation to treat their slaves charitably.[30]

By the mid-1840s, however, Pendleton had no choice but to confront the slavery issue head on. In 1844 he personally experienced the events that led to the creation of the Southern Baptist Convention, witnessing firsthand what he saw as abolitionist radicalism. Pendleton's own antislavery position was still undeveloped in 1844, but his displeasure with abolitionism was already beginning to congeal. That April he traveled to Philadelphia as a delegate to the triennial convention of the American Baptist Home Mission Society (ABHMS). As was the case in the nation's other major Protestant bodies, slavery had become a contentious religious issue for the nation's Baptists. The meeting's attendees might have agreed in principle with Pendleton's view that "discussion of the [slavery] question in the Home Missionary Society is out of order," but that did little to keep the issue from dominating the tenor of the conference. Pendleton's experience in Philadelphia shaped his religious opinion of abolitionists and contributed to his antislavery conservatism.[31]

Leading up to 1844, northern abolitionist Baptists had been pushing for the denomination to articulate a denunciation of slaveholding, and they argued that slaveholders should not be missionaries. Ever since the 1840 American Baptist Anti-Slavery Convention, a meeting of northern abolitionists in New York City, sectional tensions had been building. The 1840 convention produced a treatise entitled "An Address to Southern Baptists" that denied the biblical sanction for slavery and called on Baptists in the South to repent for perpetuating the institution. Moreover, the abolitionists demanded that southerners immediately move toward emancipation or face being cut off from fellowship. As expected, the ultimatum did little to motivate slaveholding Baptists to free their slaves and only increased sectional friction. In between the northern and southern factions, the ABHMS attempted to hold a middle ground. At its 1841 meeting, its executive committee passed a resolution that implored both sides to avoid bringing extrareligious affairs to the center of Baptist life. Whatever political differences might separate Baptists, the committee urged, they ought to be bound together by a sense of unity shaped by adherence to the same Christian tradition.[32]

This spirit of tension marked the 1844 meeting Pendleton attended. As did the leaders of the convention three years prior, Pendleton tried to maintain a neutral stance on the slavery question. Nevertheless, Pendleton's journal

---

[30] Victor B. Howard, "James Madison Pendleton: A Southern Crusader against Slavery," *Register of the Kentucky Historical Society* 74 (July 1976): 193–4.

[31] Journal of James Madison Pendleton, April 26, 1844, Department of Library Special Collections, Manuscripts, Western Kentucky University, Bowling Green.

[32] Goen, *Broken Churches*, 92–3.

reflected a noticeably negative tone toward abolitionists at the convention. Pendleton's record of the event tells of the slavery question being introduced at the convention on April 26 and recounts some of the argumentation. The notable South Carolina minister Richard Fuller (1804–76) "remarked impressively," according to Pendleton, "that there must be a new Bible before it could be proved that slavery is a sin – for where there is no law there is no transgression." Moreover, by Pendleton's estimation, the chief abolitionist spokesman, Nathaniel Colver (1794–1870), pastor of Boston's Tremont Street Baptist Church and a long-term associate of James G. Birney, was "exceedingly rough & uncourteous" and failed to argue "with fairness and magnanimity." Despite these opinions, Pendleton refrained from taking sides. Because the ABHMS had not been organized to deal with such "extra-constitutional" questions, there was no reason to debate them. Although Pendleton briefly mentioned another debate over slavery on April 29 and the vote on April 30 that continued to allow ministers from slave states to become missionaries, he provided no further analysis of the matter.[33]

Clearly Pendleton thought the issue had been tabled, but that fall a group of Alabama Baptists decided to test the resolution. They appealed to the General Convention, asking what it would do if a slaveholder attempted to become a missionary. Though stated cautiously, the executive committee effectively ended its neutral stance when it replied that it would not appoint a slaveholder to such a post. Northern Baptists were still a relatively conservative group, and this was no sanctioning of abolitionist principles. Still it was a definitive antislavery statement, and that alone was enough to raise the ire of southern Baptists in late 1844. It decisively rent the fabric of Baptist America that had, in the years leading up to their decision, somehow managed to hold together.[34]

In May 1845 southerners held a meeting in Augusta, Georgia, to discuss splitting from the national convention and forming a new body comprised of Baptists from the slave states. The Upper South was vastly underrepresented – only one representative from Kentucky attended and no one came from Tennessee – and these states argued against immediately leaving the national denomination. For its part, the flagship newspaper of Kentucky Baptists, the *Baptist Banner and Western Pioneer*, signaled much support for the southern position throughout 1844 and 1845, but it also "hope[d] our brethren in the South will pause and seek God for wisdom before they take the step, in this matter, which cannot be contracted." Still, Baptists farther south understood

---

[33] Pendleton Journal, April 26, 29, and 30, 1844. Colver served with Birney as a representative to the 1840 World Anti-Slavery Convention in London. See Fladeland, *Birney*, 196. In only a few years, Colver would achieve even greater acclaim as an abolitionist spokesperson with the publication of his sermon, *The Fugitive Slave Bill: Or, God's Laws Paramount to the Laws of Men. A Sermon, Preached on Sunday, October 20, 1850* (Boston: J. M. Hewes, 1850).

[34] Goen, *Broken Churches*, 95–6; McKivigan, *War against Proslavery Religion*, 90–2.

that their coreligionists in the Upper South agreed in principle with the convention's purpose. Thus confident of southern solidarity on the issue, the meeting went forward and formed the Southern Baptist Convention.[35]

Pendleton himself did not defend slavery, but he nonetheless followed his fellow white southerners into the Southern Baptist Convention. The reason had much to do with his baseline ecclesiastical principles as a Baptist. More than any other American denomination, Baptists maintained a rigid commitment to the autonomy of local congregations. Unlike Protestant counterparts in the Episcopal, Methodist, or Presbyterian traditions, Baptists had no authoritative body that exercised congregational oversight. For Baptists, "congregational autonomy" was neither mere lip service nor a simple catch phrase. Baptists such as Pendleton believed, as a matter central to the way they practiced their faith, that Christian identity was an individual matter expressed through the local congregation. Naturally, different practices and interpretations grew from different churches. This view of congregational polity is precisely what made the abolitionists' raising of the slavery question so offensive to Pendleton. Slavery – in fact, all questions of moral and political import – was a matter to be sorted out in local churches, not aired in the context of denominational debate.[36]

William C. Buck (1790–1872), editor of the *Baptist Banner and Western Pioneer*, said as much in an 1845 plea for preserving unity with conservative Baptists in the North: "The mission belongs to [national Baptists] and not to the Boston Board; *and that Board has neither the right nor the power to dictate to the churches the terms and conditions upon which the mission is to be conducted or the union of the denomination preserved.*" The Home Mission Society existed to support and discuss missionary endeavor, and not affairs properly relegated to the congregational level.[37]

Pendleton's disdain for northern abolitionist Baptists was not limited to their cavalier attitude toward congregational autonomy. As was the case with Kentucky gradualists in Methodist and Presbyterian circles, abolitionist biblical interpretations proved heretical as well. Although by the date of the Baptist schism evangelical abolitionists had abandoned the Garrisonians, the radical Boston abolitionist still provided a convenient foil for religious conservatives. Garrison in fact agreed with the proslavery assertion that the Bible did sanction slavery. By 1845, however, he concluded that biblical sanction meant not that slavery was right, but that the Bible was wrong. Garrison's enlightened, rational

---

[35] Goen, *Broken Churches*, 96–7; William Wright Barnes, *The Southern Baptist Convention, 1845–1953* (Nashville: Broadman Press, 1954) 10, 16, quote 28.

[36] On Baptist ecclesiological principles, see Philip N. Mulder, *A Controversial Spirit: Evangelical Awakenings in the South* (New York: Oxford University Press, 2002), 53. Although Mulder's account is mainly devoted to eighteenth-century developments, he nonetheless provides an apt description of Baptist congregational principles. See also Gregory A. Wills, *Democratic Religion: Freedom, Authority, and Church Discipline in the Baptist South, 1785–1900* (New York: Oxford University Press, 1997), 26–36.

[37] Buck quoted in Barnes, *The Southern Baptist Convention*, 27–8.

reading of the text led him to conclude, "The God, who in America, is declared to sanction the impious system of slavery . . . is my ideal of the Devil." Rather than the authoritative source of truth most Americans saw in the Bible, Garrison read the book to be "a lie and a curse on mankind." He went further in other essays, claiming that "[t]o say everything contained within the lids of the Bible is divinely inspired," such as the notion, for example, that slavery was a necessary part of God's ordained social order, "is to give utterance to a bold fiction, and to require the suspension of the reasoning faculties." Although he succeeded in rallying some support within abolitionist circles – Wendell Phillips, Theodore Parker, and Ralph Waldo Emerson all voiced agreement – the lingering effect of Garrison's scandalous anti-biblicism was to alienate from the abolitionist movement many who affirmed the high place of Scripture.[38]

In this key respect, Kentucky's colonizationist-emancipationists followed much of the proslavery logic. For the Methodists who had collectively affirmed abolitionism as error in 1836, opinions changed relatively quickly. Over the next eight years, northern attitudes shifted decidedly against slavery until American Methodism reached its breaking point. In 1842, abolitionist Methodists in the North withdrew from the national denomination because of its toleration for slaveholding members and formed the Wesleyan Methodist Church. By the end of 1844, some 15,000 northerners had joined the Wesleyans. Those numbers were significant, but not overwhelming given Methodism's more than 1.1 million members – which made it the largest denomination in the United States. Rather, it was events within the nation's largest religious denomination itself that caused much more notice and ultimately fractured the Methodist Episcopal Church into two sectional branches.[39]

The issue that ultimately brought about schism concerned the right of Methodist bishops to hold slaves. Georgia bishop James O. Andrew had acquired slaves through marriage, years after his 1832 ordination as bishop, and the laws of his state barred him from emancipating them. Although Andrew had violated no laws of the church, an increasingly antislavery northern faction could not stomach the idea of a slave-owning bishop. For his part, Andrew

---

[38] J. Albert Harrill, "The Use of the New Testament in the American Slave Controversy: A Case History in the Hermeneutical Tension between Biblical Criticism and Christian Moral Debate," *Religion and American Culture* 10 (2000): 149–86, quotes 159–60; and quotes from William Lloyd Garrison, "No Union With Slaveholders!," *The Liberator*, September 19, 1851; "Thomas Paine," *The Liberator*, November 21, 1845. For other examples, see also H. C. Wright, "The Bible a Self-Evident Falsehood, If Opposed to Self-Evident Truth," *The Liberator*, September 29, 1847; "The Bible," *The Liberator*, November 24, 1848; and "The Bible Not an Inspired Book: A Sermon," *The Liberator*, November 14, 1851; "Plenary Inspiration of the Bible," *The Liberator*, July 1, 1853.

[39] Goen, *Broken Churches*, 81–3; McKivigan, *War against Proslavery Religion*, 84–7. For a longer account of the 1844 General Conference and its significance for American Methodism, see Donald G. Matthews, *Slavery and Methodism: A Chapter in American Morality, 1780–1845* (Princeton: Princeton University Press, 1965), 246–82. For 1844 Methodist Episcopal Church membership numbers, see *Minutes of the Annual Conferences of the Methodist Episcopal Church, for the Years 1839–1845*, vol. 3 (New York: T. Mason and G. Lane, 1840), 603.

offered to resign his office, but southern Methodists refused to accept his offer. The situation proved intractable, and at the 1844 General Conference in New York City, the northern majority passed a motion calling on Andrew to "desist from the exercise of his office" so long as he remained a slave owner.[40]

Southern Methodists were apoplectic. The situation was much the same as with the Baptists: the General Conference was not an abolitionist body. It had voted for resolutions that called their ruling in the Andrew case "advisory only, and not . . . a judicial mandate," but southerners did not see it that way. Rather, in a minority protest penned by Kentuckian Henry B. Bascom, they opined that "the abolition and anti-slavery principles of the north will no longer allow them [the northerners] to submit to" what southerners saw as the Methodist Episcopal Church's traditional non-meddling approach to the slavery question. For southern Methodists, that approach had long been sanctioned by their denomination's official moral and legal standard, the *Book of Discipline*. Because northerners "will no longer . . . submit to the law of the Discipline on the general subject of slavery and abolition," the southern minority wing interpreted the 1844 Methodist General Conference's rulings as an omen of abolitionist aggression to come. Rather than wait around for compromise, southerners argued, "*the south cannot submit, and the absolute necessity of division is already dated.*" In light of the acrimony, the General Conference resolved that because "the Annual Conferences in the slaveholding states find it necessary to unite in a distinct ecclesiastical connection," a separate fellowship, south of the slave-free line, needed to be created.[41]

Northern Methodists had not necessarily abandoned their earlier moderate approach to slavery, nor did they summarily reject slaveholders from their ranks. However, from the perspective of southern Methodists, the denomination's failure to defend slaveholding as specifically Christian meant that the shadow of abolition nonetheless clouded northerners' spiritual vision. And so southerners began immediately to coordinate efforts to withdraw their 500,000 members from the denomination. Meeting in Louisville one year later, in May 1845, the Methodist Episcopal Church, South (MECS), was born in Kentucky – and with it the largest Christian fellowship in the United States was torn in two.[42]

---

[40] Goen, *Broken Churches*, 81–3; Matthews, *Slavery and Methodism*, 264–9. Goen quotes the 1844 General Conference's resolution, which can also be found in *History of the Organization of the Methodist Episcopal Church, South* (Nashville: South-Western Christian Advocate, 1845), 23. See pp. 68–9 for voting records in the Andrew case. Some northern Methodists did side with the South in the vote, but no southerners voted against Andrew.

[41] *Journal of the General Conference of the Methodist Episcopal Church, Held in the City of New York, 1844*, in *Journals of the General Conference of the Methodist Episcopal Church*, Vol. 2: *1840, 1844* (New York: Carlton and Phillips, 1856), 135, 198.

[42] On the relative conservatism of northern Methodists, despite the southern interpretation at the time, see McKivigan, *War against Proslavery Religion*, 86–7. Some four thousand slaveholders remained in the northern church, convinced, as McKivigan argues, "that the northern Methodist church was not an abolitionist body." See also Mathews, *Slavery and Methodism*, 276–9.

Superficially, it appeared that the MECS was born of white southern solidarity in defense of slavery. In some sense, that was true. Yet it was also true that the new denomination, like the new polities created by the Baptist and Presbyterian schisms, was born of an uneasy gradualist-proslavery coalition. The southern minority's protest at the 1844 General Conference masked the fact that its ranks included many antislavery voices, albeit – much like the American Colonization Society – conservative, not radical ones. In fact, the primary architect of the southern protest, Henry Bascom, was among them. At the time of the 1844 meeting, Bascom served as president of Transylvania University in Lexington and was widely known throughout the United States as a first-order preacher. His 1850 appointment as a bishop in the Methodist Episcopal Church, South, was affirmation of a highly influential career. In his early ministry as an itinerant in 1820s Ohio, Bascom had made quite an impression on Henry Clay, who succeeded in seeing the minister named chaplain of the U.S. House of Representatives in 1823. After a brief stint as the president of Pennsylvania's Madison College from 1827 to 1829, Bascom took a position as an agent of the American Colonization Society, before accepting a post in 1832 on the faculty of Augusta College, located roughly forty miles up the Ohio River from Cincinnati, in the town of Augusta, Bracken County, Kentucky.[43]

Founded in 1822, the college was established, given its location, under the auspices of both the Kentucky and Ohio Methodist conferences. However, as the slavery question came to be debated with increasing fervor through the 1830s, the college's status grew more and more tenuous. Although Augusta College saw no massive student uprising of abolitionists as had occurred at Lane Seminary, the school featured a number of debates about slavery and abolition. Its president, Joseph S. Tomlinson, espoused antislavery views, as did a number of the students from Ohio. By the early 1840s, the Ohio Conference no longer felt it could send its students to Augusta, and in the fall and winter of 1841–2 it withdrew its financial support and established Ohio Wesleyan University. In the meantime, citing "the well known division of opinion and feeling in Kentucky and Ohio, in relation to the existing controversy on the subject of slavery," the Kentucky Conference chose to redirect its funds to Transylvania University. A leading figure in this decision, Bascom assumed the Transylvania presidency in 1842, and half the Augusta College faculty followed him.[44]

[43] M. M. Henkle, *The Life of Henry Bidleman Bascom* (Nashville: M. E. Church, South, 1894), 135–6, 183–203, 230; Harold D. Tallant, *Evil Necessity: Slavery and Political Culture in Antebellum Kentucky* (Lexington: University Press of Kentucky, 2003), 20–5.

[44] Kenneth H. Wheeler, "Higher Education in the Antebellum Ohio Valley: Slavery, Sectionalism, and the Erosion of Regional Identity," *Ohio Valley History* 8.1 (Spring 2008): 8–12; Walter H. Rankins, *Augusta College, Augusta, Kentucky: First Established Methodist College, 1822–1849* (Frankfort, KY: Roberts Printing, 1957), 47–50; Redford, *Life and Times of H. H. Kavanaugh*, 264–71; *Communication from Commissioners of the Kentucky Conference to the Legislature of Kentucky, in reply to a memorial from the Trustees of Augusta College* (Lexington: Observer and Reporter, 1843), 3.

Stripped of nearly all its funding, Joseph Tomlinson did his best to keep Augusta College operational. The effort did not last long, and the state of Kentucky revoked the school's charter in 1849. However, that did not stop Tomlinson from trying to resist what he saw as the proslavery bent of Kentucky Methodism. He and his church in Augusta refused to join the MECS when it was created in 1845, and at the 1848 General Conference of what was then a mostly northern Methodist Episcopal Church, he blasted Bascom and southern Methodists for their sanction of slaveholding. In contrast to southern apologists, who viewed Tomlinson as a "deranged" leader whose "empire of reason was tottering to its fall," northern Methodists saw no problems with his mental faculties. He accepted an appointment to Ohio Wesleyan in 1850 and left Kentucky.[45]

The rift between Bascom and Tomlinson over slavery had not always existed, however. In several speeches supporting colonization in 1832 and 1833, Bascom contended that his auditors needed to "exert yourselves in wiping away the most defacing stain – that of slavery – that is seen lingering in the azure heaven of your country's reputation." That claim was only a small part of a larger argument calling for the expatriation of African Americans to Liberia; however, like his fellow leading religious whites in Kentucky, Bascom believed colonization a serious attempt to provide American blacks "what the declaration of our nation's independence broadly avouches *all men* have a right to be – the subjects of a government of their own choice and ordination!" Bascom called, as did John C. Young and Robert J. Breckinridge, for a whites-first view of emancipation that would gradually remove blacks to what he saw as their native land. Following the conservative logic, he argued, "I *do not*, I *will not* meddle with the question of domestic slavery, as sanctioned by law in this country. I speak of the oppression of Africa as a country," which he argued had been despoiled by the slave trade, against the will of Africans themselves. As was the case with other colonizationists, Bascom would not address the moral right of slavery to exist in the United States. That was an abolitionist move. He was antislavery, but he was no radical.[46]

As the author of the document that distilled proslavery southern Methodists' complaints against their northern counterparts in 1844 and ultimately led to southern separation, Bascom appeared to become a stronger supporter of slavery over time. To be sure, after writing the southern minority protest at the 1844 General Conference, Bascom published a lengthier condemnation of northern Methodists' record on slavery, *Methodism and Slavery* (1845). The treatise achieved a wide readership throughout the United States

[45] Wheeler, "Higher Education in the Antebellum Ohio Valley," 10–11, 21n16; Redford, *Life and Times of H. H. Kavanaugh*, 211–13.

[46] Henry B. Bascom, "Claims of Africa; Or an Address in Behalf of the American Colonization Society," in *Posthumous Works of the Rev. Henry B. Bascom*, ed. Thomas N. Ralston, 4 vols. (Nashville: E. Stevenson and F. A. Owen, 1856), 2:253–3, 266–70, 277, 285.

and drew the attention of several leading politicians, including John C. Calhoun (1782–1850) and Henry Clay, who found much to praise in Bascom's argument.[47]

The Transylvania University president blasted abolitionism for advancing a variety of different social ills, as well as a heretical view of the development of Christian doctrine. He contended that "slavery is a civil relation, with which Christianity does not meddle, and as such is not to be interfered with on the part of the Church. From Moses to Christ, slavery, perpetual slavery for life, existed in the Church, even in connection with the Priesthood in all its grades, and God, equal and infinite in wisdom and goodness," allowed and "enforced its relations." The practice was furthermore sanctioned by the Christian Church's "early and later fathers" of antiquity, including "Ignatius, Chrysostom, and Jerome" who "denounce[d]" attempts to "interfere, so as to disturb the civil and domestic relations between master and slave." As Bascom maintained, "unless it can be shown to be inconsistent with the word of God, and so forbidden to the Christian, we maintain that any authoritative interference with the relation by the Church, is a usurpation of right that ought to be resisted." What was true for "the great head of the Church general, Prophets and Apostles, the Scriptures of the Old and New Testaments, the principal fathers and writers of the Church, since the days of inspiration" was, in Bascom's reading, no less true in 1845.[48]

Given Bascom's earlier work as a colonization agent who publicly opposed slavery, it might appear that the Methodist had reversed his earlier position. But that was not the case. Instead, his trajectory revealed just how closely much proslavery and gradualist religious thought aligned. As he explained early on in *Methodism and Slavery*, Bascom applied "the term *abolition*, in the plain, obvious and general sense, in which I have always understood and used it, to denote *any interference or meddling with the question of slavery, contrary to the intention and beyond the provisions of law, civil and ecclesiastical – that is, the law of the land and the law of the Church*." By contrast, "the principles and actions of those who seek the removal or regulation of slavery, in strict and respectful accordance with law, as above, I have always regarded and spoken of as *conservative* in character and decency, and shall do so in this discussion."

[47] Henry Clay, letter to Thomas B. Stevenson, August 12, 1845, in *The Papers of Henry Clay*, vol. 10: *Candidate, Compromiser, Elder Statesman, January 1, 1844–June 29, 1852*, ed. Melba Porter Hay (Lexington: University Press of Kentucky, 1991), 236; John C. Calhoun, letter to Thomas B. Stevenson, July 7, 1845, in *The Papers of John C. Calhoun*, vol. 22: *1845–1846*, ed. Clyde N. Wilson (Columbia: University of South Carolina Press, 1995), 13–14. See also Bridget Ford, "Black Spiritual Defiance and the Politics of Slavery in Antebellum Louisville," *Journal of Southern History* 78 (February 2012): 80–3.

[48] Henry B. Bascom, *Methodism and Slavery: with Other Matters in Controversy between the North and the South; Being a Review of the Manifesto of the Majority, in Reply to the Protest of the Minority, of the Late General Conference of the Methodist E. Church, in the Case of Bishop Andrew* (Frankfort, KY: Hodges, Todd, and Pruett, 1845), 62, 65, 66.

The result was a chastened account that allowed much room for the gradualist antislavery position.[49]

Methodism and Slavery was no rabid proslavery document, and Bascom spilled much ink showing readers that southern Methodists were not even necessarily a proslavery faction. As Bascom maintained, "A very large proportion of the Minority of the South, in the late General Conference, have no connection with slavery," and some "never expect to have any. Many of them have done much, and expect to do more, for the freedom of the negro." The Kentuckian even claimed that many southern Methodists "had themselves manumitted a large number of slaves, and had been the means of securing the freedom of many others" through gradual means. They were thus "not prepared to submit to be libeled and proscribed by those who never *have* and are never *likely* to do any thing for the negro, and whose zeal seems to derive its principal pabulum from the success of their efforts, in preventing others from doing any thing." The fact was that many such conservative emancipationists came from the border slave states of "Maryland, Western Virginia, Kentucky, and Missouri." This "great mass of non-slave holding citizens" did not fit the picture that painted the South with a broad proslavery brush.[50]

Bascom's conception of white southern views was not wishful thinking. Many southerners clearly understood the distinction Bascom made. There was no uniform opinion on slavery in the slaveholding South, and the Deep South's planting elite remained suspicious of those on the border. Although he initially supported Bascom, John C. Calhoun's opinion of Bascom's argument soon became more complex, thanks to an exchange of letters with fellow South Carolina slaveholder James Henry Hammond (1807–64) – the state's former governor as well as past and future U.S. congressman – who read *Methodism and Slavery* far more negatively. Calhoun argued that, although "[Bascom] does not agree with us on the subject of abolition," the Kentuckian got so much right "that it is calculated to do a vast deal of good in portions of the South." For Calhoun's part, he "thought it highly desirable, that publick attention should be called to it."[51]

Hammond was less sanguine. He drew no distinction between conservative, gradualist positions, such as those held by Bascom and Henry Clay, and those of abolitionists. Although few abolitionists ever existed in Kentucky, Henry Clay's cousin, slaveholder Cassius M. Clay, was frequently charged as such. The same year that *Methodism and Slavery* appeared in print, in 1845, Cassius Clay began publishing his antislavery newspaper, the *True American*, in Lexington. The paper was devoted to whites-first gradual emancipation, and in

---

[49] Bascom, *Methodism and Slavery*, 11.

[50] Ibid., 75–6.

[51] See John C. Calhoun, letter to James Henry Hammond, August 2, 1845, *Papers of Calhoun*, 22:50. For another discussion of this exchange and its significance for Kentucky gradualism, see Tallant, *Evil Necessity*, 23–5.

1846 Clay enlisted with the Kentucky militia to fight in the Mexican-American War, which ultimately significantly increased the United States' slaveholding lands. For his part, Clay claimed that he went to fight for patriotic reasons and did not believe the war would "strengthen" slavery. Although northern abolitionists criticized his decision to fight, the fact was that Clay held closer ties to northern immediatists than almost any other Kentuckian. He corresponded with Garrisonians – which was enough to draw suspicion on its own – and also with leaders in the Liberty Party, who had once again nominated James G. Birney as their presidential candidate in 1844, though Clay did not support their efforts directly. Cassius Clay disavowed colonization and often questioned white supremacy in ways few other gradualists would. Taken together, this approach set him apart from the majority of antislavery southerners and drew ire from most conservatives inside and beyond Kentucky's borders.[52]

Clay did not simply skirt close to the line of abolitionism; his *True American* also published articles by avowed immediatists. One of these individuals was John G. Fee, Kentucky's delegate to the Liberty Party's Southern and Western Convention in Cincinnati in June 1845 – where Birney presided in his last major public appearance before suffering a debilitating horse-riding accident – and the state's most outspoken abolitionist in the late 1840s and 1850s. An evangelical who converted to abolitionism through studies at Augusta College and Lane Seminary in the late 1830s and early 1840s, Fee had much difficulty securing a pastorate in Kentucky because of his antislavery views. He, like abolitionists elsewhere, had come to believe that it was his duty to reject fellowship with slaveholders. Fee did not keep these views a secret, and his New School Presbyterian presbytery, populated by a number of slaveholders, censured him in September 1845. Moreover, Fee's public lectures and writings in northern Kentucky provoked numerous instances of mob violence.[53]

---

[52] On Cassius Clay's antislavery record, see Jacob F. Lee, "Between Two Fires: Cassius M. Clay, Slavery, and Antislavery in the Kentucky Borderlands," *Ohio Valley History* 6.3 (Fall 2006): 50–70. On his correspondence with Salmon Chase of the Liberty Party, who had invited him to attend their Southern and Western Convention in Cincinnati in June 1845, see "Cassius M. Clay's Letter," in *The Address of the Southern and Western Liberty Convention, to the People of the United States* (Cincinnati: Gazette, 1845), 20. Stanley Harrold has argued persuasively that Cassius Clay's motivations were less stridently racist than those of more conservative opponents of slavery, suggesting that the whites-first antislavery argument could be marshaled for more radical, if not integrationist, ends. Indeed, Cassius Clay was often labeled "the 'fanatic'" among Kentucky's opponents of slavery." See Harrold, "Cassius M. Clay on Slavery and Race: A Reinterpretation," *Slavery and Abolition* 9.1 (May 1988): 42–56, quote 44.

[53] See Richard Sears, *The Kentucky Abolitionists in the Midst of Slavery, 1854–1864: Exiles for Freedom* (Lewiston, NY: Edwin Mellen Press, 1993), 39–57; Victor B. Howard, *The Evangelical War against Slavery and Caste: The Life and Times of John G. Fee* (Selinsgrove, PA: Susquehanna University Press, 1996), 19–35; John G. Fee, *Autobiography of John G. Fee* (Chicago: National Christian Association, 1891), 24–49; *Address of the Southern and Western Liberty Convention*, 13; Fladeland, *Birney*, 252–7.

In the *True American*, Clay published a series of articles that Fee later revised and expanded as *An Anti-Slavery Manual* (1848). Fee argued that, although it was the case that the Bible contained many references to slavery, it was not true that the Holy Writ sanctioned American slavery. Against conservative hermeneutical principles, Fee drew on the Philadelphia New School Presbyterian Albert Barnes' famous 1846 *Inquiry into the Scriptural Views of Slavery*. Barnes himself had been a major precipitant factor in the Presbyterian Old School/New School schism because many conservatives saw him as a heretic for his denial of original sin – a charge cleared by vote of the 1836 Presbyterian General Assembly thanks to a noted preponderance of New School votes. Following Barnes, Fee advocated a reading of the text that highlighted its spiritual intent over against its literal word. This approach was far more liberal than conservative readers allowed, but Fee did not care: "We *need . . . a different kind of teaching.*" The slavery that existed in America did not line up with "the sum and essence of all religion," which he contended Jesus taught in Luke 10 and Mathew 22. True Christians were to offer "supreme love to God, and equal love to our neighbor." Yet on a "practical" level, American slavery "is the opposite of all this and yet it is alleged to be in accordance with the religion of the Bible."[54]

Fee noted that American Christians had no trouble pointing to 1 Corinthians 6:10 – "Nor thieves, nor covetous, nor drunkards, nor revilers, nor extortioners, shall inherit the kingdom of God" – as support for bringing church discipline against those who used alcohol to the point of intemperance. Certainly the passage denounced drunkenness, Fee wrote, and no one would argue that the teaching only applied to the biblical era. But in interpreting the passage, the American church was terribly inconsistent. Believers overlooked the implications of the verse's condemnation of extortion because, he claimed, "few will deny" that "slavery is the worst form of extortion." American Christians had fallen under the influence of a "delusive Gospel," one that sanctioned a practice severely out of step with the teaching of Scripture.[55]

In the main, Fee argued that biblical slavery and American slavery were not the same entity. In a lengthy section of his *Anti-Slavery Manual*, Fee compared Mosaic slavery with that in nineteenth-century America. In the biblical account, the requirement of Jubilee guaranteed that cyclically, every seven years, all slaves would go free. Furthermore, Deuteronomy 23:15–16 taught the ancient Hebrews not to return an escaped servant to his master, so that the servant might not be oppressed. The Bible demanded that masters treat

---

[54] John G. Fee, *An Anti-Slavery Manual: Being an Examination in the Light of the Bible, and of Facts into the Moral and Social Wrongs of American Slavery, with a Remedy for the Evil* (1848; New York: Arno Press, 1969), vii, ix; Albert Barnes, *An Inquiry into the Scriptural Views of Slavery* (Philadelphia: Perkins and Purves, 1846); Moorhead, "Restless Spirit of Radicalism," 24–5.

[55] Fee, *Anti-Slavery Manual*, ix–x.

slaves with charity. Fee cited Exodus 21:26–7, which said that if a master physically abused a servant, the servant was free to leave his or her master. In contrast, there was no regular, cyclic manumission of slaves in the American context. Fugitive slave laws compelled runaway slaves to be returned to oppressive masters. And furthermore, masters had no compunction about physically assaulting their slaves.[56]

Citing chapter and verse, Fee maintained that there was only one solution to the problem as he saw it: slavery was sin, and "as in every other sin, we must abandon it." There was only one plausible alternative to slavery: immediate emancipation for all slaves and non-fellowship with slaveholders. Such argumentation led him into direct conflict with the New School Presbyterians, who ultimately withdrew their support in late 1848. To continue funding his ministry, Fee turned to Lewis Tappan. Tappan was the treasurer of the newly formed abolitionist American Missionary Association (AMA) – an amalgam of the Union Missionary Society, the Committee for West Indian Missions, and the Western Evangelical Missionary Society – whose leadership also included William Goodell, George Cheever, Amos Phelps, Gerrit Smith, and other prominent immediatists. Although the AMA's early leadership identified themselves as Congregationalists or Presbyterians, the organization maintained a nondenominational stance. For Fee, this nonsectarian attitude fit perfectly; it allowed him freedom to promote his abolitionist agenda without having to answer to the authority of a narrow religious body that might question his decisions, as had been the case with the New School Presbyterians.[57]

By the standards of the slaveholding South, or even the standards of gradual emancipationists in the border states, John G. Fee was a radical. Cassius Clay may have given Fee a platform, but he did not always agree with the evangelical abolitionist. And certainly southern-supporting divines such as Henry B. Bascom were no friends of Fee or Clay's cause.

But living on the border and espousing gradualist antislavery views meant that conservatives might be targeted as sympathetic toward abolitionists. For his part, Bascom never signaled support for Cassius Clay's antislavery vision, but as far as James Henry Hammond of South Carolina was concerned, the Methodist was guilty by association. The college president came from

---

[56] Ibid., 23, 54–58. The text of Deuteronomy 23:15–16 reads: "Thou shalt not deliver unto his master the servant which is escaped from his master unto thee: He shall dwell with thee, even among you, in that place which he shall choose in one of thy gates, where it liketh him best: thou shalt not oppress him." The text of Exodus 21:26–7 reads: "And if a man smite the eye of his servant, or the eye of his maid, that it perish; he shall let him go free for his eye's sake. And if he smite out his manservant's tooth, or his maidservant's tooth; he shall let him go free for his tooth's sake."

[57] Fee, *Anti-Slavery Manual,* 154; Howard, *Evangelical War against Slavery and Caste,* 31–6; Bertram Wyatt-Brown, *Lewis Tappan and the Evangelical War Against Slavery* (1969; Baton Rouge: Louisiana State University Press, 1997), 292–3; Lewis Tappan, *History of the American Missionary Association: Its Constitution and Principles* (New York: n.p., 1855), 17–20.

Kentucky, where Hammond saw "growing up a powerful abolition excite-ment" under the leadership of "Cassius Clay, differing no way *in principle* from Dr. Bascom & Henry Clay." Hammond claimed that Cassius Clay was "making the most powerful appeal in his new paper 'The True American' to the nonslaveholders of Kentucky, & preaching insurrection to both black & white." For reasons of political expediency, gradualists pretended that their goals differed from those of radicals, but that was all a ruse: there was no real difference. In the South Carolinian's reading, *Methodism and Slavery* masked the fact that Bascom and his fellow Kentuckians were only "*pseudo* friends of Slaveholders" who grasped for "an overwhelming domination over So[uthern] Methodism, which would soon become as dangerous to us as that of the North." From James Henry Hammond's vantage point, all antislavery was an undifferentiated mass. He could not, as Calhoun hoped, endorse *Methodism and Slavery* because of Bascom's "unsound views of Slavery." In Hammond's assessment, "sound [M]ethodists" were "neither abolitionists nor *colonization-ists.*" Antislavery of any kind could not be countenanced.[58]

Hammond's skeptical reading of Bascom's work contrasted with Calhoun's. In his final letter on the subject to Hammond, Calhoun's assessment was chas-tened. The elder statesman contended that, although Hammond made some good points, "I think you do not do the Doctor [Bascom] justice, in identi-fying his opinions with either Cas[s]ius [M.] or Henry Clay on the subject of abolition. The former is one of the most rabid of the fanaticks, and goes all lengths against the South and its institutions. I do not think the latter an abolitionist, but I should be glad to think him as sound, as Dr. Bascom on all points." Although Calhoun could see the difference between gradualism and abolitionism, that distinction never made sense to Hammond. If Bascom was what he said he was – and if Kentucky was truly allied with the Deep South on the slavery question – Cassius Clay "could not be tolerated a moment, if Kentucky was sound or his friends less powerful."[59]

When Hammond wrote those words, he could not have known the future. If he had, he might have seen that not only did few Kentucky whites approve of Cassius Clay's activities but they also proceeded just as Hammond had hoped. Just one year after Hammond wrote to Calhoun about *Methodism and Slav-ery*, in August 1846 a mob forced the closure of the Clay's *True American* office in Lexington. Owing largely to Clay's status as a member of the planter elite, his printing press was not sacked and destroyed, but he was nonetheless forced to relocate the paper north of Kentucky's border to Cincinnati, where it floundered due to financial problems. This development probably would have pleased Hammond, but he nonetheless remained convinced that Bascom

[58] James Henry Hammond, letter to John C. Calhoun, August 18, 1845, in *Papers of Calhoun,* 22:79–83, quotes 80.
[59] Hammond, letter to Calhoun, August 18, 1845; and Calhoun, letter to Hammond, August 30, 1845, in *Papers of Calhoun,* 22:80, 100–1.

deserved no support from the Deep South. Bascom's attempt to link grad-ual emancipationism with strident proslavery arguments proved impossible to Hammond.[60]

Still, in the context of the church fights of 1845, Bascom showed that he was no enemy of the slaveholding South. As much as he had argued that Border South Methodists were not necessarily proslavery, he also challenged the view that gradualists were a secret abolitionist faction. If immediatists in the North hoped to find allies among the Border South's gradualists, they were "sadly mis-taken." Bascom's constituency had no "sympathy with Northern interference respecting slavery." As he put it, "This class of citizens may not approve – may even be opposed to slavery, but knowing the rights and cherishing the interests of the States to which they belong, they will always be found ready to resist any interference with them." It might have been the case that "[t]housands" from the border states, "ninety nine in the hundred," wanted "to see slavery extinct in the land." But they would all the same "never consent to emancipation except upon the condition, that as rapidly as the slaves are freed, they shall be removed from the State. Remove them with the prospect that they will do well, and very few will object to their freedom." The dictates of Holy Scripture and the laws of their home states bound white southern believers. They would not resist them, regardless of their personal views. By raising the slavery question in the General Conference, northern Methodists had shown no respect for these baseline conservative principles.[61]

As a leading light in the southern Methodist exodus from the northern church, Bascom's nuanced position was an important one. The white South's quarrel – as Bascom understood it, though not in the eyes of Calhoun or Hammond – was not with antislavery per se. Provided it came gradually and included black removal, slavery might end some day in America. Still, that day was a long way off. Anyone who called for a more expedient solution remained guilty of violating the laws of God and human society. In short, Bascom and his fellow southern Methodists maintained that fellowship with slaveholders and gradualists could be easily maintained. Abolitionists were another matter.

Thus when it came to the affairs of the church, gradualists and proslavery believers shared significant common ground. Yet, as Henry Bascom's reception by James Henry Hammond indicated, not all defenders of slavery found the gradualist–proslavery alliance palatable. Outside the sphere of church politics, conservative as such an emancipationist agenda was, it often proved too radical for contemporaries of a more decidedly proslavery conviction.

---

[60] Lee, "Between Two Fires," 62–3. Hammond remained firm in his conviction that Bascom and border state southerners could claim no affinity with the Deep South. See William W. Freehling, *The Road to Disunion*, vol. 2: *Secessionists Triumphant, 1854–1861* (New York: Oxford University Press, 2007), 32.

[61] Bascom, *Methodism and Slavery*, 76.

A public war of words – both written and spoken – in early 1840s Lexington revealed just this point. Just a few years after Robert J. Breckinridge's debate with George Thompson, the Presbyterian found himself embroiled in another conflict, this time with Robert Wickliffe – an affluent Lexington attorney who by the early 1850s was the state's largest slaveholder, owning nearly two hundred slaves. A one-time supporter of emancipation and colonization, the former state senator Wickliffe came to reject all antislavery initiatives. The hot-tempered slaveholder also held a long-standing grudge against Breckinridge. In the late 1820s the two had squared off in the state legislature over the slavery question, and Breckinridge's 1830 *Hints on Slavery* articles (republished as a pamphlet in 1843) included a number of personal references to Wickliffe. In 1840 Wickliffe gave a public speech in Lexington in which he attacked the gradualist-supported Law of 1833 banning slave imports into Kentucky. More important, he lambasted the antislavery sentiments that had been developing in the state for years.[62]

Though it included many issues, both political and personal, the Wickliffe–Breckinridge exchange showed a major semantic fault line about what terms such as abolition and emancipation ultimately meant. According to Wickliffe, emancipationists promised to lead Kentucky into a tumultuous future. "Suppose," Wickliffe asked, "that gentlemen gain their point and set our negroes free, do they benefit the slave or the condition of society?" Knowing that anti-slavery folk would answer in the affirmative, Wickliffe asserted, "I beg leave to differ from them." Manumitted blacks would, he continued, "become masses of vagrants," and Kentucky the scene of "a war of extermination [to] settle which race shall possess" it. Wickliffe then launched an attack on local opponents of slavery and in the process drew Breckinridge into the debate. Defining an "abolitionist" as "[o]ne who intends to abolish negro slavery, by an immediate or a slow process – by a direct attack upon the tenure of slavery, or by an indirect mode," Wickliffe smeared Breckinridge with a word the Presbyterian despised: abolition. Wickliffe, however, went further. If the conservative minister insisted that he was not an abolitionist, then he aimed to delude the public. In fact, Wickliffe contended, Breckinridge, whom he linked with Cassius Clay, was an abolitionist "in disguise."[63]

Within a few months, Breckinridge appeared at Lexington's courthouse to offer a rebuttal. He opened with a pro forma introduction in which he noted his "surprise" at being caught up in "political agitations." Thereafter, he preserved few niceties. In the 1820s, the Breckinridge family had employed Wickliffe to

---

[62] Robert J. Breckinridge, *Hints on Slavery* (Lexington: n.p., 1843); Klotter, *Breckinridges of Kentucky*, 70–1; Lowell H. Harrison and James C. Klotter, *A New History of Kentucky* (Lexington: University Press of Kentucky, 1997), 168–9.

[63] Robert Wickliffe, *Speech of Robert Wickliffe Delivered in the Court House, in Lexington, on Monday, the 10th day of August, 1840, Upon Resigning His Seat as Senator from the County of Fayette, More Especially in Reference to the "Negro Law"* (Lexington: Observer and Reporter, 1840), 16–19.

help handle the management of the family estate, but by the early 1830s the family was questioning Wickliffe's ethics and the arrangement ended bitterly. Breckinridge wanted to tell the "complete" story of his history with Wickliffe, but doing so would personalize and embitter the tone of the debate.[64]

Breckinridge called Wickliffe's definition of abolitionist "as insidious as it is absurd." Abolitionists, he argued, promoted "*immediate* emancipation" and rejected on principle "gradual and remote results." To Breckinridge they were "public enemies," individuals who should be "treated as conspirators against the peace and safety of your families; hunted down as the instigators of arson, rape, and murder." Abolitionists advocated "a heresy," of which the chief "doctrine" was racial "*amalgamation*." "*Against* this horrid doctrine," Breckinridge argued defiantly, "I have fought without intermission." Resorting to hyperbole, Breckinridge mocked the idea that he might also be considered a "conspirator": "[n]ow we understand" Wickliffe's point, he said. "[W]hoever *intends* that a day shall ever come in the distant future, when true, real, and general freedom shall dwell amongst the children of men and cover the earth with peace and blessedness – that man is a traitor." Wickliffe, as was also the case with James Henry Hammond, saw no nuance in antislavery positions. Despite the fact that Breckinridge was no friend of abolitionists – and had traveled to Scotland to debate George Thompson to make the point – there was no room for antislavery of any kind in Wickliffe's proslavery worldview.[65]

A month later, Wickliffe went back to the Lexington courthouse to "reply to the billingsgate and filth with which the reverend slanderer has bespattered me." Wickliffe mocked Breckinridge's professed spirit of piety, saying, "He came here . . . with uplifted hands and eyes, declares, by the Providence of God, to defend himself against the gross slanders on his pure and immaculate character and *his beloved Church*. And how does this saint commence? Why, by bringing up my private and individual affairs before you." The personal attack did not end there. Wickliffe derided Breckinridge's emancipation and colonization plans throughout the speech, but he also besmirched Breckinridge's conduct and character before he entered the ministry. To Wickliffe, Breckinridge "resembles another great man – an excellent hypocrite, in more respects than one. I mean Oliver Cromwell. Oliver was a great gambler before he joined the church," he said, but at least Cromwell returned all that he had won after coming to faith. In contrast, Breckinridge "gambled off several of" his family's slaves. Driving home the point, Wickliffe noted that one of these slaves, "the *namesake* of the gentleman, was a listener to him on yesterday, when he quoted from [Cassius] Clay his sentiment on slavery, and proclaimed himself the universal champion of universal emancipation." Wickliffe concluded by warning

---

[64] Robert J. Breckinridge, *Speech of Robert J. Breckinridge, Delivered on the Courthouse Yard at Lexington, KY. On the 12th day of October, 1840, In Reply to the Speech of Robert Wickliffe . . .* (Lexington: N. L. and J. W. Finnel, 1840), 5–6.

[65] Ibid., 20, 23–4.

Breckinridge that he should put his own affairs in order before bringing up the "sins of other people."[66]

Despite counsel from family and friends, Breckinridge published a pamphlet denouncing Wickliffe. Wickliffe responded with his own leaflet, and it was clear that by this point the debate had degenerated into a vitriolic stalemate. Breckinridge fired back his *Third Defence* (1842), wherein he warned of God's judgment on slanderers, but Wickliffe would have the last word. In many ways, the title of his final pamphlet captures the disdain he held for the Presbyterian minister: *A Further Reply of Robert Wickliffe to the Billingsgate Abuse of Robert Judas Breckinridge, Otherwise Called Robert Jefferson Breckinridge* (1843). In it, Wickliffe likened Breckinridge's attacks on slavery to the behavior of Judas, Jesus of Nazareth's betrayer. Judas, Wickliffe noted, was often "represented with a downcast, sly, doggish countenance, with a pair of huge whiskers, treating with the Jews for the thirty pieces of silver to betray the Saviour.... I have no drawing of" Breckinridge "when he was negotiating with the universal emancipating society," Wickliffe added, but the deceptive facial expression adopted by Judas when "kissing the Saviour, and slyly handing him over to a Roman soldier" was the same face Breckinridge "assumes when he salutes a former companion at farro and poker."[67]

Wickliffe's character assassination did not stop here. He intimated that Breckinridge had carried on an interracial sexual relationship with some of his slaves. The first was a house servant, "Miss Milly," owned by Breckinridge's father, with whom "Judas" had a dalliance during his teenage years. No child resulted from this relationship, but Wickliffe strongly "suggested" that the minister had "sired" two "almost white" children with a mulatto slave, Louisa. She never admitted who the father of her children was, but that did not hide Breckinridge's "fame as a *Bocanegra*." With these charges, Wickliffe decided "to nauseate the reader" no farther. Breckinridge never responded.[68]

As the debate between Breckinridge and Wickliffe showed, the distinction between Kentucky's defenders of slavery and the state's gradualist emancipationists was often quite profound. If the churches provided a haven for gradualists to make common cause with proslavery believers, this alliance was far harder to sustain when it came to debates about practical politics. Antebellum Kentucky's white conservatives made the Commonwealth a remarkably volatile ideological environment when it came to the slavery question. As a border slave state, Kentucky's context enabled gradual emancipationists to develop

[66] Robert Wickliffe, *Speech of Robert Wickliffe, In Reply to the Rev. R. J. Breckinridge, Delivered in the Court House, in Lexington, on Monday, the 9th November, 1840* (Lexington, Ky.: Observer and Reporter, 1840), 3–4, 49–50.

[67] Robert J. Breckinridge, *The Third Defence of Robert J. Breckinridge Against the Calumnies of Robert Wickliffe* ... (n.p., 1842), 90; Robert Wickliffe, *A Further Reply of Robert Wickliffe to the Billingsgate Abuse of Robert Judas Breckinridge, Otherwise Called Robert Jefferson Breckinridge* (Lexington: Kentucky Gazette, 1843), 7.

[68] Ibid., 55–7.

an alternative to the white southern Protestant reading of the Bible that drew divine sanction for American slavery. Geographically located in the middle ground, these conservatives found a way to carve out a middling antislavery position that, if unpersuasive to more committed proslavery coreligionists, did not sacrifice the evangelical Protestant orthodoxy of the day.

Nevertheless, even as Kentucky's border location afforded emancipationists the freedom to maintain antislavery political and theological convictions, that freedom had its limits. Although their gradualist antislavery approach offered a way to uphold nineteenth-century standards of evangelical orthodoxy while still dismissing abolitionism out of hand, the era's prevailing racial orthodoxy offered no such flexibility. Kentucky's emancipation-colonization movement shared with its proslavery opposition an all-encompassing faith in white superiority. Kentucky's white emancipationists would remain a vocal presence in the late 1840s and 1850s, and their gradualist stance marked them as distinct from more decidedly proslavery religious adherents. Still, the foundation of evangelicalism, white supremacy, and anti-abolitionism allowed for a greater degree of unity with other conservative whites – proslavery whites – than the antebellum context of debate over slavery otherwise allowed. In the years that followed, Kentucky's white population would assess politically the merits of gradual emancipation, in particular by vote in 1849. Overwhelmingly, the state's whites found the program wanting, and in the near future conservative Christian antislavery would reach its political and theological limits. Nonetheless, emancipationism remained a fixture in the pre–Civil War Commonwealth.

3

The Limits of Christian Conservative Antislavery

White Supremacy and the Failure of Emancipationism, 1845–1859

> The abolitionist and the pro-slavery man, agree in nothing but the final result of their principles. . . . They both contend that the black man and white ought to abide together forever; whereas if reason or experience teaches us any lesson, it is that they ought not. God has been pleased to distinguish the races of men inhabiting this earth. . . . For Kentucky, there is no condition of her high and lasting progress more obvious to me, than the removal from her bosom of the black race.
>
> – Presbyterian minister Robert J. Breckinridge,
> *The Question of Negro Slavery and the New Constitution of Kentucky* (1849)[1]

For Kentucky's antebellum history of slavery, 1849 was a signal year. Earlier, during its session of 1846–7, the Commonwealth's legislature had called for a public referendum to vote on whether the state should revise its constitution, which had been in place unmodified since 1799. Overwhelmingly, the state's electorate endorsed the idea of revision, with more than 67 percent voting for change. To proceed with the creation of a new constitution, Kentucky law required a follow-up referendum, and, in 1848 the proportion supporting revision grew to more than 72 percent of the voting populace. Thus, as per the mandate of the people, a constitutional convention was called to meet in August 1849.[2]

Although a range of political issues prompted Kentucky officials to propose revising the state's outdated constitution, slavery overshadowed them all as the

---

[1] Robert J. Breckinridge, *The Question of Negro Slavery and the New Constitution of Kentucky* (Lexington: n.p., 1849), 14.

[2] Harold D. Tallant, *Evil Necessity: Slavery and Political Culture in Antebellum Kentucky* (Lexington: University Press of Kentucky, 2003), 133–6; Lowell H. Harrison and James C. Klotter, *A New History of Kentucky* (Lexington: University Press of Kentucky, 1997), 176–8.

major point of debate in the late 1840s campaign. For proslavery Kentuckians, revising the constitution presented an opportunity to expand the political reach of the slaveholding class. They had already succeeded in February 1849 in repealing the 1833 Slave Nonimportation Act; constitutional revision, it seemed, offered a way to secure slave owners' interests for the long term.[3]

By contrast, the repeal of the Law of 1833 served to further galvanize the state's already active emancipationist movement. The ending of the ban on slave importation constituted, in the words of the Commonwealth's visible and committed minority of white antislavery activists, "part of a system designed to terrify and crush the emancipation party of this State." With such a dire assessment of their political standing, emancipationists thought the time ripe to insert a gradual emancipation clause into the constitution, thereby resisting what they saw as a proslavery conspiracy. As a result, from 1847 to 1849, the Commonwealth's opponents of slavery conducted a public campaign they hoped would shape the constitutional convention. On April 25, 1849, the state's most influential politician, Henry Clay, led a statewide emancipationist convention in Frankfort. Numerous leading "Friends of Emancipation" from religious and political ranks attended the meeting, including Presbyterians Robert J. Breckinridge and his brother William, John C. Young, and Stuart Robinson (1814–81); Baptist James M. Pendleton; the nonsectarian abolitionist John G. Fee; the abolition-minded political activist Cassius M. Clay; and former Whig representative to the U.S. Congress, William P. Thomasson (1797–1882) of Louisville. Henry Clay later declined to represent the newly formed emancipationist party at the state's constitutional convention because he believed it would compromise his standing as a U.S. senator. As a result, Robert J. Breckinridge, then pastor of Lexington's First Presbyterian Church, accepted an offer to take charge of the party. At the same time, local emancipationist meetings convened around the state, and they succeeded in nominating antislavery candidates in twenty-nine counties.[4]

The emancipation canvass of 1849 proved the apogee of Kentucky's antebellum antislavery movement. Showing just how unwilling most white Kentuckians were to embrace even the most conservative and modest of antislavery proposals, the 1849 emancipationist effort fell far short of its supporters' expectations. Antislavery Kentuckians found themselves beset by outbreaks of

---

[3] Tallant, *Evil Necessity*, 134–42.

[4] Lowell H. Harrison, *The Antislavery Movement in Kentucky* (Lexington: University Press of Kentucky, 1978), 53–60; Tallant, *Evil Necessity*, 136–45. The phrase "friends of Emancipation" is from James M. Pendleton, *Reminiscences of a Long Life* (Louisville: Press Baptist Book Concern, 1891), 92; "Convention of the Friends of Emancipation in Kentucky," *The Examiner*, May 5, 1849; "Convention of the Friends of Emancipation in Kentucky," *National Anti-Slavery Standard*, June 21, 1849; and Breckinridge, *The Question of Negro Slavery*, quote 3. See also Victor B. Howard, "The Kentucky Presbyterians in 1849: Slavery and the Kentucky Constitution," *Register of the Kentucky Historical Society* 73 (July 1975): 217–40.

violence in Louisville, Paducah, and in rural areas. In the most notorious incident, at a June debate in Madison County a proslavery mob assailed Cassius Clay before he used his bowie knife to cut out the intestines of one of his assailants, Cyrus Turner, who died ten hours later. Moreover, a cholera epidemic in the state may have kept citizens from voting. In the end, the Commonwealth's generally proslavery populace voted unambiguously against emancipation. The highest estimates show that emancipationists garnered just 14,801 votes – or 9.7 percent of the total ballots cast – and succeeded in getting only two delegates elected to the constitutional convention. Moreover, the constitution that the state did approve in May 1850 strengthened the rights of slaveholders, essentially barred free blacks from the state, and guaranteed slavery's survival in Kentucky well into the future.[5]

The emancipationist constitutional campaign of the late 1840s – and its legacy into the 1850s and 1860s – demonstrates the limits of Christian conservative antislavery in antebellum Kentucky because it so closely mirrored the arguments marshaled by gradualists in this period. Given the overwhelmingly conservative nature of Kentucky's white Christian majority, emancipationists in the 1840s continued to draw on arguments crafted in prior years that emphasized fidelity to evangelical standards, the superiority of the white race, and the detrimental nature of abolitionist schemes. As was the case in earlier years, these antislavery canons did not allow for a radical paradigm, but they did permit the ideological leeway to politically pursue an emancipationist program. Particularly, in the drive of the late 1840s, evangelical emancipationists used these conservative ideas to advocate free labor as a form of economic and social organization superior to slave labor.

Still, if gradualists did not violate robust orthodoxies on religion and race, their program remained untenable to most white Kentuckians. The failure of the 1849 emancipation canvass showed that the work already done in the churches – the unification of proslavery believers and conservative emancipationists on matters theological – remained undone in society writ large. Emancipationism did not succeed in Kentucky, but it was not, as its abolitionist critics charged, proslavery.

Long-standing rifts were apparent among antislavery Kentuckians in 1849. Most Commonwealth emancipationists favored ending slavery gradually, with compensation to owners and the colonization of free blacks. But a minority of antislavery Kentuckians disagreed with such an approach. Notable among white dissidents at the April emancipation convention were the abolitionists

---

[5] Harrison and Klotter, *New History of Kentucky*, 117–19; and Tallant, *Evil Necessity*, 145–60, who provides the higher voting statistics on pp. 149 and 251n30. James C. Klotter, *The Breckinridges of Kentucky* (Lexington: University Press of Kentucky, 1986), 76, offers the more common conservative estimate of roughly ten thousand voting for emancipation. See also Jacob F. Lee, "Between Two Fires: Cassius M. Clay, Slavery, and Antislavery in the Kentucky Borderlands," *Ohio Valley History* 6.3 (Fall 2006): 64–5.

John G. Fee and Cassius Clay, who opposed the gradualists' insistence on black removal. Clay spoke for those who thought the emancipation program "too moderate," but who also believed "[t]he party in favor of freedom is growing everywhere." For the purposes of building what Clay hoped would be a workable political antislavery coalition, he admitted, "We *fanatics* are willing to take your compromise." The Kentucky emancipation movement, narrow as its vision was to Clay and Fee, seemed in the heat of the 1849 emancipation canvass to represent an advancing southern wing of the cause of liberation. However, when the cause stood defeated and there appeared no purpose in trying to mend the rifts among emancipationists, Clay and Fee continued to advocate for immediatism and rejected colonization.[6]

The leaders and members of Kentucky's growing independent black congregations joined Clay and Fee in protesting a white supremacist social order. Like most in the slaveholding South, the majority of enslaved Kentuckians worshiped with whites in biracial segregated churches. Yet Kentucky also claimed an established presence of free African American churches with black pastors, located largely, though not exclusively, in the state's urban centers. This pattern differed from elsewhere in the South. Such spaces had existed more widely in the early national period, but by the mid-nineteenth century, through a variety of tactics, they had been forced to close or house worship only under the authority of a white minister – especially in the wake of Nat Turner's 1831 rebellion in Southampton, Virginia.[7]

In Kentucky, the paramount example of an independent congregation was the First African Baptist Church of Lexington, which was the largest church of any kind in the antebellum Commonwealth and claimed well over 2,000 members by 1860. Formed in 1801 by a non-ordained slave named Peter, probably the first black preacher in the state and colloquially called "Old Captain," the church maintained uneasy linkages to white Baptists who refused to recognize baptisms performed by a non-ordained minister. In 1824 the Elkhorn Association, the oldest association of Baptist churches west of the Allegheny Mountains dating to 1785, received the First African Baptist Church into fellowship after ordaining London Ferrill, a free black man. By 1860, in part due to internecine quarrels, Lexington was home to two other independent black Baptist churches, as well as two black Methodist churches. Moreover,

[6] "Convention of the Friends of Emancipation"; "Emancipation in Kentucky," *The Examiner*, February 3, 1849.

[7] Marion B. Lucas, *A History of Blacks in Kentucky*, vol. 1: *From Slavery to Segregation, 1760–1891* (Frankfort: Kentucky Historical Society, 1992), 118–22; Charles F. Irons, *The Origins of Proslavery Christianity: White and Black Evangelicals in Colonial and Antebellum Virginia* (Chapel Hill: University of North Carolina Press, 2008), 48–51, 183–84; Mechal Sobel, *Trabelin' On: The Slave Journey to an Afro-Baptist Faith* (Westport, CT: Greenwood Press, 1979), 201–10; and J. H. Spencer, *A History of Kentucky Baptists: From 1769 to 1885*, 2 vols. (Cincinnati: J. R. Baumes, 1885), 2:7–44, 653–7.

in 1851 the city saw the formation of an independent black Christian church when thirty-five members withdrew from white churches in the city.[8]

In addition to the major cities of Louisville and Lexington, separate black churches began to appear after 1840 – though in some cases earlier – in Bowling Green, Danville, Frankfort, Maysville, Paris, Richmond, and elsewhere. These congregations were composed of both free and enslaved members, and they operated with varying degrees of freedom from white religious authorities. Although the pastors were black, in most cases the churches were adjuncts of, and financially supported by, white churches or denominational associations or boards.[9]

In other cases, they were completely autonomous, although such ecclesiastical freedom did not come without struggle. In 1840s Louisville pastor Henry Adams (1803–72) of the First African Baptist Church and teacher William H. Gibson (1829–1906) of the Fourth Street Colored Methodist Episcopal Church worked to effect withdrawal from the oversight of the proslavery white churches that participated in their founding in the 1830s and 1840s. The Fourth Street Church in particular began the process after the 1845 creation of the expressly proslavery Methodist Episcopal Church, South; it endured an intense legal battle for its property before a sympathetic – and likely antislavery – judge ruled in its favor. In 1849, Gibson led his fellow parishioners into the United States' oldest black denomination, the famously abolitionist African Methodist Episcopal Church. Thereafter the church took the new name of Asbury Chapel and included among its pastors Hiram R. Revels, who much later, in 1870, achieved renown as the first African American to serve in the U.S. Congress as a senator from Mississippi. By 1860 nine free black churches operated in Louisville, and at least four were completely independent of white oversight. This number included the overtly antislavery Quinn Chapel African Methodist Episcopal Church, which a number of enslaved Louisvillians were prohibited from attending.[10]

Even if these black churches were not part of the official political activities of the emancipation party, their drive toward spiritual autonomy coalesced

---

[8] Lucas, *History of Blacks in Kentucky*, 118–22; George W. Ranck, *"The Travelling Church": An Account of the Baptist Exodus from Virginia to Kentucky in 1781 under the Leadership of Rev. Lewis Craig and Capt. William Ellis* (n.p., 1910), 22–3; Sobel, *Trabelin' On*, 201–10; and Spencer, *History of Kentucky Baptists*, 2:7–44, 653–7.

[9] Lucas, *History of Blacks in Kentucky*, 118–30. Spencer, *History of Kentucky Baptists*, 2:653, counted seventeen independent black Baptist churches with more than 5,000 members at the time of the Civil War. Sobel, *Trabelin' On*, 333–43, counted eighteen, though that number counts First African Baptist of Lexington twice due to the complexities of the church's early history and its relationship to the Elkhorn Association.

[10] See Bridget Ford, "Black Spiritual Defiance and the Politics of Slavery in Antebellum Louisville," *Journal of Southern History* 78 (February 2012): 69–106; Bridget Ford, "American Heartland: The Senimentalization of Religion and Race Relations in Cincinnati and Louisville, 1820–1860" (Ph.D. diss., University of California, Davis, 2002), 49–62, 148–57; and Lucas, *History of Blacks in Kentucky*, 118–30.

in the Commonwealth at the same time as the state was debating antislavery measures. For a small number of white Kentuckians, such affirmations of independence showed the limitations of the gradualist paradigm, which denied the possibility of equal social standing regardless of race. For the greater white majority, however, free black churches contributed to their hardening opposition to any form of emancipationism. By their very existence, these black churches visibly rejected white arguments for a proslavery gospel in ways that were more than symbolic.

Certainly antebellum African Americans faced reprisals for excessive assertions of freedom, and for the enslaved no threat loomed larger than the threat of being sold. Even though the Law of 1833 banned the importation of new slaves from outside the state, and despite a professed widespread aversion to the idea of the slave trade among religious whites, there was no prohibition against Kentucky masters selling their slaves within the state or "down river." In the region, often among neighbors, a localized trade thrived throughout the antebellum era. And over the same period, according to the leading estimates, Kentucky exported 77,000 souls – a traffic in persons that began before statehood in 1792 and persisted during the Civil War. From 1830 until 1860, Kentuckians sold between 2,000 and 3,400 slaves every year. Thus, although not every slave was sold, none were exempt from the slave trade's presence.[11]

Despite much white Christian writing that emphasized the sacredness of marriage and family, the law in the South did not recognize these categories for slaves, and they were not taken into consideration when prospective sales loomed. The hypocrisy of such a slaveholding system that drew much of its justification from Christian sources was not lost on those who were enslaved. Two of Kentucky's most famous fugitive slaves, who were also both deeply connected to the Methodist Church, made differing versions of this argument. Josiah Henson, born in Maryland before being relocated with his master to Daviess County, Kentucky, was ordained as a Methodist preacher in 1828. In his 1849 life narrative, Henson depicted his childhood experience witnessing his own father's sale, which was followed by that of his brothers, sisters, and mother. In 1828 Henson watched the process play out again among his fellow slaves in Daviess County: "Husbands and wives, parents and children were to be separated forever. Affections, which are as strong in the African as in the European were to be cruelly disregarded; and the iron selfishness generated by the hateful 'institution' was to be exhibited in its most odious and naked deformity." It was the threat of sale and separation from his own wife and children that compelled Henson to lead his family to Upper Canada in 1830. Henson's story was so moving that it apparently served as a primary inspiration for the most prominent antislavery publication to emerge from an Ohio Valley

---

[11] Lucas, *History of Blacks in Kentucky*, 88–89, 99–100, breaks the statistics down by decade, showing approximately 2,300 slaves sold annually in the 1830s, 2,000 per year in the 1840s, and 3,400 annually in the 1850s.

context – or anywhere else in the United States – Harriet Beecher Stowe's *Uncle Tom's Cabin* (1852).[12]

Active at the same time as Henson, former Kentucky slave Henry Bibb made similar – and bolder – arguments. He escaped several times from various masters before moving to Detroit, Michigan, in 1842. From there, he began lecturing on his life's travails for various abolitionist organizations, including the Liberty Party and American Missionary Association. Those lectures ultimately appeared in an edited form – thanks to the editorial assistance of his wife, Mary E. Bibb, a free woman from Rhode Island – in the book he is best known for, his *Narrative of the Life and Adventures of Henry Bibb* (1849). The following year, in 1850, Henry and Mary Bibb emigrated across the Detroit River to Windsor, Canada West, where they established a newspaper, *Voice of the Fugitive*, in 1851.[13]

As a devout Methodist, Bibb regularly used the pages of his paper to condemn proslavery Christianity. In a series of notable "letters" he blasted his former Kentucky master, a member of the Methodist Episcopal Church, as a "hypocrite." Bibb argued that his former master "profess[ed] to be a Christian – a leader in the M. E. Church, and a representative of the Lord Jesus Christ, and yet you sold my mother from her little children... you sold my brother George from his wife and dear little ones, while he was a worthy member, and Clergyman of the same Church, to which you belong." Bibb's former master "profess[ed] to take the Bible, as [his] standard of christian duty." But slaveholding, in Bibb's view, violated several key teachings in Scripture: "Listen to the language of inspiration: 'Feed the hungry, and clothe the naked:' 'Break every yoke and let the oppressed go free.' 'All things, whatsoever ye would that men should do unto you, do ye even so unto them, for this is the law and the prophets.'" Slavery was abominable, Bibb argued: "you shall know that there is a God in heaven, who cannot harmonise human slavery with the Christian religion;... you shall know that there is a law which is more binding on the consciences of slaves than that of Congress, or any other human enactment."[14]

It is worth noting that Henson and Bibb's experiences as fugitive slaves were somewhat anomalous. Although Kentucky slaves engaged in manifold forms of resistance – including slowing down the pace of their labor, breaking farm implements, committing arson, and even engaging in direct acts of violence – running away drew the most attention and most directly shaped whites' perceptions about the types of controls needed to maintain slavery. Yet, in 1850

---

[12] Ibid.; and Josiah Henson, *The Life of Josiah Henson, Formerly a Slave, Now an Inhabitant of Canada, as Narrated by Himself* (Boston: Arthur D. Phelps, 1849), quote 27–8.

[13] C. Peter Ripley, et al., eds., *The Black Abolitionist Papers*, Vol. 2: *Canada, 1830–1865* (Chapel Hill: University of North Carolina Press, 1986), 109–12n1–4; Henry Bibb, *The Life and Adventures of Henry Bibb, An American Slave*, intr. Charles J. Heglar (Madison: University of Wisconsin Press, 2001).

[14] Henry Bibb, "A Letter to my Old Master," *Voice of the Fugitive*, September 23, 1852; Bibb, "Letter to my old Master. No. 2," *Voice of the Fugitive*, October 7, 1852.

less than one-twentieth of 1 percent (96 of 210,981), and in 1860 just more than one-twentieth of 1 percent (119 of 225,483), of Kentucky slaves success-fully ran away. Such numbers do not account for the untold many who were truant – who shirked their duties or temporarily escaped, often for the purposes of visiting family – but later returned. There can be no doubt that Henson and Bibb spoke for many enslaved people in their written and verbal excoriation of the slave system. Yet, understandably, their condemnations came only after they were outside Kentucky's borders.[15]

Within the confines of the Commonwealth, such direct language had reper-cussions. It is with that reality in mind that Kentucky's free black churches' challenge to the slaveholding order becomes even more apparent. Although much of the enslaved religious experience occurred out of the sight of whites, in an "invisible institution" practiced secretly in hush arbors, the very visible presence of African Americans in more traditional church and denominational settings should not be minimized. A major pretense of the proslavery gospel was that African Americans were not simply racially inferior, but spiritually inferior as well. White oversight was thus required for black spirituality, and "missions to the slaves" were needed to ensure right belief as much as social control. But by their existence, independent black churches with black minis-ters confounded such logic. The "missions to slaves" were thus long challenged in Kentucky, and the work of claiming an emancipatory history – via religion – began long before white Americans in the Commonwealth or elsewhere came to embrace widespread, legal emancipation.[16]

That point could not have been more clear in the 1849 campaign for con-stitutional revision, where Kentucky's white emancipationists were essentially oblivious to African Americans' own assertions of independence. To advocate for constitutional emancipation in the Bluegrass State, the functional leader of Kentucky's emancipationist movement, Robert J. Breckinridge, penned a series of articles outlining the antislavery platform that he and other gradualists had been developing for nearly two decades. Just before the mid-1849 formation of the emancipationist party, the minister wrote an article for the Lexington Observer and Reporter under the pen name "Fayette." The essay followed many of his earlier colonization arguments and stated as baldly as ever Breck-inridge's version of the whites-first emancipationist agenda. "Emancipation is not the main thing," he contended. In fact, ending slavery was "not even a main

[15] Lucas, History of Blacks in Kentucky, 57–62. On the significance of running away in a different, yet parallel, context, see William A. Link, The Roots of Secession: Slavery and Politics in Antebellum Virginia (Chapel Hill: University of North Carolina Press, 2003), 97–119.

[16] See Ford, "Black Spiritual Defiance"; Lucas, History of Blacks in Kentucky, 118–45; Albert Raboteau, Slave Religion: The "Invisible Institution" in the Antebellum South (New York: Oxford University Press, 1978); and John B. Boles, ed., Masters and Slaves in the House of the Lord: Race and Religion in the American South, 1740–1870 (Lexington: University Press of Kentucky, 1988). On white missions to the enslaved and the proslavery gospel, see Irons, Origins of Proslavery Christianity, esp. pp. 169–209.

thing except as it may aid an object more important than itself." That "object" instead was the *"Unity of race, and that the white race for Kentucky."*[17]

Yet, in spite of his emphasis on white concerns, Breckinridge did argue in a subsequent pamphlet, *The Question of Negro Slavery and the New Constitution of Kentucky* (1849), for the basic religious rights of African Americans. Proslavery believers, he noted, have "invoked" "our divine religion . . . against us. God, the creator of man, and his infinite benefactor, it is constantly alleged, is the great author of the institution by which man has the most effectually defaced God's image in man." Such ideas, Breckinridge argued, were wrong. Every black slave, he suggested, "was, like us, created in the image of God; has, like us, an immortal soul; is, like us, capable of joy and sorrow." Slaves may be "property; but they still are our fellow-men, our fellow-sinners, many of them our fellow-christians." Breckinridge succinctly rejected the religious proslavery argument when he wrote, "The master may serve God – so may the slave. Both it may be, might serve him better if the relation did not exist." The biblical mandate for slavery, as gradualists had argued for years, did not apply to the institution's American form.[18]

Without a doubt, Breckinridge's form of antislavery rested on a conservative, racially paternalistic foundation, but it still proved too extreme a position for much of the minister's southern audience. Not only did the idea of gradual emancipation prove unconvincing to Kentucky voters but Breckinridge himself also ran afoul of dedicated proslavery Presbyterians. Just after the defeat of emancipation in Kentucky in the fall of 1849, the *Princeton Review* – nineteenth-century American Presbyterianism's flagship theological journal, edited by one of the nation's most influential antebellum evangelical divines, Charles Hodge – published an editorial essay favorable toward Breckinridge's *The Question of Negro Slavery and the New Constitution of Kentucky.* Lauding gradualism and the emancipationists' goals in the constitutional revision process, the *Princeton Review* celebrated that Kentucky "Presbyterians have taken the lead in this [emancipationist] struggle." The editorial did acknowledge that "the cause of emancipation in Kentucky has failed for the present," but it held out hope for future gains for the emancipationist cause in the Bluegrass State.[19]

Such praise from the North, however, preceded an anonymous 1850 proslavery pamphlet written by "A Presbyterian in the Far South." The unnamed author assaulted Breckinridge's emancipationist agenda and the *Princeton Review* for supporting it: "In sober truth, it is melancholy as well as surprising,

---

[17] Quoted in Victor B. Howard, "Robert J. Breckinridge and the Slavery Controversy in Kentucky in 1849," *Filson Club History Quarterly* 53 (October 1979): 333.

[18] Breckinridge, *The Question of Negro Slavery*, 13–15.

[19] Charles Hodge, "Emancipation: Art. VI.—*The Question of Negro Slavery and the New Constitution of Kentucky.* By Robert J. Breckinridge, D.D.," *Biblical Repertory and Princeton Review* 21 (October 1849): 581–606, quotes 585.

that a man of the grasp of mind of Robt. J. Breckinridge, in urging the adoption of a favorite theory, should blindly rush into difficulties that are palpable to the plainest subject." Breckinridge, the pamphleteer charged, had proposed a plan that might hold merit in Kentucky but that lacked any support in the rest of the South. Breckinridge and the *Princeton Review* should realize that they were faced with the "WHOLE SOUTH WANTING SLAVE LABOR," and that the institution looked very different in the Deep South than in Kentucky. The author conceded that Breckinridge was more than likely aware of the difference – even if the *Princeton Review*'s Yankee editor Charles Hodge was not – and he was even willing to grant that Breckinridge's scheme only pertained to Kentucky. Yet any attempt to extend privileges or rights to blacks was necessarily destined for failure: "God has doomed the African race to slavery, for ages past, and so far as we can see, for ages to come." By pushing for Christians to recognize the need for African American emancipation – even as he presumed African American inferiority and advocated black expatriation – Breckinridge distanced himself and the gradualist position from the view held by proslavery clergy.[20]

The Holy Bible, proslavery advocates contended, established the righteousness of slaveholding. The South's leading expositor of proslavery Christianity, James Henley Thornwell – a friend of Breckinridge – made this point clear in an 1851 report to the Presbyterian Synod of South Carolina titled "Relation of the Church to Slavery." In this report Thornwell expressed lucidly what most proslavery clerics already believed: "The Bible, and the Bible alone, is [the church's] rule of faith and practice.... Beyond the Bible, [the church] can never go, and apart from the Bible she can never speak." And what did the Bible say about slavery, Thornwell asked? "Certain it is that no direct condemnation of Slavery can anywhere be found in the Sacred Volume.... it is truly amazing that the Bible, which professes to be a lamp to our feet and a light to our path, to make the man of God perfect, thoroughly furnished unto every good work, nowhere gives the slightest caution against this [supposedly] tremendous evil." Jesus never condemned slavery and the prophets never condemned slavery; in the case of the laws of Moses and the New Testament works of Paul, slavery often appeared to earn direct approval. The only way a person could demonstrate that slavery, inherently, was a sin would be to rely on the "spirit of speculation," not on the hard evidence that the revealed Word of God offered.[21]

[20] A Presbyterian in the South, *A System of Prospective Emancipation, Advocated in Kentucky, By Robert J. Breckinridge, D.D., and Urged and Supported in the Princeton Review, in Article VI.—October, 1849* (Charleston: Walker & James, 1850), quotes 15, 16, 22.

[21] James Henley Thornwell, "Relation of the Church to Slavery," in *The Collected Writings of James Henley Thornwell*, eds. John B. Adger and John L. Girardeau, 4 vols. (1873; Carlisle, PA: Banner of Truth, 1974), 4:383–5. The Synod of South Carolina unanimously approved Thornwell's paper. On Breckinridge and Thornwell's friendship, see Klotter, *The Breckinridges of Kentucky*, 54, 56; and correspondence between Thornwell and Breckinridge in *The Life*

For Kentucky's religious white emancipationists, such logic proved convincing. However, as gradualists affirmed the proslavery approach to reading the biblical text, they tended to disagree that the conclusions proslavery divines reached about contemporary slavery arrangements were in fact the scriptural message. Where proslavery clergy found biblical sanction through a literalist reading of the text, gradualist believers saw good reasons for slavery's end. Like their opponents such as Thornwell, theological conservatives such as Robert J. Breckinridge resisted the temptation to move toward a "spirit of speculation" on the Holy Writ's meaning to achieve near-term political gains. Yet arguments about the nature of Scripture and how it might be applied to public affairs notwithstanding, evangelical antislavery conservatives in the Commonwealth saw American slavery as a deeply flawed system that needed to end. Although the proslavery religious argument was never absolutely ironclad, it was difficult for white theological conservatives to sidestep the proslavery implications of an interpretative method that they themselves employed. Yet that was precisely what evangelical emancipationists attempted in refuting American slavery.

It was just this subtle interpretive maneuver that the Baptist minister James M. Pendleton brought to bear in his most compelling piece of antislavery writing, *Letters to the Rev. W. C. Buck* (1849), a pamphlet that appeared in response to a series of proslavery newspaper articles published by his friend and colleague in the Baptist pulpit, William C. Buck, pastor of Louisville's East Baptist Church. Pendleton spelled out explicitly his primary reason for seeking slavery's end: American slavery was not the same as biblical slavery, and no amount of hermeneutical gymnastics could convince him that the institution should be preserved in the United States. The righteousness of "slavery in the abstract," as the proslavery mantra went, ignored the injustice of slavery as it was actually practiced. For Pendleton, "a great deal of sin" marked American slavery, and that was enough to justify ending the evil practice altogether.[22]

By April 1849 Buck had served nearly a decade as editor of the *Baptist Banner*, the chief organ of Kentucky Baptists. Hoping to prompt thoughtful Christian reflection about the political issue of slavery, the Louisville minister wrote a series of articles that, months later, he republished in pamphlet form as *The Slavery Question* (1849). He circulated five thousand copies of the pamphlet with the intent of discouraging support for the Commonwealth's emerging emancipation party.[23]

For his part, Buck saw no reason to reject slavery as a means of social organization. The Bible, especially the Old Testament, was full of descriptions

and *Letters of James Henley Thornwell*, ed. Benjamin M. Palmer (1875; Edinburgh: Banner of Truth, 1986), 257–66.

[22] James M. Pendleton, *Letters to Rev. W. C. Buck, In Review of His Articles on Slavery* (n.p., 1849), 10. Pendleton and his wife were regular guests of Buck's at his church in Louisville, and the two worked together in state-level Baptist efforts. See Pendleton, *Reminiscences*, 59–60.

[23] Victor B. Howard, "James Madison Pendleton: A Southern Crusader against Slavery," *Register of the Kentucky Historical Society* 74 (July 1976): 200–1.

of master–slave relationships. That relationship, Buck wrote, was designed for a specific purpose: "*benevolence to the poor and defenceless, and religious instruction to Idoliters.*" God had instituted slavery for reasons of moral uplift, to enable those with means to take care of those without. "Slavery was never intended by God to minister to the cupidity and luxury of the master without an adequate, and even more than an adequate return of good to the slave." Yet this "perverted and abused" form was exactly what much of American slavery looked like. Buck did not want to defend slavery as an "apologist" for the system as it existed at the time, because he freely admitted that slavery "has been the occasion of enormous and crying sins."[24]

Such admissions, however, did not compel Buck to reject slavery out of hand. One did not have license to proclaim that "slavery is a sin in itself" just because "wicked men have sinned." As was the case with biblical slavery, American slavery could be rescued from sinful implementation. The biblical slave was "*the gainer* by his enslavement; so that the master is guilty of no moral wrong" because "the condition of his slave is better than it otherwise would have been." Indeed, Buck wrote, this was true of much of American slavery. Was not America a better place than Africa? That continent "from time immemorial, has been inhabited by a population of the most degraded, ignorant, barbarous, and cruel of any other quarter of the world." Africans were "pagan idolaters, enveloped in the thickest moral darkness" who needed to be brought into the light – that is, introduced to Christianity. Whatever its abuses, had not slavery done that for blacks? Truly, Buck wrote, "American slavery assimilates with what we have seen to be an important constituent of the slavery recognized in the scriptures – *effecting the good of the enslaved.*" Despite such feelings, Buck did not unequivocally endorse American slavery as it existed. Seemingly similar to Pendleton, Buck wrote that the "[s]lavery in this country" was not the same as "the slavery of the Bible."[25]

Yet Buck, regardless of his opinion that American slavery was sinful in practice, did not agree with the emancipationists that universal manumission was the best solution to the problem. Buck had long been a defender of a colonization scheme, writing, "Compared with the natives of Africa, the Africans in this country are a civilised and christianised people; and are rapidly approaching that state of intellectual improvement and moral refinement which will fit them for *self-government and national independence.*" These opinions very closely lined up with the colonization-emancipation agenda of Kentucky's emancipationists, but Buck rejected the Kentucky emancipationists' 1849 program. There were three primary reasons Buck withheld his support. First, each slaveholder had to be compensated "for the loss of the estate which he holds in his slave property." Second, even though many colonizationists supported the

[24] William C. Buck, *The Slavery Question* (Louisville: Harney, Hughes and Hughes, 1849), 10, 12.
[25] Ibid., 12, 15, 16, 22.

emancipationist party, the party platform itself contained no plan to colonize formerly enslaved African Americans once manumitted. Colonization had to be part of the plan or "the country is to be infested with multitudes of lawless and irresponsible hirelings for a half century to come." Third, Buck wrote, no one had considered how to ensure the continuing moral and civil development of blacks once free, so that once colonized they could properly "exercise the right of self-government." Thus, in the end, although not an uncritical supporter of slavery, Buck refused to see how emancipation would improve on the current social system of relations.[26]

Buck's rejection of emancipation aroused James M. Pendleton's antislavery sensibilities. Pendleton responded to Buck's writing with a series of letters he intended for publication in Buck's *Baptist Banner*. When he was denied a forum there, the letters ended up appearing in an emancipationist newspaper, the Louisville *Examiner*, founded in 1847 by John C. Vaughan with the support of such northern opponents of slavery as Salmon Chase, Charles Sumner, Lewis Tappan, and Gerrit Smith – and seen as the successor to Cassius Clay's *True American* as a leading voice of Kentucky's antislavery movement.[27]

Pendleton's *Letters to the Rev. W. C. Buck* (1849) was aimed directly at the heart of the Louisville Baptist's argument. Buck had written that "*God approves of that system of things which, under the circumstances, is best calculated to promote the holiness and happiness of men.*"[28] The idea that slavery, as it existed in Kentucky, "promote[d] the 'holiness and happiness' of slaves," was ludicrous to Pendleton. To demonstrate that slavery had a pernicious influence, Pendleton wrote, "would be like showing that the sun is not the source of cold and darkness." That idea was "an insult to the good sense of [Buck's] readers," as was the idea that American slavery had a positive value.[29]

Buck and many of those advancing the proslavery argument claimed that the institution of slavery was sanctioned in the Bible and, as evidence, pointed to the fact that Abraham had servants. That explanation did not satisfy Pendleton. "If the term 'servant,' as used in the Scriptures, is synonymous with the term 'slave' as used among us," he queried, "is it not remarkable that the Hebrew and Greek words translated servant are in no instance rendered slave?" In addition to the issue of translation, Pendleton argued, "it does not follow necessarily that Abraham's servants were slaves in the American acceptation of the word." For example, he wrote, in Genesis 14, Abraham armed his servants for battle, whereas in mid-nineteenth-century America "many of our states make it a penal offence for a slave to carry a weapon." Moreover, "Abraham held his slaves for *their* benefit." In what instance, he asked, have "American

---

[26] Ibid., 22, 27–9.
[27] Howard, "Pendleton: Southern Crusader against Slavery," 200–1; Tallant, *Evil Necessity*, 126–8.
[28] Buck, *The Slavery Question*, 4.
[29] Pendleton, *Letters to Rev. W. C. Buck*, 2–3.

slaveholders [been] influenced by considerations of benefit to their slaves to hold them in bondage?"[30]

Content with his arguments regarding Abraham, Pendleton moved on to Moses, who "says, 'He that stealeth a man and selleth him, or if he be found in his hands, shall surely be put to death.'" In Pendleton's view, if Americans were truly following a biblical model in their slave practice, they would sentence slave traders to death. "How were Africans first introduced into this country? They were stolen from their native land and brought here in chains." Continuing, Pendleton asked where in American slavery the concept of the Jubilee year might be found. In ancient Israel, under Mosaic Law, every seventh year all slaves were to be set free. "How would American slaveholders fancy a periodical manumission of slaves?" he inquired. They would "resist," naturally. Compared with the American system, "servitude under the Mosaic law was indeed benevolent."[31]

The rest of Pendleton's *Letters* attacked the proslavery argument in a more general sense. The Bowling Green pastor noted that many people, Buck included, argued that slavery was not wrong "in the abstract." What, he asked, did that mean? He supposed it referred to "slavery separated from its abuses." But there was no such thing. That kind of slavery, he argued, did not exist in reality. "[P]ro-slavery men most ridiculously transfer their idea of the innocence of slavery in the abstract to slavery in the concrete," he wrote. According to Pendleton, defenders of slavery frequently said, "The slavery which sacredly regards the marriage union, cherishes the relation between parents and children, and provides for the instruction of the slave, is not sinful." Yet the proslavery argument from Scripture was at base fallacious when applied to the local situation, Pendleton wrote. The "system of slavery in Kentucky . . . *does none of these things.*" Slave masters made no "provision" for the "improvement and moral training of the slave," and no law compelled masters to do so. Furthermore, marriages between slaves were completely "disregarded." Whatever case proslavery champions might make for their cause, Pendleton believed, was confounded by the immorality of the system as it operated in practice.[32]

On these latter points about the nature of slavery in practice, Pendleton would have earned Buck's agreement. However, the two differed greatly about what constituted the most Christian way to order a society. Before his confrontation with Buck, Pendleton, in a series of anonymous articles in the *Examiner*, had tipped his hand in that regard. The Bowling Green pastor signaled his support for a free labor society. Because of Adam's biblical fall, detailed in Genesis' third chapter, and the subsequent curse placed on humanity as a result, all people were required to labor. Yet slavery kept some people from contributing their rightful amount of work. Slavery, Pendleton, wrote, upset the providential

[30] Buck, *The Slavery Question*, 9–10; Pendleton, *Letters to Rev. W. C. Buck*, 1–4.
[31] Pendleton, *Letters to Rev. W. C. Buck*, 4–5.
[32] Ibid., 9–10.

design, and as such, free labor was a matter of religious importance.[33] More-over, the presence of slavery in southern states explained why they failed to progress at the rate of northern states, Pendleton wrote. Considered in terms of political economy, Georgia did not lag behind Massachusetts because of "the inequality of the action of tariff laws." No, Pendleton said, the reason was that "one is a free state, the other is cursed with slavery. In one labor is considered honorable; in the other disgraceful – the business of slaves."[34]

Lethargy in economic development was only a part of the problem, Pendle-ton wrote. The even greater tragedy was that the southern states, because of slavery, had become dependent on the North for their very survival. The lack of a developed manufacturing industry had made Kentucky wholly "depen-dent" on northern industry. "Is not Kentucky compelled to admit, humiliating as the admission is, that she is tributary to the free states? She depends, in a great degree, on the fabrics of the free states to clothe her population – *even her slaves.*" That Kentucky could not provide its own economic sustainability was a scandal in Pendleton's mind. Slavery had so enfeebled Kentucky that the Commonwealth was forced to give up its "independence and self-subsistence." In truth, Pendleton wrote, Kentucky was stuck in a "colonial condition." Citing a speech given by the U.S. senator from Bowling Green, Joseph Underwood, Pendleton wrote that Kentuckians were "looking to the mother country for supplies."[35]

Such bold arguments for free labor would have aroused the suspicions of proslavery Christians. Obviously, the idea of eliminating slavery was an affront to white southern order, but the issue was not that simple. Although proslav-ery clerics rested their defense of slavery in large part on biblical injunction, they also saw free labor as a pernicious, destructive, and unambiguously anti-Christian way to organize a society. Much historical work has shown how deeply the antebellum South was connected to global markets; not only was the slave system fully capitalist, but also in many locales it existed hand-in-hand with wage labor arrangements. Nonetheless, even as Pendleton might have seen "a great deal of sin" in master–slave relations, most white southerners did not share his appraisal of its implications. What concerned proslavery Christians, in other words, was not capitalism in the abstract but specifically free labor. They saw no reason to believe that free labor economies were inherently more

[33] A Southern Kentuckian (Pendleton), "Thoughts on Emancipation – No. 7," *The Examiner,* November 6, 1847.

[34] A Southern Kentuckian (Pendleton), "Thoughts on Emancipation – No. 9," *The Examiner,* December 4, 1847. In many ways, Pendleton's defense of free labor aligned with an argument that had been developing for several decades in the North and would serve as the basis for the 1848 emergence of the Free Soil Party. See Jonathan H. Earle, *Jacksonian Antislavery and the Politics of Free Soil, 1824–1854* (Chapel Hill: University of North Carolina Press, 2004).

[35] A Southern Kentuckian (Pendleton), "Thoughts on Emancipation – No. 13," *The Examiner,* January 1, 1848; A Southern Kentuckian (Pendleton), "Thoughts on Emancipation – No. 14," *The Examiner,* January 8, 1848.

righteous than slave systems. Northern and European capitalism destroyed familial and communal ties, slaveholders wrote; it preyed on the weak. "Free labor" was a phantasmal concept that replaced one form of subjugation with another. The difference was that outside the South laborers thought they were free, but no moral impetus compelled capitalists to treat their workers with magnanimity. White southerners wanted to find an alternative to this social design, and they had one in their slave society. They could ostensibly preserve paternalism and benevolence, and furthermore, proslavery southerners could claim the biblical high ground.[36]

William C. Buck said as much in *The Slavery Question*. Free labor was a tragic concept because there was always an inequitable power relationship: "the rich have the control, not only of the amount of labor to be performed, but of the wages to be paid for it." Employers could keep wages low while prices for staples like food rose to exorbitant levels. Workers "labor[ed] sixteen hours out of the twenty-four" and then were not "able to supply themselves with bread." The immorality of this arrangement appalled Buck, especially when there was a more Christian alternative. People may be "fallen" sinners, incapable of true moral behavior, but God, in spite of human nature, had provided all the resources necessary to create a just society. It was a truism that "in all ages and countries, those who are in affluence and power have oppressed the helpless and poor." The only way that such oppression could be overturned, Buck wrote, was if "*by some benevolent arrangement, the interests of the poor and helpless are identified with the interests of the powerful and wealthy.*" Biblical slavery was "such an institution." There was no master in the South who would let his slave go hungry, according to Buck. The same, the Louisville pastor contended, could not be said of industrial Europe or of "the populous cities of the [American] East." Slavery may have had its sinful excess, Buck admitted, but those shortcomings were nothing compared to the sort of social upheaval brought on by free labor.[37]

Buck spoke to an opinion widespread among proslavery whites, who saw the North's free labor system as a threat to their slave-driven society. Part of

---

[36] Pendleton, *Letters to Rev. W. C. Buck*, 10. On the proslavery critique of free labor, see Eugene D. Genovese, *The Slaveholders' Dilemma: Freedom and Progress in Southern Conservative Thought, 1820–1860* (Columbia: University of South Carolina Press, 1992), 3–8. On capitalism and the nineteenth-century American slave economy, see David Brion Davis, *Inhuman Bondage: The Rise and Fall of Slavery in the New World* (New York: Oxford University Press, 2006), 175–92; Seth Rockman, *Scraping By: Wage Labor, Slavery, and Survival in Early Baltimore* (Baltimore: Johns Hopkins University Press, 2009); Anthony Kaye, "The Second Slavery: Modernity in the Nineteenth-Century South and the Atlantic World," *Journal of Southern History* 75 (August 2009): 627–50; L. Diane Barnes, Brian Schoen, and Frank Towers, eds., *The Old South's Modern Worlds: Slavery, Region, and Nation in the Age of Progress* (New York: Oxford University Press, 2011); and on the Kentucky slave trade in particular, see Benjamin Lewis Fitzpatrick, "Negroes for Sale: The Slave Trade in Antebellum Kentucky" (Ph.D. diss., University of Notre Dame, 2008).

[37] Buck, *The Slavery Question*, 13.

the reason for this proslavery rejection of free labor had to do with what one historian has described as a consistent, profound, southern Christian disdain for "mammonism": southerners believed "that the economic enthusiasm of the day was leading to a deadly indifference toward higher, spiritual things." No serious proslavery clergyman doubted that the slave system as it existed was in need of reform, but demands for the generation of more capital stymied any attempts to make slavery more just. By this assessment, the proslavery rejection of free labor was only part of a larger proslavery attempt to create a moral order rooted in biblical values.[38]

James M. Pendleton, a Christian supporter of free labor, did not agree with proslavery views that asserted the advantages of slave labor over free labor. Moreover, he did not think, as proslavery advocates did, that the Christian God had sanctioned the sort of slavery that existed in the United States. Dissent against slavery on these grounds, however, did not lead Pendleton to take what he and other evangelical gradualists would have seen as a radical step and join the ranks of immediate abolitionists. For Pendleton, slavery was always a complex matter, laden with complicated factors. He may have opposed slavery, but he opposed even more strongly the work of abolitionists.

In point of fact, in the Kentucky context, free labor ideology quite comfortably complemented the whites-first antislavery argument of the state's religious conservatives. Fellow gradualist Robert J. Breckinridge's 1849 pamphlet, *The Question of Negro Slavery and the New Constitution of Kentucky*, reasserted the racist rationale for opposing American slavery by suggesting exactly how and why emancipation would benefit Kentucky whites. It was important, the divine contended, for "*the great non-slaveholding interest*" – Kentucky whites who comprised "seven-eights of the whole population, the overwhelming majority of the voters of the State" – to understand the personal losses they faced due to the labor problem created by slavery. Breckinridge and other gradualists wanted to see the end of slave importation into Kentucky and to slowly kill off the institution because, as the Presbyterian viewed the matter, slavery considerably harmed the white population. If slavery kept African Americans in a "degraded state," it also hurt whites by taking away probable sources of gainful employment. "The white laborer," Breckinridge claimed, had the right "to make his living by the sweat of his brow." Some Kentuckians might wonder what would happen in the labor "vacuum" created by the absence of slavery, but Breckinridge did not worry: jobs would be taken "by our own children," and the practice of "preferring our neighbor's slaves to our own flesh and blood" would cease.[39]

---

[38] Kenneth Startup, "'A Mere Calculation of Profits and Loss': The Southern Clergy and the Economic Culture of the Antebellum North," in *God and Mammon: Protestants, Money, and the Market, 1790–1860*, ed. Mark A. Noll (New York: Oxford University Press, 2001), 217–35, quote 218.

[39] Breckinridge, *The Question of Negro Slavery*, 2–5.

The end of slavery, in short, would open a labor market for Kentucky's economically disadvantaged whites. "For my part," he wrote, "I so greatly desire to see this noble State made the exclusive abode of the free white man" that "one of the leading motives of all my conduct connected with [emancipation] has been the hope of substituting the race of negro slaves with the race of free whites." According to the minister, the slaveholding class that would "plead for protection in the enjoyment of [its] slave property" aimed to "cut short at every step, the hopes, the rewards, and the privileges of the free." Indeed, the preservation of slavery would come "at the expense of the white people of the State." If slaveholders did not see an economic reason to emancipate their slaves, perhaps they would be motivated by a notion of racial solidarity.[40]

Baptist minister Pendleton never pushed as far as Breckinridge did with this sort of racist analysis, but it can be assumed that the Presbyterian clergyman represented Kentucky's antislavery, anti-abolitionist, anti-black populace with such white supremacist sentiments, Pendleton included. Although less overt on racial matters, many of Breckinridge's themes informed Pendleton's antislavery writings. From September 1847 to June 1848, Pendleton published a series of pro-emancipationist articles under the pen name, "A Southern Kentuckian," in the Louisville *Examiner*. In those essays, the Baptist opposed the extension of slavery into the American West and called for a program of emancipation, but he also made sure to distance himself from the agenda of more radical abolitionists to the north. Pendleton generally avoided overtly racist statements and even appealed to the Declaration of Independence's line that "all men are created equal" to undermine the white supremacist assumption of black inferiority. "Africans are not excepted," Pendleton wrote. "There is no allusion to their inferiority."[41]

Still, in the midst of such broad-minded opinions, Pendleton also followed Breckinridge in placing white concerns at the center of the issue. One essay lamented that slavery perpetuated idleness among Kentucky's free population and asked, "Who" could "not deplore slavery as a great calamity, the effect of which is decidedly unfavorable to the interests of our white population?"[42] Questions such as this one, which implicitly asserted the whites-first antislavery position, aligned Pendleton closely with the racist ideology of the bulk of Kentucky's emancipationists.

In addition to such white supremacist argumentation about labor and slavery, Pendleton also supported other conservative antislavery measures. Along with attending Henry Clay's April 1849 state emancipation meeting in

---

[40] Ibid., 9, 10.

[41] Tallant, *Evil Necessity*, 59–90; Howard, "Pendleton: Southern Crusader against Slavery," 195; Pendleton, *Reminiscences*, 93; A Southern Kentuckian (Pendleton), "Thoughts on Emancipation – No. 15," *The Examiner*, January 22, 1848.

[42] A Southern Kentuckian (Pendleton), "Thoughts on Emancipation – No. 7," *The Examiner*, November 6, 1847.

Frankfort, in May he helped lead a meeting of Warren County emancipationists that included Bowling Green senator Joseph Underwood. There Pendleton
joined the others in resolving not to "disturb, or to aid others in disturbing
the right of masters to their slaves now in being in Kentucky." At the same
time, they advocated entering a clause into the Commonwealth's constitution
opposing "any increase of slaves in this state," agreeing that to do so would be
"highly detrimental" to Kentucky's free black population. Furthermore, they
agreed to a platform of gradual emancipation connected to the colonization
effort.[43] As these activities and writings indicate, Pendleton's rejection of abolitionism and acceptance of conservative antislavery ideas placed him on an
intellectual trajectory that followed the bulk of Kentucky's conservative emancipationists. The message of his *Examiner* articles, stated even more openly by
the Warren County emancipationists, was that Pendleton promoted gradual
emancipation connected to colonization, a position laden with a belief in black
inferiority. Perhaps Pendleton muted the racist implications of his gradualist
position more than most of his fellow antislavery conservatives, but that did
not mean he escaped racism altogether.[44]

Few white Kentuckians did. Perhaps the lone exception to the belief in white
supremacy that marked the bulk of Kentucky's antislavery advocates was the
abolitionist John G. Fee. As with other abolitionists, black and white, who did
not find receptive audiences for their arguments until they left the state, few of
Fee's antislavery works were published within the Commonwealth. In contrast
with Robert J. Breckinridge and many other gradualists who had ready publish-
ers in Louisville and Lexington, Fee looked to presses in Cincinnati and New
York to circulate his views. As opinions on slavery ossified, so did the boundaries of acceptable discourse on slavery. Print culture networks corresponded
to the geographic boundaries of the slave–free line.

---

[43] Clement Eaton, ed., "Minutes and Resolutions of an Emancipation Meeting in Kentucky in
1849," *Journal of Southern History* 14 (November 1948): 543–4.

[44] Pendleton's affinity for the colonizationist aspect of the gradual emancipationism scheme always
remained less overt than other Kentucky emancipationists, but he still endorsed it in his antislavery writings. See his "Thoughts on Emancipation" series, Nos. 11–14, *The Examiner*, December
18 and 25, 1847; January 1 and 8, 1848.

   As anecdotal evidence that directly demonstrates Pendleton's support for colonization, it is
possible that Pendleton intended to colonize the one slave he owned. According to historian
Victor B. Howard, the Baptist divine inherited a slave boy from his father in the late 1840s
and sought to free him for passage to Liberia. Before the boy could go, however, he died. See
Howard, "Pendleton: Southern Crusader against Slavery," 194. Howard's record differs from
Pendleton's own narrative about his slave. According to Pendleton himself, the slave he acquired
was a young female, whom he did not obtain until 1863, when the minister's mother died. By
law, he could not emancipate the slave girl so the "best [he] could do was to hire her out"
and add 10 percent to whatever she earned. Pendleton wrote that he was "not a slave-holder
morally, but *legally*," and when the institution "was abolished I rejoiced in the severance of the
relation I had sustained to her." See Pendleton, *Reminiscences*, 127–8. Pendleton left the South
in 1862, so there is some reason to believe Howard's account over that recorded in Pendleton's
memoirs.

In his 1854 anti-colonizationist book, *Colonization. The Present Scheme of Colonization Wrong, Delusive, and Retards Emancipation*, Fee followed a well-trod path of anti-gradualist argumentation and claimed that the American Colonization Society contributed to the perpetuation of slavery in the United States. The ACS promoted the view that blacks were inferior to whites, which "fosters *caste*," Fee asserted. Colonizationists claimed that blacks would never have a chance to succeed in a white society because of "prejudice against them." In Fee's reading, however, "prejudice" was really just a code word for "caste." Caste existed around the world, Fee wrote, in India and Europe, "among people of the same color." Was it right? Not according to the biblical record:

> Did Christ, the Saviour of the world, sanction it in his acts toward the daughter of Samaria, the Canannitish woman? Did he, when he mingled and dined with publicans and sinners – Gentiles – as much despised by Jews then, as colored persons are now by some white persons?
>
> Does the Holy Spirit sanction caste, when it dwells alike with every holy heart, irrespective of color?
>
> Does God, the Father, sanction it, when he declares he loves the whole world, and is no *respecter* of persons?

Colonizationists ignored such biblical examples, Fee wrote. "Colonization makes *war* upon God" by promoting social division. In the face of Scripture, colonizationism "teaches that we should have respect to persons, and give to the white man privileges here we should not give the colored man." In his argument against caste, Fee also appealed to "free white laborers." Surely they could see how their lack of wealth precluded them from the "first table, and from the family of many slaveholders and aristocrats." If free white laborers thought they were free because they were white, they were mistaken, Fee wrote. The American caste system thus extended to whites as well.[45]

Fee's solution to the problem of caste pushed much further than many whites, including many abolitionists, were prepared to go. Interracial mixing was desirable for Fee: "Better that we have black faces than bad hearts, and reap eventually the torments of hell. We may have pure hearts if our faces should, after the lapse of a century or two, be a little tawny." For Fee, the destruction of racial caste would come through a means and method repulsive to most white Americans, not simply those in Kentucky: amalgamation via interracial sex.[46]

Such a view certainly put Fee out of step with gradual emancipationists in Kentucky, to say nothing of the state's general white population. However, not even Fee was so enlightened during the late 1840s emancipationist canvass, when he opposed amalgamation, speaking against it in his 1848 *Anti-Slavery*

---

[45] John G. Fee, *Colonization. The Present Scheme of Colonization Wrong, Delusive, and Retards Emancipation* (Cincinnati: American Reform Tract and Book Society, [1854]), 17–22.

[46] Ibid., 27.

Manual. But within three years, in the revised 1851 version of the volume, Fee changed his mind and argued that amalgamation was "no sin, no crime."[47]

No other white antislavery Kentuckian seems to have ever felt that way in the antebellum era. For gradualists, their racism carried forward into the next decade. An 1850 proslavery report characterized Kentucky's 1849 defeat of emancipation as "very decisive," showing definitively that the "agitation of the matter was uncalled for" and offering "small encouragement" to those emancipationists who might ever hope for a "renewal" of political debate on the question. However, despite the political setbacks, many gradualists attempted to carry on the cause in Kentucky. For his part, Robert J. Breckinridge remained committed to theologically and racially conservative antislavery. In 1851 he spoke before the Kentucky Colonization Society and argued that "the life and doctrine of Jesus Christ" taught right-minded believers that all humanity shared a "universal brotherhood." The idea, "which nature teaches – and all knowledge fortifies," the minister contended, was in fact, "a precious, living truth." Nevertheless, a seeming contrast was also apparent: "The reality of immense diversities in the condition, development, character, and destiny of different portions of our race, must be accepted as a truth, even more obvious than its unity." Breckinridge claimed that African Americans represented "part of an immense race, embracing an eighth part of the human family," but still they remained "a race doomed" in his view "to general degradation and personal servitude; long outcast from the family of man and from the great common brotherhood." Yet, after more than two centuries of the slave trade and American slavery in practice, a "grand era in the world" had finally arrived. The future of the African American population had become completely entwined with that of the United States' whites, and that racial reality was an immense blessing to the inferior population. Breckinridge zealously and paternalistically explained the providential benevolence that now extended to enslaved and free blacks:

> The parasite has clung to the wall of adamant – the African is bound to the car of the Anglo-American! He must bear him through in triumph – he must perish with him by the way – or he must destroy him outright. That car cannot pause to re-adjust this doomed connection, any more than the adamantine spheres can cease to wheel unshaken in the hand of God, that the planets may adjust their casual perturbations. Bear him through in triumph – perish with him by the way – or destroy him outright!

To prevent the impending disaster of a racial – if not a total human – holocaust, Breckinridge proposed, as he had for twenty years, that African Americans should "be restored to their father land." The colonization imperative, in

---

[47] See Tallant, *Evil Necessity*, 175–80; John G. Fee, *An Anti-Slavery Manual, Being an Examination in the Light of the Bible, and of Facts into the Moral and Social Wrongs of American Slavery, with a Remedy for the Evil* (1848; New York: Arno Press, 1969), 176; and Fee, *An Anti-Slavery Manual*, 2nd ed. (New York: William Harned, 1851), 172.

the minister's eyes, was in fact a divine calling for American whites. "Can the Anglo-American," Breckinridge asked of his audience, "bear through in triumph, not his own destiny only, but that of the black race also?" The "notable conjunction of many acts of God and man" had forced the question on American whites. To ignore the emancipation-colonization program was to ignore the will of the Christian God for the human race.[48]

Such argumentation was on its face untenable to proslavery believers, but the same was also true for abolitionists in the Commonwealth, if for different reasons. Marginalized by the mainstream of Kentucky antislavery, John G. Fee responded by directly attacking the emancipation party's leaders in *The Sinfulness of Slaveholding* (1851). Many affiliated with the party, including Breckinridge certainly, claimed that slavery was not sinful in and of itself, even though they wanted it ended in Kentucky. Such thinking appalled Fee: "If they do not know better, acting as they do, they should be nailed to the wall." Fee wanted to set the public straight. With *The Sinfulness of Slaveholding* he sought to provide "arguments" for "the people" by "which to thus nail" emancipationists who waffled on the nature of slavery.[49]

In Fee's view, emancipationists erred by simply acknowledging the proslavery insistence on slavery's scriptural mandate. As he had a few years earlier in *An Anti-Slavery Manual*, Fee claimed that the essence of Scripture taught against slavery. The primary *"principles of the Bible"* were "Justice and Mercy," yet the proslavery exegesis did not fall in line with those principles. Proslavery divines interpreted certain texts to sanction slavery, when the whole of the Bible presented a message that undermined the sort of oppression and inequality woven into the fabric of American slavery.[50]

If general concepts about the nature of biblical teaching were not enough for his readers, Fee also referenced specific texts that he believed undermined slaveholding. Pointing to the Genesis creation story, Fee noted that God gave humanity "dominion over the fish of the sea, the birds of the air, and the beasts of the field; but over man he gave not dominion." Furthermore, the fact that God delivered Israel from Egyptian slavery "is a declaration of his abhorrence to the principle of oppression, too clear ever to be misunderstood." Indeed no support for oppression could be found in Scripture. The gospel taught "that God is no respecter of persons" and that "there is no difference between Jew and Gentile." If God, "who is unchangeable," had obliterated distinctions during the biblical era, why, Fee asked, did anyone think they could oppress others in the nineteenth century?[51]

---

[48] Robert J. Breckinridge, *The Black Race: Some Reflections on its Position and Destiny, as Connected with Our American Dispensation* (Frankfort, KY: A. G. Hodges, 1851), 5, 7, 12.

[49] John G. Fee, *The Sinfulness of Slaveholding Shown by Appeals to Reason and Scripture* (New York: John A. Gray, 1851), 3.

[50] Ibid., 15.

[51] Ibid., 10–11, 15.

In this way Fee condemned American slavery for its most manifestly oppressive deviation from its ancient form: racism. In his reading, American slavery was distinct from the institution as described in Scripture, where in the New Testament Rome enslaved those peoples it conquered, many of whom came from Europe: "[W]hat was the complexion of these nations? . . . THIS SLAVERY WAS WHITE SLAVERY; that is, the large portion of those enslaved were *as white, and many of them whiter than their masters.*" Accordingly, defenders of slavery in America could not justify the practice by referencing its sanction during the biblical era. Slavery then had little to do with race.[52]

Ideologically, Fee's arguments sounded like those made north of the Ohio River by many of his associates in the evangelical abolitionist movement. A year before publishing *The Sinfulness of Slaveholding*, Fee joined a number of northern abolitionist leaders at the April 1850 Christian Anti-Slavery Convention in Cincinnati. This convention opened in the midst of the national crisis over the expansion of slavery precipitated by California's application to Congress to enter the United States as a free state. That state's application also raised the question of what to do with the other territories acquired in the Mexican-American War, and the congressional compromise that resulted included the 1850 Fugitive Slave Act authorizing the arrest of any African Americans anywhere in the United States suspected of being escaped slaves. The Fugitive Slave Act furthermore did not allow blacks to testify on their own behalf and imposed significant fines and penalties on those accused of helping fugitives.[53]

The 1850 Christian Anti-Slavery Convention in Cincinnati drew on evangelical abolitionist history. Similar conventions had occurred in the 1840s in New England and upstate New York, and several others in the Old Northwest states during the 1850s also followed the Cincinnati meeting. This convention was decidedly evangelical in its tone and aim, and it minimized the role of and speaking opportunities for Garrisonian abolitionists who challenged traditional Protestant orthodoxies.[54]

In that sense, the convention that came together in Cincinnati in 1850 showed the results of earlier fissures among abolitionists over religion. It also bore the influence of its abolitionist forebears in the Ohio Valley in other ways. Although James G. Birney was in failing health and unable to attend, his presence was felt. He sent a letter commending the work of the meeting and decried the Compromise of 1850 as a call for "the liberty to enslave their fellow-creatures, or to send back into slavery those who are endeavoring to escape from it." Birney also criticized Henry Clay – a major architect of the

---

[52] Ibid., 28–9.
[53] John R. McKivigan, *The War against Proslavery Religion: Abolitionism and the Northern Churches, 1830–1865* (Ithaca: Cornell University Press, 1984), 128–32.
[54] Ibid.

Compromise of 1850 – for "trying again to compromise the matter of Slavery." As Birney had done years earlier in attacking colonizationists like Clay, the convention declared "that the American Colonization Society is a twin sister to Slavery, and has done incalculable injury to the free colored man, and should not be countenanced by the Christian Churches." Furthermore, the convention showed Birney's influence in its attitude toward American denominations. Where Birney had, a decade prior, condemned churches as the bulwarks of American slavery, the Christian Anti-Slavery Convention in Cincinnati followed this logic to its conclusion. The convention approved a resolution by John G. Fee that not only condemned slavery as "sin in itself" but also argued that the "friends of a pure Christianity ought to separate themselves from all slaveholding churches, and from all churches, ecclesiastical bodies, and missionary organizations, that are not fully divorced from the sin of slaveholding." Not only was slaveholding a sin but also religious fellowship with any who held slaves – even if that did not include one's own local congregation – was sin as well. The meeting's conclusion encouraged a rising impulse among Christian abolitionists: it was their duty to "come out" from and leave behind offending churches.[55]

Fee amplified the arguments made at the Cincinnati Christian Anti-Slavery Convention one year later in *Non-Fellowship with Slaveholders the Duty of Christians* (1851). Published the same year as *The Sinfulness of Slaveholding*, Fee's *Non-Fellowship with Slaveholders* argued exactly what the title suggested: no one who claimed to be a Christian ought to keep fellowship with a slaveholder. The integrity of Christianity was under attack because of proslavery believers, he wrote. Referring to religiously skeptical abolitionists such as those of the Garrisonian variety, who claimed the Bible lacked "divine authenticity" because "it sanctioned human slavery," Fee said that the truth about Scripture needed to be told. How could the Bible hold the standard for integrity and justice when it supported slavery? The real threat to Christianity was not abolitionism but "the pro-slavery teaching of the churches." It was possible, Fee facetiously conceded, that apart from holding other humans in bondage, slaveholders were probably in general "virtuous, industrious, humane, and amiable persons." But proslavery Christianity, a "false religion," had perverted slaveholders' understanding of truth. Categorically, slaveholders "have become oppressors and extortioners in the worst form, violating the plainest principles of natural justice." Slaveholders were like the biblical Hebrews during the reign of Manasseh, Fee wrote. People who seemed perfectly "amiable and humane would dash their innocent offspring into the flames of burning

---

55 *The Minutes of the Christian Anti-Slavery Convention, Assembled April 17th–20th, 1850. Cincinnati, Ohio* ([Cincinnati]: Franklin Book and Job Rooms, 1850), 14, 19, 22–3, 61. See also McKivigan, *War against Proslavery Religion*, 128–32.

[pagan deity] Moloch." A sin, slavery, had pervaded the church. It was the church's responsibility to get rid of it.[56]

For Fee, slavery represented "the worst form of extortion practiced by men." Since 1 Corinthians 5 commanded believers "not to keep company . . . no not to eat" with extortioners, Fee argued that slaveholders should be banned from fellowship. Going further, Fee directed his readers to Revelation 18, which called Christians to "[c]ome out of [Babylon], my people, that ye be not partakers of her sins, and that ye receive not of her plagues." Babylon, Fee wrote, was an allegorical reference "used to designate corrupt churches in general." The Revelation chapter described Babylon as involved in all sorts of trade, including, according to verse 13, "slaves, and souls of men." "The sin of mystic Babylon," Fee asserted, "was slaveholding; and God commands his people to come out from such a church, 'from all who copy her example.'" In Fee's reading, these passages demonstrated not only the sinfulness of slaveholding but also the sin of maintaining Christian fellowship with slaveholders.[57]

Fee's *Sinfulness of Slaveholding* and *Non-Fellowship with Slaveholders* appeared in the midst of what amounted to a last-ditch effort on the part of antislavery Kentuckians to gain public acceptability. In 1851, Cassius Clay ran for governor as the candidate of the emancipation party that did not see its work accomplished in 1849. Clay aimed to build up from the very low electoral returns of 1849 with the hope of establishing a viable third party in the state. Despite his own disdain for colonization, Clay supported gradualism and advocated making the Commonwealth freer – and whiter – by selling Kentucky's slaves south. If this platform might have sounded familiar to Kentucky's conservative emancipationists, they nonetheless largely abandoned Clay. In 1851 the result was even worse than 1849; Clay and the emancipation party received only 3 percent of the vote.[58]

The failure of gradualism in Kentucky marked a major turning point in the state's antebellum history. Not only had emancipation gone down in political defeat but also within a few years a slave insurrection scare would serve to confirm for many whites the futility of any antislavery scheme. The scare began in December 1856 in Christian County, bordering the Tennessee state line in southwestern Kentucky. Reports from the towns of Hopkinsville and LaFayette suggested that enslaved ironworkers intended to organize on Christmas Day and march to freedom in Indiana, slaughtering any whites who stood in their way. Between thirty and fifty African Americans were arrested and jailed in Hopkinsville, and coerced "confessions" produced stories of the insurrection plot. Yet no rebellion materialized. By February 1857, after the calming of

[56] John G. Fee, *Non-Fellowship with Slaveholders the Duty of Christians* (New York: John A. Gray, 1851), 3, 13–14.
[57] Ibid., 4, 8–9.
[58] Freehling, *Road to Disunion*, 471–72; Tallant, *Evil Necessity*, 160–1; Lee, "Between Two Fires," 65–6.

whites' passions, those slaves held in custody were discharged back to their masters.[59]

Clearly the insurrection panic of 1856 owed much to overblown white fear. After the fact, many Kentucky whites admitted as much. In so doing, such an acknowledgment served as the basis for an emboldened proslavery religious argument. As one believer wrote in the *Western Recorder* – the new name for the *Baptist Banner* after 1851 – slavery "must always continue to be a curse to the white as well as to the black man, if the proper distinction between master and slave is not kept up. That distinction is recognized in the Bible," and thus, as William C. Buck had argued against James M. Pendleton, it was not slavery that was wrong, but the current American form.[60]

Buck had claimed following his debate with Pendleton that the failure to reform American slavery fell squarely on the shoulders of abolitionists. These radicals agitated the slavery question "and sought to stir up insurrection and bloodshed among [Kentucky's] slaves." White Kentuckians may have once been interested in gradualist measures, but the "fanaticism" of immediatism had led to an "increase of proslavery feeling in the South." Abolitionists were thus "the authors of all the ills and evils which may result from their violent and lawless practices." Buck's 1849 analysis was foreboding: "We have warned them of this result, and for years past urged them to a different, and wiser, and more christian policy; but still they seem determined to pursue their former blind and ruinous plan."[61]

That interpretation of antislavery activism was pervasive in 1850s Kentucky. Thus, when Hopkinsville slaves appeared ready to throw off their chains in 1856, the *Western Recorder*'s account of the event argued that the rebellion plot emerged because too much freedom was in the air. In this view, the Hopkinsville insurrection scare taught "a useful lesson" about the social control of the enslaved. "In former years" – presumably in the late 1840s emancipation canvass and earlier – "hundreds of negroes were permitted to attend political barbecues, and not only listen to all the excited discussions which politicians engaged in upon the subject of slavery, but they were permitted to come under the demoralizing influences consequent upon high political excitement." Kentucky's political climate had been marked by an "extravagance of feelings of liberality" when it came to the slavery debates. Too much discussion of the question had occurred in public by "those opposed to the institution of slavery, and even those professing abolition proclivities... without regard to the fact whether negroes were present or not."[62]

---

[59] Charles B. Dew, "Black Ironworkers and the Slave Insurrection Panic of 1856," *Journal of Southern History* 41 (August 1975): 321–38; and Lucas, *History of Blacks in Kentucky*, 59–60.

[60] "Insurrection," *Western Recorder*, January 21, 1857.

[61] B. (William C. Buck), "Correction," *Baptist Banner*, October 3, 1849.

[62] "Insurrection."

The upshot was plain. Public antislavery debate of any kind was to be squelched: "the farmers of Christian county will never again suffer this subject to be argued before their negroes." White believers in southwestern Kentucky "intend[ed] to preserve the institution of slavery" and "guard it with the utmost vigilance." The *Western Recorder* essay thus ended with a threat: "If politicians desire notoriety as anti-slavery men, or as Abolitionists, we do not think Kentucky is the proper theater in which they should acquire it. The safety of the institution of slavery, and the safety of their families, demand that the citizens of this commonwealth should no longer permit slavery agitation to be mingled in their political struggles." In this understanding, gradualism and abolitionism were one and the same. Conservative whites were saying to anyone who opposed slavery in Kentucky: get out. It became clear that slow means of ending slavery, connected to colonization, were no more palatable than stark abolitionism to most white Kentuckians. Emancipationists wanted to remove the state's slaves, but the state wanted to remove emancipationists.[63]

Those whites who persisted in agitating the slavery question in the 1850s tended to be individuals who fell outside the mainstream of white Kentucky society. Their number included the community of German immigrants who settled in Louisville after the failed German Revolution of 1848. Opposed to the expansion of slavery in the western territories and supportive of gradual emancipation as well as racial equality under the law, these German émigrés came to serve later as the base for Kentucky's small Republican Party.[64]

Persistent critics of Kentucky slavery also included individuals active in locales that bordered the Ohio River. There abolitionists tended to exist only in enclaves, which they themselves described as "colonies" of freedom designed to push against the boundaries of the increasingly narrow political and geographical space where antislavery views might be found. William S. Bailey, who founded the *Newport Daily News* in 1850 – called the *Free South* after 1858 – in northern Kentucky, carried on the tradition of John Vaughan's Louisville *Examiner* into the 1860s. Also active was Delia Webster, who in 1852 founded an abolitionist colony on 600 acres in Trimble County. Webster had served time in prison for participating in 1844 with Ohio Methodist minister Calvin Fairbank in a widely publicized slave-rescuing mission around Lexington. In 1854, after several arrests on suspicion of aiding fugitives, Webster left for Indiana. Lewis Tappan of the American Missionary Association hoped to renew interest in the Trimble County abolitionist colony, but it met with little success.[65]

More significant was the effort by Cassius Clay and John G. Fee to establish an abolitionist colony in the interior of the Commonwealth. Clay had a grand

---

[63] Ibid.
[64] Tallant, *Evil Necessity*, 162.
[65] Ibid., 162; Stanley Harrold, *The Abolitionists and the South, 1831–1861* (Lexington: University Press of Kentucky, 1995), 26–30, 120–1; and Harrold, *Border War: Fighting over Slavery before the Civil War* (Chapel Hill: University of North Carolina Press, 2010), 122–3, 175–6.

vision for an antislavery community in Kentucky from which he could draw a political support base. He owned a 600-acre tract of land in southern Madison County, located on a ridge of Appalachian foothills. Clay encouraged Fee to move to Madison County, and Fee, once he received approval from the American Missionary Association, accepted Clay's offer. In 1853 the AMA established an antislavery church that rejected fellowship with slaveholders, and in 1854 Fee took over as its pastor. Fee named the community Berea, derived from those biblical Jews in Acts 17 who listened to the teachings of the apostles Paul and Silas and "received the word with all readiness of mind." The name itself was, like Fee's ministry more broadly, a sharp rebuff to a white supremacist state fixated on the Bible. In the biblical account, Bereans "searched the scriptures daily." In nineteenth-century Kentucky, Bereans would do the same – and conclude that the sins of slavery and racial caste could not stand in God's sight. Under Fee's leadership, the modest but growing community laid plans for anti-caste, anti-sectarian churches and schools. In his appeals for northern support, Fee made it clear that he hoped to build a free-soil colony in the midst of a slave state to abolish the evil institution from within.[66]

Although Clay and Fee had worked closely together in the past, and Fee lived on land Clay provided, the two were unable to reach an accord on the best way to carry out an antislavery platform in Kentucky during the 1850s. Clay wanted to unite with northern Free Soilers and those committed to ensuring that slavery was not extended into the western American territories. In broad relief, this was the group that provided the base for what became the Republican Party, which Clay stumped for in the Old Northwest and joined in its earliest days. By the spring of 1856, a Republican branch operated in Kentucky and sought Fee's support. However, for Fee, Republicanism did not go far enough in its antislavery ambitions. It was built as a national party on a common-denominator platform that denounced the extension of slavery but did not call for immediate abolition, and Fee balked.[67]

Privately, Fee and Clay quarreled about party politics. After years of disagreement, their two paths finally diverged publicly on July 4, 1856. The two were scheduled to give speeches at an event at Slate Lick Springs that commemorated the holiday. Clay insisted that Fee go first. Fee ascended the pulpit

---

[66] John G. Fee, "Emigration to Kentucky," December 13, 1856, *American Missionary* 11 (January 1857): 21; and Fee, "A College in Kentucky – needed," January 14, 1857, *American Missionary* (March 1857): 65–6. Both letters in typescript "Letters and Articles by and about Rev. John G. Fee, his life and work in the *American Missionary*," 56–8, RG 1.02, Series III, Box 5, Folder 7, Berea College Archives, Berea, KY. See also Marion B. Lucas, "John G. Fee, The Berea Exiles, and the 1862 Confederate Invasion of Kentucky," *The Filson History Quarterly* 75 (2001): 156; and Harrold, *Abolitionists and the South*, 121–6. The biblical text is Acts 17:11.

[67] Lucas, "Fee and the Berea Exiles," 157–9; Harrold, *Abolitionists and the South*, 146–7; and Victor B. Howard, "Cassius M. Clay and the Origins of the Republican Party," *Filson Club History Quarterly* 45 (January 1971): 49–71.

and delivered a message straight out of his abolitionist repertoire. Claiming the egalitarian language of the Declaration of Independence and the moral authority of Holy Scripture, Fee assaulted slavery with rhetoric he had been using for more than a decade. When it was Clay's turn to speak, he denounced Fee's immediatist position as extreme. Furthermore, after the July 4, 1856, celebration, Clay cut Fee and the Berea community off from his support – financial, as well as physical, which had kept at bay violent assaults on the Berea community. In short order, the specter of violence would drive Fee and the Bereans from the Commonwealth.[68]

For Kentucky's more conservative antislavery activists, the 1850s were a time of little activity on the issue. Robert J. Breckinridge's 1850s career followed the trajectory of the Bluegrass State's larger emancipationist movement. His was a limited voice for the antislavery cause in this decade. His political and religious responsibilities account for part of this change, including serving as Kentucky's secretary of public education from 1847 to 1853, followed by the founding of Danville Theological Seminary in 1853 with the ambition of building it into the Presbyterian Church USA's premier center for ministerial education in the American West. He also published two major theological tomes, *The Knowledge of God, Objectively Considered* (1858) and *The Knowledge of God, Subjectively Considered* (1860). In spite of these pressing duties, however, it was also true that the Presbyterian backed away from his earlier antislavery views in the 1850s. Following an increasingly conservative trajectory, he continued to rebuke publicly his old enemies, the immediate abolitionists, and even wrote that slavery was improving in the South through the "power of the Gospel." Breckinridge never officially renounced his early antislavery positions, but by the start of the Civil War, he was willing to mute his opposition to slavery in the interest of preserving the Union.[69]

Other conservative emancipationists also found themselves marginalized in the wake of the 1849 defeat, even if they followed a different path than Breckinridge. In his memoirs, James M. Pendleton recorded that his "spirit sank" with the failure of the emancipation movement. The Baptist lamented that he "saw no hope for the African race in Kentucky, or anywhere else without the interposition of some Providential judgment." Knowing how visible he had

[68] Lucas, "Fee and the Berea Exiles," 157–9; Tallant, *Evil Necessity*, 193–7; and Harrold, *Abolitionists and the South*, 146–7.

[69] Klotter, *Breckinridges of Kentucky*, 58–60, 76; Robert J. Breckinridge, *The Knowledge of God, Objectively Considered: Being the First Part of Theology Considered as a Science of Positive Truth, Both Inductive and Deductive* (New York: Robert Carter, 1858); and Breckinridge, *The Knowledge of God, Subjectively Considered: Being the Second Part of Theology Considered as a Science of Positive Truth, Both Inductive and Deductive* (New York: Robert Carter, 1860). On Breckinridge's 1850s involvement in theological debates, many of which took on a sectional cast, see Elizabeth Fox-Genovese and Eugene D. Genovese, *The Mind of the Master Class: History and Faith in the Southern Slaveholders' Worldview* (New York: Cambridge University Press, 2005), 542–56.

been in the emancipation drive, Pendleton counted the many slaveholders in his Bowling Green congregation and came very close to accepting a pastorate in Springfield, Illinois, in order to take his family away from the slavery agitation and to raise his children in a free state. His church in Kentucky, however, refused to accept its pastor's resignation, and Pendleton remained at the post for several more years.[70]

The 1850s were no less contentious times for Pendleton. His profile grew in Southern Baptist circles due to his ecclesiological tract, *An Old Landmark Re-set* (1854). The treatise became a foundational text for the Landmark Baptist movement, which was highly influential in the Middle and Upper South and claimed a pure and unbroken line of succession from Jesus Christ to particular contemporary Landmark churches, thereby rejecting non-Landmark churches as valid arbiters of the gospel.[71] As a result of his rising prominence in Southern Baptist life, Pendleton received an appointment in 1857 as a theology professor at Union University in Murfreesboro, Tennessee. His continuing antislavery principles, however, drew routine public criticism, especially as sectional tensions between South and North intensified during the late 1850s. When the

---

[70] Pendleton, *Reminiscences*, 93–4, 102–3; Pendleton, "Correction," *Baptist Banner*, October 3, 1849; and Howard, "Pendleton: Southern Crusader against Slavery," 201–2. In 1850, Pendleton did leave his Bowling Green congregation for a pastorate in Russellville, Kentucky. From all indications, this move had nothing to do with Pendleton's antislavery stance. He helped start Bethel College in Russellville and then returned to Bowling Green's First Baptist Church in 1851.

[71] Landmarkism made several sweeping claims about the nature of Baptist Christianity. Chief among them were the rejection of the historic concept of an invisible and universal church; a view that a truly spiritual church could only be found within local, autonomous congregations; the rejection of any forms of baptism other than those performed by immersion; and the assertion that Landmarkism stood in a historic line of "succession" that extended from Jesus Christ through the "true church" over time to the contemporary Landmark Baptist churches. This final point, and the collective weight of the Landmark movement, drove home the notion that only Landmarkists – and no other Christian adherents, even some Baptists – were actually Christians. Landmarkism was a tremendously controversial movement with ramifications for all sorts of Baptist practices through the latter half of the nineteenth century and well into the twentieth.

Pendleton remains associated with Landmarkism because his *An Old Landmark Re-set* (Nashville: Graves & Marks, 1854) gave the movement its name. Pendleton was one of the three pillars in the early Landmark triumvirate; James R. Graves, long-time editor of the *Tennessee Baptist*, and A. C. Dayton were the other early leaders of the movement. Keith Eitel, "James Madison Pendleton," in *Baptist Theologians*, ed. Timothy George and David S. Dockery (Nashville: Broadman Press, 1990), 188–204, argues that Pendleton was not as thoroughgoing in his Landmarkism and suggests that Pendleton disagreed with Graves and Dayton on several key points, especially the existence of a universal church. For more on the foundations and platforms of Landmarkism, as well as its three leaders, see this series of articles: James E. Tull, "The Landmark Movement: An Historical and Theological Appraisal"; Harold S. Smith, "The Life and Work of J. R. Graves (1820–1893)"; Bob Compton, "J. M. Pendleton: A Nineteenth-Century Baptist Statesman (1811–1891)"; and James E. Taulman, "The Life and Writings of Amos Cooper Dayton (1813–1865)," all in *Baptist History and Heritage* 10 (1975): 3–18; 19–27, 55–6; 28–35, 56; 36–43.

Civil War broke out, Pendleton feared for his life and fled to the North, accepting a pastorate in Hamilton, Ohio.[72]

By the late 1850s, Kentucky's religiously conservative antislavery movement had shown its limits. Unable to make a compelling religious case for free labor designs and failing in 1849 to achieve a decisive political victory for their agenda, emancipationists could not influence more committed proslavery theological minds to abandon the idea of the righteousness of slaveholding. Kentucky continued in the late 1850s to experience public dissent against slavery, but it required the Civil War to force slavery's end – an end that would come via cataclysm and upheaval, not in the gradualist-colonizationist mode preferred by conservative white Kentuckians. Those white believers in antebellum Kentucky who opposed slavery held commitments to evangelicalism, white supremacy, and anti-abolitionism in common with their proslavery opponents. Yet that common ideological ground would not become apparent until after the death of American slavery. Then, ironically, it was proslavery evangelicals who convinced the gradualists to join their side. In Kentucky, the future of conservative Christian antislavery resided with the proslavery movement.

---

[72] Pendleton, *Reminiscences*, 112–14. John E. Dawson, an editor of the Alabama newspaper the *South Western Baptist*, charged Pendleton as an "abolitionist" and argued that no person with antislavery views ought to hold a post in a southern university. Howard, "Pendleton: Southern Crusader against Slavery," 206–10, discusses the great number of papers that came out against Pendleton. Interestingly, one of his main defenders was William C. Buck. Despite the public debate, the two remained friends, and Buck charged Pendleton's detractors with wrongly connecting Pendleton to abolitionist John Brown.

4

The Abolitionist Threat

Religious Orthodoxy and Proslavery Unionism on the Eve of Civil War, 1859–1861

> The great heresy of the North is abolitionism. The creed founded on it discards many of the fundamental doctrines of the Bible. As a morbid sentiment, it naturally tends to socialism, rationalism, and infidelity. Elevating its own lawless impulses and dictates above the Biblical standard of truth, it necessarily rejects the Word of God as a guide. Prescribing its own passion as a condition of religious fellowship and church membership it repudiates the charity of the Gospel, rejects the doctrines of Christ, and excludes the people of God from its communion. This explains all.... Abolitionism is the cancer at the very heart of America.
>
> – "Northern Apostacy,"
> *Western Recorder*, May 26, 1860[1]

On May 6, 1861, just a few weeks after Confederate artillery fired on Fort Sumter and initiated the Civil War, Kentucky's annual statewide meeting of Baptists, the General Association, petitioned the state legislature to "preserve the peace of the state." A report in the *Western Recorder*, formerly named the *Baptist Banner* and the voice of the denomination in the Commonwealth, took great pride in noting that the document lacked partisan animus. Demonstrating that Baptists were not "attempt[ing] to make political capital" in that moment of sectional strife, the petition had been affirmed by coreligionists from all variety of perspectives, "Secessionists and Unionists, women and children." The appeal itself called on Kentucky's politicians to "rise above the excitement and confusion of party, and of the times, and deliberately, in the fear of God, seek only, first, the good, the very best possible good, of our Commonwealth, and, then, of other portions of our country." The logic of this argument was straightforward: Kentucky Baptists hoped "to avert from our soil, our homes,

---

[1] "Northern Apostacy," *Western Recorder*, May 26, 1860. This article was reprinted from the Richmond, Virginia, *Christian Advocate*, the official newspaper of the Virginia Conference of the Methodist Episcopal Church, South.

our women, and our children, the dreadful scourge of civil war." In the coming conflict, they wanted to remain neutral.[2]

That opinion was common among Kentucky's religious whites, and among white Kentuckians as a whole, who labored to remain detached from the divisive sectional controversy. Their sentiment of neutrality had stood out vividly in the notably complicated and controversial presidential election of November 1860. A majority of the Commonwealth's electorate (45.2%) sided with the conservative Constitutional Union Party candidate, slaveholder John Bell of Tennessee, over the southern Democratic Party nominee, native Kentuckian John C. Breckinridge (36.3%). The other two candidates, Democrat Stephen A. Douglas and Republican Abraham Lincoln – the eventual winner – both from Illinois, received 17.5 and 0.9 percent, respectively. Almost everywhere else in the United States, Constitutional Unionists were unpopular; Kentucky joined only Tennessee and Virginia in giving a majority vote to Bell. The party itself was an amalgam of former Whigs and Know Nothings and famously ran on a platform that "recognize[d] no political principle other than *the Constitution... the Union... and the Enforcement of the Laws.*" Most significantly, Constitutional Unionists took no stance on the most pressing issue of the day – slavery.[3]

Such reluctance to speak on the slavery question, if unappealing almost everywhere else in the United States, singularly suited a border slave state unwilling to push for secession but also unwilling to tamper with the institution within its boundaries. Slavery, in fact, had much to do with white Kentucky's variety of political conservatism. If the Union was to be preserved, it was the Union without modification: that is, the Union as it existed in 1860. Neutral Kentuckians defended, in other words, a slaveholding nation they refused to leave and opposed changing.[4]

White Kentucky's political neutrality drew considerable justification from religious sources. For the state's substantial constituency of evangelical whites,

[2] "The Lexington Memorial," *Western Recorder*, May 25, 1861.

[3] Lowell H. Harrison, *The Civil War in Kentucky* (Lexington: University Press of Kentucky, 1975), ix, 4–5; Lowell H. Harrison and James C. Klotter, *A New History of Kentucky* (Lexington: University Press of Kentucky, 1997), 183–6; James M. McPherson, *Battle Cry of Freedom: The Civil War Era* (New York: Oxford University Press, 1988); quote 221. The 1860 presidential election figures were taken from the American Presidency Project, University of California, Santa Barbara, http://www.presidency.ucsb.edu/showelection.php?year=1860.

[4] Historians Lowell Harrison and James Klotter cogently capture the irony of Kentucky's attempt to remain disengaged from the sectional crisis: "neutrality was attractive to many Kentuckians who were uncertain of the path their state should take, although a state had no more right to declare neutrality than it did to secede." See Harrison and Klotter, *New History of Kentucky*, 187; Gary R. Matthews, "Beleaguered Loyalties: Kentucky Unionism," in *Sister States, Enemy States: The Civil War in Kentucky and Tennessee*, eds. Kent T. Dollar, Larry H. Whiteaker, and W. Calvin Dickinson (Lexington: University Press of Kentucky, 2009), 9–24; and Jacob F. Lee, "Unionism, Emancipationism, and the Origins of the Kentucky's Confederate Identity," *Register of the Kentucky Historical Society* 111.2 (Spring 2013): 206–9.

God had ordained slavery as a properly Christian institution. To be sure, debate persisted in Kentucky throughout the antebellum era over the relative merits of slavery in the Commonwealth. Yet no religiously conservative white Kentuckian disavowed the biblical mandate for the institution in the abstract. Moreover, none from that group dared question the racist foundation on which antebellum white American society was based. Biblically considered and divorced from practical reality, slaveholding represented for white evangelical Kentuckians the supreme application of divine political economy.

On the eve of the Civil War, the United States remained a nation that protected the rights of slaveholders. Given that, when most religious whites in Kentucky spoke of loyalty to the Union, they spoke of a nation they believed served as the civil protector of conservative Christian values, including slavery. Their Unionism, in other words, was a proslavery ideal. It was this belief that drove their commitment to political neutrality in the sectional conflict. From such a perspective, threats to neutrality constituted threats to their faith or, at the very least, threats against the nation that secured their conservative Christian faith. As the Kentucky Baptist press contended in early 1860, "God has chosen these United States as the theater" of divine beneficence. The American nation stood "elevat[ed] among the kingdoms of the earth," "a monument of the power of Christianity and civilization," "reserved for some grand and holy purpose" by "our great Creator." To rend the national fabric would prove disastrous, especially if that rending came through violent and bloody means.[5]

From the viewpoint of religiously and politically neutral Kentucky, two major factions were poised to fight. On one side were southern proslavery secessionists; on the other were northern abolitionists. Both were evil because both sought to destroy the Union as it presently existed, but Kentuckians were not evenly poised between the two options. Secession, however undesirable and extreme it might have seemed to many white evangelical Kentuckians in 1860 and 1861, served to preserve Christian slavery and the white supremacy that attended the institution. If disunion was wrong, Kentucky's religiously conservative whites at least identified with and understood the position of their coreligionists in the South.

They offered no such empathy for the hostiles from the North. To Kentucky conservatives, secession remained far less of an evil than that foisted on the American public by a radical antislavery faction hell-bent on tearing down the most basic foundations of Christian America: its faith, its unity, and its racial stratification, all of which the slavery system secured. As a Virginia Methodist bluntly contended, and Kentucky Baptists heartily endorsed in May 1860, "Abolitionism is the cancer at the very heart of America."[6] It thus constituted

---

5 "Prayer for the Preservation of the Union," *Western Recorder*, January 9, 1860; "Thoughts upon the Present Condition of our Country," *Western Recorder*, August 18, 1860.
6 "Northern Apostacy."

the primary threat to Christian America and, by extension, to Kentucky's political neutrality.

In early January 1860 the *Western Recorder* published an article by a venerable founder of the Southern Baptist Convention, Baltimore pastor Richard Fuller, which quickly set the terms of debate on the sectional crisis for religious conservatives in white Kentucky. The essay initially appeared in the Boston *Courier* as a defense of the Christian slaveholding South against the assaults of northern abolitionists. Fuller's pen had been quickened by the late workings of John Brown, the infamous abolitionist who, in October 1859, led twenty followers to raid a federal armory in Harper's Ferry, Virginia. This "insane outbreak of fanaticism," as Fuller called it, had been interpreted by many in the North as an act of heroism. From Fuller's viewpoint in Baltimore, that sort of "sympathy" for a man who had a long record of excessively violent reaction against proslavery opponents and who had recently been hanged for committing a treasonous "deed of violence and blood" had no place in the United States. Rather, the positive response to Brown in the North was cause for "amazement and alarm." For generations, Yankee abolitionists had "inflame[d] the imagination of women and children" and "misled multitudes of men – most excellent and pious – but utterly ignorant as to the condition of things at the South." In Fuller's own purple prose, quoted here at length, the northern position on the slavery–abolition controversy, as exemplified by what he saw as enthusiasm for John Brown-style antislavery, was encapsulated as follows:

> The South is denounced for not at once immolating four thousand millions of property guaranteed to them by the Constitution; for not at once abandoning to weeds and brambles millions of fertile acres; for not breaking up their entire social system, and either driving their servants from their comfortable homes, to become vagabonds in other States, which will again drive them out of their borders – or else harboring in their midst hordes of discontented, indolent vagrants, utterly unfit for freedom, who would certainly be exterminated unless in mercy they were again reduced to servitude. Because they will not do all this – will not inflict this suicidal wrong upon themselves, and try this fatal experiment upon the servants they love; because they will not thus ruin their families, and desolate their hearths and homes, and all this in violation of their best convictions of duty, they are to be the objects of incessant calumny, to be pillaged and murdered in cold blood by their own fellow citizens, who are heroes and martyrs for doing this butchery.[7]

Such arguments were not mere abstractions in the Kentucky context. Although Kentucky's white abolitionists never sought to foment rebellion as did Brown, their presence alone proved provocative to the state's conservative whites. And in the wake of Brown's raid, Kentucky abolitionists appeared even more threatening. Over the years of antebellum struggle, antislavery immediatists in the Commonwealth had claimed the right to wage armed resistance to

---

[7] Richard Fuller, "Letter of Dr. Fuller on Union," *Western Recorder*, January 21, 1860.

slavery and proslavery forces. That was especially the case for Cassius Clay, but by the late 1850s it also applied to William S. Bailey, whose *Newport News* defended the actions of slave insurrectionists. It also was true of members of John G. Fee's Berea community, who faced frequent mob assaults after Clay's withdrawal of protection in 1856. Such attacks led the community members, although pacifist in stance, to arm themselves for the purposes of self-defense.[8]

Kentucky was never a hospitable place for abolitionists, but the events at Harper's Ferry confirmed widespread suspicion about immediatists in the state. In the aftermath of the raid, John Copeland, a freeborn African American member of Brown's party, reportedly confessed to authorities that a similar rebellion was planned to take place simultaneously in Kentucky, led by the state's abolitionists. Copeland's story was corroborated by an anonymous report to Virginia governor Henry A. Wise, supposedly written by a former Brown-affiliated abolitionist. The informant claimed insider knowledge about the ongoing training of two thousand men north of the Ohio River for an abolitionist force to invade Kentucky and overthrow slavery with the help of the Commonwealth's enslaved – who would be led by the state's abolitionists. Wise sent the report of the plot on to Kentucky governor Beriah Magoffin, and copies soon circulated in Kentucky's major newspapers.[9]

Such reports were largely baseless, but that mattered little in the heat of such a moment. Kentucky's conservative whites knew that abolitionism would be the downfall of their Christian slaveholding republic. Brown's raid provided part of the proof of that belief. Further confirmation came from John G. Fee; the result was hostile.

At the time of Brown's failed rebellion, Fee was traveling throughout the North, attempting to raise money from evangelical abolitionists to establish one of the key institutions he long believed necessary for the success of the Berea community: an antisectarian college that rejected racial caste and followed the model of Oberlin. In 1858 that vision received a boost with the arrival of John A. R. Rogers, an Oberlin-trained and American Missionary Association–connected minister from Illinois, to establish a "higher school" at Berea. On his fundraising trip, Fee was not shy about voicing support for John Brown, doing so on multiple occasions in November 1859, including in New

---

[8] Stanley Harrold, *Border War: Fighting over Slavery before the Civil War* (Chapel Hill: University of North Carolina Press, 2010), 185–90. For reports of mob violence against Fee and the Bereans, see John G. Fee, letter, June 21, 1857, *American Missionary* (September 1857): 211–12; Fee, "Mob – Outrages – Reaction," August 14, 1857 and September 4, 1857, *American Missionary* (October 1857): 230–2; Fee, letter, February 9, 1858, *American Missionary* (April 1858): 88; and Fee, letter, February 12, 1858, *American Missionary* (April 1858): 88–90. All in typescript "Letters and Articles by and about Rev. John G. Fee, his life and work in the *American Missionary*," 66–7, 68–9, 79–80, 81–3, RG 1.02, Series III, Box 5, Folder 7, Berea College Archives, Berea, KY.

[9] Marion B. Lucas, "John G. Fee, The Berea Exiles, and the 1862 Confederate Invasion of Kentucky," *The Filson History Quarterly* 75 (2001): 158–60.

York City at two of the most famous churches in the United States: Henry Ward Beecher's Plymouth Congregational Church in Brooklyn and George B. Cheever's Congregational Church of the Puritans in Union Square.[10]

Such open support for Brown by Fee incited a December mass meeting in Madison County that called for the expulsion of the Bereans from the Commonwealth. As the meeting was reported in Kentucky's political press, Fee was characterized as having "proclaimed from the pulpit and the desk, his sympathy for and approbation of the late notorious John Brown, asserting that we needed more Browns in Kentucky, and asked for a donation of two or three thousand dollars only, to revolutionize the State." Yet that was not quite the full story. Replying from Pittsburgh, Pennsylvania, Fee maintained that his fellow Kentuckians misunderstood his position on Brown and failed to fully quote his arguments to northern antislavery audiences: "I have said, 'we need more John Browns – not in the MANNER OF HIS ACTION, BUT IN HIS SPIRIT OF CONSECRATION' – 'men who would go not to entice away a few slaves, for that would not remove the difficulty – men who would go, not with carnal weapons but with the "sword of the spirit," the Bible.'" Fee had intended his statements in the North to be a tempered call for Christian abolitionists to go south to bring about the end of slavery. As one committed throughout his career to principles of nonviolence and moral suasion, Fee claimed that he had disavowed Brown's brutal measures.[11]

Most white Kentuckians, however, had little concern for Fee's intentions. As his opponents in Madison County contended about the Bereans, "there has come amongst us a set of men, not citizens of this county, and with the exception of one [Fee], not of the State" who were "agents and emissaries of Northern Abolition societies." As the conservatives put it, "these societies are our enemies, if indeed they are not the enemies of all mankind." Abolitionists were guilty of "teaching a new religion, to be propogated by the pike, with a baptism of fire and blood." These radicals, moreover, "worship[ed] a new God – not the God of our revolutionary fathers, from whom we derive all our blessings and whose wise and beneficent will is the peace and happiness of the whole family of man." Antislavery immediatists were, instead, fanatics

[10] John G. Fee, "Emigration to Kentucky," December 13, 1856, *American Missionary* 11 (January 1857): 21; Fee, "A College in Kentucky – needed," January 14, 1857, *American Missionary* (March 1857): 65–6; John G. Fee, letter, July 9, 1858, *American Missionary* (September 1858): 232–3; "Prayers for John Brown," *American Missionary* (November 1859): 283–4; John G. Fee, letter, December 1859, *American Missionary* (December 1859): 277–8. All in "Letters and Articles by Fee," 56–8, 88–9, 105, 106–7. "County Meeting," *Kentucky Messenger*, December 23, 1859, in RG 1.01, Folder 1, BCA. See also Shannon H. Wilson, *Berea College: An Illustrated History* (Lexington: University Press of Kentucky, 2006), 1–21; and Lucas, "Fee and the Berea Exiles," 160–2.

[11] "County Meeting"; John G. Fee, "To the Citizens of Madison County, Kentucky," December 14, 1859, RG 1, Box 5, Folder 2, BCA; Wilson, *Berea College*, 20–1; and Lucas, "Fee and the Berea Exiles," 160–2.

who disavowed truth. Fee and his ilk claimed something more: "a higher law than any known to the Constitution, under which we live, justifying plunder, treason, and servile insurrection." It was well known that abolitionists were heretics. But their false belief did more than violate theological standards. The problem was not simply one for churches: abolitionism's heterodoxy threatened society as a whole. There could be no toleration for such aberrant belief, which inspired such subversive action.[12]

On December 23, 1859, an extralegal mob of sixty armed Madison County men rode into the Berea community and gave its residents ten days to leave the state. Fee was then still traveling in the North. Upon receiving word of this action against his community, he again wrote publicly to defend his abolitionist principles, saying the Bereans believed in "us[ing] only moral means" to end slavery. However, he also warned that failing to allow slavery to "pass away peaceably" would mean that "God will let loose his judgments." Yet Fee himself did not fear such a potentially cataclysmic consequence. "I would be willing to bleed at every pore," he maintained, "if by so doing I could induce Southern men to come to a fair investigation of truth on this and other subjects. Then we might indeed expect union and salvation." Although Fee rejected those who saw him as the harbinger of violent upheaval, such language only served to underscore conservative Kentuckians' fears that abolitionists – and Fee particularly – sought revolution in the name of a Christianity that bore no resemblance to the true faith. After all, they had already denounced his abolitionist belief as false doctrine.[13]

The fate of the abolitionist community in Madison County was sealed. The Bereans appealed the threat of forced expulsion to Kentucky governor Magoffin, but it came to nothing. On December 29, thirty-six people – including all of Fee's family – left the state, crossing into Cincinnati, where they reunited with Fee. When several of the Berea exiles attempted to reenter Kentucky a month later, a mob of more than a thousand opposed them in northern Kentucky.[14]

Forced expulsion did not put an end to Fee's desire to work in Kentucky, however. Indeed, he renewed his activities at Berea and in central Kentucky only a few years later. Yet, with the Civil War beginning in the near future, the end to slavery that Fee had spent almost two decades working for was on the horizon, though he – like all Americans – was probably not aware of the fact in 1860.

In his defense of the Berea community, Fee had argued that there would be no stemming the tide of abolition: "An attempt to suppress agitation by banishing a few abolitionists, is vain. All slaves are abolitionists – all

---

[12] "County Meeting."
[13] John G. Fee, "Circular No. 2. To the Citizens of Madison County, Kentucky," December 27, 1859, RG 1, Box 5, Folder 2, BCA.
[14] Lucas, "Fee and the Berea Exiles," 162–5.

masters – all men are abolitionists so far as *their* liberty is concerned. They want freedom for themselves – now – and that too without expatriation." In Fee's view, the truth was plain, and it came from Christian moral teaching. As he put it, "Just so fast as men shall have courage to speak out the monitions of a natural conscience, and just so far as they shall really embrace that religion which requires us to do unto men as we would they should do unto us, thus far will men agitate and oppose every system of slavery." The basic desire of every human being, in other words, was for freedom. There could be no avoiding this aspect of the divine order.[15]

But religious conservatives saw this matter entirely differently. For the Baptist editors of the *Western Recorder* who published Richard Fuller's missive against John Brown, abolitionists such as Fee misunderstood God's political economy, specifically the necessity of racial hierarchy. The basic flaw in immediatism, as Fuller saw it, was that abolitionists cared little for African American souls. If his northern antagonists did, they would push for less extreme ends to slavery and work to ensure that the South's racial dependents were actually prepared for freedom. The northern populace, Fuller wrote, "wasted large sums for Abolition books and lectures," but they never spent that money where it really mattered, nor even so much as inquired of a white southerner – those who knew from their day-to-day existence – "what could be done to promote the happiness and welfare of these slaves." What needed to be done, Fuller argued, was to provide gospel-based education for slaves. In an ostensible show of fairness to certain abolitionist claims, Fuller admitted that there were immoral laws on southern books that had impinged on the right of slaves to freely assemble. Yet, as a right-minded minister who placed his own higher calling ahead of temporal decrees, Fuller reported that he willingly broke those laws, "meeting thousands from different plantations and preaching to them" while also teaching many other slaves to read. His own example, he argued, ought to prove to his abolitionist readers that the white southerner was the "true friend" of "the African." As he saw it, "the guardianship of a kind master" represented the best hope – "a great blessing" – for the future of the black race. Freedom would come, but only through the civilization that white Christianity would bring. Moreover, "[i]f the gospel is to emancipate slaves," Fuller contended, "it would be, not by insurrection and massacre, but by a love which will melt off their bonds." Those who assailed slavery, Fuller believed, misunderstood its Christianizing and civilizing import.[16]

This 1860 defense of the slaveholding South contra radical abolitionism resonated with a widely accepted Christian proslavery position that Fuller, along with many of his colleagues in southern pulpits, had maintained for years. Indeed, Fuller was commonly regarded – certainly in the South, but also in the North – as one of the finest, most careful, and judicious interpreters

[15] Fee, "Circular No. 2."
[16] Fuller, "Letter of Dr. Fuller on Union."

of the biblical record's application to American slavery. The signal moment
in Fuller's securing of this reputation came in 1845 when he engaged Brown
University president Francis Wayland in a written debate over the Christian
merits of the American slave system. In Baptist circles, the moment was rife with
contention, as the denomination careened toward sectional cleavage over the
slavery question. In response to antislavery critics in northern circles, Fuller –
at that time pastor in Beaufort, South Carolina – gave as much ground to his
opponents as he believed the Bible would allow on the issue.[17]

Fuller, like many proslavery clerics in Kentucky pulpits, did not deny that
injustice infected American slavery. Yet, like his fellow southern proslavery
clerics, he could not avoid the fact that the Bible "condemn[ed] the abuses of
slavery, but permit[ed] the system itself." The burden of proof, Fuller contended
in 1845, rested on opponents of slavery. Antislavery activists could not escape
the clear message of both the Old and New Testaments: slavery was a properly
Christian institution. However, as a human reality, slavery could not avoid
the taint of original sin. Because human beings could not avoid imperfection –
sin – all human endeavors were necessarily flawed. The inevitable sinfulness of
human actors, however, did not mean that believers gave up attempts to work
for good in the world. As such, the reality of a slavery system compromised by
sin did not impugn the idea of Christian slavery itself. Making the point, Fuller
asked his readers, "will it not be laboring in the vocation of the infidel, to assert
that the Bible does not condemn slavery, especially when we know that in the
times of the Apostles, masters were allowed to torture their slaves, and starve
them, and kill them as food for their fish?" Admitting the moral gravity of this
question, the southern divine answered, "[T]he enormities often resulting from
slavery, and which excite our abhorrence, are not inseparable from it – they
are not elements in the system, but abuses of it." American slavery had flaws,
but so too did all human institutions. To dismiss slavery out of hand meant
dismissing the biblical record as well.[18]

Francis Wayland, Fuller's Rhode Island opponent, found himself compelled
by the force of the southerner's argument. "Never before," Wayland wrote,
"has the defence of slavery on Christian principles been so ably conducted."
An evangelical emancipationist, Wayland, like many Kentuckians, held a conservative, white supremacist antislavery position and rejected immediatist abolitionism. Thus, it is not surprising that he found aspects of Fuller's argument,
especially his strict biblicism, convincing. Yet Wayland refused to concede to

[17] For the broader significance of this debate for antebellum America, see Mark A. Noll, *The Civil War as a Theological Crisis* (Chapel Hill: University of North Carolina Press, 2006), 36–8. Noll considers the Fuller-Wayland dispute one of the last public religious discussions of slavery where opponents exercised "reasonable restraint" and avoided devolving into heated polemic.

[18] Richard Fuller and Francis Wayland, *Domestic Slavery Considered as a Scriptural Institution: In a Correspondence between the Rev. Richard Fuller of Beaufort, S. C., and the Rev. Francis Wayland, of Providence, R. I.* (New York: Lewis Colby, 1845), quotes 4, 7.

Fuller that all forms of slavery were implicitly righteous, simply due to the biblical warrant for an abstracted version of the institution. Wayland contended that, taken to its logical conclusion, Fuller's argument meant that blacks could enslave whites as much as whites had enslaved blacks in American society. Making his own use of biblical chapter and verse to show the error of Fuller's logic, Wayland explicated his point about nonracial slavery, citing 1 Peter 2:18: "[I]f the slaves of any state or plantation should rise and enslave their masters, this precept would justify them; and yet more, the other precepts, according to your interpretation, would oblige the masters as Christians to obey them, 'doing service from the heart, not only to the good and gentle, but also to the froward.'" In point of fact, Wayland admitted that such a racially revolutionary notion of American slavery "goes very far beyond any thing that I ever before heard claimed for the slaves." And the Brown president did not actually believe "slaves had a right to rise and emancipate themselves by force," because "it would be a great calamity were [slavery] to terminate by violence, or without previous moral and social preparation." In other words, as was the case with most American whites, the prospect of slave insurrection alarmed Francis Wayland. The Brown University president may have disagreed with Fuller over the nature of American slavery, but they reached common ground on the duties of Christian masters to bonded souls.[19]

Indeed, in Wayland's closing correspondence, he repeatedly remarked how closely his view aligned with Fuller's, especially their agreement on the extent of corruption in American slavery. Slaveholders, Wayland asserted, were compelled by the words of Holy Scripture to treat their slaves as Christian equals. Stated baldly, such a view required what were then illegal matters: slave marriages had to be honored, family structures could not be compromised by separating children from parents, slaves should receive full educational access, their testimony should stand in secular as well as church courts, and slaves should be given the ability to freely assemble for worship. "[I]n a word," Wayland wrote, a robustly Christian conception of slavery, which he believed Fuller was advancing, understood that slaves deserved "the full benefit of equal law in all cases whatsoever, save only that he is under obligation to render reasonable and cheerful service to his master." Insofar as Fuller worked toward these aims, Wayland could scarcely complain about the southerner's version of proslavery doctrine.[20]

In his response, Wayland did not concede the righteousness of slavery and – while endorsing aspects of Fuller's argument – he did not compromise his

[19] For an extended treatment of Wayland's conservative antislavery views, see Deborah Bingham Van Broekhaven, "Suffering with Slaveholders: The Limits of Francis Wayland's Antislavery Witness," in *Religion and the Antebellum Debate over Slavery*, eds. John R. McKivigan and Mitchell Snay (Athens: University of Georgia Press, 1998), 196–220; Fuller and Wayland, *Domestic Slavery Considered*, 226, 237, 238, 252.

[20] Fuller and Wayland, *Domestic Slavery Considered*, 226–54, quote 234.

antislavery principles. Instead, Wayland's attitude toward Fuller can be explained along religious and political lines. First, although the Rhode Island divine believed in the evil of American slavery – in his words, "I believe that I should sin willfully against God, if I ever promulgated a slaveholding Christianity" – Wayland believed more fervently in the importance of preserving religious unity. Thus, in condemning slavery, Wayland avoided using invective against Fuller and sought to mollify differences between pro- and antislavery religious factions. Second, Wayland was a committed evangelical and a conservative emancipationist. As remained the case with coreligionists in Kentucky, that amalgam made him unwilling to support abolitionist schemes that would have radically called for the immediate end of slavery or a cavalier attitude toward the biblical record on slavery. As Wayland saw it, abolitionists had so "commonly indulged in exaggerated statement, in violent denunciation, and in coarse and lacerating invective" that they had poisoned the nation's religious discourse on the issue and threatened the peace of society.[21]

Fifteen years after Wayland and Fuller squared off, the issues at stake in their 1845 debate were still very much alive, especially from the perspective of white religious Kentuckians. Much like Fuller and Wayland more than a decade prior, Kentucky's religious conservatives agreed about who were the primary agitators in the sectional crisis. When contrasted with abolitionists, the differences that proslavery and emancipationist Kentuckians saw between themselves became inconsequential.

From the perspective of those white evangelicals who considered themselves true believers in 1860, there was right and wrong on the slavery question – and abolitionism was wrong. Thanks to that "alarming" fiction, as one *Western Recorder* article contended, "Orthodox churches have been affected" by the "corrupt current of mingled errors." The essay – republished from the Richmond *Christian Advocate*, the chief organ of the Virginia Conference of the Methodist Episcopal Church, South – saw the "evangelical ministry" now warped by "widespreading heresies." Classic doctrines of Christianity, including "a particular providence, the special agency of the Spirit in regeneration, the inspiration of the Scriptures," to say nothing of "depravity, regeneration, and the atonement," had all been subverted by abolitionism's wayward theology. And that theological problem was freighted with tremendous social and political baggage. "Heresy in religion is a portentous omen," the article's Methodist author argued. Assuming the orthodox Christian foundation for nineteenth-century American society, he wrote, "A corrupt public conscience is a throne on which Satan sways a terrible dominion. . . . Religion in America has more to fear from the abolition speculations of the North than from any other source in the whole world." True Christians needed to band together to defeat such

---

[21] Van Broekhaven, "Suffering with Slaveholders," 207–8; Fuller and Wayland, *Domestic Slavery Considered*, quotes 13, 123.

threats. Such unified orthodoxy might not simply preserve the faith. It might also protect the life of the American nation.[22]

It was precisely this sort of religious solidarity against abolitionism that prompted the Baptist *Western Recorder* to publish, in early January 1861, a redacted version of a sermon by Henry J. Van Dyke (1822–91), noted minister of the First Presbyterian Church of Brooklyn, New York. In the sermon delivered less than a month earlier, Van Dyke labored to show "The Character and Influence of Abolitionism." The New York Presbyterian's religiously conservative message registered a clear ecumenical appeal, apparent in the strong approbation given by the *Western Recorder*'s editors in their introduction to the reprinted sermon. Van Dyke, they wrote, delivered a "discourse characterized by the loftiest Christian patriotism, and by its fearless advocacy of God's truth." Indeed, they had "seldom seen a more faithful revelation of the true character of abolitionism." Although a Presbyterian in the heart of Yankeedom, Van Dyke's commitment to foundational principles of conservative Protestantism offered a guiding light to Kentucky Baptists.[23]

In Van Dyke's discourse that followed this introduction, the Presbyterian pastor plainly defined an abolitionist as one who "believes that slaveholding is sin, and ought therefore to be abolished." That was quite a different position from the one occupied by emancipationists, who, for example, might "believe on political or commercial grounds that slavery is an undesirable system" or find the U.S. Constitution unduly disposed toward "the rights of slaveholders." That antislavery impulse could be tolerated, according to Van Dyke. One was not an abolitionist "unless he believes that slave holding is morally wrong." Advocates for that extreme view, he argued, had no Christian basis for such a claim.[24]

Van Dyke's argument unfolded directly. Abolitionism failed as a properly Christian ideology because it had "no foundation in Scriptures." It was "a historic truth," he contended, that "at the advent of Jesus Christ slavery existed all over the civilized world, and was intimately interwoven with its social and civil institutions." On such a purportedly evil institution, the New Testament record remained silent. "Drunkenness and adultery, theft and murder – all the moral wrong which have ever been known to afflict society, are forbidden by name." Somehow, however, slavery, "according to abolitionism, this greatest of all sins – this sum of all villainies – is never spoken of except in respectful terms. How," Van Dyke asked his sermon's auditors, "can this be accounted for?"[25]

[22] "Northern Apostacy."

[23] "Character and Influence of Abolitionism," *Western Recorder*, January 5, 1861.

[24] Ibid. Quotes from longer printed version of the sermon, published as, Henry Jackson Van Dyke, *The Character and Influence of Abolitionism!: A Sermon Preached in the First Presbyterian Church, of Brooklyn, on Sunday Evening, December 9th, 1860*, 2nd ed. (Baltimore: Henry Taylor, 1860), 5.

[25] "Character and Influence of Abolitionism."

The answer was obvious. Abolitionism led "to utter infidelity." Those under its spell operated from the "assumption, that men are capable of judging beforehand what is to be expected in a Divine revelation." Abolitionists "did not try slavery by the Bible," but rather "tried the Bible by the principles of freedom." Theoretically those "principles of freedom" drew from the laws of "nature." Yet really, Van Dyke surmised, natural law was merely code language for "preconceived notions." Abolitionists, in other words, committed the classic first error on the path to heterodoxy: a human believing he or she understood the mind of God was "the cockatrice's egg, from which in all ages heresies have been hatched. This is the spider's web," the Brooklyn divine argued, "which men have spun out of their own brains, and clinging to which, they have attempted to swing over the yawning abyss of infidelity." Van Dyke admitted that not all "abolitionism is infidelity," but the "tendencies" within the system were too much to ignore: "Wherever the seed of abolitionism has been sown . . . a plentiful crop of infidelity has sprung up." True believers needed to avoid the bitter "fruit of such principles." Orthodox faith, Van Dyke asserted, demanded no less.[26]

The Brooklyn pastor gained less traction for his perspective among his northern coreligionists, but in white evangelical Kentucky, it achieved extensive appeal. Moreover, Van Dyke's was not the only opinion about abolitionism from above the Mason-Dixon line that white religious Kentuckians found laudable.[27] Van Dyke's sermon only briefly alluded to the white supremacist foundation of American slavery, but for the many white Americans – South and North – who agreed with him, it was impossible to extract racism from their critique of abolitionism.[28] Indeed, just a few months after publishing Van Dyke's sermon, the *Western Recorder* published a defense of slavery that originally ran in the *Christian Observer*, a Philadelphia-based New School

---

[26] Ibid.

[27] As a result of his open denunciation of abolitionism, many in the North argued that Van Dyke was a proslavery southern sympathizer. Van Dyke's Unionist credentials, however, had long been established, and his opinion on abolitionism does not seem to have affected his Brooklyn congregation's opinion of his pastoral abilities, where he served until his death in 1891. See Lewis G. Vander Velde, *The Presbyterian Churches and the Federal Union, 1861–1869* (Cambridge, MA: Harvard University Press, 1932), 285; Peter J. Parish, "From Necessary Evil to National Blessing: The Northern Protestant Clergy Interpret the Civil War," in *An Uncommon Time: The Civil War and the Northern Home Front*, eds. Paul A. Cimbala and Randall M. Miller (New York: Fordham University Press, 2002), 78–9; and "Tablet to the Rev. Dr. Van Dyke: Formally Unveiled in the Second Presbyterian Church, Brooklyn," *New York Times*, October 2, 1894.

[28] It is no reach to assume that Van Dyke's own sense of racial superiority pervaded his analysis. In briefly saying that he would bracket questions of race in his sermon, he alluded to a classic racist defense of slavery: its utility as a Christian instrument for the improvement of benighted Africans: "I shall not attempt to show what will be the condition of the African race in this country when the Gospel shall have brought all classes under its complete dominion." Van Dyke, *Character and Influence of Abolitionism*, 11–12.

Presbyterian paper that earned a reputation as the only publication in that mostly northern denomination to overtly endorse secession.[29] Written anonymously by "A Christian" from the City of Brotherly Love, the article contended, as did a slew of other anti-abolitionist writings, that "[t]he advocates of the 'higher law' in regard to slavery" rejected the Holy Writ and were only able to "contend against the institution on conscientious grounds." The truth of the biblical record on slavery, however, became apparent, the author argued, when rational minds looked at the very practical racial need for slavery. Despite possessing "every opportunity," "the African has no where risen, to any extent in civilization." Freedom was no blessing to American blacks, and the writer knew as much, living as he did on the free soil of Philadelphia. "There is a homely adage that 'the proof of the pudding is in the eating,' and when we in Philadelphia see around us a population of at least ten thousand persons of color, the mass of them born in our own State, and enjoying every advantage of civilization," it was impossible for the white mind to countenance that "we find them, with a few avocations, [living] in poverty." If the "degenerate" state of "the free black man, with the great advantage he has in Philadelphia," proved any indication, the writer asked, "how can it be expected that the liberated slave could succeed?" As the northern author contended, and his white Kentucky readers understood, African Americans constituted an unavoidably degraded race. Those abolitionists who argued otherwise rejected "common sense" and "God's law" only to uphold "their pride of opinion." As "A Christian" put it, God, "for his wise purposes, permitted the African for centuries to be a barbarian in his own country, and a slave when he left it. Why," he asked, would anyone "rebel and cavil with the great decree?" American slavery served a fundamentally Christian purpose by "now bringing thousands" of African Americans "to the knowledge of the truth as it is in Jesus." It made little sense that immediatist antislavery activists "'calling themselves Christians' and ministers of Christ interfere to prevent this glorious cause." Abolitionism, asserted the writer, ludicrously pursued the wrongheaded ideal "of giving freedom to the contented and happy slaves." God had chosen one superior race to work for the elevation of another far more inferior: to act against that divine imprimatur represented nothing less than an affront to the will of God.[30]

Historians have debated the extent to which racism pervaded proslavery Christianity, particularly as it concerned readings of Genesis 9:18–27, where the biblical patriarch Noah pronounces the "Curse of Canaan" or "Curse of Ham" on his son.[31] Although no allusion to race, in any modern sense of the

---

[29] On the record of the *Christian Observer* in the sectional crisis, see Vander Velde, *Presbyterian Churches*, 370–1.

[30] A Christian, "The Bible and Slavery," *Western Recorder*, March 9, 1861.

[31] Mark Noll has argued that the reason the proslavery–antislavery debate was so fierce was because of a "theological crisis" over biblical interpretation and the role of Providence in the world. In Noll's formulation, because northern and southern Protestants both read the Bible the same way – through the lens of what he calls a "Reformed, literal hermeneutic" – religion

term, exists in the passage – and although there existed little historical precedent for a racialized reading of the text – white nineteenth–century American interpretations ubiquitously read African American inferiority into the curse, finding therein a foundation for black enslavement.[32]

was central in the rise of sectional strife: "Two cultures, purporting to read the Bible the same way, were at each other's throats." See *America's God: From Jonathan Edwards to Abraham Lincoln* (New York: Oxford University Press, 2002), 396. Noll is somewhat sanguine about the possibilities of alternative hermeneutics in the period to solve the Bible-and-slavery dilemma. In *America's God* and also *The Civil War as a Theological Crisis*, Noll makes this point about African American, Catholic, and some high-church Reformed traditions. In short, the dilemma was profound, but perhaps not entirely intractable. There were religious contingencies, though few Americans heeded those voices. Thus, in large part according to Noll, the Civil War came about because of the hermeneutical failures of American Protestantism.

Eugene Genovese and Elizabeth Fox-Genovese disagree. The sum of the Genoveses' point is that it has always been impossible to craft an antislavery agenda rooted in the Bible: "Noll offers the arresting argument that a faulty hermeneutic imposed severe rigidity on both proslavery and antislavery theologians and that peculiarly American conditions prevented a turn to the alternative hermeneutics offered by African Americans, Catholics, and certain Reformed Protestants. Noll's illuminating discussion clarifies much, but does not demonstrate how any of the alternatives could ground antislavery Christian doctrine in Scripture." See Elizabeth Fox-Genovese and Eugene D. Genovese, *The Mind of the Master Class: History and Faith in the Southern Slaveholders' Worldview* (Cambridge: Cambridge University Press, 2005), 526–7.

Molly Oshatz pushes the debate further. Implicitly, she agrees with the Genoveses. Her essay "The Problem of Moral Progress: The Slavery Debates and the Development of Liberal Protestantism in the United States," *Modern Intellectual History* 5 (2008): 225–50, and book, *Slavery and Sin: The Fight against Slavery and the Rise of Liberal Protestantism* (New York: Oxford University Press, 2011) show how northern Protestants' inability to ground their antislavery claims in Scripture led to the rise of theological innovation and the concept of "moral progress," which gave rise to theological liberalism. However, Oshatz is careful to distance herself from both the projects of Noll and the Genoveses in "The Problem of Moral Progress," 227n5, where she contends: "Noll's focus on hermeneutical and moral failure, and the Genoveses' disparaging characterization of the incipient liberalism of antislavery Protestants, do not account for the ways in which the slavery debates necessitated theological innovation."

Charles Irons comes at the issue from a different direction and focuses primarily on the role of race. He argues that Noll is right about the white Protestants' "faulty hermeneutic," which is most blatantly obvious to Irons in proslavery whites' racialized readings of the biblical texts. Although they claimed to be reading Scripture at face value, the Bible contains no references to race. For Irons, "White evangelicals did not constantly adjust their defense of slavery because they discovered new passages in the Bible or developed new modes of interpretation, but because the terms of their relationship with black evangelicals changed." See Charles F. Irons, *The Origins of Proslavery Christianity: White and Black Evangelicals in Colonial and Antebellum Virginia* (Chapel Hill: University of North Carolina Press, 2008), 16.

32 On the origins of the Curse of Ham and its connection to slavery, see David M. Whitford, *The Curse of Ham in the Early Modern Era: The Bible and the Justifications for Slavery* (Surrey: Ashgate, 2009). Stacy Davis, *This Strange Story: Jewish and Christian Interpretation of the Curse of Canaan from Antiquity to 1865* (Lanham, MD: University Press of America, 2008), also provides a thoroughgoing analysis of the origins of the nineteenth-century racist, proslavery reading of the Curse of Canaan.

The full text of Genesis 9:18–27 reads: "And the sons of Noah, that went forth of the ark, were Shem, and Ham, and Japheth: and Ham is the father of Canaan. These are the three sons

As a pseudonymous "Nannie Grey" contended in a February 1860 *Western Recorder* essay (reprinted from the Richmond, Virginia, *Whig*), God's providential racial design for humanity, set forward in Genesis 9:27, had only recently been fulfilled. The text – "God shall enlarge Japheth, and he shall dwell in the tents of Shem; and Canaan shall be his servant" – contained a direct, prophetic application to American race relations. The North American continent's first peoples, American Indians, "are, undoubtedly, the descendents of Shem." Likewise, Japheth was progenitor of "the Europeans" who had conquered the North American continent and "now dwell in the homes of the Indians." Finally, Canaan's "sons" constituted the population of black slaves. Once, according to Grey, they "lived in the degraded wilds of Africa," but now they had received the "blessing" of becoming the "servant" of Japheth's white offspring – "to be civilized by the enlarged brain of Japheth, for God enlarged him mentally as well as physically." Africa's "miserable inhabitants," Grey argued, had been offered divine provision. Sparing no shortage of abhorrently imaginative racist language, Grey portrayed indigenous Africans to the *Western Recorder*'s white readers as "the thick-lipped, black skinned and wooly headed negro, in a state of barbarism, more degrading than of the brute creation; for he has neither the ingenuity of the beaver, nor the industry of the bee; for he provides neither food nor shelter for himself; but [is] guided by brute instinct alone." The Genesis curse, Grey explicated, had so "literally" and obviously "been fulfilled" that no one could doubt the "truth" the Christian God revealed in "the Bible." Racial distinctions, biblically considered by white religious conservatives in nineteenth-century America, were a providential gift.[33]

Some elite proslavery divines, as one historian has maintained, found such a strained application of the text for racist ends "feeble." But most contemporary southern whites did not. Drawing from a deep religious well of "intuitive racism," proslavery believers read white supremacy directly into the biblical texts they charged their abolitionist enemies with perverting. Relying on their

---

of Noah: and of them was the whole earth overspread. And Noah began to be an husbandman, and he planted a vineyard: And he drank of the wine, and was drunken; and he was uncovered within his tent. And Ham, the father of Canaan, saw the nakedness of his father, and told his two brethren without. And Shem and Japheth took a garment, and laid it upon both their shoulders, and went backward, and covered the nakedness of their father; and their faces were backward, and they saw not their fathers nakedness. And Noah awoke from his wine, and knew what his younger son had done unto him. And he said, Cursed be Canaan; a servant of servants shall he be unto his brethren. And he said, Blessed be the Lord God of Shem; and Canaan shall be his servant. God shall enlarge Japheth, and he shall dwell in the tents of Shem; and Canaan shall be his servant."

[33] Nannie Grey, "The Origin of Slavery," *Western Recorder*, February 25, 1860. Versions of this article circulated through a number of southern newspapers in the period. In addition to its interpretation of African American inferiority, the article's exegesis of the Curse of Canaan was also applied broadly to justify Indian subjugation and, hence, manifest destiny. See William G. McLoughlin and Walter H. Conser Jr., "'The First Man Was Red' – Cherokee Responses to the Debate over Indian Origins, 1760–1860," *American Quarterly* 41 (June 1989): 252.

own commonsense understanding of black inferiority, most whites required no fancy hermeneutical scaffolding to build a racialized theological structure. Simply put, white southerners – as well as many white northerners – were unwilling to accept a Bible that was not racist.[34]

A late March 1861 *Western Recorder* article, also reprinted from the New School Presbyterian, Philadelphia-based, *Christian Observer*, demonstrated this point succinctly: "The descendants of Ham are yet in slavery as God willed it, and they will be so until he changes their condition." The divine division of the races led to a "natural dislike or antipathy in the white race to the black, which prevents the amalgamation of the races." Although racial hostility would not be permanent, it would persist until the end of humanity as the writer knew it, invoking the historic Christian notion of millennial global peace at the end of time "when the Lion and the Lamb lie down together." Until then, however, American slavery, "which is now in a very ameliorated form," served as a socially stabilizing force of Christian benevolence. In this writer's telling, African Americans were an uncontrollable people when left to their own, baser passions. The enslaved were "happy where they are," "restrained by their owners from the vices so common with the free black man in our cities." Those "vices" included a host of the most critical problems facing American urban populations: "details of murders, poisonings, arsons" filled the "daily papers.... Our streets at night swarm with prostitutes, swindling in high and low places, dram-drinking, gambling, and every vice that can be enumerated." Comparatively considered, slavery could not be so bad – after all, the Bible approved of it. The Christian God had offered slavery as a means by which whites could socially control an inferior race unfit, as the example of northern free blacks confirmed, for the responsibility of freedom. Slavery may have been evil, the author opined, but it was certainly "the least of evils."[35]

Obviously, the proponents of abolitionism did not see the matter that way. "This self-righteous and Pharisaic spirit impedes the cause of the church," a pro-southern northern voice contended. By pushing a racially and theologically heterodox agenda, as a like-minded Presbyterian put it, abolitionists ventured to "plunge our happy nation into a fraternal war." Abolitionism "would let

---

34 For the first quote, see Eugene D. Genovese, *A Consuming Fire: The Fall of the Confederacy in the Mind of the White Christian South* (Athens: University of Georgia Press, 1998), 4. On "intuitive racism," see Stephen R. Haynes, *Noah's Curse: The Biblical Justification of American Slavery* (New York: Oxford University Press, 2002), 126. Part and parcel of the Christian proslavery exegesis of the Curse of Canaan as connoting racial difference was a defense of monogenetic accounts of human origins, as explained in the biblical record. Reaching for an explanation of a white-dominated racial hierarchy that also upheld the Genesis record on common human ancestry, the racialized interpretation of the curse proved a convincing narrative. See Colin Kidd, *The Forging of Races: Race and Scripture in the Modern World, 1600–2000* (Cambridge: Cambridge University Press, 2006), 137–51; and David N. Livingstone, *Adam's Ancestors: Race, Religion, and the Politics of Human Origins* (Baltimore: Johns Hopkins University Press, 2008), 180–6.
35 A Christian Father, "Christian Charity," *Western Recorder*, March 23, 1861.

loose the passions and prejudices of men and all the evils which [include] civil war, the slaughter of men and of innocent women and little children." White Kentuckians, long assured of the rationality and importance of neutrality – and equally convinced of abolitionism's syllabus of errors – did not need persuading on this point.[36]

Three days before the secession of South Carolina on December 20, 1860, Duncan Robertson Campbell (1814–65) penned a letter to the *Western Recorder* addressed to a readership broadly defined as the "Christian public, North and South." Campbell, well known to his audience as president of Georgetown College – located in central Kentucky, roughly ten miles north of Lexington and the state's flagship institution of Baptist undergraduate education – did not achieve such a prominent position by holding extremist opinions.[37] His assessment of the sectional crisis was, like that of many white Christians in Kentucky, characteristically moderate. A civil war need not occur, Campbell assured his readership, but it would only be avoided if extreme partisans on both sides of the divide would give up their grievances. Those grievances were manifold, but it was clear from the tone of Campbell's letter that one side had been injured far more than the other. Campbell's prose took up more than three lengthy newspaper columns, and it did offer words of opprobrium for the South's secessionists, whom he saw as inaugurating nothing less than "revolution." That rebuke of disunionists, however, accounted for only a small fraction of the space devoted to condemning the North's "crusade of abuse" of southern patriots.[38]

Southerners charged that "the present troubles originated with the North." By and large, Campbell wrote, they were correct. Because they lived on free soil, northerners "have ungenerously and offensively assumed to themselves a higher grade of moral Christian character." There had been no shortage of "torrents of abuse and insult" from Yankee "pulpits," "platforms," and "presses" in the "last fifteen or twenty years." It was not only the "peculiar institution" of the South that came under attack but "our character also." However, those same northern Christians, the college president argued, needed to consult the Bibles they believed carried so much authoritative value. After a close reading of the text, Yankee believers would have to ask themselves "if the supercilious and proscriptive course" toward abolition, which included much invective "towards Christians at the South, is warranted by the spirit and conduct of Christ and his apostles towards the slaveholders of their day?" On this matter, the slaveholding South could remain assured: the answer was no. Abolitionism drew no "warrant from Scripture." As Hopkinsville educator J. W. Rust, one of the most prominent lay Baptists in Kentucky, claimed, "The

[36] Ibid.; A Christian, "The Bible and Slavery."

[37] For biographical information on Campbell, see J. H. Spencer, *A History of Kentucky Baptists: From 1769 to 1885*, 2 vols. (Cincinnati: J. R. Baumes, 1885), 1:603–4.

[38] D. R. Campbell, "To the Christian Public, North and South. *Must the Union be broken up?*" *Western Recorder*, December 22, 1860.

pulpit at the North" labored under the "pressure of the 'higher law power.'" It had thus become corrupted: "The great *animus* of the Northern pulpit has been hostile, and in constant activity against the institution of slavery in the South." Abolitionism was a heretical disease that had infected northern churches and twisted traditional Christian messages of love into harangues of hate.[39]

According to Campbell, Northerners thus bore the responsibility for "driv[ing] the South to revolution." With the rise of the abolition-minded Republican Party to political dominance in the North, a "section" was now "wholly controlling" national politics with the "single sentiment of antislavery." Thus, as Campbell explained, the South had no recourse, no way to protect its own interests – slavery – but war. The dominant section, the North, held the slave that would heal the nation's deep wounds: they had to "retrace their steps of aggression" and recognize the rights of masters in the South, secured both by the Bible and the U.S. Constitution. Because the abolitionist North had provoked the animosity between the sections, it was the North that needed to repent. After that – and after "a reasonable time" passed – sectional hostility would cease.[40]

Presbyterian Samuel R. Wilson (1818–86) presented a similar argument in a November 1860 sermon on the sectional crisis: "I believe that in this whole affair Northern men have been really the aggressors, and impartial history will so attest." Wilson, pastor of Cincinnati's First Presbyterian Church, claimed his "life-blood" came through "Southern veins," despite being born in the Queen City, having received his education in northern schools, and only holding pastorates to date on free soil. To be sure, Wilson claimed a sizable audience in Kentucky, so much so that he assumed the pulpit of Shelby County's Mulberry Presbyterian Church in 1863 before moving to Louisville's First Presbyterian Church for a thirteen-year pastorate beginning in 1865. Like religiously conservative Kentuckians, Wilson, just north of the slave line, espoused a conservative Unionist viewpoint. The Presbyterian contended that the election of Lincoln, although it was the "*immediate occasion*" of the "present threatening movements in the country," was "not the *cause*." Sectional strife came from a deeper source, rooted in the rampant tripartite American sins of "Pride," "Oppression," and "Lawlessness." No region claimed a monopoly on these wrongs, according to Wilson.[41]

---

[39] Ibid; J. W. Rust, "'My Kingdom is Not of this World.' The Irrepressible Conflict," *Western Recorder*, January 5, 1861. In 1864, Rust assumed the presidency of Hopkinsville's Bethel Female College, a boarding school sponsored by his local Bethel Association of Baptist churches, and in 1869, he became co-owner of the *Western Recorder*. See Spencer, *History of Kentucky Baptists*, 1:727.

[40] Campbell, "To the Christian Public."

[41] Samuel R. Wilson, *Causes and Remedies of Impending National Calamities* (Cincinnati: J. B. Elliot, 1860), 7–11, 16. For biographical information on Wilson, see William Elsey Connelley and E. M. Coulter, *History of Kentucky*, ed. Charles Kerr, 5 vols. (Chicago: American Historical Society, 1922), 3:364–5.

Still, the Ohio minister's message of sectional conciliation tended, like that of his Kentucky coreligionists, to highlight the record of northern wrongs. On southern plantations, there persisted "the degradation and oppression" of the enslaved, of which most Americans had been well informed. Yet "[i]n New England, with the paeans of liberty sounding in his ears, the emancipated slave freezes and starves and sinks into imbecility; and the philanthropy of his boasted Northern friends, having exhausted itself in denunciation of his master, leaves him to the tender mercies of time and chance." In truth, Wilson allowed, "the black man in our midst is subjected to many unjust disabilities." That acknowledgment, however, did not mean that the Cincinnati pastor advocated, as did apostate abolitionists, "either social or civil equality" of the races. Simply, Wilson wanted to point out the hypocrisy of northern immediatist antislavery voices. "The taunting finger," as he put it, "may point to the slave-mart, the whipping-post, and the loose marriage-tie of the slave; and the taunt may be hurled back by an appeal to the pauperism, prostitution, homicides, and divorces of those who, in the philanthropic zeal, have forgotten the admonition of Jesus: 'Judge not, that ye not be judged.'" Southern secessionists, according to Wilson, were guilty of trying to "break up the national Covenant" and could not be lauded for launching a "rebellion" that, if failed, "is treason." In Wilson's telling, however, the South had been provoked by "[a] pulpit teaching the infidel doctrine of a Higher law than God's word residing in the instincts and rational consciousness of man's own soul." If bloodshed were to come from the impending crisis it would be on abolitionist hands.[42]

In an attempt to avoid the mass spilling of American blood, as well as preserve slavery and the Union, Kentucky senator John J. Crittenden (1786–1863) – like much of his constituency, a Constitutional Unionist – proposed to Congress a famously flawed eleventh-hour compromise on slavery in December 1860. Through a series of constitutional amendments, the slave–free line would be set at 36°30′: Deep South states could keep slavery; the Fugitive Slave Act would be more strictly enforced; future states entering the nation could determine for themselves whether or not they wanted slavery; and – according to a final provision – these amendments could not be overturned in the future and Congress could not interfere with slavery. Republicans in both houses of Congress rejected the Crittenden Compromise outright, which smacked overtly of other failed attempts to mollify sections of the country on the slavery question and looked obviously similar to the Missouri Compromise of 1820. Moreover, it did nothing to stave off the secessionist impulse. Two days after Crittenden submitted his proposal for consideration, South Carolina left the Union.[43]

Still, if the Crittenden Compromise proved offensive beyond Kentucky's borders, within the state it seemed the only hope for saving the Union.

[42] Wilson, *Causes and Remedies*, 4, 10, 11, 15.
[43] Harrison and Klotter, *New History of Kentucky*, 185–6.

Particularly among Kentucky's leading religious bodies, neutrality remained the watchword of the day. As right-minded conservatives, Kentucky's religious whites would not follow the path to bloodshed or national destruction. Yet they clearly believed that there were zealots in both the North and South who would.

Robert J. Breckinridge, at that time Kentucky's most prominent Presbyterian cleric – and also the state's most cantankerous – argued in a widely published sermon following South Carolina's secession that warfare would be all but unavoidable "if, the Cotton States, [follow] the example of South Carolina – or the Northern States adher[e] to extreme purposes in the opposite direction." Such insanity was to be avoided at all costs. As was the case with Crittenden, Breckinridge held the "unalterable conviction" that "the slave line is the only permanent and secure basis of a confederacy for the slave States" and "that the union of free and slave States, in the same confederacy, is the indispensable condition of the peaceful and secure existence of slavery."[44]

Similarly, in a late 1861 article in the *Danville Quarterly Review*, the theological journal associated with the Old School Presbyterian Danville Theological Seminary and known for its Unionist tone, Breckinridge contended that the only sure security for American slavery came through a collectively unified nation. Breckinridge's antebellum conservative emancipationism resolutely led him to call for the "whitening" of the Commonwealth. He had long affirmed, on the one hand, a commitment both to the maintenance of white supremacy in Kentucky through the colonization of African Americans in Liberia and, on the other, a version of states' rights doctrine that did not interfere with the interests of slave states farther south. The U.S. Constitution, Breckinridge argued in 1861, had guaranteed the rights of southern slaveholders from its inception. The Union, moreover, which enforced those constitutional assurances, had provided Americans with "more than seventy years of unparalleled prosperity." Given these historical and contemporary political realities, according to the Presbyterian divine, the "madness of the whole secession conspiracy" made little sense. Southerners would leave the Union to protect their right to hold slaves, a right they already enjoyed.[45]

A letter by one of Kentucky's emerging Baptist orators, Henry McDonald (1832–1904), asked in the *Western Recorder*, "Are Christian men prepared for secession and its bitter fruits? What evil will disunion remedy? As men, as patriots, as Christians, let us weigh well what we do. Are any so blind as to suppose that our rights, civil and religious, can live in the engulfing maelstrom of disunion?" No, the state's white religious conservatives maintained, Kentucky

---

44 Robert J. Breckinridge, *Discourse of Dr. Breckinridge Delivered on the Day of National Humiliation, January 4, 1861, at Lexington, KY* (Baltimore: John W. Woods, 1861), 15.
45 Robert J. Breckinridge, "The Civil War: – Its Nature and End," *Danville Quarterly Review* 1:4 (December 1861): 645.

would have no part in the endeavor to wreck the Union. In the sectional crisis, moderation was key.[46]

For religious Kentuckians, these matters were never purely political, nor were they only responding to secular developments. Indeed, much of the context for white Kentucky's religious statements on disunion came from coreligionists elsewhere in the nation. With regard to secession, Kentucky Baptists in particular were acutely aware of developments in Alabama, where the state's Baptist convention endorsed a secessionist resolution at its November 1860 meeting. The Alabama Baptist statement was an almost immediate response to the election of Abraham Lincoln, widely believed in the South to signal an open assault on the southern way of life enshrined in slavery and, thus, cause to break with the North.[47] Writing to a broad audience of Kentucky Baptists, Henry McDonald found such argumentation tenuous at best. Nothing had happened yet, he contended. "The rights of the people are represented as not merely endangered, but destroyed." Yet Lincoln "has not yet assumed the position to which he has been constitutionally elected," nor had he "done one official act, good or bad." The opinions emanating from Baptists farther South could be characterized unambiguously: "Rhetoric, not reason, war, not peace, angry agitation, not conservatism, rule the day." Disunion – and certain warfare to follow – needed to be considered far more carefully by Baptists in the United States, McDonald argued.[48]

Unlike any other nation in world history, McDonald reminded his readers, the United States had afforded Baptists incredible religious liberties. By contrast, "[p]agan, papal, and too often Protestant nations have united to exterminate Baptists." As the historical record showed, "There is hardly a country

---

[46] Henry McDonald, "The Resolution of the State Convention of Alabama Baptists," *Western Recorder*, December 8, 1860. At the time, McDonald was serving as pastor of Greensburg Baptist Church in south central Kentucky. His star would rise considerably in the coming years, when, beginning in 1870, he served (at times contemporaneously) as pastor of Georgetown Baptist Church, professor of theology at Western Baptist Theological Institute, and professor of moral philosophy at Kentucky's Georgetown College. By 1880, he had accepted the pastorate of the Second Baptist Church of Richmond, Virginia, and held a position at Richmond College. From 1882 to 1900 he led the Second Baptist Church of Atlanta and also served as president of the Southern Baptist Convention's Home Mission Board. See Spencer, *History of Kentucky Baptists*, 2:211; and George Braxton Taylor, *Virginia Baptist Ministers*, 5th ser., 1902–14 (Lynchburg, VA: J. P. Bell, 1915), 99–102.

[47] For the broader context on the Alabama Baptist resolution, see Wayne Flynt, *Alabama Baptists: Southern Baptists in the Heart of Dixie* (Tuscaloosa: University of Alabama Press, 1998), 109–13. On broadly southern attitudes toward the election of Lincoln as a rationale for secession, see Charles B. Dew, *Apostles of Disunion: Southern Secession Commissioners and the Causes of the Civil War* (Charlottesville: University of Virginia Press, 2001). One representative opinion, among the many presented by Dew, is that of John Archer Elmore, secession commissioner from Alabama to South Carolina, who on December 17, 1860, argued, "The election of Lincoln [is] 'an avowed declaration of war upon the institutions, the rights and the interests of the South'" (p. 27).

[48] McDonald, "Resolution of the State Convention of Alabama Baptists."

in Europe but what has drunk the blood of Baptists, and kindled the fires of persecution against us." In the divinely favored United States, however, "True soul freedom, the yearning of every Baptist heart, and for which we have so nobly suffered, is now realized." "In no other land," McDonald maintained, "is there such fullness of religious freedom." The work of nation-making had been a distinctively Baptist enterprise, as "Baptist blood was shed on every revolutionary battle field." Why, he asked, would American Baptists now choose to "desecrate the land where [our forebears] sleep by destroying what their lives help to purchase?" It was unimaginable to McDonald that his coreligionists elsewhere in the South could forget the labors of such a significant generation from less than a century earlier. Moreover, considered theologically from a Baptist perspective, the Union stood guardian of an essential doctrinal principle: the liberty of believers to practice their variety of faith as they pleased. By dismissing the Union so cavalierly, as Alabama Baptists did in their resolution against the Union, secessionists risked key aspects of their religious lives.[49]

The *Western Recorder*'s editors enthusiastically endorsed Henry McDonald's conservative Unionist article. Indeed, the paper argued, as did McDonald, that Abraham Lincoln's election, however unpopular, provided no just provocation for secession. Even as late as March 9, 1861 – days after Lincoln took the oath of office on March 4 – the Baptist newspaper remained positive in support of the Union. In addition to publishing the full text of the new president's inaugural address, which tried to strike a conciliatory tone toward the South, the paper asserted its viewpoint on the matter: even "though in the estimation of many" civil war was irrepressible, the editors chose "to look on the bright side" and refused to "give up the hope but that all may be well with our whole country." At the time these words appeared in print, however, seven southern states had already exited the Union, and it appeared increasingly less plausible that such longing for peace would be realized in the near term.[50]

Moreover, if the *Western Recorder* was the primary dispenser of Baptist opinion in the Commonwealth, its editors certainly did not speak for all Kentucky Baptists. Just a week after McDonald's December 1860 article appeared in print, the newspaper published an altogether different perspective on "The Crisis" by A. D. Sears (1804–91), a well-known pastor in the southwestern Kentucky town of Hopkinsville. As Sears interpreted the troubles of the day, the nation had been on a collision course since 1845 – the year Baptists split along the Mason-Dixon line over the slavery question and saw the creation of the Southern Baptist Convention. Baptists in the South, who affirmed the biblically sanctioned Christian right of masters to hold slaves, had been pushed far enough throughout the course of the antebellum era. Given "the aggressions upon the institution of slavery, so constantly and violently made by the people of the North," it was no surprise to Sears that "we would reach the present

[49] Ibid.
[50] "Apologies," *Western Recorder*, March 9, 1861.

crisis." Rather, he contended, "The wonder to me is that the people of the South have kept quiet so long." Sears found no "fault" in the action of the Alabama Baptists. "They are not traitors," he asserted. "[W]e should remember that the men of Alabama and South Carolina are but men, and that as men they have been goaded on by the wrongs of the Northern States to a determination to resist aggression, and to defend their rights at all hazards." Any talk of patriotism, Sears argued, ignored the role of "a mad and infuriated sectional party" – apparent to any reader as abolitionist-influenced Republicans – who had forced the hand of southern secessionists.[51]

The question now before citizens of the Bluegrass State, according to the Hopkinsville pastor, was whether or not it would follow the lead of slaveholding states to the South. Kentuckians had a choice. They could "remain silent, and thus lead both the people of the North as well as the South astray." Or, by contrast, Kentucky could take a stand and show that it "would not countenance any attempt to invade the soil of any of the States of the South by Federal troops and that in no event will Kentuckians endorse or sustain measures calculated to involve any of the states in the calamities and horrors of civil war." From Sears' point of view, the choice was plain: "if we are not blind to the spirit of the religion of our Saviour, as well as utterly destitute of all regard to the interests of mankind, we will adopt the latter answer." White Kentucky had not yet made such a decision, but according to Sears, protecting the interests of the white Christian South could not be wrong. Sears did not advocate that Kentucky secede, but he did insist that the state oppose actions to militarily resist the secession of its sister states to the south.[52]

Kentucky never came to officially endorse the southern cause, but Sears otherwise reflected clearly the political opinion of the state's whites. On April 15, 1861, Kentucky governor Beriah Magoffin famously rebuffed Lincoln's call to send 75,000 troops to support the war effort, four militias of which would come from the Bluegrass State. Magoffin minced no words in replying to the president: "I say emphatically, Kentucky will furnish no troops for the wicked purpose of subduing her sister Southern states." Then, a month later, the governor followed with a broadcast declaration of the state's neutrality, opposing the use of any of the "State Guard" for any purpose other than to "prevent encroachments upon [Kentucky's] soil, her rights, and her sovereignty by either of the belligerent parties." The Kentucky militia, he asserted, existed only to "preserve the peace, safety, prosperity, and happiness and strict neutrality of her people." As a matter of official state policy, Kentucky neither supported southern secession nor northern military efforts to reunite the Union.[53]

[51] A. D. Sears, "The Crisis," *Western Recorder*, December 15, 1860. Sears ranked as one of the more prominent Baptist ministers in Kentucky and Tennessee, carrying on an active ministry in the region for more than forty years. See Spencer, *History of Kentucky Baptists*, 1:267–8.

[52] Ibid.

[53] "President Lincoln to Gov. Magoffin," *Western Recorder*, April 20, 1861; "Proclamation of Gov. Magoffin," *Western Recorder*, May 25, 1861. See also Harrison and Klotter, *New History of Kentucky*, 186–9.

For the state's conservative whites, Magoffin's declarations represented the political application of the religious values they steadfastly held. Interpreting the war, which had only just begun, Joseph Otis, editor of the *Western Recorder*, wrote that the paper had "but one mission and that mission is peace." Otis fervently declared himself "loyal to the Union," but refused to take sides in the fight. Explaining his position, Otis asked his readers, "Shall the cause of Christianity be set back a hundred years to appease fanaticism on one hand or build up a sectional administration on the other? Shall the benign influence of Christian America be forever destroyed throughout the world" simply to achieve "political ends?" "Shame," Otis wrote, "on the Christianity which requires the sword to uphold it; and thrice cursed is that nationality which can live only at the cost of their own citizens, immolated upon the altar of sectional bigotry." As a Methodist essayist put it, evangelical northerners and southerners were bound together by a bond that transcended sectional allegiance: their faith. As "the cry for blood, blood, blood, comes from one section and is sent back with terrible defiance by the other, shall we lift up our voice to augment the wrath and swell the fury? By the grace of God, *never*." Neutrality in warfare, thus understood, was an important religious value because it meant refusing to take arms against fellow members of a broader Christian fellowship.[54]

At the same time, however, it remained clear whom white religious Kentuckians blamed for stoking the embers of sectional conflagration. Abolitionists, with their heretical views of Christian truth, could never stake claim to a broader fellowship of the orthodox. Right-thinking believers understood that Christian America had been a divine gift. "[W]e were unwilling," Joseph Otis wrote, summing up the late antebellum political attitude of white religious Kentuckians, "to give our sanction to building up a sectional Christianity, based upon an unrelenting hostility to [the] wise and beneficent institution" of slavery. That is, he could not sanction abolitionism or the political consequences of its principles. After all, slaveholding had been "protected by the Constitution, and blessed and owned of God in the enlightenment and regeneration of many of Africa's sons, who are now heralds of the cross in their benighted fatherland." As religious conservatives in white Kentucky had consistently contended, slavery was a Christianizing force, a quintessential institution for a nation shaped by faith.[55]

The Civil War, brought on by abolitionist agitation, thus threatened the core of Christian America. There was only one solution to the mounting strife, according to Otis. "Christianity, pure and undefiled," was all that could "save our country and once again unite every section in sweet communion." Unfortunately, it seemed to the editor that the moment of Christian influence had

---

[54] Joseph Otis, "WHO WILL WRITE THE CHAPTER?," *Western Recorder*, June 1, 1861; "Our Brethren," *Western Recorder*, June 1, 1861.

[55] Otis, "WHO WILL WRITE THE CHAPTER?"; Otis, "OUR NATION'S GROUND OF HOPE," *Western Recorder*, June 8, 1860.

passed. In allowing the slavery question – which true believers did not agitate – to fuel sectional antagonism, the properly orthodox had compromised their formidable antebellum base of cultural unity and power. Now, however, "a heterogeneous mass, composed of natives and foreigners, and sects of every shade and color, abolitionists, proslavery demagogues, rip-raps, zouaves and infidels" had "assumed a guardianship over the nation." Christian America had been compromised. Otis worried "that the nation's ground of hope, the only palladium of a free people" – white evangelical Christianity – "is forever buried." For the godly in the Commonwealth, the open fighting between sections represented the worst of American life. Because of the war, the nation that had served as the guarantor of Christian values could no longer made such assurances.[56]

For this reason, in June 1861 the *Western Recorder* announced in its pages, "SINK OR SWIM, LIVE OR DIE, SURVIVE OR PERISH, WE ARE OPPOSED TO THIS WAR." That sentiment prevailed broadly in the state throughout the course of the conflict, but Kentucky's political neutrality came to an end in September 1861. At that date, following contentious debate between a Union-minded legislature and a southern-sympathizing but neutral governor, the state's House and Senate passed resolutions against the wishes of Magoffin demanding the removal of Confederate forces that had entered the southwest part of the state. Formalized support for the Union soon followed, and Kentucky remained with the Union throughout the course of the war. A sizable group of secessionists did hold conventions in Russellville in October and November 1861; those meetings led to the organization of a provisional Confederate government in Bowling Green in October 1861, but it operated ineffectually for the next year and only under the protection of the nearby Confederate army. When Confederate forces withdrew from Kentucky the next year, after the battle of Perryville in October 1862, Confederate Kentuckians had to rule from beyond state lines and did so with little consequence. Despite its official Unionism, Kentucky retained a visible minority of Confederate sympathizers within its borders and sent between 25,000 and 40,000 volunteer soldiers to fight for the South. However, more than three times that number fought for the Union – including, after the landmark Union decision in early 1864 to enlist black troops, more than 23,000 once-enslaved African Americans who fought for their own freedom and that of their dependents – and the state continued to be dominated politically by conservative Unionists.[57]

By the summer of 1861, no one in the Commonwealth was certain of the future the Civil War would bring. Yet war had come, and from the perspective of conservative white religionists in the state, it was an unwelcome presence. They were confident that the fighting, which had only just begun, had

[56] Otis, "OUR NATION'S GROUND OF HOPE"; Otis, "WHO WILL WRITE THE CHAPTER?"
[57] Harrison and Klotter, *New History of Kentucky*, 179–80, 190–5.

irreparably sundered Christian America – the only viable basis for North–South unity. But in point of fact, they argued, it was abolitionism that was responsible for the initial breach.

Conservative Kentuckians had long held antipathy toward those radicalized northern opponents of slavery whom they believed created the tension between the sections – and they carried that belief with them in the coming years. As the war progressed and turned from a war to preserve the Union to a war to abolish slavery, white Kentuckians grew increasingly convinced that their antebellum fears of an abolitionist threat were being realized. The religious interpretation of the righteousness of slavery and the inequality of the races, developed and in place before emancipation, thus provided a compelling narrative by which white religious Kentuckians could remain neutral in language and support the preservation of the Union on Christian slaveholding grounds – even as they sided socially and culturally with the South. Thus white evangelicalism also drove the developments that were to come in the postbellum years, when white Kentucky ultimately embraced a Confederate memory of the war.

5

Competing Visions of Political Theology

Kentucky Presbyterianism's Civil War, 1861–1862

> It is easy to say that [disloyalty to the Union] is *political* – all this difficulty is *personal*. . . . On the contrary, it is *sin*. It is heresy and schism in the Church; it is conspiracy and treason in the commonwealth; it is malice, and false witness, and hatred, and envy, against God's children. It is sin – *grievous sin*. And God will require it of his servants, and will exact it both of the Church and State – if the leaders in such sins go uncensored and unpunished.
>
> – *Danville Quarterly Review*, June 1862[1]

In early March 1862, noted Old School Presbyterian polemicist Robert J. Breckinridge published an article in the Louisville *Journal* soliciting subscriptions for the *Danville Quarterly Review*. Conditions were dire for the fledgling theological journal. Founded just more than a year earlier by Breckinridge and an "association" of eleven like-minded ministers, the publication was connected to central Kentucky's Danville Theological Seminary and Centre College, both aligned with the Old School Presbyterian Church. In early 1862, however, five members of the editorial board – Stuart Robinson, Thomas A. Hoyt, John H. Rice, Robert L. Breck, and J. M. Worrall – had left the *Review* under protest. Now, the publisher, Richard H. Collins – closely connected with the departed editors – refused to continue printing the journal and would not release the mail book that contained the names of subscribers. According to Breckinridge, the departure of the editors and publisher could be explained straightforwardly: "they were secessionists" who disapproved of Breckinridge and the *Review*, which, in a number of articles, had overtly and consistently advocated Unionism over the past year.[2]

[1] "The Late General Assembly of 1862, of the Presbyterian Church in the United States of America," *Danville Quarterly Review* 2.2 (June 1862): 370.
[2] Robert J. Breckinridge, "The Danville Review," Louisville *Journal*, March 5, 1862, Stuart Robinson scrapbook, Stuart Robinson Papers, Box 1, The Filson Historical Society, Louisville. Also

Breckinridge's brief article achieved a twofold purpose. For the short term, it secured the *Danville Quarterly Review*'s solvency. Yet much more significantly, it inaugurated a theological war among Kentucky Presbyterians over two competing ideas about the relationship of the church to the state. For Breckinridge's perspective only represented one side of the story. Within days of the initial article, responses from several of the former *Review* editors appeared, all of whom disavowed secessionist sympathies. As Covington, Kentucky, minister J. M. Worrall argued, "I have never done, or left undone, anything...that ought subject me to the epithet of 'Reverend Secessionist,' or any other kind of Secessionist."[3] More vociferously, Stuart Robinson – popular pastor of Louisville's Second Presbyterian Church, a proponent of emancipation in the late 1840s canvass, and a late 1850s colleague of Breckinridge at Danville Theological Seminary – who would soon emerge as Breckinridge's foremost opponent, retorted that "Dr. B.'s charges, and infatuations" were "wholly untrue." Continuing, he pressed further: "As to the unworthy cry of 'secessionist,' I know of no ground for Dr. B.'s charge, except that I do not concur in Dr. B.'s despotic and intolerant spirit, nor in his Jacobinal contempt for courts' and judges' decisions, nor in his judgment of the ability and importance of his articles, in which I have discovered few important ideas."[4] Robinson, Worrall, and the former editors may have disagreed with the tone of the *Danville Quarterly Review*'s Unionist stance, but that, they argued, did not make them disloyal to the United States.

Rather, they maintained deeper reasons for their dissent. First, they contended that Breckinridge had moved the *Review* away from its initial terms of incorporation. As Thomas A. Hoyt explained, when the *Review* was founded in October 1860, weeks before the November 6 election of Abraham Lincoln to the U.S. presidency, "no one dreamed of a theological review plunging into the arena of party politics." Hoyt, along with the other *Review* expatriates, acknowledged that the journal's founding principles allowed any of the editors "to publish whatever he chose."[5] But the *Review* also called for a "prohibition of direct controversy...between its different contributors."[6] In the very first issue of the publication in March 1861, Breckinridge had opted to publish a militantly Unionist article and, knowing he advocated a debatable position,

published verbatim in Breckinridge, "In Memoriam. A Tribute to the Rev. Stuart Robinson: With Notices of the Rev. J. M. Worrall, the Rev. T. A. Hoyt, the Rev. R. L. Breck, and some others," *Danville Quarterly Review* 2.1 (March 1862): 140–2.
3 J. M. Worrall, "Danville Review," Cincinnati *Gazette*, n.d., Stuart Robinson scrapbook.
4 Stuart Robinson, "Dr. Breckinridge and the Danville Review Again," Louisville *Journal*, n.d., Stuart Robinson scrapbook. Robinson also reprinted the article in his newspaper, see "Dr. Breckinridge and the Danville Review Again," *True Presbyterian*, April 3, 1862.
5 Thomas A. Hoyt, "Rev. Dr. Breckinridge's Card," Louisville *Bulletin*, n.d. (March 7, 1862), Stuart Robinson scrapbook.
6 "Explanatory Note," *Danville Quarterly Review* 1.1 (March 1861): ii.

asked his fellow editors to contribute a dissenting essay. Rather than create tension among editors in the pages of the *Review*, Robinson and Hoyt claimed they chose to live up to the original terms of agreement, avoid controversy, and opted to leave the journal. John H. Rice, J. M. Worrall, and Robert L. Breck soon followed.[7]

The point of division, however, could not so easily be reduced to a fight about the *Review*'s original principles. Much more fundamentally and much more critically, the former editors rejected the sort of Unionist political theology advocated by Breckinridge and the journal. J. M. Worrall denied that he ever "tried to dispense the Gospel" of "Jeff. Davis, or the Cincinnati Gazette, or any other so fallible guides." No, Worrall argued, he simply followed his "best understanding of the sacred Word of God."[8] In Stuart Robinson's language, "there is an important difference between Dr. B.'s views and my own, but one with which 'secession' has nothing to do." Robinson had "for years" believed, "taught, and practiced the doctrine that Ministers of the Gospel, Professors of Theology, and teachers of religion generally have no right to use a position given by the church to inculcate political dogmas, either Northern or Southern." The "confounding" of the distinction between the "spiritual and secular" was "the great bane of religion and of the church."[9] When politics and religion were too closely mingled, the *Review*'s former editors argued, the true faith suffered. Breckinridge and the *Danville Quarterly Review* had shown no respect for this principle. As a result, the departed editors could no longer endorse or participate in the journal's efforts.

It was the beginning of a division over religion and politics that would only get wider. On one side were those led by Breckinridge and affiliated with the *Review* – those committed to the northern-based Old School Presbyterian Church in the United States of America, which throughout the course of the Civil War expressed manifestly nationalist statements of loyalty to the U.S. government. Against this stance, Stuart Robinson was by far the most prominent voice of opposition. Along with his fellow *Danville Quarterly Review* expatriates, Robinson deployed a conscientiously theological argument about the relationship between church and state, arguing that the church was a wholly "spiritual" institution that could not speak to matters of politics. For one party the greater sin was rending church and nation. For the other it was mixing politics and religion. Over the course of the Civil War, hostility among Kentucky Presbyterians over these two visions of political theology increased exponentially.

It was no minor internecine squabble. Indeed, during the Civil War, Kentucky became the site of a major debate over the relationship between church and state that had significant implications for future interactions

---

[7] Hoyt, "Breckinridge's Card"; Robinson, "Breckinridge and the Danville Review."
[8] Worrall, "Danville Review."
[9] Robinson, "Breckinridge and the Danville Review."

between religion and American politics. Ideas have never been formulated in cultural, political, or social isolation. In the context set by the American Civil War, Kentucky's Presbyterians found answers to questions of loyalty and disunion to the United States – as well as answers to closely related questions about the righteousness of slavery – in the realm of ecclesiological debate. The answers they reached did not simply divide Kentucky Presbyterians into feuding camps. Unlike the state's Methodists and Baptists, the majority of whom were already affiliated with southern sectional denominations as a result of divisions over slavery in 1844 and 1845, the Old School Presbyterians – the most populous form of American Presbyterianism – remained united across sectional boundaries until late 1861. As Kentucky Presbyterians sorted out their sectional loyalties along theological lines, the intrastate debate spilled into the General Assembly – the highest, nationwide, ruling body of the Presbyterian Church. In the postwar years, the controversy ultimately fractured the Synod of Kentucky, with the majority of the state's presbyteries leaving the Unionist denomination for the Southern Presbyterian Church by 1869. Thus, for Bluegrass Presbyterians, theological answers to questions about Union or secession proved decisive in setting the tone for the future of American Presbyterianism.

But these Civil War debates established even more than that. In a much broader sense, they also paved the way for the future shape of American religious engagement with political matters, and not only for Presbyterians. If Kentucky's Methodists and Baptists did not fight among themselves over political theology, the answers reached by Bluegrass Presbyterians about the relationship between religion and politics nonetheless spoke to opinions widespread among the state's – and the South's – influential white Protestant denominations in the wake of the Civil War. Kentucky Presbyterianism's civil war thus underscores the broad factors that prompted white Kentucky's ideological embrace of the Confederacy after the fact.

Robert J. Breckinridge and his cohort of Unionist Presbyterians retained a robustly providential view of the United States' place in world history. Such a conviction resonated broadly with a theological understanding of the church's relationship to the state that had persisted north of the Mason-Dixon line, inherited from seventeenth-century Puritans. For many northern Protestants, the Civil War represented the culmination of a millenarian vision, a necessarily violent hurdle to be cleared before inaugurating an age of peace and ultimate divine favor upon the American people. Because the slaveholding South rejected the providentially ordained United States by seceding, the Protestant North, understanding itself as participating in a divine covenant with the Christian God, believed that the rebellious elements of society required eradication in an "American Apocalypse," as one historian memorably put it. It was this sort of vision that led Robert J. Breckinridge to write in late 1862 that, although he did not initially desire the sectional conflict, it had come with the promise that "our glorious country, baptized indeed in blood," would be afterward "purged, united, and safe." As a result, Breckinridge and his fellow

Danville Presbyterians remained loyal to the United States until the end of the war.[10]

In the war's early years, that Unionist vision prevailed in white Kentucky. However, Kentucky's border state identity and location also fostered a political-theological understanding of the American nation's place in Christian history that rivaled the post-Puritan ideal. If the Commonwealth claimed adherents to northern-style Protestant theologies of church and state, there were also those in Kentucky who followed political theologies regnant in more southern locales.

White Protestant theology, as several decades of careful scholarly analysis has established, was foundational to the making of Confederate identity. When the Confederate States of America ratified its constitution in March 1861, the southern document – in sharp contrast to the nonsectarian and religiously neutral U.S. Constitution – signaled to all readers that the new nation was "invoking the favor and guidance of Almighty God." Like northerners, white southerners developed the belief that they were a chosen people who participated in a covenantal relationship with God. From this southern religious perspective, the Confederate cause – and the war in its name – was a Christian one. White southerners entered the Civil War convinced that God was on their side.[11]

Yet that politicized understanding of white southern religion was a departure from historic patterns. For at least a century, dating to the colonial era, southern evangelicals had refrained from wielding religion in direct political engagement, believing the church to be a purely spiritual institution that should not meddle with the purely secular affairs of state. That pervasive southern Protestant doctrine, which achieved its fullest articulation as the "spirituality of the church" (or nonsecularity of the church), was implicitly proslavery: it asserted that the church's proper role was to aid in the saving of souls and the cultivating of individual piety, not to work for the Christianization of society at large. In other words, white southerners could be certain of slavery's morality because of the institution's biblical foundation. As a result, they argued, churches ought not haggle over and meddle with the legality of slavery. It was a righteous institution, but as a legal matter was best left to the state. Shifting definitions of the "political" rendered a commitment to the spirituality of the church somewhat arbitrary in practice, but that does not change the fact that many white southerners nonetheless insisted that they lived by the doctrine.

[10] See James H. Moorhead, *American Apocalypse: Yankee Protestants and the Civil War* (New Haven: Yale University Press, 1978); Robert J. Breckinridge, "Negro Slavery and the Civil War," *Danville Quarterly Review* 2.4 (December 1862): 686.

[11] See Drew Gilpin Faust, *The Creation of Confederate Nationalism: Ideology and Identity in the Civil War South* (Baton Rouge: Louisiana State University Press, 1988), 22; Mitchell Snay, *Gospel of Disunion: Religion and Separatism in the Antebellum South* (1993; Chapel Hill: University of North Carolina Press, 1997); and Harry S. Stout, *Upon the Altar of the Nation: A Moral History of the Civil War* (New York: Viking, 2006), 47–52.

"Spirituality" was always a belief fraught with tension, but in a United States that constitutionally affirmed the rights of slaveholders, that tension remained sublimated.[12]

However, with the rise of more aggressive antislavery activism in the 1830s and the rhetorical attacks on southern society that followed, southern Protestants became increasingly vocal about supposedly secular political affairs. Slavery, the bedrock of antebellum white southern society, was ordained of God. It was not the South that had erred, but the North, which southerners believed ignored the plain, commonsense, literal teaching of the Bible about slavery. Thus, the election of Abraham Lincoln to the U.S. presidency in November 1860 proved decisive in securing southern religious support for the Confederacy. White southerners convinced of the righteousness of slavery came to believe that an abolitionist conspiracy had taken over the American government. In 1861 the evangelical South suddenly laid claim to the same sort of politicized religious identity that had persisted in the Protestant North for more than two centuries.[13]

In the border slave state of Kentucky, however, the pattern was slightly different. Without question, evangelical whites denounced abolitionism with ubiquitous vigor. However, because the slaveholding state had not entered the war on the side of the Confederacy, many in the Commonwealth retained the older southern Protestant understanding of the relationship between church

[12] Much historiographic debate has surrounded the "spirituality of the church" doctrine, its sources, and its legacy. Jack Maddex, "From Theocracy to Spirituality: The Southern Presbyterian Reversal on Church and State," *Journal of Presbyterian History* 54 (1976): 438–57, has argued that the Presbyterian idea of the church's "spirituality" was a particular postbellum innovation, but other historians tend to disagree in varying ways. Several historians contend that the Civil War–era doctrine drew from historic roots in colonial America. For example, see Preston D. Graham Jr., *A Kingdom Not of this World: Stuart Robinson's Struggle to Distinguish the Sacred from the Secular during the Civil War* (Macon, GA: Mercer University Press, 2002), 169–73; James Oscar Farmer Jr., *The Metaphysical Confederacy: James Henley Thornwell and the Synthesis of Southern Values* (Macon, GA: Mercer University Press, 1986), 256–60; and John B. Boles, *The Irony of Southern Religion* (New York: Peter Lang, 1994). For the most recent and cogent explanation for the complex series of ecclesiological negotiations that led white southern evangelicals to arrive at the "spirituality of the church" stance in the post-Revolutionary era, see Charles F. Irons, *The Origins of Proslavery Christianity: White and Black Evangelicals in Colonial and Antebellum Virginia* (Chapel Hill: University of North Carolina Press, 2008), 55–96, esp. p. 66.

[13] On the transformation of a historically apolitical southern religion to politicization on slavery and the sectional crisis, see Boles, *Irony of Southern Religion*. Analyzing the emergence of religious Confederate rituals in Richmond, Virginia, Harry Stout and Christopher Grasso compellingly explain the transformation in white southern church–state ideas: "Where the Puritans had taken two generations to invent a rhetoric of nationhood and war around the ritual convention of the fast and the thanksgiving day, the Confederacy would achieve it in a year, and it would grow thereafter until the very last battles were lost." Stout and Grasso, "Civil War, Religion, and Communications: The Case of Richmond," in *Religion and the American Civil War*, eds. Randall M. Miller, Harry S. Stout, and Charles Reagan Wilson (New York: Oxford University Press, 1998), 320.

and state. Thus, the 1862 *Danville Quarterly Review* controversy exposed a rift between two competing visions of political theology. The years 1861 and 1862 represented only the beginning of hostilities in a fight that would not be resolved until well after the Civil War itself ended.

If the 1862 quarrel over the *Danville Quarterly Review* exposed a rift between rival political theologies, signs of fracture had been visible, as former *Review* editors noted, for more than a year. On January 4, 1861, Breckinridge ascended a pulpit in his native Lexington to preach on the growing sectional crisis. Calling for humility and repentance for national sins, Breckinridge hoped that armed conflict might be avoided. "These are but the beginning of sorrows," he exhorted. "If we desire to perish, all we have to do is leap into this vortex of disunion. If we have any conception of the solemnity of this day, let us beseech God that our country shall not be torn to pieces."[14] Elsewhere, the minister lashed out at the "spirit of lawlessness and anarchy" running rampant in both North and South. Whether in the form of radical abolitionism and its "systematic and persistent agitation connected with the Black Race" or southern secessionism's inane pretension to "obstruct the execution of the laws of the United States" and "nullify them absolutely," both extremes were marked by the same "universal tendency to disintegrate all things."[15]

The message may have been one for a nation careening toward civil war, but Breckinridge fashioned it singularly for his Kentucky audience. He argued that Kentucky and other states along the border of the "slave line" held the key to preserving national unity. He believed it was those states – the free states of Ohio, Indiana, Illinois, Pennsylvania, and New Jersey, along with the slave states of Maryland, Delaware, Virginia, Kentucky, and Missouri – that were most politically moderate. The border states rejected "the passionate violence of the extreme South" and refused to follow "the turbulent fanaticism of the extreme North." Breckinridge minced no words: it would be "suicidal" to embrace secession and deviate from the moderate course. The minister had one main argument: "the chief aim... should be the preservation of the American Union, and therein of the American nation."[16] It was a goal to be pursued at all costs.

To be sure, there would be costs. Breckinridge recounted the flashpoints in the recent American history of turmoil over slavery and politics: "the unjust, offensive, and unconstitutional enactments by various [northern] State Legislatures" in refusing to cooperate with the 1850 Fugitive Slave Act; the Supreme

[14] Robert J. Breckinridge, *Discourse of Dr. Breckinridge, Delivered on the Day of National Humiliation, January 4, 1861, at Lexington, KY* (Baltimore: John W. Woods, 1861), 4. For other sermons on the sectional crisis, see *Fast Day Sermons: Or the Pulpit on the State of the Country* (New York: Rudd & Carelton, 1861).

[15] Robert J. Breckinridge, "Our Country – Its Peril – Its Deliverance," *Danville Quarterly Review* 1.1 (March 1861): 74–5.

[16] Breckinridge, *Discourse of January 4, 1861*, 2, 14. Though farther south, Breckinridge also included Tennessee and North Carolina as "moderate" states that he hoped would not join the secession effort.

Court's decision in the Dred Scott case (1857), which had attempted "to settle" once and for all the status of slavery's legality and, in so doing, led to the "repeal of the Missouri Compromise"; the "conduct of the Federal Government and of the people in Kansas," where through vigilantism they attempted to resolve slavery's fate; "the total overthrow of the Whig and American [Know-Nothing] parties, the division and defeat of the Democratic party, and the triumph of the Republican party"; and, lastly, the "secession of South Carolina." In spite of these travails, Breckinridge contended, there remained "no justification for the secession of any single State of the Union – none for the disruption of the American Union." People needed to bury their "unhallowed passions" and the "fanaticism of the times." The different sections of the country were distinct, and Breckinridge saw no "reason why States with slaves and States without slaves, should not abide together in peace . . . as they have done from the beginning." Such forbearance, however, required personal sacrifice.[17]

In the name of Union, Breckinridge seemed willing to make such sacrifices. Significantly, those sacrifices included his earlier antislavery stance. Although the cleric never repudiated his career of antislavery activity, with the sectional crisis impending he did subtly alter his position. Up until the start of the Civil War, no religious Kentuckian more clearly embodied the complexities and contradictions of white Border South ideology than Robert J. Breckinridge. The slaveholding Presbyterian spent more than three decades arguing for a program of gradual emancipation. The approach was conservative to the core, focusing primarily on the interests of Kentucky's white population and rejecting all calls by abolitionists for an immediate end to the institution. Yet by early 1861, Breckinridge sought to bracket the discussion of slavery with hopes of allaying sectional strife and thus preserving the Union. It was an approach that, if inconsistent with his antebellum politics, followed a similar ideological trajectory. The minister had long denounced "extreme" approaches to the slavery issue, and in that respect his views never changed – to fight a civil war over slavery would be the very definition of extreme.

Still, in January 1861 he admitted that he "[knew] of no way" that "slavery" in the "Cotton States" could "be dealt with at all."[18] Breckinridge had long defended a form of states' rights doctrine, and this statement reflected that position. At the same time, it also spoke to Breckinridge's conservative Presbyterian theological view of the world, which assumed that human individuals and societies were inescapably corrupted by sin and thus forced to employ some form of social stratification. As he wrote in an essay just a few months later, slavery was "utterly incapable of being permanently and universally abolished" so long as humanity "continues in a state of sin and misery." Slavery itself was amoral in the same way that "sickness" – "the product of God's just sentence of death upon our sinful race" – was amoral. "Sorrow and affliction are brought

---

[17] Breckinridge, *Discourse of January 4, 1861*, 9.
[18] Ibid., 12–13.

on us in innumerable forms," Breckinridge wrote. Directly put, he offered "the simple, the rational, and the scriptural account of human servitude." The idea that one could escape slavery or, at the very least, an unequal division of labor and society, was, theologically considered, incomprehensible.[19]

Along with political and theological motives for muting his opposition to slavery in 1861, Breckinridge added racist reasons. The Presbyterian's white supremacy had always loomed at the forefront of his antebellum antislavery arguments. On the eve of the Civil War, Breckinridge also invoked white trepidation about blacks in the name of preserving the Union. He put the question to his audience: "Do you want some millions of African cannibals thrown amongst you broadcast throughout the whole slave States?"[20] Shortly thereafter, the minister wrote in a Unionist *Danville Quarterly Review* essay that "the only infallible rule of conduct, God's blessed Word," spoke against the kind of radicalism – "upon which the public mind has been lashed into madness" – that had infected the North and South. White Americans should be worried about the "triumph" of an "anarchical spirit," Breckinridge wrote. If "this nation is destroyed," the country's whites would have to deal with "the real problem": a war over slavery would force "the cotton region of this continent" to decide whether "the ultimate dominion of the white race" would prevail or if "a mixed race essentially African" would come to rule. "Is the inaugurating of that problem worth the ruin of this great nation?" Civil war over the question of slavery would no doubt prompt a dialogue on race that Breckinridge knew his white readers, comfortable like him in their racial superiority, were not willing to have.[21]

Breckinridge never moved toward a direct, explicit endorsement of American slavery, but for Unionism's sake he edged closer than ever before toward endorsing some form of a proslavery position. Indeed, it was just that kind of white supremacist argument that motivated the southern secessionists to abandon the Union for the Confederacy.[22] The development was not lost on critics. Benjamin Morgan Palmer (1818–1902), a prominent New Orleans Presbyterian cleric, one of the South's leading champions of slavery, and a hardened secessionist, responded to Breckinridge's 1861 ideas with surprise and approval. The Kentuckian who had once argued that slavery was "inconsistent with a state of sound morality" now made assertions congruent with the proslavery position "held by Christian men throughout the South for many years." In point of fact, Breckinridge's shifting opinion on slavery reflected less hypocrisy than a realignment of his religio-political priorities. In that moment of sectional crisis, when strife over slavery threatened to destroy the nation that

[19] Breckinridge, "Our Country," 92–3.
[20] Breckinridge, *Discourse of January 4, 1861*, 13.
[21] Breckinridge, "Our Country," 94.
[22] See Charles B. Dew, *Apostles of Disunion: Southern Secession Commissioners and the Causes of the Civil War* (Charlottesville: University Press of Virginia, 2001).

Breckinridge believed was uniquely favored by the Christian God, he privileged the Union over gradual emancipation. Nevertheless, to Palmer, it was "a sign of progress" in Breckinridge's Christian thought. Proslavery believers should "have no strictures to make upon his present exposition of negro slavery," Palmer maintained. Breckinridge's current view was "condemned neither by the clear teachings of revelation on the one hand, nor by the confused utterances of the law of nature on the other."[23]

Breckinridge, however, had not attempted to curry favor from divines like Palmer, rejecting as he had the "fanaticism" of secessionist excitement – and Palmer did not miss the point. If the Kentuckian won support from proslavery ranks for his religious and racial orthodoxy, his strident Unionism spoiled whatever goodwill he had acquired. "The cloak of the philosopher," Palmer inveighed, "has been too scant to hide the burly form of the partisan." Breckinridge "pours forth his defamatory charges upon the seceding States with a wealth of expression only at the command of this great mast of the English tongue." Palmer, proving every bit Breckinridge's polemical equal, continued: "Anarchy, disloyalty, revolt, revolution, rebellion, fanaticism, sedition, form the alphabet of an almost exhaustless invective, which, by endless transposition and iteration, make up a description so hideous that its very deformity should prove it a caricature." As he agreed with Breckinridge's theological and racial view of slavery, so Palmer also endorsed the Kentuckian's depiction of abolitionism as the radical harbinger of chaos. Yet he saw no ground for secession to be "lashed together" with the "Abolitionism of the North." Secessionism, far from the fanatical crusade depicted by Breckinridge, was largely a conservative movement led by southerners committed to a true application of the U.S. Constitution. Writing just before the April 12, 1861, Confederate attack on Fort Sumter that started the Civil War, Palmer contended that any rational person knew what was happening in the Charleston harbor: the federal fortification of the fort "meant" northern "coercion" of the South. To Palmer, the message was clear. The "imbecile and treacherous Government" of the North "could not be trusted." In such a political situation, secession was not rash: it was the only proper course of action.[24]

The political realities of southern disunion and military confrontation with the United States were not immediately manifest in the Old School Presbyterian Church. Although theological differences of opinion on slavery undeniably contributed to the 1837–8 Old School–New School Presbyterian schism, that division was not clearly sectional. A few southern presbyteries initially joined the New School, but in the next decade agitation over slavery proved too much stress for the denomination. In 1857 the New School condemned slaveholding as sinful, prompting twenty-one southern and border state

[23] Benjamin Morgan Palmer, "A Vindication of Secession and the South," *Southern Presbyterian Review* 14 (April 1861): 142–3.
[24] Ibid., 144–5, 158–9.

presbyteries – containing approximately 15,000 members – to leave the denomination, making the New School a wholly northern denomination. At the same time a tenuous alliance, comprised of both southern and northern churches, preserved the Old School Presbyterian Church USA until the start of the Civil War.[25]

Thus, even though some Confederate clergy advocated Presbyterian denominational schism, the impact of the war on ecclesiastical relations remained unclear in the first few months of 1861. All that changed after the May meeting of the Presbyterian Church USA's General Assembly in Philadelphia. Slave state Presbyterians, who accounted for roughly a third of all American Presbyterian communicants, were conspicuously absent at the meeting, with more than half of all southern presbyteries (33 of 64) unrepresented. Still, representation was strong from the Border South states that had remained with the Union: the Kentucky and Missouri synods sent representatives from every presbytery (six of six and five of five, respectively), whereas the Baltimore and Upper Missouri synods each only lacked representation from one presbytery (four of five and three of four, respectively).[26]

As expected, the General Assembly called for a statement on the sectional crisis. With representation from the Confederate states weak, it overwhelmingly approved a starkly nationalist declaration. Known as the "Spring Resolutions," they were named for the minister who proposed the statement, New York City's Gardiner Spring (1785–1873). Like Breckinridge, Spring had long opposed abolitionism, but he also ardently supported the national government. The Spring Resolutions had two parts. The first called for a "day of prayer" on July 1, 1862, when Presbyterian clergy and laity were to "humbly confess and bewail our national sins; to offer thanks to the Father of light for his abundant and undeserved goodness toward us as a nation; to seek his guidance and blessing upon our rulers and their counsels, as well as on the Congress of the United States." These prayers were to be uttered with the hope that the Christian God might "turn away his anger from us, and speedily restore to us the blessings of an honorable peace."[27]

Spring's second resolution built on the nationalism expressed in the first. It noted, "That this General Assembly, in the spirit of that Christian patriotism which the Scriptures enjoin ... do[es] hereby acknowledge and declare our obligations to promote and perpetuate, so far as in us lies, the integrity of these United States." Moreover, the statement asserted, upstanding Presbyterians were "to strengthen, uphold, and encourage the Federal Government in the exercise of all its functions under our noble Constitution," to which they

[25] C. C. Goen, *Broken Churches, Broken Nation: Denominational Schisms and the Coming of the American Civil War* (Macon, GA: Mercer University Press, 1985), 68–78.

[26] See Lewis Vander Velde, *The Presbyterian Churches and the Federal Union, 1861–1869* (Cambridge, MA: Harvard University Press, 1932), 42–5, numbers from p. 43.

[27] Joseph M. Wilson, *The Presbyterian Historical Almanac, and Annual Remembrancer of the Church, for 1862* (Philadelphia: Joseph M. Wilson, 1862), 73. See Vander Velde, *Presbyterian Churches*, 46–87, for extensive discussion of the Spring Resolutions.

had to give their "unabated loyalty." To avoid misconceptions, the resolution clarified that the term "Federal Government" meant the "central administration... prescribed in the Constitution of the United States," which was "the visible representative of our national existence." American Presbyterians did not have the freedom to pick and choose "particular administration[s]" or "the particular opinions of any particular party." No, the nation always required their loyalty, regardless of controversial governmental policy.[28]

The Spring Resolutions only passed after days of debate. Even then, prominent denominational leaders registered significant dissent. Principally, that dissent came from Princeton's Charles Hodge, the most distinguished Presbyterian theologian of the nineteenth century. Hodge's protest conceded that "loyalty to the country" was "a moral and religious duty, according to the word of God, which requires us to be subject to the powers that be," but the Spring Resolutions had demanded far more than loyalty to government. Those Presbyterians in seceded states no longer lived under the authority of the United States. By forcing them to assent to the Spring Resolutions, the General Assembly was, in effect, coercing Confederate Presbyterians to commit treason against their new government. Confederate Presbyterians would be "forced to choose between allegiance to their States and allegiance to the Church." It was a choice they should not have to make. It "violated the Constitution of the Church, and usurped the prerogative of the Divine Master." As Hodge put it in a counter resolution to Spring's, "The General Assembly is neither a Northern nor Southern body; it comprehends the entire Presbyterian Church, irrespective of geographical lines or political opinion." Now, with the Spring Resolutions, political allegiance became a test of membership. That move represented "a departure" from historic Presbyterianism. "The General Assembly has always acted on the principle," Hodge argued, "that the Church has no right to make anything a condition of Christian or ministerial fellowship, which is not enjoined or required in the Scriptures and the Standards of the Church." In previous years, numerous partisans had pushed for authoritative statements on controversial issues such as temperance and slaveholding. The General Assembly, to its credit, had always "resist[ed] these unscriptural demands." In so doing, Presbyterians "preserved the integrity and unity of the Church." A political dilemma as fraught as the sectional crisis was "clearly beyond the jurisdiction of the General Assembly." Political stances did not determine the state of souls and should not become a test of church membership. The Spring Resolutions threatened an already weak relationship between sectional Presbyterians. Hodge's dissent received endorsement from fifty-eight commissioners to the General Assembly, a majority of whom hailed from slave states (34 of 58). That number remained far less than the 156 who affirmed the Spring Resolutions, but the disapproval was worth noting.[29]

---

[28] Wilson, *1862 Presbyterian Historical Almanac*, 73.
[29] Ibid., 70, 76–7. For the sectional breakdown of signers of the Hodge protest, see Vander Velde, *Presbyterian Churches*, 69.

Border State Presbyterians, particularly Kentuckians, met the action of the 1861 General Assembly with stated discontent. By and large, Kentucky Presbyterians voiced their agreement with the Hodge protest. In September 1861 the Presbytery of West Lexington, in language largely composed by Robert J. Breckinridge, denounced the Spring Resolutions. "It is undoubtedly certain," the presbytery argued, "that the General Assembly had no authority, either from Christ or from the Constitution of the Church, to require, or even advise, the tens of thousands of Presbyterians who are citizens" of the Confederate states "to revolt against the actual governments under which they live." Just a few months later, the Synod of Kentucky issued a similar statement, calling it "incompetent" of the "Assembly, as a spiritual court, to require, or to advise acts of disobedience to actual governments." The Synod registered its "grave disapprobation" of the Spring Resolutions and declared them "to be repugnant to the word of God, as that word is expounded in our Confession of Faith." Like Charles Hodge, Kentucky Presbyterians believed the General Assembly acted in error.[30]

Compared to the reaction of Presbyterians in slave states farther south, however, the Kentucky response was staid. Almost immediately after the General Assembly, Presbyterians in Confederate states began pushing for a denominational exodus. On December 4, 1861, the aim was achieved. A number of prominent southern Presbyterians met in Augusta, Georgia, and founded the Presbyterian Church in the Confederate States of America.[31]

Although Kentuckians denounced the decisions of the 1861 General Assembly supporting the Spring Resolutions, denominational schism proved too extreme a solution at that date. Yet Kentucky Presbyterians remained anxious about the action taken by the national governing body. Indeed, it was in response to the 1861 General Assembly that fault lines in Kentucky Presbyterianism began to appear. Yet it was not until the meeting of the 1862 General Assembly that the Kentucky Presbyterians began to choose political-theological sides.

The 1862 national meeting came in the immediate wake of the *Danville Quarterly Review* controversy. Robert J. Breckinridge, who had initiated the war of letters with Stuart Robinson and other former editors of the *Review* by

[30] Reports of the Presbytery of West Lexington and the Synod of Kentucky excerpted in "Jurisprudence, Sacred and Civil. – The published Criticisms on some of the Principles heretofore discussed in the Danville Quarterly Review," *Danville Quarterly Review* 2.1 (March 1862): 170–3. This article in the *Review* appeared as a response to an article in Louisville's *Presbyterian Herald*, which accused the *Review* of coming too close to supporting the Spring Resolutions. The *Review* denounced the *Herald* and endorsed the decisions of the West Lexington Presbytery and Synod of Kentucky. The *Herald*, which was a Unionist, but theologically conservative newspaper – and thus supported the Hodge protest – folded in early 1862. It was purchased by Stuart Robinson, who began publishing the *True Presbyterian* as an outlet for his version of apolitical Christianity.

[31] Vander Velde, *Presbyterian Churches*, 88–102.

calling them secessionists, showed little patience for their denials of national disloyalty. He launched a fiery missive against his former colleagues in the pages of the March 1862 *Review*. Breckinridge reprinted word for word his article from the Louisville *Journal*, which had called for support for the failing theological publication, followed immediately by a verbatim copy of Robinson's reply. In the end, Breckinridge proposed to bring the whole *Danville Quarterly Review* matter before the 1862 General Assembly, so that the divisive issue might be adjudicated. If the church decided in his opponents' favor, he would resign his post at Danville Theological Seminary. Before making that promise, however, Breckinridge delivered an invective so severe that it could have only served to exacerbate tensions among Bluegrass Presbyterians.[32]

Breckinridge argued that the former *Review* editors had, because of their secessionist politics, engaged in a conspiracy to destroy the journal and the unity of national Presbyterianism. Disregarding the clerics' words to the contrary, Breckinridge directed most of his ire toward Robinson, whose "series of insolent and calumnious insinuations, turgid in expression, and sprinkled with few pious words," were "like salt on spoiled meat." Breckinridge had made the truth of his opponent's political loyalty plain; Robinson, when faced with that uncomfortable truth, had "resort[ed] to unworthy subterfuges and evasions." Rather than "honestly owning" his secessionist views, Breckinridge accused Robinson of "interlarding various misstatements of fact" and acting as if the debate between the two divines had something to do with the superiority of Robinson's "high spiritual" theology. In fact, Robinson was a secessionist. Breckinridge said that he had no qualms about admitting he was a "Union man." Why, Breckinridge asked, would Robinson not do the same?[33]

To be sure, Breckinridge knew the answer to that question. Robinson claimed he had long advocated a stark separation of church and state. The claim was not disingenuous. In 1855, Robinson and his colleague Thomas Peck initiated *The Presbyterial Critic and Monthly Review*, a short-lived journal that often advocated nonpolitical Christianity.[34] Then, in 1858, during a brief stint as Breckinridge's colleague at Danville Theological Seminary, Robinson published a widely circulated volume on ecclesiology, *The Church of God*. In that book, Robinson offered a sweeping statement on the theological foundations of the church and argued that the church's "power" was "wholly spiritual," consistent with Jesus Christ's "idea of a kingdom not of this world." The church and state had "nothing in common except that both powers are of divine authority" and "both were instituted for the glory of God." Other than that, Robinson wrote, "they differ fundamentally." The church existed to save souls and dealt with "things unseen and spiritual." The "scope and aim"

[32] Breckinridge, "In Memoriam."
[33] Ibid., 149, 151.
[34] See "Our Idea," *The Presbyterial Critic and Monthly Review* 1:1 (January 1855), in Graham, *A Kingdom Not of This World*, 193–9.

of "civil power," by contrast, pertained only to "things seen and temporal."[35] Moreover, in a well-known 1859 lecture, Robinson praised "the American theory of Church and State," which, enshrined in the U.S. Constitution, kept the institutions separated. Robinson saw himself as a true disciple of the sixteenth-century Protestant Reformation, which rescued true Christianity from "the pagan Rome idea of religion as part of the State." There was a difference between the action of individual believers and those of ecclesiastical bodies. As free citizens in a democratic society, individuals could believe and advocate for whatever causes they wished. However, Robinson argued, "The Church has no right to decree touching civil affairs, nor to teach politics." A mixing of the two only perverted the true church.[36]

The *Danville Quarterly Review* and Breckinridge flatly rejected Robinson's political theology. The church, a *Review* essay argued in response to the Spring Resolutions, is "bound to recognize the state as an ordinance of God; to render to it a true allegiance and obedience." Where Robinson saw the church and state divided under particular offices of the Trinity – the church under Jesus Christ, the redeemer of a "peculiar people"; the state under God, "the author of nature," as a way of ordering of societies "for the preservation of the race" – the *Review* separated the categories far less clearly.[37] It found Robinson's "distinctions" lacked "the least foundation in the word of God."[38] The "church and state," according to the *Review*, "are coordinate jurisdictions under the same divine charter – analogous to the executive, legislative, and judicial departments of government, under the Constitution of the United States." The church had an obligation to act "[w]hen a political question enters the sphere of morals and religion." As such, the contentious 1861 General Assembly erred "not in *speaking*, but in speaking unwisely. The Assembly had a right to make a [political] deliverance; the misfortune is, it made an erroneous one." Like the Synod of Kentucky and the leading denominational light, Charles Hodge, the *Review* rebuked the Spring Resolutions for encouraging rebellion against established governments. The *Review* article, however, refuted the idea that the church existed as a solely spiritual institution, unqualified to pronounce on secular, political measures.[39]

Agreeing with his journal, Breckinridge believed Robinson's nonsecular theory of the church was a grave mistake. But he set the stakes much lower in the 1862 *Danville Quarterly Review* controversy: Robert J. Breckinridge simply did not believe Robinson practiced what he preached. He saw Robinson's

[35] Robinson, *The Church of God as an Essential Element of the Gospel, and the Idea, Structure, and Functions Thereof* (Philadelphia: Joseph M. Wilson, 1858), 84–5.

[36] Stuart Robinson, *The Relations of the Secular and Spiritual Power* (Louisville: Bradley & Gilbert, 1859), 6, 20; Robinson, "Breckinridge and the Danville Review."

[37] Robinson, *Relations of Secular and Spiritual Power*, 20.

[38] "Politics and the Church," *Danville Quarterly Review* 2.4 (December 1862): 629.

[39] E. E., "The Late General Assembly. – Church and State," *Danville Quarterly Review* 1.3 (September 1861): 501, 505, 511.

"endeavor to develop and enforce a higher spiritual life" as nothing more than "a thin varnish of piety over a turbulent spirit," a patina of theological posturing to mask "his schismatical and disloyal schemes."[40] Truth be told, Breckinridge asserted, Robinson had sent him a letter dated January 24, 1861, which offered "three reasons" why Robinson could no longer serve on the *Danville Quarterly Review*'s editorial board. The first two were practical concerns: Robinson saw little hope for the future success of the journal, and it had not secured the number of subscribers it had hoped.[41]

The third reason, however, revealed Robinson's secret political motives. Robinson stated that, although he held "no special sympathy with South Carolina" – which had seceded a month prior – he could not endorse Breckinridge's Unionism. Robinson believed that Kentucky's future, "or rather the least of evils," lay with "a Southern Confederacy." Although Robinson maintained that, "as a minister of the Gospel," he had "studiously avoided becoming partisan on the subject," he simply did "not accept" Breckinridge's "views, in so far as they look hostile to the South." Grandstanding aside, this private letter exposed Robinson's deepest political and theological loyalties. As Breckinridge interpreted for his readers, even if Robinson denied his secessionism, "his best possible defense is, that he did nothing" to help preserve the Union. That was enough. In Breckinridge's dualistic world, there was no defense for removing oneself from politics in the face of a "bleeding country" that "needed" any and all help to ensure its preservation. Robinson's so-called "doctrine" of a non-secular church really meant nothing more than "the treason of his comrades." The issue was black and white: refusal to aid the Union was an endorsement of secession.[42]

It is impossible to know if Robinson actually sent Breckinridge such a letter. Certainly Robinson kept company with some of southern Presbyterianism's most prominent and enthusiastic secessionists, clergy such as Benjamin Morgan Palmer and the venerable James Henley Thornwell of South Carolina. Perhaps, as Breckinridge charged, Robinson meddled in schismatic church politics behind closed doors. Robinson, for his part, flatly denied the charge.[43]

Yet whether or not Robinson ever actually endorsed the Confederacy was not important. Rhetorically Breckinridge had lumped secessionists, pacifists, and neutrals – in general anyone not solidly committed to the future of the national unity of the United States – into one undifferentiated anti-American mass. Those who questioned the Union – or the *Review*, or Breckinridge, or the Presbyterian General Assembly – became enemies. Breckinridge's conduct toward the other *Danville Quarterly Review* editorial expatriates reveals as

---

[40] Breckinridge, "In Memoriam," 154.
[41] Ibid., 154–9.
[42] Ibid.
[43] For Robinson's denial, see Robinson, *An Appeal to the Christian Public, and All with Whom Loyalty is not Madness* (Louisville: Hanna & Co., 1862), 9–10.

much. Presumably, he did not hold the same sort of damning private correspondence from Thomas A. Hoyt, Robert L. Breck, J. M. Worrall, or Richard H. Collins. Yet that did not prevent Breckinridge from going after them with the same sort of aggressive linguistic hostility he displayed toward Robinson.

The case of Breck is particularly telling. A founding member of the *Review*'s editorial board, the Maysville, Kentucky, pastor served the journal throughout 1861. He tendered his resignation when, in late 1861, the rest of the editors rejected unseen an article he wrote attacking President Abraham Lincoln's famously unpopular April 1861 suspension of habeas corpus in Maryland, followed in May by the imposition of martial law to quell dissent in Union areas – decisions notably unpopular to Kentuckians because Maryland, as a border state, shared many social and political characteristics with the Bluegrass. Concerned that Breck's thesis "might appear unfriendly to the action of the General Government," the editors asked Breck to "withhold" the essay until a future date less burdened with "political stress." Breck replied to the *Review* board that, although he did not know what everyone else thought politically, he was no radical and did not suppose his views were "materially different" than those of the other editors. Still, Breck assured his colleagues that he did not seek to disturb the peace among editors. Rather than force the issue, he withdrew his article and left the board. The *Review*'s editors responded that they hoped Breck would stay, but the Maysville minister declined, saying that he wanted to remain on good terms.[44]

Richard H. Collins, the *Review*'s publisher in 1861, did not like the way Breck had been treated. Not only did he decide to stop publishing the *Review* but he also opted to publish Breck's article in pamphlet form as *The Habeas Corpus, and Martial Law* (1862). In his preface, Collins wrote that Breck was "a loyal citizen" of Kentucky and the United States, but that loyalty and patriotism did not demand approval of all government actions. Breck made a straightforward point: it was important to save the Union, but there were certain "inalienable rights" that mattered more than national unity. What, Breck asked, was the Union worth if it did not protect "the great underlying principles of our liberty"? Surveying recent legal writings on the issues, Breck concluded that habeas corpus was the constitutionally guaranteed security against despotism. Revoking it, combined with the declaration of martial law, meant "the enforcement of the arbitrary will" of a "dictator" and signaled the abrogation of fundamental American freedoms.[45]

Breck's pamphlet largely avoided taking sides in the Civil War. But his opinions still raised Breckinridge's antipathy. Throughout the course of the Civil War in Kentucky, there remained a significant number of Confederate

[44] See correspondence between Robert L. Breck and Jacob Cooper, October 29, 1861, November 4, 1861, November 8, 1861, in Robert L. Breck, *The Habeas Corpus, and Martial Law* (Cincinnati: Richard H. Collins, 1862), 5–8.
[45] Ibid., 4, 10, 32.

supporters who opposed any sort of federal intervention in the Bluegrass State. At the same time, Kentucky also claimed a significant number of Unionists who, as loyal citizens of the nation, opposed the governmental suppression of civil rights in the name of perpetuating that Union. It is hard to determine where Breck's loyalties resided in 1861. Breck ended his essay on a cautious note, arguing that the Union was better lost if it meant abandoning the Constitution's guaranteed protection of basic rights. Still, he carefully avoided endorsing the Confederacy. In fact, he turned the words of strident Unionists such as Robert J. Breckinridge around. According to Breck, those who would reject the "supremacy" of the Constitution by suspending habeas corpus were the real traitors.[46]

Breckinridge had no time for such an opinion. By his dualistic rubric, Breck had all but joined the Confederacy. No "loyal man" could "even appear to endorse" Breck's drawing of "the faintest possible line, between loyalty and treason." Breck did not mention Breckinridge by name, but according to the senior cleric, Breck's "attack" was intended to "harm" Breckinridge and the *Danville Quarterly Review*. That was a particularly regrettable development because Breckinridge felt a strong bond of friendship to Breck's family, and Breck himself never received "anything but proofs of respect and affection" from Breckinridge. Still, the doyen of Danville felt the need to issue a warning: Breck was "co-operating" with "men" in "business" that was "[un]worthy of his race, or his former self." Anyone who would attempt to take on the *Danville Quarterly Review* served "directly" the ends of "the detestable secession conspiracy." For Breckinridge, the Union, the *Review*, and the General Assembly of the Presbyterian Church were all constituent parts of the same organism. Battling one meant battling all. And Breckinridge ensured a fight would happen at the 1862 General Assembly.[47]

Stuart Robinson proved more than eager to engage Breckinridge. In early May, a week before the 1862 General Assembly met in Columbus, Ohio, Robinson published a thoroughgoing rebuke of Breckinridge in his newly launched newspaper, the *True Presbyterian*. The newspaper's title spoke to its platform: Robinson wanted a paper that would advocate doctrines on church and state consistent with what he saw as "true" and historic Presbyterianism. The article, republished in pamphlet form in advance of the General Assembly, continued to make Robinson's case against Breckinridge.[48]

The essay added little of theological substance to Kentucky Presbyterianism's fight over political theology. It did, however, offer insights into Robinson's

---

[46] For more on Kentucky attitudes toward the suspension of habeas corpus and martial law in the Civil War, see Lowell H. Harrison and James C. Klotter, *A New History of Kentucky* (Lexington: University Press of Kentucky, 1997), 205–7; Breck, *Habeas Corpus*, 38–9.

[47] Breckinridge, "In Memoriam," 141, 146, 163–5.

[48] Stuart Robinson, "To the Christian Public – and all with whom loyalty is not Madness," *True Presbyterian*, May 8, 1862. For the pamphlet form, see Robinson, *Appeal to the Christian Public*.

political sentiments, delivered in the form of polemical fireworks. Breckinridge had dishonestly misled the public with a "meretricious array of bedizzened billingsgate and gilded defamation." Breckinridge had completely misrepresented Robinson's political allegiances, which Robinson had never attempted to hide. According to the Louisville pastor, he was a "Border State man against Abolitionism" and "the atheistic tendencies of that fanaticism." He stood *"against* the Black Republican platform" but also *"against* the theory of secession." Robinson believed in the "Union on the basis of the Crittenden Compromise," the 1860 proposal offered to Congress – and rejected by both the House and Senate – by Kentucky Senator John J. Crittenden, which would secure and preserve slavery for the Deep South and, in so doing – according to proponents – stave off secession.[49]

In bringing up the Crittenden Compromise, Robinson hinted at how closely the contours of his fight with Breckinridge followed the ebb and flow of Kentucky politics. "[U]p to six months ago," Robinson wrote, no one in Kentucky would have considered his politics the least bit suspicious. It was not much of a reach to think that as many as "nine-tenths of the people of Kentucky" might have agreed with Robinson's opinions. Without getting into specific details, Robinson spoke to the Unionist change that occurred in Kentucky's government in the latter months of 1861. Up until the summer of that year, many of Kentucky's main political leaders, including Governor Beriah Magoffin, were members of the State Rights party. Although Magoffin and his fellow party members often spoke in terms of stark neutrality – so much so that in May 1861 Magoffin and the state legislature refused to raise troops to fight for the United States – many believed it only a matter of time before Kentucky followed the rest of the slaveholding South and joined the Confederacy. Starting in July, however, when representatives to the U.S. House were elected, and through the August state legislature elections, Kentuckians overwhelmingly chose Unionist candidates. Part of the reason for Kentucky's strong endorsement came from very low voter turnouts; most states' righters, arguing for strict neutrality, did not participate in the elections. The result was a landslide for Unionism. For his part, Robinson may have disagreed with the "wisdom" of the Kentucky electorate, but he "abided by, respected and obeyed the laws" in the state he called home.[50]

In the same way, Robinson continued to spell out his Border State convictions when it came to the church. Although he "opposed, and very earnestly," the Spring Resolutions, Robinson planned to remain within the Presbyterian Church USA "unless" the General Assembly would make it "impossible for

---

[49] Robinson, *Appeal to the Christian Public*, 4–5.

[50] Ibid., 4; Harrison and Klotter, *New History of Kentucky*, 185–90. Contrary to traditional explanations that suggest Kentucky Unionism masked a silent majority of Confederate sympathizers, Thomas C. Mackey argues that most Kentuckians were legitimately Unionist. See Mackey, "Not a Pariah, but a Keystone: Kentucky and Secession," in *Sister States, Enemy States: The Civil War in Kentucky and Tennessee*, eds. Kent T. Dollar, Larry H. Whiteaker, and W. Calvin Dickinson (Lexington: University Press of Kentucky, 2009), 25–45.

the Kentucky Slave-holding Churches to continue their connection with it." Robinson was no earnest secessionist, nor did he desire to fracture the church, despite the claims of his antagonist in Danville.[51]

At the 1862 General Assembly, the Breckinridge–Robinson dispute often took center stage. As promised, Breckinridge brought the *Danville Quarterly Review* controversy before the Assembly. Told from his perspective, Breckinridge had been unfairly maligned by Stuart Robinson and Thomas A. Hoyt "without any provocation on my part" – a claim that flatly ignored his March article in the Louisville *Journal* that started the fight. His opponents had charged Breckinridge with abusing his position as a professor of theology at Danville Theological Seminary and using the post "to the advancement of improper public objects, and unworthy personal aims." Breckinridge, however, maintained, as he had all along, that his political activities fell well within the bounds of his office. As such, Breckinridge tendered his resignation from the seminary, effective September 1, 1862. Robinson and Hoyt both issued rebuttals, arguing that it was they who had been attacked and denying that they did anything other than respond in "self-defence." Robinson maintained that this "personal controversy" should not even have entered the General Assembly – the matter was not one for such a high court. It dealt with "charges of moral delinquency" among pastors. Such charges, according to the constitution of the church, had to be sorted out at the local presbytery level.[52]

The entire controversy went before a committee of seven ministers and elders for arbitration. The committee agreed with some of Robinson and Hoyt's concerns, particularly that the General Assembly was not the forum for dealing with personal squabbles. Yet, in the main, Breckinridge emerged victorious. The Assembly ruled that "no facts" had come to light that "impair[ed] their confidence in Dr. Breckinridge as a Professor in the Danville Seminary." As such, the church refused to accept his resignation. Moreover, they agreed with Breckinridge that theology professors did not have to sit silent on political "matters of great national concernment." Indeed, Breckinridge deserved "the gratitude of the Church and the country" for his "bold and patriotic stand" over the past year of civil war and church schism.[53]

That resolution did not mark the end of the fighting. Breckinridge and Robinson collided once more at the 1862 General Assembly. The second time, the issue cut straight to their differences over political theology. On the fourth day of the meetings, Breckinridge issued a paper on the "State of the Country and the Church" for the Assembly to consider. The document was overtly Unionist and not markedly different from the previous year's Spring Resolutions, which Breckinridge had denounced. Breckinridge's paper contained no sentiments that would encourage revolution – the feature of the Spring Resolutions

---

[51] Robinson, *Appeal to the Christian Public*, 5.
[52] Joseph M. Wilson, *Presbyterian Historical Almanac and Annual Remembrancer of the Church, for 1863* (Philadelphia: Joseph M. Wilson, 1863), 118–22.
[53] Ibid., 122.

he had most stridently objected to – but much of the rest was the same. Indeed, in what was a significantly longer document, Breckinridge's tone was equally, if not much more, harsh than that of the Spring Resolutions. "This whole treason, rebellion, anarchy, fraud, and violence, is utterly contrary to the dictates of natural religion and morality and is plainly condemned by the revealed will of God," the professor argued. "If, in any case, treason, rebellion, anarchy can possibly be sinful, they are so in the case now desolating large portions of this nation, and laying waste great numbers of Christian congregations." Then, in a statement that can only be read in light of Breckinridge's past year of theological-political disputation, he brought down a rhetorical hammer: "Disturbers of the Church ought not to be allowed – especially disturbers of the Church in states that never revolted." No ministers were mentioned by name, but Breckinridge's argument sounded quite similar to the ones he had deployed in Kentucky against Robinson and his cohort. Those "disturbers who, under many false pretexts, may promote discontent, disloyalty, and general alienation, tending to the unsettling of ministers, to local schisms, and to manifold trouble" could not be tolerated in the Presbyterian Church.[54]

Such words were not lost on Stuart Robinson. The Louisville pastor argued that the language "concerning 'disturbers of the Church,' acting 'under false pretexts'" would no doubt "be taken by the public as practically a judgment against some one." Yet because "not a single fact in the paper itself" explained what was meant by these statements, it would be left "to the prejudices and passions of the public, to any Synod, Presbytery, or person" to decide how to rule against such violators of the church's peace. Continuing his argument about the church's spiritual character, the Louisville pastor protested an Assembly that "declare[d] 'loyalty' to be in common with orthodoxy and piety." The Breckinridge paper took the "authority given to the Spiritual Courts" and turned it on its head. It "render[ed] to Caesar the *things that are God's*" and also presumed that the church had the God-given "authority" to lead affairs of state, rather than remain "subject to the powers that be." Both were "contrary to Scripture" and, thus, errant decisions.[55]

Despite Robinson's protest, the Breckinridge paper easily passed. Since most slave-state Presbyterians had left the General Assembly for the Presbyterian Church CSA, little sympathy remained for opinions that appeared less than fully committed to the United States. By an overwhelming vote of 206 to 20, Breckinridge's political theology proved victorious at the 1862 General Assembly. Robinson's dissent was recorded, but left unanswered and received no formal discussion.[56]

---

[54] Ibid., 123–4. For more on the discussion of the Breckinridge paper, see Vander Velde, *Presbyterian Churches*, 110–14.
[55] Ibid., 126–8.
[56] Ibid., 126, 129.

After Breckinridge's paper was endorsed by the General Assembly in May, the *Danville Quarterly Review* followed in June with a celebratory, triumphalist account of the controversy with the "diabolical" Robinson and his "secret helpers." The "coarse and vulgar element in Mr. Robinson's nature" had been exposed. The "assumed grandeur and spirituality" of his theology was a ruse for his anti-Unionism. Robinson had been proven a "sham spiritual hero." The article claimed it could not be certain how many of Robinson's fellow "secessionists" remained willing to help the Louisvillian destroy Breckinridge and Danville, but the *Review* believed that number was shrinking. Writing as if its own conduct stemmed from the purest of motives, the *Review* suggested that it would not pursue "vengeance" against Robinson and his associates: "God has said it is his." The true Christian God would judge "those who abuse his name and outrage his laws." Robinson and his compatriots would receive their due. Justice would come and God would honor those who lived for right.[57]

Just a month later it appeared that some form of justice had been done: Robinson left Kentucky in July 1862. On a trip to Ohio to visit the home of his ailing brother, the minister received word from friends in Kentucky that it would be best for him not to return. Local Union troops had deemed his writings in the *True Presbyterian* inflammatory, and they had seized copies of the paper. Robinson's comrades feared that the minister would be jailed on charges of sedition if he returned to the Falls City. Although he maintained his connections to the Bluegrass State and continued to edit the *True Presbyterian*, Robinson exiled himself to Toronto for the duration of the war.[58]

With Robinson out of the way, by mid-1862 Breckinridge appeared destined to win the Kentucky fight over political theology. Indeed, with Unionism ascendant in Kentucky politics, guaranteed by a mandate of the electorate in the fall of 1861, Breckinridge's nationalist political theology seemed perfectly suited to carry the day. All that, however, would change within a few short months. Breckinridge's political theology was tied to the fortunes of the United States. That made it an imperfect fit for a border slave state such as Kentucky. So long as the Union made decisions that comported with the will of white Kentucky, Unionism succeeded.

On September 22, 1862, President Abraham Lincoln issued the preliminary Emancipation Proclamation, which guaranteed freedom to all slaves who were in Confederate lands as of January 1, 1863. It did not alter slavery's status in states like Kentucky that remained with the Union. Nevertheless, white Kentucky perceived quickly the significance of the Proclamation. In some sense, it recognized a process that was well underway thanks to the actions of the Union army, the U.S. Congress, and the enslaved themselves in destroying

---

57 "The Late General Assembly of 1862, of the Presbyterian Church in the United States of America," *Danville Quarterly Review* 2.2 (June 1862): 363–9.
58 See Vander Velde, *Presbyterian Churches*, 168; Louis B. Weeks, *Kentucky Presbyterians* (Atlanta: John Knox Press, 1983), 86–7; and Graham, *A Kingdom Not of This World*, 53–9.

slavery as it had existed prior to 1861. Where for whites in Kentucky, the Civil War was once intended to preserve the Union alone, it had now become a war about slavery. From their vantage point, that change was unacceptable. Suddenly, the idea of Union became less and less appealing. With slavery's end impending, racist white Kentuckians no longer found a political theology resolutely committed to Union as compelling as it had once appeared.

Breckinridge himself never gave up his Unionism, but he also never expressed any desire to see emancipation – that is, until he had no choice but to accept what the war had unleashed. And even then it was an acceptance in the name of Union. By the end of 1862, Kentucky Presbyterians had declared no winner in their civil war over political theology. But as emancipation loomed closer on the horizon, the less certain it seemed that Breckinridge's vision would prevail.

6

The End of Neutrality

Emancipation, Political Religion, and the Triumph of Abolitionist Heterodoxy, 1862–1865

> [I]n times to come scholars and historians shall be treating abolition as the great fanaticism of the nineteenth century.... As a politics, history will write it down as below the intellect and contrivance of a bedlamite. As a religion, it will go down to posterity as a mongral exhibition of all the mongral infidelisms of the times – infidelism which cheated the churches and ruined them.
>
> – "Abolition and the Future," *True Presbyterian*, March 3, 1864[1]

In mid-October 1862, the white minister William Thomas McElroy (1829–1910), pastor of Louisville's Walnut Street Presbyterian Church, lamented the course of the "dreadful war" presently tearing apart "our country + state." McElroy was a resolute Unionist, and at the time, he and his wife Eliza were residing in the home of her father, the prominent Louisville merchant and philanthropist Samuel Casseday. McElroy's brother-in-law Alex had already joined the "Rebel" war effort as an officer in Kentucky Confederate general Simon Bolivar Buckner's brigade, and it distressed McElroy that "every member of [Samuel Casseday's] family" – all of the seven Casseday children, except the oldest brother "Ben + my wife," as McElroy wrote in his journal – "is strong for the rebellion." Against the family's prevailing opinion, the minister argued, "I cannot, + will not countenance any measure subversive of the good government under which we have lived." McElroy remained loyal to the United States, and stood "for 'The Union, The Constitution, + The enforcement of the laws.'" Convincingly, he wrote, "I am as I have been from the start, + ever expect to be." In late 1862, the state's formal political support for the Union had been secured, but there obviously remained strong Confederate sympathies among many in the Bluegrass State. Many Kentuckians – including McElroy's

---

[1] Philos, "Abolition and the Future," *True Presbyterian*, March 3, 1864.

own family members – had questioned their state's official commitment to the Union, but this minister was not one of them.[2]

That opinion soon changed, however. Just a few months later, in December 1862, after reading "with great care" the text of President Abraham Lincoln's Emancipation Proclamation for the first time, McElroy found himself appalled. The document "looks far too much like abolition for me to endorse," he explained. Where the minister might have supported Lincoln's efforts to preserve the Union, McElroy now worried that the president's "whole cabbinet is so [abolitionist] that I fear the war will degenerate from a lofty + noble struggle for the nations life, to a brutal <u>war</u> over the negroes." He continued, "[I]f the war be simply for the <u>Union</u> the <u>constitution</u> + the <u>enforcement</u> of the <u>laws</u> – they will be maintained, if on the other hand it becomes a war for abolition it will be long, fatal to the country, + fail of its object." McElroy's language reflected how much he, like many white religious Kentuckians, retained the conservative, proslavery Unionist interpretation of the cause of the Civil War. He contended that slavery had nothing to do with the issues at stake in the war. McElroy argued that he was for the Union "but not for the [abolitionist] policy advocated by some of the cabinet." In other words, he could not accept that the Civil War was a conflict about anything other than the preservation of national unity.[3]

Things were different for McElroy before the war. Like a visible minority of Kentucky clergy, the minister embraced gradual emancipation. However, when, in 1856, he was accused of preaching "an abolition sermon," McElroy took great care to show that his views were actually "the reverse" of any radical scheme to immediately free slaves into white American society. As was the case for the overwhelming majority of Kentucky's religious whites, the divine had no vision for the future political equality of the nation's enslaved African American population – indeed, he could not imagine such a possibility.[4]

So strong was McElroy's antipathy to the idea of immediate emancipation without colonization that it undermined his commitment to the Unionist cause. By early 1863 – in other words, just a few short months after declaring his undying loyalty to the Union – he began preaching pro-Confederate sermons

[2] William Thomas McElroy Journal, October 17, 1862, William Thomas McElroy Papers, Folder 10, The Filson Historical Society, Louisville. On Samuel Casseday and his family, see Lucien V. Rule, "Review of Fannie Casseday Duncan, *When Kentucky Was Young* (Louisville: John P. Morton, 1928)," *Filson Club History Quarterly* 2 (July 1928): 184–5. Alex Casseday began the war, as did Simon Bolivar Buckner's unit more broadly, as a member of the Kentucky State Guard and thus neutral in the sectional conflict. Buckner opposed Kentucky's late 1861 end of political neutrality, rejected a Union commission, and accepted a Confederate generalship, taking most of his unit with him, including Alex Casseday. See Arndt M. Stickles, *Simon Bolivar Buckner: Borderland Knight* (Chapel Hill: University of North Carolina Press, 1940), 51–91, esp. p. 67 on Alex Casseday's defense of neutrality.

[3] McElroy Journal, December 1862.

[4] Ibid., July 7, 1856; October 17, 1856.

from his Louisville pulpit. By the end of the war, his thinking about race and politics proved cause for religious disunity along sectional and racial lines. In 1865 and 1866, McElroy led the majority of his congregation to end fellowship with the Presbyterian Church USA. In this move, McElroy joined the bulk of Bluegrass Presbyterians, who between 1865 and 1869 voted overwhelmingly to reject their ties to the northern church – a connection all the state's presbyteries had maintained through the war – and align with the southern sectional branch of the denomination, known during the war as the Presbyterian Church in the Confederate States of America.[5]

William Thomas McElroy's Civil War–era career is indicative of a much broader cultural and political transformation that occurred among Kentucky whites in the period. The years from 1862 to 1865 were critical in this transformation. For the majority of such believers, emancipation – and the way it came about – meant that the United States had become a different country from the one they knew in 1860. Emancipation, severed from gradual implementation and black deportation, signaled to Kentucky's white religious conservatives that abolitionist heterodoxy had triumphed at the highest levels of American public office, as well as on the ground and, most pressingly, in their midst. By 1862, therefore, as the long work of black and white abolitionists became to be realized, the specter of emancipation served to unite the Commonwealth's white evangelicals around a common cause that they had collectively agreed upon long before the Civil War: their putative racial and theological superiority. Starting in late 1862, white Kentuckians drew on long-standing theological proslavery arguments – aggressively anti-abolitionist and explicitly racist – to distance themselves from Union policy and, more generally, the North. That region, they argued, had become infected with an abolitionist heresy that had perverted its religion and society.

---

[5] On McElroy and the move of Kentucky's Presbyterians to the Presbyterian Church in the United States (or Southern Presbyterian Church), see the brief account in Louis B. Weeks, *Kentucky Presbyterians* (Atlanta: John Knox Press, 1983), 79–107.

McElroy's role was a great deal more significant and complicated than this brief description suggests. In 1865 and 1866, McElroy, several lay leaders, and a sizable majority of his parishioners at Walnut Street Presbyterian Church initiated a congregational split over an intricate set of questions pertaining to Presbyterian denominational polity, the most glaring and crucial of which was whether the church could tolerate its pastor's southern sympathizing from the pulpit. Because McElroy and his supporters chose to leave the northern Presbyterian church – the owner of the church's property "in trust" – the split created a knotty legal battle over who could claim control of the physical church property. After much wrangling, both in church and civil courts, the case reached the U.S. Supreme Court in the landmark case, *Watson v. Jones* (1871). The court's ultimate decision – which ruled that because Presbyterianism was a hierarchical form of government, the denomination that originally claimed the church was the rightful owner of its property in an "implied trust" – set precedent for more than a century of complicated American church–state property law. See Ronald W. Eades, *Watson v. Jones: The Walnut Street Presbyterian Church and the First Amendment* (Lynnville, TN: Archer Editions Press, 1982).

Kentucky's most visible abolitionist, John G. Fee, certainly did not see it that way. Fee had returned to the state from exile in 1863, and he resumed his labors in central Kentucky, especially at Berea but also at Camp Nelson, in Jessamine County. The camp was established in 1863, and because it was located in the heart of the state's most concentrated slaveholding region, it became one of the principal sites of black troop enlistment – as well as emancipation more generally, with more than 13,000 African Americans finding freedom there in the next two years. After leading a Christian worship service held at the camp in October 1864, Fee documented the spirit of liberation and Christian abolitionist unity that he witnessed in that moment:

> In the midst of this slaveholding State was a crowded assembly, listening to ministers from the North and the South, white and black. In the congregation, as in the church newly formed [at Camp Nelson], were persons from the East, the West, the North, the South. There were male and female, soldier and citizen, and every grade of complexion, from the fairest Caucasian to the darkest African – all blended together on the one common basis of manifested faith in Christ. Therein, the person of every freedman was a practical demolition of that hated monster, slavery; and there, in the blending association, was a practical crucifixion of that great and virulent enemy of the Gospel – caste. I thank God that I have lived to see this day.[6]

This account was published in the American Missionary Association's monthly journal; many of its evangelical abolitionist readers would have absolutely agreed with Fee's assessment. The death of slavery – and as Fee saw happening, the racism that supported social inequality – was cause for celebration and Christian worship.

But emancipation indicated something very different to Kentucky's white religious conservatives. As they responded to emancipation, abolitionism, and what they saw as politicized religion, it became increasingly clear that the possibility of maintaining an ostensibly neutral, proslavery Unionist stance on the meaning of the war and the American nation no longer existed. For a white population long prepared to see abolition as evil, it was as if an antebellum prophecy of doom had become manifest before their eyes. White evangelical Protestantism, in other words, served a primary ideological role in the making of Kentucky's postwar Confederate identity. Although that view of the war would not fully flourish in the Commonwealth until after the fact, its seeds were sown long before. And emancipation marked the beginning of their flourishing.

---

[6] John G. Fee, letter, October 10, 1864, *American Missionary* (November or December 1864): 294, in typescript "Letters and Articles by and about Rev. John G. Fee, his life and work in the *American Missionary*," 147, RG 1.02, Series III, Box 5, Folder 7, Berea College Archives, Berea, KY. On Camp Nelson, see Richard D. Sears, ed., *Camp Nelson, Kentucky: A Civil War History* (Lexington: University Press of Kentucky, 2002), xix.

Early on in the war, Kentucky remained steadfast in its claims for neutrality. That changed when the state was invaded by Confederates – first on a small scale in southern Kentucky in the fall of 1861, and then with a broader and larger effort led by Braxton Bragg and E. Kirby Smith in the central part of the state in the summer of 1862. In this way, though much of Kentucky never saw Union troops during the war and many slaves remained in bondage long after 1862, Confederate invasion ironically represented the first assault on Kentucky's slavery system because of the social upheaval that came with it.[7]

The second assault came later in 1862 with Lincoln's preliminary Emancipation Proclamation. The enslaved constituted nearly 20 percent of Kentucky's population in 1860 – roughly 225,000 souls. And although some 65,000 people endured as slaves in the Bluegrass State until the ratification of the Thirteenth Amendment in December 1865 – which Kentucky rejected – the Emancipation Proclamation nonetheless registered a decisive impact. The document did not apply to Kentucky, but it still signaled much there. Not only did it permanently free the many slaves who had escaped bondage for the protection of Union military camps elsewhere in the occupied South but it also offered those still enslaved a promise of approaching liberation – thereby encouraging and hastening southern blacks' escape from enslavement.

In Kentucky, fugitives began fleeing slavery for the protection of Union Army camps in small numbers in the summer of 1861, a process that accelerated rapidly by the end of the year as the Civil War's fighting came to the Commonwealth. For the enslaved, the Union Army always represented freedom – even as military officials did not often see themselves as agents of liberation. Lacking a clearly defined federal policy toward fugitives, especially in loyal states, the Union response toward Kentucky fugitives was haphazard at best. Slaves often traveled to Union lines in whole family groups, and although work for men was readily available, women and children proved more difficult to manage under existing policies. Because Kentucky was a Union state where slavery remained legal until 1865, the great majority of Union officers were unwilling to offer even minimal social support for those African Americans who served no military purpose, regularly turning away fugitive Kentuckians who sought refuge in their camps. At Camp Nelson, for example, where the number of refugees swelled at times to more than 5,000, officers routinely expelled African Americans. The most notorious incident occurred in November 1864 when more than 400 women and children family members of black

---

7 See Marion B. Lucas, *A History of Blacks in Kentucky*, vol. 1: *From Slavery to Segregation, 1760–1891* (Frankfort: Kentucky Historical Society, 1992), 146–51; Aaron Astor, *Rebels on the Border: Civil War, Emancipation, and the Reconstruction of Kentucky and Missouri* (Baton Rouge: Louisiana State University Press, 2012), 108–10; and Ira Berlin et al., eds., *Freedom: A Documentary History of Emancipation, 1861–1867*, Ser. 1, Vol. 2: *The Wartime Genesis of Free Labor: The Upper South* (Cambridge: Cambridge University Press, 1993), 625–7.

soldiers were sent out into freezing temperatures without adequate clothing or provisions, which resulted in many deaths.[8]

In cases where military value might be derived, fugitives were used as laborers or impressed into menial service in military camps – digging trenches, building fortifications, clearing roads, cutting timber, performing servant duties in camps, and conducting similar activities. Impressment was not limited to the Union Army; Confederates engaged in the practice as well, although African Americans did everything in their power to escape the grip of the southern army. While in many instances Union officials compensated loyal owners for their slaves' labor, impressment often meant that slaves never returned to their masters. For the many loyal slaveholders in Kentucky, that reality was grating – clearly the Union military violated masters' constitutionally guaranteed rights of property.[9]

Impressed slaves and refugees were the vital, irreplaceable source of labor that made the Union military cause possible – and successful – in Kentucky. Yet even if the Union war effort spelled emancipation in the end, for those impressed into service it did not necessarily appear that their labor would produce some kind of utopian future of freedom. At least some African Americans in Kentucky questioned the work of the Union Army in direct terms. One anonymous correspondent to the African Methodist Episcopal *Christian Recorder* argued that the arrival of "the Northern army" had resulted in a crackdown on free blacks in Louisville under the pretense of keeping peace and maintaining the slaveholding constitutional order: "Kentucky has been redeemed; 'her white people are free' and her 'free blacks are enslaved,' and they have no more 'rights that white men are bound to respect.'" As the writer explained, Louisville's' free blacks, who had otherwise been loyal citizens and worshiped freely, now found themselves in a "condition" that was "worse than before the war. Our churches are closed, and a free man cannot walk after dark though he has his free papers." Moreover, impressed African Americans regularly were required to complete harder tasks in worse working conditions than under slavery. Although some received compensation for their labor, it was often a pittance. Most significantly, and in continuity with the long history of slavery to date, impressment frequently meant forced separation from family and community networks, with little sense of when reunions might occur.[10]

---

[8] Lucas, *History of Blacks in Kentucky*, 147–51; Berlin et al., *The Upper South*, 625–8; Sears, *Camp Nelson*, l–li; Amy Murrell Taylor, "How a Cold Snap in Kentucky Led to Freedom for Thousands: An Environmental Story of Emancipation," in *Wierding the War: Stories from the Civil War's Ragged Edges*, ed. Stephen Berry (Athens: University of Georgia Press, 2011), 191–214; and Richard D. Sears, "A Long Way from Freedom: Camp Nelson Refugees," in *Sister States, Enemy States: The Civil War in Kentucky and Tennessee*, eds. Kent T. Dollar, Larry H. Whiteaker, and W. Calvin Dickinson (Lexington: University Press of Kentucky, 2009), 219, 231–3.

[9] Lucas, *History of Blacks in Kentucky*, 147–51; Berlin et al., *The Upper South*, 625–8.

[10] Ibid.; and An Observer, "A Letter from Kentucky," *Christian Observer*, April 5, 1862.

By the first months of 1863, the problems of Kentucky fugitive laborers and impressed slaves grew even more complicated for Union officials. Thousands of former slaves entered Kentucky from the South, having traveled with the Union Army of the Ohio, which had been in Tennessee. These "contrabands," so named by Union commanders – and distinguished from Kentucky fugitives and impressed blacks who remained enslaved by law – came as laborers from Tennessee, Mississippi, and Alabama. Since they originated from rebellious states, they were often presumed free because of the Emancipation Proclamation or earlier congressional confiscation acts, which seized property of Confederate slaveholders as war materiel. But black Kentuckians performing similar tasks for the Union Army were not accorded the same status because they did not come from a rebellious state. Moreover, loyal slave owners objected to the use of these fugitives, complaining to Union officers "that the slaves in Kentucky would become demoralized and worthless by coming into contact with the contrabands." For military officials, however, there seemed no better options available.[11]

It was in this context that the Emancipation Proclamation took on particular urgency in Kentucky. Its preliminary version, issued in September 1862, coincided with Confederate invasion. With a growing manpower shortage throughout the Union Army, Lincoln authorized the enlistment of black troops in December 1862. Unlike earlier federal policies that were uneven and unclear about the status of contrabands and fugitives, this move was sweeping and expressly connected emancipation with Union service: enlistment meant freedom. Worried about the reaction from loyal white slaveholders, however, Lincoln exempted Kentucky. Leading Kentucky politicians, especially Governor Thomas E. Bramlette, remained steadfast in opposing the enlistment of Kentucky blacks, but that did not stop African Americans themselves – both free and enslaved – from traveling to places where black enlistment was permitted. Thus, an untold number of black Kentuckians went north of the Ohio River and also to the occupied South, especially Tennessee, and signed up as Union soldiers.[12]

So long as Kentucky did not fail to meet its draft quotas using only whites, Lincoln promised Bramlette that the Bluegrass State would not be called on to send black soldiers to the Union Army. However, by early 1864 white recruitment flagged in the Commonwealth, which spoke generally to the increasing unpopularity of the war, and to emancipation specifically, among Kentucky whites. According to the best estimates, 71 percent of military-aged white males – 18 to 45 – refused to serve either the Union or Confederacy. Throughout the war, only 25 percent of drafted white Kentuckians ever showed up to fight for the Union. The rest avoided federal enlistment by

---

[11] Berlin et al., *The Upper South*, 627–9; Speed S. Fry, letter to Ambrose Burnside, October 24, 1863, in Sears, *Camp Nelson*, 26.
[12] Lucas, *History of Blacks in Kentucky*, 151–2.

finding substitutes, buying their way out of service, or simply dodging the draft outright.[13]

The state's more than 40,000 enslaved men of military age therefore proved too valuable a resource for federal officials to ignore. Bramlette won his 1863 gubernatorial election in a landslide, but only because the Union Army had declared martial law to suppress disloyalty just before the election, thereby disfranchising about a third of potential voters. As a Unionist Democrat, Bramlette was beholden to Kentucky's many Unionist slaveholders; he intended to resist federal pressure to enlist blacks, perhaps even to the point of taking arms. An intense private meeting with leading Kentucky Unionists, including Robert J. Breckinridge and the Kentucky district military commander, General Stephen Gano Burbridge, ultimately convinced the governor of the folly of opposing federal mandates. By all accounts, however, Bramlette was hard to convince. As Breckinridge later wrote to Burbridge, "Nothing I was ever engaged in seemed more providential, or more surprising, or indeed more opportune," but it took much work on the part of these individuals. Bramlette thus agreed in March 1864 to allow for black enlistment, and black recruiting in Kentucky began at military camps throughout the state.[14]

The linkage between military service and emancipation became even clearer and more complete the next year. In March 1865 federal legislation freed enslaved wives or children of black Union soldiers. This law came about in no small part due to widely published accounts of the horrors faced by refugee families of black soldiers; especially influential was the story of the expelled Camp Nelson refugees who died from exposure the previous November. Thus, in Kentucky, outside the bounds of the Emancipation Proclamation, the connection between black Union enlistment and freedom was more profound than anywhere else: it was the only path to freedom. The state's African Americans knew as much and enlisted in record numbers. Nearly 24,000 black Kentuckians came to fight for the Union. That number was more than 10 percent of the state's overall African American population and also more than 10 percent of all blacks in the Union Army. But even more substantially, it included a staggering 57 percent of military-aged black men in the Commonwealth – a higher proportion than in any other slaveholding state.[15]

[13] Anne E. Marshall, *Creating a Confederate Kentucky: The Lost Cause and Civil War Memory in a Border State* (Chapel Hill: University of North Carolina Press, 2010), 20; Lucas, *History of Blacks in Kentucky*, 146–77.

[14] Victor B. Howard, *Black Liberation in Kentucky: Emancipation and Freedom, 1862–1884* (Lexington: University Press of Kentucky, 1983), 45–90; Lucas, *History of Blacks in Kentucky*, 146–77; James C. Klotter, *The Breckinridges of Kentucky* (Lexington: University Press of Kentucky, 1986), 84–5; and Lowell H. Harrison and James C. Klotter, *A New History of Kentucky* (Lexington: University Press of Kentucky, 1997), 206. See also John David Smith, "Self Emancipation in Kentucky," *Reviews in American History* 12 (June 1984): 225–9. Robert J. Breckinridge, letter to S. G. Burbridge, March 26, 1864, Stephen Gano Burbridge Papers, FHS.

[15] On black enlistment in Kentucky, see Astor, *Rebels on the Border*, 124–31. Kentucky was second only to Louisiana in the number of black enlisted men. For comparative totals of black

Abolitionists perceived clearly what was happening. At Camp Nelson, former Berea exile and John G. Fee's associate, John A. R. Rogers, associated black enlistment with the advance of "the future progress of Christianity." Quoting the biblical text of Matthew 20:16, Rogers wrote, "'The last shall be first, and the first last.' God often chooses the weak things of the world to confound the mighty." In Rogers' telling, it had taken him some time to reach the "conclusion" that "all that is good depended in this State as much on the black race as the white." Yet what he saw in the midst of the Civil War showed him "that the black men to whom Brother Fee preaches [at Camp Nelson] – and he preaches to not a few of either the black or white race – are destined to exert great influence. Colored soldiers will be leaders among colored men."[16]

None understood better than enlisted African American Kentuckians what the Civil War meant for their lives. As Baptist and former slave Elijah P. Marrs (1840–1910) explained after the war about his enlistment in Louisville in September 1864, "We were all new men, and we soon expected to be sent to the front." The prospect of fighting was a frightening one: "We had just left our homes, and though out of slavery we loved the place of our birth." However, Marrs and his fellow freedpeople "were loth to return" to bondage, "and a thought seemed to come to the mind of every Christian, that though the Civil War between the North and South had separated us from home and friends, yet the protecting hand of the United Government of God was still over us all." Federal policy had given authoritative force to what was playing out on the ground. The United States' war to preserve the Union was also being fought to destroy slavery.[17]

Among Kentucky's religiously conservative whites, this latter point was not lost, and they did not welcome emancipation. Although he came to change his opinion, in December 1862 thoroughgoing Unionist Presbyterian and slaveholder Robert J. Breckinridge wrote derisively "that neither *the Constitution as it is*, nor yet *the Union as it was*, is compatible with the state of things" the Emancipation Proclamation set in motion. The war had entered a new era, and as the white minister put it, "it is perfectly obvious to every sane man ... who is not an ultra Abolitionist" that the prospects were dire. The war was now being prosecuted to "establish the freedom and supremacy of the black race in the South, and confer on free negroes ... that perfect equality with ourselves, whether personal, social, civil, or political." Supporting the Union in "a war for the maintenance of a Constitution that allowed and protected slavery" was a noble cause. But fighting "a war against slavery" – the federal placation of

---

enlistments, see Ira Berlin et al., *Slaves No More: Three Essays on Emancipation and the Civil War* (New York: Cambridge University Press, 1992), 203. See also Taylor, "How a Cold Snap in Kentucky Led to Freedom for Thousands."

16 John A. R. Rogers, letter to the Secretaries of the American Missionary Association, August 27, 1864, in Sears, *Camp Nelson*, 116.

17 Elijah P. Marrs, *Life and History of the Rev. Elijah P. Marrs, First Pastor of Beargrass Baptist Church and Author* (Louisville: Bradley & Gilbert, 1885), 23–4.

"the abolition cry" that had grated on the nation for "a whole generation" – was not an endeavor Breckinridge believed worth defending.[18]

Breckinridge's argument appeared in the pages of his theological journal, the *Danville Quarterly Review*, which had maintained a strongly Unionist stance since its founding in January 1861 and addressed theological and political matters of central significance to the Ohio Valley region. From his editorial position, Breckinridge argued that he was well qualified to speak on behalf of the "loyal slaveholders of the nation, and especially of the Border States," who believed unequivocally that the secessionist "engines of revolutionary fanaticism" and "treason" should be quashed. Unlike their abolition-minded counterparts, however, these more moderate Unionists held the "profound conviction" that ending American slavery "can have no beneficial effect whatever" toward "crushing the rebellion, and preserving the nation." At the moment of secession, the Danville divine argued, Confederates responded in the most "extreme reaction" imaginable to the ascendancy of the free-soil–based Republican Party and the election of its candidate, Abraham Lincoln, as president. Now, however, with emancipation proclaimed, loyal Americans were forced to accept a likewise "subverted and abused" understanding of the U.S. Constitution, a view that only an antislavery radical could find tolerable. The *Review* editorial contended that the vast majority of Unionists were conservative in nature, which meant they would "not permit a party at the South to create a new nation," but neither would they "permit a party at the North to destroy the Constitution under the pretext of maintaining the Union." Both secessionists and abolitionists operated from the same extremist impetus, but from "opposite directions," the editor argued: "They both agree that our system is a failure, and must be abandoned or greatly modified." A properly conservative and theologically informed view of the American nation, however, understood that neither course should be followed. "Here we plant ourselves with confiding faith in God," Breckinridge insisted. "His dealings with the American people have been wonderful, from their first settlement on this continent, [and in the] nearly two and half centuries since."[19]

This was a decidedly whitewashed picture of American history. In Breckinridge's own case, his attempt to maintain Unionism on the one hand and slaveholding on the other proved futile. In May 1864, four male slaves and their families absconded from Breckinridge's Lexington farm to enlist at Camp Nelson. Two months later, in July 1864, Breckinridge showed up at the camp, demanding a total of seventeen slaves who had fled his ownership for freedom. Breckinridge did not oppose the enlisting of his adult male slaves. After

---

[18] Robert J. Breckinridge, "Negro Slavery and the Civil War," *Danville Quarterly Review* 2.4 (December 1862): 673, 676, 708.

[19] Ibid., 671–3, 676, 678, 684; "The Secession Conspiracy in Kentucky, and its Overthrow: with the Relation of both to the General Revolt," *Danville Quarterly Review* 2.1 (March 1862): 121.

all, Breckinridge's Unionist politics were a key reason Kentucky blacks could become soldiers in the first place: just a few months earlier he had emphasized to Governor Thomas E. Bramlette Union military necessity over the rights of slaveholders.[20]

But in July 1864, the clergyman demanded the return of those women and children who had also fled for the Union Army's protection. As one former slave wrote to the Presbyterian minister, "i lef for A good cause," but Breckinridge appears to have been confounded by the entire affair. He had devoted the better part of the last four decades arguing that slavery needed to be ended, but only gradually – not in the immediatist forms favored by abolitionists. Although the process of emancipation in Civil War–era Kentucky was more protracted than anywhere else, Breckinridge's own slaves came to their liberation through no gradual means. One day in March 1864 they walked away from slavery and claimed freedom for themselves. This was not the slow death to slavery Breckinridge had in mind for Kentucky or the United States, let alone for the slaves he personally held.[21]

Fundamentally, conservative religious whites in Kentucky rejected the Emancipation Proclamation and subsequent black enlistment because they did not see African Americans as rightful, equal participants in the American political system. Indeed, Breckinridge wrote that "the black race" "for nearly two and a half centuries" had been "hanging upon" the United States' white population "like a parasite upon a noble oak." Emancipation had been declared without fully coming to terms with the consequences of "bestowing a qualified freedom upon several millions of an inferior and subject race." The reality, according to the white minister's assumption about post-emancipation American society, was that "utter ruin would overwhelm the black race" and "indescribable shock" would overtake "every element of prosperity – nay, even of civilization, throughout every region where the black race approximated the whites."[22]

In other words, as had been argued among white Kentuckians for decades, the abolition of slavery would inaugurate a race war.[23] Once the Civil War had a noble purpose – protecting the interests of a white Christian republic that maintained slavery. That prospect, however, was all but gone. Lincoln's "proclamation of September" threatened to "sweep this nation, already convulsed, into new convulsions, the depth of which no modern sufferings of nations have fathomed." No doubt the South had erred in seceding from the Union, and undeniably secessionists deserved just punishment. Yet the Danville

---

[20] Klotter, *Breckinridges of Kentucky*, 84; and Amy Murrell Taylor, *The Divided Family in Civil War America* (Chapel Hill: University of North Carolina Press, 2005), 145.

[21] Ibid., quote from Taylor, *Divided Family*, 145.

[22] "Negro Slavery and the Civil War," 679, 707–8.

[23] Ibid., 679, 681, 708. Breckinridge's argument was not new. The fear that abolitionism would lead to race warfare was ubiquitous throughout the slaveholding South before the Civil War and, according to Charles R. Dew, drove the secessionist impulse in the Confederate states. See Dew, *Apostles of Disunion: Southern Secession Commissioners and the Causes of the Civil War* (Charlottesville: University Press of Virginia, 2001).

Presbyterian found himself wondering "if it is *worthy of us*" – loyal whites – "to inflict such a fate" as black liberation "on an immense portion of our own race." It was one thing to punish the South and crush an impertinent rebellion against God's chosen nation. But it was quite another to allow "an alien and inferior race" to make war on fellow whites. No one "with Saxon or Norman or American blood in their veins" could, according to Breckinridge, be a party to "the slaughter" of whites at the hands of blacks. No cause, no matter how ostensibly moral – not "the pretext of loyalty and patriotism" to the nation nor the subduing of "rebels and traitors" – could justify that kind of racial treason. "We are not even able to see" how the war "in any way involves or affects the black race," the cleric contended. "The nation is fully able – irrespective of all questions about the black race – yea, is better able without than with most of these intricate questions – to conquer its rebellious citizens" and "restore peace and public order." The president and the abolitionist North, however, disagreed. With emancipation announced, the fundamental terms of the war changed, and the white Unionist Presbyterian minister feared that the country he believed in fighting to preserve no longer existed.[24]

Race war was not the only catastrophe that emancipation raised in the minds of Kentucky's white evangelicals. Conservative whites had no doubt that, even if an all-out racial holocaust failed to occur, their race would be marred forever by the looming prospect of interracial sex. Although many white Americans, especially after the Civil War, were convinced by scientific and theological polygenesis arguments designed to demonstrate the bestial origins of African Americans and other non–Anglo-Saxon peoples, most religious conservatives in the Civil War era – and especially proslavery theologians – did not accept such logic because it contravened the scriptural record on a single source of human ancestry. As biblical literalists, southern proslavery divines linked polygenesis to other forms of infidel understandings of the world – including abolitionism – and saw ideas affirming a multiplicity of human progenitors as part of an ongoing liberalization of Western social norms and Christian truth.[25]

Yet social ordering based on race did not depend on the new science to sustain its legitimacy. The Bible itself, read literally and commonsensically, spoke to and defined a world of stratification. Even if race per se was not in the text, whites' commonsense theology affirmed that racialized hierarchies were God-given. For evangelical whites it was therefore possible to maintain a commitment to a theory of the unity of the human race and yet still believe firmly in a providential design for racial hierarchy, which secured whites' sense of racial superiority.[26]

[24] "Negro Slavery and the Civil War," 686, 708
[25] Christopher Luse, "Slavery's Champions Stood at Odds: Polygenesis and the Defense of Slavery," *Civil War History* 53 (December 2007): 379–412.
[26] See Colin Kidd, *The Forging of Races: Race and Scripture in the Protestant Atlantic World* (Cambridge: Cambridge University Press, 2006), 147–51; and David N. Livingstone, *Adam's Ancestors: Race, Religion, and the Politics of Human Origins* (Baltimore: Johns Hopkins University Press, 2008), 186–200. Kentucky's religiously conservative whites maintained a

It was this perspective that led Presbyterian Stuart Robinson, Breckinridge's most virulent and long-standing critic, to lash out in April 1864 at abolitionism for advancing the "God-defying depravity" of "intermarriage between the white and the negro races of the country." Robinson "had supposed that no thing could any longer surprise us in the way of demented, depraved and debasing 'ism' from" the North, "the great hot-bed of effete, putrid and fermenting Puritan infidelism" – which, because of its historic linking of religion and politics, represented nothing more than an apostate region. Nonetheless, northern heretics had managed such a feat by advocating "*miscegenation*" as the means for the "elevation of the negro" and "a policy for the improvement of the white race." Surely no "American, and especially" no "Christian American" found such "degraded and debasing fooleries of men" attractive. From a certain point of view, the white minister could imagine interracial sex leading to at least some social benefit, but that perspective also imagined African Americans as docile, infantile submissives to the dictates of white orthodox Protestantism. "We can see how the Yankee's selfishness might be supplemented by the negro's generosity," the cleric sarcastically conjured. Or, perhaps the northern abolitionist's "Chinese self-conceit" might be mollified "by the negro's humility; his infamous faithlessness by the negro's fidelity; his niggard meanness by the negro's generosity; his innate coarseness and vulgarity by the negro's passion for the refined and beautiful, his God-defying infidelity by the negro's whole-hearted faith in Christ; – and perhaps a score of other points to contrast."[27]

Those seemingly positive reasons for integrating the races, however, counted for little in the face of the glaring problems of mixing two populations given to depravity. "What shall be the result," Robinson queried, "of adding the Yankee's natural propensity to thievery to the negro's passion for pilfering; to his cringing cowardice the negro's abject fear; to his inveterate lying, the negro's natural mendacity; to his natural vulgarity the negro's animalism; to his treachery and bloodthirst, the negro's savagery – and so of other points of resemblance?" In answering this question, the minister opined that "true philanthropy" required that a superior people protect a "helpless race" "from contact with influences" that would do little more than "degrade them" further.[28]

Race mixing, Robinson argued, was a critical issue that bore on the future of the country. If Kentuckians thought they could remain aloof, they were misguided. Robinson did not pause here to consider what most abolitionists had long noted: that the South's master class had long taken sexual advantage of enslaved women and produced their own mixed-race progeny. Instead, it

biblically informed monogenesis view of human origins. See, for example, "The Unity of the Human Race," *Danville Quarterly Review* 2.3 (September 1862): 395–406; and "'How much is a Man better than a Sheep.' – The Sacredness of our Common Humanity," *True Presbyterian*, September 24, 1863.

[27] "Rapid Progress of the Northern Infidel Negrophilism to Utter and Shameless Depravity," *True Presbyterian*, April 14, 1864. Certainly Robinson drew on an older tradition in making this argument. See Dew, *Apostles of Disunion*, esp. pp. 51–8.

[28] "Rapid Progress of Northern Infidel Negrophilism."

was obvious that abolitionists themselves were the problem. The "most radical Abolitionist" conspiracy to "coerce both Church and State into submission" had already been inaugurated. "Kentucky" and "other Border States" needed to remain vigilant. Once the "emancipation scheme is successful," the white minister argued, the division between the races would be the next bastion of American civil society to fall. Abolitionists had already succeeded in destroying slavery. They could not be permitted to assault the rampart of white hegemony as well.[29]

In spite of an omnipresent sense of racial superiority among Kentucky's white evangelicals, however, not all white voices were so assured of their race's special, divinely elevated character. According to a February 1864 editorial in the *Western Recorder*, the state newspaper of Kentucky Baptists, "The Anglo-Saxon race, indeed, has much to distinguish it from the general mass of mankind." Whites had been so important and influential in world history that they had "played a conspicuous part in the world's progress in intellectual culture, inventions, enterprise, and wealth." The superiority of the white race was so plainly obvious, the *Western Recorder* editors wrote, that many believed "that the perpetuation and spread of our particular ideas and institutions are so linked with the civilization, enfranchisement, and conversion of the world, that we certainly are safe, whatever may transpire." It was a common viewpoint, but such a notion, according to the Baptist newspaper, was "entirely a delusion." "With all the godliness, faith, saintship, missionary fervor, and real nobility which have been developed among the Anglo-Saxons," despite "their superior privileges," the fact remained that "the most wicked, godless, hypocritical, atheistic, and heaven defying-people on earth have been, and to this day are, these self-same Anglo-Saxons." It could not be denied, the article claimed, that "the Anglo-Saxon race is an embodiment of the same depraved humanity found everywhere upon earth." Perhaps whites were "only a little better cloaked with Pharisaism, a little more thoroughly pervaded with Satanic subtlety," or "a little more pietistically sentimental," but they were also "a little in advance in the procession of apostate nations on their way to the judgments of God Almighty." For those readers who doubted this truth, the legacy of the Civil War was proof enough to make the point: "The Anglo-Saxon race professes to be the messenger of peace, yet carries a sword ever warm with blood, and often with the blood of its own immediate kindred." The *Western Recorder* was by no means suggesting that whites should give up their place of privilege nor that emancipation was a proper policy decision. The essay was, however, a sober and commonsensical reflection on the carnage that supposedly enlightened white Americans had brought on themselves.[30]

Moreover, rather than challenging the white supremacy that so defined Kentucky's conservative religion, the *Western Recorder* was actually questioning

[29] Ibid.
[30] "Our Country: What Is to Become of It?," *Western Recorder*, February 13, 1864.

the foundations of U.S. civil society. American whites were complicit in an "idolatry of self and country." They had chosen the "substitution of human devices, agencies, and arrangements in the place of the proper Saviour." This flawed religious approach – "such mischievous delusion" – had been enshrined, the Baptist paper argued, in the *entirely atheistic* U.S. Constitution. "The deepest principles upon which the whole machinery of our Government is built," the article maintained, "is a theological falsehood. – a Pelagian heresy." Invoking the fifth-century theologian who battled with Augustine of Hippo over the nature of grace and salvation – and was deemed a heretic by the ancient church for advancing that human free will remained unstained by original sin – the American constitution "assure[d] that the majority of men are pure, intelligent, right-minded, virtuous, and governed by reason and truth; which is contrary to all Scripture, experience, and fact." In sum, "the framework of our institutions" was "subversive of the divine order, and embraces all the elements of apostasy from God, and ultimate destruction."[31]

The opinion of the *Western Recorder* revealed a burgeoning hostility to the American nation among white Kentucky evangelicals. That acrimony was connected directly to the conservative white impression of abolitionism. If at one time there existed a Christian America, a properly righteous nation, biblical in shape, it had been directly undermined by the "radicalism" of "the abolition effort." That movement had "for years declared that the accomplishment of its designs could only be achieved *over the ruins of the American church and the American union.*" Abolitionism, as Kentucky's religiously conservative whites had long maintained, fomented the Civil War by forcing the hand of secession-leaning southerners. It appeared, from the perspective of early 1864, that these radical antislavery activists "have succeeded" in their plan to undermine the foundations of Christian America – its national unity and its churches.[32] In the wake of emancipation, and as Civil War–era politics tended to lean toward abolitionist-influenced policy, evangelical whites in the Commonwealth increasingly questioned the basis for their loyalty to the national Union. That religious understanding was an important precursor to white Kentucky's broader identification with the Confederacy after the Civil War.

During the conflict itself, however, as the earlier internecine squabbles between Presbyterian factions in the state revealed, those white evangelicals in Kentucky who retained an affinity for southern forms of belief expressed their hostility toward Unionism through the language of the "spirituality of the church." In July 1862, months before the Emancipation Proclamation would animate Kentucky whites, the *True Presbyterian* – the weekly newspaper edited by Stuart Robinson, founded just a few months earlier to directly oppose the Unionist political theology advocated by Robert J. Breckinridge and

[31] Ibid.
[32] "The Church and the War," *Western Recorder*, January 16, 1864.

the *Danville Quarterly Review* – published a pseudonymous article that made
the point directly: "Christ's kingdom is not of this world, nor of the nature
of the governments of this world," the essay argued. "Its actions and theirs,
its principles and theirs, its governors and theirs are wholly different, and all
attempts to work them together, or to identify them, is utter folly and certain
injury to each." The implication could not be more obvious, the author contended: "To weave the web of Church and State . . . together is not patriotism,
but phrenzy, and will end as all phrenzy does end." Mixing politics and religion
led to a perversion of both entities, and it had extreme, violent implications for
society at large.[33]

Just a month earlier, in June 1862, the newspaper had published an essay
by an unidentified minister concerned that the war effort had impinged upon
his apolitical pastoral call. It was no longer enough, the writer asserted, "to
preach a pure gospel, to bring men to Christ, and" to teach "obedience to the
laws of God and man." The clergyman stood incredulous that, in the moment
of war fervor, preachers "must define and teach the political creed also, the
creed most in favor, *our* political creed, and this even at the risk of driving
off your hearers from God's house." Noting the New Testament example of
the Apostle Paul, the anonymous correspondent wrote, "The great model, ever
before held up for all preachers said, 'For I determined *not* to know *any thing*
among you, *save Jesus Christ and him crucified.*'" Now, the minister believed,
"we must know something more; Jesus Christ and him crucified are to be held
in abeyance – thrust in the background, in deference to the superior claims of
[national] loyalty."[34]

In the reading of these evangelical Kentucky whites, those Unionist believers who overtly mixed politics and religion constituted a "Satanic School." As
one of Robinson's *True Presbyterian* editorials contended, Christian Unionists
were a "class of religionists in all churches, who, under guise of zeal for the
government," issued a "war-cry against the South." Additionally, those "of
their fellow-citizens of the North" who held questionable Unionist credentials
faced "fierce 'breathings out of threatenings and slaughter.'" Robinson's argument drew directly from biblical exegesis. In the New Testament book of John,
Jesus of Nazareth had lashed out at his Pharisee opponents for "falsehood
and blood-thirst." Those Jewish officials, famously depicted in the Gospel as
responsible for Jesus' crucifixion, were, in Robinson's interpretation, the biblical parallel to his nineteenth-century pro-Union, abolition-minded, politicized
religious opponents. Quoting the text, Robinson showed that Jesus had called
the Pharisees for what they clearly were: "ye are of *your father the devil*, and
the lusts of your father ye will do. HE WAS A MURDERER from the beginning AND
ABODE NOT IN THE TRUTH, because there is no truth in him. When he speaketh
a lie, he speaketh his own, for he is a liar, and the father of it." Robinson's

---

[33] Junius, "Church and State: Chapter 1," *True Presbyterian*, July 17, 1862.
[34] Z., "Preaching Up to the Times – A Pastor in Trouble," *True Presbyterian*, June 5, 1862. The
quoted biblical text is 1 Corinthians 2:2.

religious enemies, who in his view twisted the truth of the gospel into fodder for a political agenda, thus represented no less of a "Satanic School."[35]

This understanding of the church's spirituality had direct implications for how white Kentucky evangelicals understood the emancipation issue. The Commonwealth's whites had deeply theological reasons for opposing radical antislavery schemes. Abolitionists, according to the state's religiously conservative whites, drew their conclusions from what they believed "the Bible *ought* to teach." The text, however, offered no succinct denunciation of slaveholding. In fact, the Scriptures affirmed the institution. By the 1860s white southerners knew this proslavery biblical litany quite well. It had been rehearsed, sharpened, and invoked countless times over the past four decades. Proslavery divines had, throughout the antebellum era, learned how to make the most of the commonsensical, literalistic biblical hermeneutic that dominated American religious culture. Now, in 1863, the *True Presbyterian* covered well-worn polemical terrain, writing that "to be consistent, [the Abolitionist] must throw away his belief, or throw away the Bible." And that, according to the newspaper, perfectly summarized "the spirit of Abolitionism." Radical antislavery activists preferred to "let the Bible burn" as they drew their arguments from "the misty regions of infidel anthropophilism and negrophilism." Abolitionism represented a "treacherous faithlessness" that drew its mission not from divine revelation but rather "the claims of philanthropy."[36]

As such, it was obvious to conservative white readers that radicalized opponents of slavery "clearly assail[ed] the actual Providential government of God over human society," in place "since ever society existed." Abolitionists, the *True Presbyterian* argued, hoped "to carry on war till God shall re-construct society." That flawed interpretation of divine work in the world "clearly impeaches the scriptures of truth by denouncing as inherently wicked a form of social organization" – slavery – that was "universal" in the biblical era but was never "denounced" by the Scriptures. Radicals, the newspaper argued, promised to "continue the carnage of civil war in the South" until "all injustice and oppression shall vanish from the earth." Not only was that vision inherently driven by a sadistic bloodlust – it was impossible, the paper argued, to eradicate evil from the world – but God had clearly ordained slavery and given humanity the Bible to make that point. Divine decrees could not, as a matter of fact, be unjust. As heretics who misconstrued the providential order, abolitionists also misunderstood the nature of justice.[37]

Radical "heresiarchs," the *True Presbyterian* argued, clamored that "'[s]lavery is the cause of all our troubles, therefore the Church must exert every energy to destroy slavery.'" That opinion, however, overlooked the "fact

---

35 "The 'Satanic School' of Religionists," *True Presbyterian*, September 24, 1863. The quoted biblical text is John 8:44.
36 "'How much is a Man better than a Sheep.'"
37 "Abolitionism Gone to Seed," *True Presbyterian*, April 16, 1863; "'How much is a Man better than a Sheep.'"

that the true origin of the [United States'] trouble, is the refusal of faithless Ahabs" – the Old Testament king of Israel who refused to heed the advice of God's prophet Elijah and brought famine and drought on his nation as a result – "to leave slavery as our fathers and the Providence of God placed it." Slavery, a public institution properly ordained by God, should not be meddled with in the courts of the church, the essay argued. Biblically considered, the covenant that God had extended to his chosen people – first to Israel and then the Christian church – did not require compromising divine truths for the sake of being "*patriotic*." So-called Christian opposition to slavery, especially in the name of war and supporting the Union, was an affront to divine order.[38]

There was ample evidence of northern believers who fit this description. In the view of many northern Protestants, the Civil War provided the occasion for the South's religious reconstruction. Principally, it meant that missionaries from the northern, antislavery faith were required to help the South make the transition from a benighted slaveholding society to one free. Outside the realm of denominational polities, the effort began in earnest when the abolitionist American Missionary Association established a school for fugitive slaves at Fortress Monroe, Virginia, in September 1861.[39]

Within a year, the North's leading Protestant denominations began like-minded efforts. An early overture came in June 1862 from the northern American Baptist Home Mission Society – the body the South's white Baptists vacated when they created the Southern Baptist Convention in 1845. Noting the advancing process of emancipation due to congressional action and military force, northern Baptists were prepared to act. By their lights, "Divine Providence" was at work in the "recent abolition of slavery in the District of Columbia, and in the setting free of thousands of bondman by the advancement of our national armies into insurgent States." The Christian God was "about to break the chains of the enslaved millions in our land," and, as a result, the ABHMS anticipated "the entire reorganization of the social and religious state of the South, which must inevitably follow the successful overthrow of the rebellion." That reorganization would inevitably bear the mark of the "Divine Hand," who would "thus furnish an unobstructed entrance for the Gospel among vast multitudes who have hitherto been shut out from its pure teachings." Northern Baptists moved to respond immediately to these new conditions. They commissioned "missionaries and teachers" for "emancipated slaves" to help usher in the new order.[40]

[38] "The real Disturbers of the Church's Peace," *True Presbyterian*, February 26, 1863.
[39] Joe M. Richardson, *Christian Reconstruction: The American Missionary Association and Southern Blacks, 1861–1890* (Athens: University of Georgia Press, 1986), 3–4.
[40] *Baptist Home Missions in North America; Including a Full Report of the Proceedings and Addresses of the Jubilee Meeting, and a Historical Sketch of the American Baptist Home Mission Society, Historical Tables, Etc., 1832–1882* (New York: Baptist Home Mission Books, 1883), 397; and Daniel W. Stowell, *Rebuilding Zion: The Religious Reconstruction of the South, 1863–1877* (New York: Oxford University Press, 1998), 27–8.

Within a few months of this resolution, Abraham Lincoln announced the preliminary Emancipation Proclamation, and the ABHMS increased its efforts. Over the next two years, they were joined in this labor by the other leading religious denominations in the North, both black and white. By the spring of 1865, the Methodist Episcopal Church, the Old and New School Presbyterian Churches, the African Methodist Episcopal Church, and the African Methodist Episcopal Zion Church had all sent missionaries to the South. Along with missionaries from the AMA and the Quaker- and Unitarian-supported American Freedmen's Union Commission, their numbers would greatly increase in the aftermath of the war.[41]

The emancipation cause was religious, and the action of northern missionaries was thus political. They often cooperated directly with the Union Army and also received the blessing of members of the Lincoln administration. From the perspective of Kentucky's evangelical whites, that was the most disdainful part of the whole northern missionary endeavor.

In their view, the most meddlesome and blatantly political features of abolitionist-influenced Protestantism appeared vividly in late 1863 and early 1864 when U.S. Secretary of War Edwin Stanton authorized several northern denominations to occupy or take control over churches in rebellious states "in which a loyal minister... does not now officiate." With the mass destruction and the social disruption to local communities brought by the Civil War, many southern churches came to be abandoned. Stanton's church orders theoretically rested on the premise that these bodies had ceased to exist. Perhaps more offensive was the related implication that no true sites of Christian worship remained in the occupied South. For denominations that had split over the slavery question – or, in the case of the Presbyterians, split over the Civil War – the orders represented a chance to reclaim a previously lost connection to old memberships.[42]

However, it was an approach that no white southerner could accept. For such believers, the orders were an affront emblematic of how little the North understood the South's commitment to orthodox, purportedly apolitical, faith. Conservative Kentuckians did not interpret the Stanton orders kindly. The

[41] Stowell, *Rebuilding Zion*, 28–9; Edward J. Blum, *Reforging the White Republic: Race, Religion, and American Nationalism, 1865–1898* (Baton Rouge: Louisiana State University Press, 2005), 51–2.

[42] The quote comes from the first of the orders, issued on November 30, 1863, and authorizing Methodist Episcopal Church bishop Edward R. Ames to occupy disloyal Methodist Episcopal Church, South, churches. For the order, see *The War of the Rebellion: A Compilation of the Official Records of the Union and Confederate Armies*, ser. 1, vol. 34, part 2 (Washington: Government Printing Office, 1891), 311. For the broader impact of these "religious Reconstruction" orders, see Stowell, *Rebuilding Zion*, 30–1; George C. Rable, *God's Almost Chosen Peoples: A Religious History of the American Civil War* (Chapel Hill: University of North Carolina Press, 2010), 330–4; and Timothy L. Wesley, *The Politics of Faith during the Civil War* (Baton Rouge: Louisiana State University Press, 2013), 67–72.

Western Recorder exploded at the notion: "'Re-Christianizing the South'!!! What a miserable burlesque on Christianity! What a vile profanity! What a stupendous arrogance! What ineffable stupidity!" Stuart Robinson's *True Presbyterian* had no difficulty identifying the development as a "shameless conspiracy" of the "Northern churches" and the "secular military power, for the propagation of their infidel negro evangel by the power of the sword." It was a "scheme as absurdly fanatical and devilish as ever disgraced the annals of Papal or Mohammedan propagandism." In other words, not only did abolitionism and politicized northern Christianity present an assault on right belief, they were in actuality false religions designed to pervert truth. For Kentucky religionists who had never taken arms against the Union, the idea of southern whites – even those secessionists conquered in war – losing their religious freedom proved inflammatory.[43]

Methodists, the largest religious body in the United States before the Civil War – and second only to Baptists in Kentucky – took the lead in religious reconstruction efforts. Part and parcel of such labors by northern religious whites was the attempt to provide education and general social relief for southern freedpeople. It was plain to the *Western Recorder*, writing in early 1864, that these Yankee interlopers had come under the sway of "[t]he New Gospel, the cornerstone of which is *Servants Obey* NOT *Your Masters.*" What struck the *Recorder* as odd, however, was that the New York *Methodist*, when reporting these early missionary efforts, wrote that the "members of the Louisville Conference" – along with the Kentucky Conference, one of two overarching Methodist ruling bodies in the Bluegrass State linked to the Methodist Episcopal Church, South – had "avowed their loyalty to the Government of the Union, and by this avowal covered themselves from the rebel part of Southern Methodism."[44]

To be sure, Kentucky Methodism, like the state's other leading white religious bodies, contained a sizable proportion of Unionists throughout the Civil War. But, was it really true, the Baptist *Western Recorder* asked of fellow Bluegrass believers, that "Kentucky Methodists" believed "that the Methodist Church North is so identified with the Federal political power that adherence to the one implies equal union to the other?" Had Kentucky's Methodist Episcopal Church, South, conferences "transferred to the Church North?" No, the *Recorder* contended. Such wishful thinking on the part of politically minded religious northerners – that Kentuckians would willingly, simply, turn their backs on their southern compatriots because they remained on the wrong side of the war – "is a little too fast." It was indeed the case that Southern Methodist conference meetings in Kentucky were rife with political acrimony during the

---

[43] "Re-Christianizing the South," *Western Recorder*, February 20, 1864; "The New Military and Ecclesiastical Combination for the Missionary Work in the South," *True Presbyterian*, March 3, 1864.

[44] "Dixie Missions," *Western Recorder*, January 30, 1864.

war, but that did not mean MECS Kentuckians supported every Union decision. When eighteen Kentucky Conference ministers left the MECS for the northern church in the spring of 1865, southern bishop and Kentuckian Hubbard H. Kavanaugh wrote that the "slight disaffections" came from expected places: the Ohio River border "cities of Covington, Newport and Louisville" as well as contested areas in "the mountains." Yet "the balance of the state," Kavanaugh argued, "are firm in their adherence to the M. E. Church, *South*." As it turned out, Baptists had accurately interpreted the opinion of most of their spiritually kindred Kentuckians. In April 1864 Louisville hosted a convention of Southern Methodist clergy in Union states that protested the political co-opting and loyalist occupation of "rebellious" churches in their denomination.[45]

The Baptist *Western Recorder* and the *True Presbyterian* might have come close to approximating the political opinion of much of white religious Kentucky. However, they did not represent the whole of the state. The rancor among the state's Southern Methodists and the ultimate withdrawal of a minority of its clergy revealed as much. And Kentucky's Methodists were not alone in their infighting.

In December 1864, Presbyterian Jacob Cooper (1830–1904), an Ohio native and professor of Greek at Centre College in Danville, forcefully denounced any who held the "spirituality of the church" doctrine in an essay published in Robert J. Breckinridge's *Danville Quarterly Review*. The "Higher Spirituality" argument, Cooper contended, had been crafted "[i]n order to strengthen the bulwarks of slavery and [to] silence" dissenting "discussion." The professor acknowledged the strength of biblical "arguments" that showed that "slavery is not a sin *per se*." Yet those hermeneutical abstractions from the Holy Writ occluded the reality that "slavery never did and never can exist *per se*. It involves an imperfect master clothed with substantially unlimited power over the body and soul of a servant." As a human institution, slavery had "consequences," and as such, it was up to the church to interpret whether it was "good or evil." Cooper himself maintained that he was "no Abolitionist" – "a name synonymous with all villainy." He claimed "no sympathy with the fanaticism frequently manifested" by radical antislavery activists and "utterly abhor[red] the infidel and blasphemous doctrines of" notorious abolitionists "[William Lloyd] Garrison, [Theodore] Parker, and their followers." That said, however, slavery presented real difficulty to American society and constituted a great moral evil. It had been the cause of the secessionist impulse, and

45 Ibid.; Stowell, *Rebuilding Zion*, 31; Ralph E. Morrow, *Northern Methodism and Reconstruction* (East Lansing: Michigan State University Press, 1956), 32–43; William Warren Sweet, *The Methodist Episcopal Church and the Civil War* (Cincinnati: Methodist Book Concern, 1912), 57; A. H. Redford, *Life and Times of H. H. Kavanaugh, D.D., One of the Bishops of the Methodist Episcopal Church, South* (Nashville: n.p., 1884), 412–13; Kavanaugh quoted in Charles T. Thrift, "Rebuilding the Southern Church," in *The History of American Methodism*, ed. Emory Stevens Bucke, et al., 3 vols. (New York: Abingdon Press, 1964), 2:261.

according to Cooper, that movement to fracture the nation was, from a Christian perspective, reprehensible.[46]

White southern believers who claimed the church had no warrant to preach to the problems of secular society were, in Cooper's telling, hypocrites. "Those men who were the most violent in their political invectives against political preaching in the North," the Presbyterian wrote, "were the foremost in urging the insurgents to revolt." The most famous of proslavery southern divines, James Henley Thornwell of South Carolina and Benjamin Morgan Palmer of New Orleans, had both asserted that the church was a wholly spiritual institution when the slavery question was agitated in the antebellum era. Then, on the eve of secession, in late 1860, both men had preached secessionist sermons designed "to consummate the accursed crime of treason without cause, and bloodshed without provocation." The nineteenth-century proponents of a nonsecular church were ironically "too holy to join with the civil power in denouncing an acknowledged evil" – slavery – "but just holy enough to aid and abet a faction in its work of sedition and blood."[47]

Robert L. Stanton, professor of homiletics and pastoral theology at Danville Theological Seminary, echoed Cooper's view in his widely published 1864 Unionist tome, *The Church and the Rebellion*. Stanton was a Connecticut Yankee, but he had spent most of the previous three decades in the Deep South. He began his ministerial career in 1839 leading churches in Mississippi before pastoring the First Presbyterian Church of New Orleans and then, in the early 1850s, presiding over Mississippi's Oakland College. Yet as *The Church and the Rebellion* indicated, Stanton was no apologist for the slaveholding South. Stanton was nowhere near as famous as his abolitionist brother, Henry B. Stanton, but Robert – like Henry – had been a student at Lane Theological Seminary during the tumultuous abolition debates of the early 1830s. Robert Stanton's career path took him into congregational ministry, not overt abolitionist activism, but he never sacrificed the immediatist antislavery beliefs forged at Lane. Although Stanton often remained closeted about his abolitionism, he likely authored the 1849 pamphlet *New Orleans as It Is*, which decried slavery and slaveholders in the city and offered a whites-first antislavery argument. Moreover, by the 1850s Stanton was well known in his closest social networks as an opponent of slavery.[48]

For Stanton, who had spent many years laboring in the same Presbyterian denomination and in the same city as the ardently proslavery Benjamin M.

[46] Jacob Cooper, "Slavery in the Church Courts," *Danville Quarterly Review* 4.4 (December 1864), 517–21, 551.

[47] Ibid., 516–17, 526. For the secessionist sermons referenced by Cooper, see J. H. Thornwell, "Our National Sins," and B. M. Palmer, "Slavery a Divine Trust," in *Fast Day Sermons: Or the Pulpit on the State of the Country* (New York: Rudd & Carleton, 1861), 9–80.

[48] See Timothy F. Reilly, "Robert L. Stanton, Abolitionist of the Old South," *Journal of Presbyterian History* 53 (Spring 1975): 33–50; and A Resident, *"Truth is Stranger than Fiction": New Orleans as It Is* (Utica, NY: DeWitt C. Grove, 1849), 41–5, 60–79.

Palmer, the time had come to denounce those who claimed that supporting slavery could be apolitical in any serious way. *The Church and the Rebellion* laid that case bare. In Kentucky, many advocates of the church's spirituality claimed no explicit affinity for secessionism. Those whites who held that belief often used it as a way of defending the rights of slaveholders, but it also was deployed as a pretext for neutrality – as much of the state hoped to remain in the early years of the Civil War.[49]

Stanton railed against such thinking. "Neutrality, at such a time, is a sin against God, and a crime against the country," he argued in 1864. "[T]here is, in fact," the professor argued, "no neutrality, regarding this contest, in the breast of any American citizen. It is an impossible thing, and every man knows and feels it." In Kentucky, proponents of the church's exclusively spiritual character – particularly Stuart Robinson and the *True Presbyterian* – were "the most powerful auxiliaries for keeping alive the spirit of the rebellion among the [state's] secessionists." Some ministers "in the Border States, and elsewhere" believed that "in this contest between loyalty and treason," one could "be 'neutral'" and have 'no opinion.'" As Stanton saw it, they were gravely misguided.[50]

Both Cooper and Stanton made their arguments from Danville, which had become one of the pronounced centers of unconditional Unionism in the state. Through the Civil War, the most significant member of the Danville Theological Seminary faculty remained Robert J. Breckinridge, and he was also Kentucky's most visible unconditional Unionist. Just as it existed elsewhere, unconditional Unionism in Kentucky elevated the Union above all else. It demanded that any factors that divided partisans be subsumed in the name of national allegiance. But in truth, there was only one divisive issue in this moment: slavery. Thus, in spite of Breckinridge's personal reservations against Civil War emancipation, he achieved wide recognition for his willingness to sacrifice even that scruple in the name of the Union. The presidential election season of 1864 revealed how highly many northerners thought of Breckinridge. As a Unionist coming from a slaveholding border state, the Kentuckian was chosen to temporarily preside over the June National Union Convention – the coalition party composed primarily of Republicans as well as Democrats who supported the federal war policy – to nominate Abraham Lincoln for a second presidential term.[51]

In his speech endorsing Lincoln, Breckinridge once again argued that loyalty to the Union must trump all other considerations. "No government has ever been built upon imperishable foundations," the Kentuckian argued, "which

---

49 Ibid.; and Robert L. Stanton, *The Church and the Rebellion: A Consideration of the Rebellion against the Government of the United States; and the Agency of the Church, North and South, in Relation Thereto* (New York: Derby & Miller, 1864).

50 Stanton, *The Church and the Rebellion*, 218, 221.

51 Klotter, *Breckinridges of Kentucky*, 85–6; and *Presidential Election, 1864. Proceedings of the National Union Convention Held in Baltimore, Md., June 7th and 8th, 1864* (New York: Baker & Goodwin, 1864), 5.

foundations were not laid in the blood of traitors." Breckinridge did not pause in explaining precisely what this harrowing contention meant: "It is a fearful truth, but we may as well avow it at once; and every blow you strike, and every rebel you kill, every battle you win, dreadful as it is to do it, you are adding, it may be a year – it may be ten years – it may be a century – it may be ten centuries to the life of the Government and the freedom of your children." For Breckinridge, all hung on the Union. He knew the assembled delegates came from a whole range of political persuasions, "primitive Republicans and primitive Abolitionists," as well as "primitive Democrats and primitive Whigs." Yet they all agreed, as National Unionists, that those markers mattered less than fidelity to their nation. And Breckinridge was eager to lead that coalition from the dais.[52]

When it came to the slavery question specifically, even as Breckinridge was in the midst of trying to reclaim many of his own fugitives in the summer of 1864, he chose not to address the specific details of Union policy on emancipation. The Presbyterian had publicly denounced the Emancipation Proclamation, but in the context of the National Union Convention, the finer points of Union slavery policy were not at issue. That was because all fault for any American problems of the day rested with the seceding South. Breckinridge professed to "believ[e] in my conscience and with all my heart, that what has brought us to where we are in the matter of Slavery is the original sin and folly of treason and Secession." Republicans had expressly claimed in 1860 "that they would not touch Slavery in the States," and yet Confederates all the same believed Lincoln's election provoked their own secession. That brazen action demonstrated that Confederates could not be trusted. They did not value the Union.[53]

Privately, Breckinridge did not agree with the way that emancipation had come about, but now, publicly, he agreed that the Civil War had brought the death of the evil institution: "I unite myself with those who believe it is contrary to the highest interests of all men and of all Government, contrary to the spirit of the Christian religion, and incompatible with the natural rights of man." Despite his own gradual emancipationism, Breckinridge sounded like an abolitionist at the National Union Convention: "I join myself with those who say, away with it forever." The Kentuckian "fervently prayed God that the day may come when, throughout the whole land every man may be as free as you are, and as capable of enjoying regulated liberty." Breckinridge's unconditional Unionism meant that there was no middle ground: there was Union above all else. To dissent on any grounds was tantamount to treason.[54]

When Breckinridge spoke these words in June 1864, he undeniably represented many Unionists. However, with the exception of his cohort in Danville

---

[52] *Proceedings of the National Union Convention, 1864*, 7.
[53] Ibid.
[54] Ibid., 8.

and a minority elsewhere in the Commonwealth, Breckinridge spoke for few in Kentucky. He maintained a close relationship with General Stephen G. Burbridge, who also in June 1864 had routed Lexingtonian John Hunt Morgan's Confederate cavalry raiders near Cynthiana, in central Kentucky. Burbridge, like Breckinridge, was unconditional in his Unionism. And the Union general also became increasingly unpopular, especially after Lincoln suspended the writ of habeas corpus in Kentucky on July 5, 1864. Where Breckinridge had called for bloodletting to curtail dissent, Burbridge had the military might to actually pull off the task. In the summer of 1864 Kentucky was in a state of "semi-anarchy," and under his notorious General Order 59, issued on July 16, Burbridge worked to quell the political disaffection and vigilantism that had engulfed the state. The general "call[ed] for the adoption of stringent measures on the part of the military authorities" to end the acts of "lawless bands of armed men engaged in interrupting railroad and telegraphic communications, plundering and murdering peaceful Union Citizens, destroying the mails," and similar anti-Union activities. Burbridge warned that "the property of rebel sympathizers" would be "seized and appropriated" so as to "indemnify the Government or loyal citizens for losses incurred by the acts of lawless men." Furthermore – and most jarring – Burbridge authorized the execution of four Confederate prisoners for every "murder" of an "unarmed Union citizen." By January 1865, sixty-seven prisoners had been executed – often based on weak evidence. In the telling of his opponents and even some of his sympathizers, Burbridge's quest for power knew no bounds. He was relieved of command in February 1865, but along with the executions, his numerous arrests and deportations of presumed disloyal Kentuckians further sullied the Union cause among whites in the Commonwealth.[55]

None of these actions appeared to bother Robert J. Breckinridge. In the fall 1864 election season, Breckinridge doubled down on the bloodthirsty language he had employed earlier at the National Union Convention. As one account from a critic documented, Breckinridge argued in a September speech, "As to these [illegal arrests], all the fault I have to find is, that more should not have been arrested than were; and many of those arrested were set at liberty too soon." The Presbyterian minister then drew on a particularly vivid historical example to make his point: "When Simon de Montfort was slaughtering the Protestants in the south of France, he was appealed to by certain persons – declaring that his men were mistaken, that they were killing many who were good Catholics. To which he replied: 'Kill them *all*; God knows his own.' And this," Breckinridge argued, "is the way we should deal with these fellows; treat them all alike." The Unionist minister supposed that there might even be some number of the accused and arrested "who are not rebels at heart." No mortal, however, could know the true condition of another person's heart. It was therefore proper to continue with indiscriminate executions. As Breckinridge saw it, "God will take care of [the falsely accused] and save [their souls] at least." But that involved the spiritual world to come. In this life they were damned.[56]

Such was the most visible religious face of unconditional Unionism in Kentucky, which most whites found increasingly unpalatable. Thomas E. Bramlette became a marked opponent of Burbridge and a leader among the state's Conservative Union Democrats. In September 1864 the governor also denounced Breckinridge as "the reverend politician who has been aptly characterized as 'a weathercock in politics and an Ishmaelite in religion.'" In a letter to Abraham Lincoln earlier the same month, Bramlette told the president that Burbridge's severe actions in the name of the Union "have been urged by the counsels of a class of men who represent the evil genius of loyalty." It was true that white Kentuckians had never supported Lincoln in any appreciable numbers, but Bramlette wanted him to know all the same that "[t]he course pursued by many of those intrusted with Federal authority in Kentucky has made to your Administration and re-election thousands of bitter and irreconcilable opponents." By contrast, "a wise and just policy and action would more easily have made friends." Such "[e]xtreme measures, by which" Union commanders "sought to break the just pride and subdue the free spirit of the people" served only to teach white Kentuckians that the Union "would have fitted them for enslavement." The cumulative result of suspending habeas corpus and allowing Burbridge to act wantonly, Bramlette explained to Lincoln, "ha[s] aroused the determined opposition to your re-election of at least three-fourths of the people of Kentucky." Bramlette knew he spoke for many white Kentuckians who did not consider themselves hostile to the Union but, given the weight of the federal military presence in the Commonwealth, found it increasingly difficult to support the cause of war in its name.[57]

Bramlette was absolutely correct about the mood of his white constituency – and he almost perfectly predicted the presidential electoral returns. The Commonwealth was one of only three Union states to vote against Lincoln; the other two were New Jersey and Delaware, and in both states the margins were

---

[56] Lewis Collins and Richard H. Collins, *History of Kentucky*, 3 vols. (Covington, KY: Collins, 1874), 1:142. It is worth noting that this quote does not appear in any other source and that Richard H. Collins, as former publisher of the *Danville Quarterly Review* and friend to Breckinridge's earlier opponents at Danville Theological Seminary, had plenty of reason to disdain Breckinridge. It is entirely plausible that Breckinridge, irascible as he was, did not utter these words. See also Klotter, *Breckinridges of Kentucky*, 86, 340n20.

[57] Collins and Collins, *History of Kentucky*, 1:142; Thomas E. Bramlette, letter to Abraham Lincoln, September 3, 1864, in *The War of the Rebellion*, Ser. 3, vol. 4, pt. 1, 689; Klotter, *Breckinridges of Kentucky*, 86; Cooling, *Franklin and Nashville*, 248–50.

far narrower. Reflecting broad dissatisfaction with the course of events, Kentucky's voter turnout for the election was 64 percent lower than in 1860. In the Bluegrass State, Democratic nominee George B. McClellan drew 69.8 percent of the vote. Only 30.2 percent went for Lincoln.[58]

White Kentuckians supported Lincoln at rates lower than any other state in the Union in 1864, but their political opinions were not simply swayed by the hard hand of General Stephen Gano Burbridge. As Bramlette argued to the president, the linkage between emancipation and the preservation of the Union had poisoned the cause for Kentucky whites. Bramlette claimed his "Unionism is unconditional," but he did not use this term in the same way as unconditional Unionists: he was not antislavery. "We are for preserving the rights and liberties of our own race and upholding the character and dignity of our position," Bramlette wrote. Sounding much like white Kentuckians prior to late 1862, the governor contended, "We are not willing to sacrifice a single life or imperil the smallest right of free white men for the sake of the negro." The problem in Bramlette's view was that the fighting that had come to Kentucky had called into question the loyalty of some whites – otherwise good Americans like himself – because they did not support the Union position on emancipation.[59]

Making the Civil War into a war about slavery meant that the conflict was about something other than the Union itself, and the majority of Kentucky whites Bramlette spoke for refused this interpretation. They deployed the language of neutrality, just as they had in 1860 and 1861:

> We repudiate the counsels of those who say the Government must be restored with slavery, or that it must be restored without slavery, as a condition of their Unionism. We are for the restoration of our Government throughout our entire limits, regardless of what may happen to the negro. We reject as spurious the Unionism of all who make the status of the negro a *sine qua non* to peace and unity. We are not willing to imperil the life, liberty, and happiness of our own race and people for the freedom or enslavement of the negro. To permit the question of the freedom or slavery of the negro to obstruct the restoration of national authority and unity is a blood-stained sin.[60]

Thus understood by Bramlette, even in late 1864, the Civil War had nothing to do with slavery. Placing slavery at the center of the conflict meant endorsing an extremist view. And what was clearly worse, making emancipation a war aim meant supporting abolitionist politics. Antislavery theologians in Danville,

[58] In Delaware, McClellan received 51.8 percent to Lincoln's 48.2 percent of the vote. McClellan received 52.8 percent to Lincoln's 47.2 percent in New Jersey; 1864 presidential election numbers taken from the American Presidency Project, University of California, Santa Barbara, http://www.presidency.ucsb.edu/showelection.php?year=1864. See also Cooling, *Franklin and Nashville*, 250–1.

[59] Bramlette, letter to Lincoln, 689.

[60] Ibid.

especially Jacob Cooper and Robert J. Breckinridge, chafed at being linked to
abolitionism. As conservatives, they had fought many years against that label
in the years before the Civil War. Yet in demanding unconditional loyalty
to the Union, even as it moved toward emancipation, that is precisely what
had happened in the minds of white religious Kentuckians. As Cooper argued
in March 1864, "There are, in truth, only two parties in our country, the
Unionists and the Secessionists – there can be no middle ground, and those who
are not for us in this struggle are against us." In white religious Kentucky, the
pretense of neutrality had disappeared. There could be no place for moderation
toward the nation or slavery. For those who opposed unconditional Unionism,
abolitionist heterodoxy now ruled the United States. To support the Union was
to support immediate emancipation; to suggest anything short of that object
was to question what that Union was all about.[61]

That development was significant. Although some Kentucky whites could
stomach such a notion of Union, most could not. Bluegrass Baptists, who at
the start of the Civil War had called for moderation and fidelity to a proslavery
Christian America, all but reversed themselves as the conflict dragged on. They
showed their own developing sense of sectional solidarity in response to an early
1864 report in the *Christian Witness*, a Chicago-based Illinois Baptist newspaper, castigating the condition of religious belief and practice in Louisville. The
Western Recorder saw fit to respond to the main charge of the *Witness*, namely
that the practice widespread in the Falls City "of ignoring politics in the pulpit"
was an "erroneous policy" that had created a "coldness" and "spiritless worship" in the city's churches. Nothing could have been further from the truth,
the *Western Recorder* contended. The fact was that "the orthodox churches in
this city have never experienced a better feeling than in the last few months."
The apolitical message preached "in their pulpits and their churches" led to a
recent wave of "revivals" that claimed "scores and hundreds" of participants.
As practitioners of true gospel Christianity, Kentucky whites knew well what
they were witnessing and its properly Christian source.[62]

The same could not be said for their fellow Baptists from Illinois.
"[S]uppose," the Kentucky paper posited, "instead of preaching the gospel,"
the Louisville clergy "had given themselves to Sabbath harangues upon the
duty of Kentuckians to give up their slaves, to discountenance the institution
and join Freedmen's societies." This approach to sermonizing, no doubt com-
monplace in the North's abolition-minded congregations, would have "driven
from church" no fewer than "Nine-tenths" of Louisville parishioners. Nothing
would be left of historic houses of worship but "desolated monuments of folly
and madness." Here was the reality, according to the *Western Recorder*: "Abolitionism, Materialism, and Politics may suit the pulpits and church-goers of

---

[61] Jacob Cooper, "The Loyalty Demanded by the Present Crisis," *Danville Quarterly Review* 4.1
(March 1864): 110.
[62] "'Louisville Correspondence' of the Christian Times," *Western Recorder*, January 16, 1864.

Boston and Chicago, but... they will not do in Louisville." In those northern locales, "[t]he house of God has been metamorphosed into an amphitheatre, and the silent devotion of religion changed into the loud plaudits of a mob." Honestly, the Kentucky Baptist press asked, what was the discernible "difference" between Brooklyn's Plymouth Congregational Church – the home of nineteenth-century America's most famous public preacher, Henry Ward Beecher, brother of antislavery littératrice Harriet Beecher Stowe and son of the deceased Lane Seminary doyen, Lyman Beecher – and New York City's notoriously corrupt political machine at "Tammany Hall"? As the Kentuckians saw it, the author of the *Christian Witness*'s report on Louisville religion "is manifestly a vagrant, desperately afflicted with the epidemic of nigger-on-the-brain, and has not sense or honesty enough to see and state things as they are here." If Louisville lacked "clerical demagogues," so be it. Abolitionism – and also the line that demarcated slave soil from free – proved too divisive an obstacle for any sense of common Christian unity.[63]

By 1865, that view was widespread among believing whites in the Commonwealth. White Kentuckians did not overwhelmingly embrace the Confederate cause during the Civil War, but after the fact they embraced Confederate religion. Rooted in antipathy for abolitionism, African American political and social equality, and so-called politicized religion, white religious Kentuckians had, in significant ways, been preparing for that development long before the sectional crisis began. The end of religious neutrality would shape the landscape of white Kentucky's politics and culture for decades to come.

[63] Ibid.; "Politics and the Pulpit," *Western Recorder*, January 23, 1864. This latter article was a reprint of the Louisville *Journal*'s response to the Chicago *Christian Times* article attacking Louisville religion.

7

Kentucky's Redemption

Confederate Religion and White Democratic Domination, 1865–1874

> Immediately after the war our brethren in the M. E. Church, North, announced our death; they published our Obituary; they preached our funeral in many of *their* pulpits... and many of their ministers have made it their especial business to declare that from and after the abolition of slavery the Southern Church had ceased to exist.... [The northern church offered sectional reunion] [u]pon the very mild and gracious terms of forsaking our sins, and "accepting the condition of things," such ... as military rule, Freedman's Bureaus, universal suffrage, negro supremacy, [and] the freedom and equality of negroes with ourselves, that is, to cease to be what we are.
>
> – "The M. E. Church, North,"
> *Christian Observer,* July 25, 1868[1]

With the surrender of Robert E. Lee at Appomattox Courthouse in April 1865, and the several other Confederate military surrenders that followed in the next few months, the formal military fighting of the Civil War came to an end. In Kentucky, however, the ideological and political battles for the loyalty of the state's white population were only beginning to escalate.[2] The sectional conflict

---

[1] "The M. E. Church, North," *Christian Observer,* July 25, 1868.

[2] The physical fighting in Kentucky also remained fierce, particularly in the form of guerilla violence, well after Confederate surrender. See Hambleton Tapp and James C. Klotter, *Kentucky: Decades of Discord* (Frankfort: Kentucky Historical Society, 1977), 5–10; J. Michael Rhyne, "A 'Murderous Affair in Lincoln County': Politics, Violence, and Memory in a Civil War Era Kentucky Community," *American Nineteenth Century History* 7 (September 2006): 337–59; Rhyne, "Rehearsal for Redemption: The Politics of Post-Emancipation Violence in Kentucky's Bluegrass Region" (Ph.D. diss., University of Cincinnati, 2006); J. Michael Crane, "'The Rebels Are Bold, Defiant, and Unscrupulous in Their Dementions of All Men': Social Violence in Daviess County, Kentucky, 1861–1868," *Ohio Valley History,* 2.1 (Spring 2002): 18–19; and T. R. C. Hutton, *Bloody Breathitt: Politics and Violence in the Appalachian South* (Lexington: University Press of Kentucky, 2013), 37–111.

resolved the fate of the national Union and, after emancipation – ultimately through the Thirteenth Amendment – the legal status of slavery. Yet in the minds of many Kentucky whites, neither issue had been resolved religiously. The Civil War destroyed slavery, but it did not destroy the faith that sustained slavery.

Kentucky's proslavery evangelicals affirmed the latter. In March 1865 Stuart Robinson was still in exile in Toronto. There he published a treatise titled *Slavery, as Recognized in the Mosaic Civil Law, Recognized . . . and Allowed, in the . . . Christian Church*. In the main, Robinson's argument was not a new one. It stood in a decades-long tradition of southern Protestant proslavery theological writing. Published just weeks after President Abraham Lincoln's Second Inaugural Address, Robinson took extreme umbrage with one of Lincoln's most famous lines. The president had "utter[ed] that blasphemous sentence, 'Yet, if God wills that [the war] continue until all the wealth piled by the bondsman's two hundred and fifty years of unrequited toil shall be sunk, and until every drop of blood drawn with the lash shall be paid by another drawn with the sword, as was said three thousand years ago, so still it must be said 'the judgments of the Lord are true and righteous altogether.'" Here was the American president, claiming that the Civil War was a kind of national atonement for the collective sin of slaveholding. It was all too much for the Kentuckian to bear. Plainly, Robinson wrote, Lincoln's words – which quoted Psalm 19:9 – could "hardly be characterized as less than impiously presumptuous perversions of the Word and Providence of God." According to Robinson, Lincoln's chief offense was that his Second Inaugural twisted the Bible – which offered obvious support for American slavery – into an abolitionist instrument.[3]

In Robinson's opinion, such religiously based political denunciations of Lincoln did not violate the spirituality of the church doctrine. Indeed, he argued that there was a difference between the actions of individual believers and those of ecclesiastical bodies. As free citizens in a democratic society, individual believers could advocate for whatever causes they wished. When he had delivered the content of his *Slavery* volume first as a series of sermons, Robinson claimed he had made no mention of the "great secular issues now pending between the slave-holding and non-slave-holding states." In book form, however, away from a formal church pulpit, the minister "felt at liberty to suggest the applications of the argument."[4]

Robinson's distinction between political opinions offered within church contexts (unacceptable) and by religious actors independent of the aegis of an organized church (acceptable) may have been too subtle. The minister's avowed apoliticism may not have been disingenuous, but he was certainly naïve about the extent to which nineteenth-century American religion was politicized – and

---

3 Stuart Robinson, *Slavery, As Recognized in the Mosaic Civil Law, Recognized also, and Allowed, in the Abrahamic, Mosaic, and Christian Church* (Toronto: Rollo & Adam, 1865), v, 20.
4 Ibid., 78.

unavoidably so. Nevertheless, Robinson's ideas about the spirituality of the church and the biblical sanction for slavery proved key to the shaping of white Kentucky's postwar embrace of Confederate identity.

It was this constellation of values that broadly characterized white religious opinion throughout the state in the years following 1865, and it fueled the Democratic dominance that marked the period. Because it remained with the Union during the war, Kentucky never faced military Reconstruction or other aspects of the 1867 Congressional Reconstruction Acts: it did not have to disenfranchise Confederates or enfranchise African American men; black testimony was not accepted equally in state courts; and Kentucky was not required to accept the Thirteenth, Fourteenth, and Fifteenth Amendments – which it voted against in every case – until they became federal law. These conditions were all required in different ways for the former Confederate states to rejoin the Union. In 1861 Kentucky had passed a state-level Wartime Act of Expatriation that denied civil and political rights to Confederates, but that was repealed by the legislature in December 1865 and liberal pardons were granted to any remaining rebels. Although a small Republican faction persisted in the face of overwhelming odds, the result was that by 1867 the state had become solidly Democratic – that year Republicans carried only 17 of 138 state legislature seats – and it would continue that way for the next thirty years. When black men in Kentucky did gain the franchise in 1870 with the Fifteenth Amendment, they injected a significant voting bloc into the state's Republican party. Yet freedom from slavery also meant freedom to leave Kentucky. The state's African American population began out-migrating in 1865, a process that accelerated as the nineteenth century wore on. In 1870 blacks remained just more than 16 percent of the Commonwealth's population, and the Democratic Party firmly held sway. Of all the former slaveholding states, Unionist Kentucky remained the most unreconstructed.[5]

With the end of Reconstruction and the restoration of the political legitimacy of former Confederates starting in the 1870s, southern whites elsewhere widely claimed to have been "redeemed." Historians have long debated the meaning of the term as it applied to the post-Reconstruction southern political order, but for a section marked by white evangelical dominance, it connoted as much religiously as it did politically. The white South's redemption drew from a deep well of religious opinion, fed by the context of antebellum debate about the nature of slavery. Because the white South's slaveholding was no sin, no atonement – contrary to the way Lincoln put it in his Second Inaugural – was

---

[5] Lowell H. Harrison and James C. Klotter, *A New History of Kentucky* (Lexington: University Press of Kentucky, 1997), 205, 216–21, 239–42; Tapp and Klotter, *Decades of Discord*, 22–8; Aaron Astor, *Rebels on the Border: Civil War, Emancipation, and the Reconstruction of Kentucky and Missouri* (Baton Rouge: Louisiana State University Press, 2012), 180–4; and B. Franklin Cooling, "After the Horror: Kentucky in Reconstruction," in *Sister States, Enemy States: The Civil War in Kentucky and Tennessee*, eds. Kent T. Dollar, Larry H. Whiteaker, and W. Calvin Dickinson (Lexington: University Press of Kentucky, 2009), 351–5.

required. Rather, the sin was destroying the thing God created for ordering human society: slavery. The sin was thus the Civil War and its aftermath, Reconstruction.[6]

In white southern ideology, this was a moment of coerced Republican rule, enforced by an overwhelming U.S. military presence. It elevated African American freedpeople to a position where they could politically dominate their former masters, and it rubbed Confederate faces in their defeat. Therefore, as former Confederate states were slowly readmitted to the Union between 1868 and 1870, and as the Democratic party regained its strength in the South – ultimately leading to Democratic control of the House of Representatives in 1874 – the term "redemption" suggested that southern, ex-Confederate whites would be allowed to rightfully participate in the national U.S. political system as recognized equals in the fabric of white American life. White southerners thus perceived redemption as the opposite of Reconstruction: redemption meant "home rule" by white southerners, no longer forced by an overreaching federal government that sought the enforcement of African American civil and voting rights.

Kentucky did not join the Confederacy during the Civil War, but it had long participated in the evangelical religious culture of the white South and zealously agreed with its views on race and slavery. In the wake of emancipation, whites in the Commonwealth made common cause with the majority of the white religious South and directed their energies toward the development of a segregationist and anti-northern theology. After the Civil War, when white religious Kentuckians confronted the prospect of an interracial, egalitarian political and social order, they overwhelmingly became a people who defined themselves forthrightly by regional and racial distinctions. That religious bond led Kentucky whites to embrace the South's Confederate cause as their own.

Without serving the Confederacy, Kentucky thus joined in redemption. For Bluegrass State whites, however, it was not redemption from Reconstruction and Republican rule – for the first was limited and the second never happened. Rather, Kentucky's redemption was a white Democratic and ex-Confederate claiming of the state's history from a Unionist past. And unlike everywhere else in the South, it began immediately after the Civil War.

There were serious efforts to challenge the rising tide of ex-Confederate domination in the war's immediate aftermath. In December 1865 General Oliver O. Howard, recognizing the dire situation in Kentucky, authorized the establishment of the Freedmen's Bureau in Louisville, Lexington, and Paducah. The Bureau operated in the state from 1866 until 1870, and for a time additional headquarters were added in Bowling Green, Danville, and Henderson. Established under the U.S. Department of War, the Bureau was staffed by the

---

[6] This series of claims follows Daniel W. Stowell, "Why 'Redemption'? Religion and the End of Reconstruction, 1869–1877," in *Vale of Tears: New Essays on Religion and Reconstruction*, eds. Edward J. Blum and W. Scott Poole (Macon, GA: Mercer University Press, 2005), 140.

military and its mandate was broad: as elsewhere in the American South, it was involved with everything from legal adjudication of labor contracts and land deeds, to education and medical care, as well as suppressing violence against African Americans.[7]

And it was violence that clearly presented the most direct challenge to the post-emancipation order in Kentucky. The Freedmen's Bureau's presence was met with great hostility by the state's whites and was seen as a reminder of the Union presence during the Civil War that had proved so incendiary. From 1866 to 1870 terrorist violence, in the name of the Ku Klux Klan or any number of other regulator bands, engulfed the state. Most of it was directed at African Americans – especially former Union soldiers or the families of enlisted blacks – or those whites who supported civil and voting rights. In 1866–7, the Bureau reported 319 incidents of racist "maltreatment" directed at Kentucky blacks, which included included 20 murders, 18 shootings, and 11 rapes. Those numbers increased in the 1867–8 reports (where there were 324 cases, 20 of which were murders) and again in 1868–9 (327 incidents, with 26 murders, 30 shootings, and 3 rapes). To be sure, the Bureau's reports vastly undercounted what was actually happening. Untold violent acts also occurred in the countryside, away from their presence. For throughout its existence, the Bureau was underfunded and undermanned. Nearly all wartime Union soldiers were demobilized from Kentucky by the middle of 1866, and clear numbers of soldiers under the Bureau do not exist. At its height in 1866 there were only twenty-one federal officers under the Bureau in Kentucky; in the next two years that number was reduced to eight. For as much as Kentucky whites may have resented its presence, the fact was that the Bureau never had enough force to keep white supremacist terrorists from attacking freedpeople or whites who worked with them as Republicans or civilian agents of the Bureau. After congressional passage of the Civil Rights Act of 1866, the Freedmen's Bureau had the ability to prosecute terrorists via federal tribunals, over state-level protest from Kentucky. However, in cases that were adjudicated locally, justice was hard to find. It was understood that terrorist violence served the aims of the Democratic Party, and most often, its white partisans were happy to ignore the consequences of such action.[8]

Elijah P. Marrs, whose Union service freed him from slavery, began working in Baptist schools for freedpeople in small towns east of Louisville in 1866. Over the next several years, as Marrs moved to different schools – all of which tended to be self-funded by African Americans – he routinely encountered white terrorists. As he explained in his memoir, "though the war was over, the K. K. K. was in full blast, and no man was safe from their depredations."

---

[7] Marion B. Lucas, *A History of Blacks in Kentucky*, vol. 1: *From Slavery to Segregation, 1760–1891* (Frankfort: Kentucky Historical Society, 1992), 185–7.

[8] Ibid., 186–95. See also the accounts in Allen W. Trelease, *White Terror: The Ku Klux Klan Conspiracy and Southern Reconstruction* (New York: Harper & Row, 1971), 89–91, 124–5, 280–4; and "Freedmen's Affairs in Kentucky," *New York Times*, March 25, 1866.

Marrs himself worked to subvert the system of white Democratic politics and extralegal vigilantism. Active in Republican politics, Marrs organized a "secret meeting at the colored Baptist church" in Shelbyville in 1869 "for the purpose of shaking up things for the election." After taking over a freedpeople's school in Newcastle, he organized a "Loyal League for self-protection," comprised of the area's African American men. Klan activity was rampant, and as Marrs explained, "we were always ready for any duty." In his telling, "For three years I slept with a pistol under my head, an Enfield rifle at my side, and a corn-knife at the door, but I never had occasion to use them." Still, Marrs understood clearly that freedom in Kentucky still required African American vigilance.[9]

In 1867 African Methodist Episcopal Church (AME) minister J. C. Embry, who in 1896 would be named an AME bishop, wrote to the denomination's flagship newspaper, the Philadelphia-based *Christian Recorder*, characterizing the progress that freedpeople's Christianity had made in Bowling Green since emancipation. In an otherwise hopeful letter that described ongoing church and school efforts, he frankly explained the context for this work among black believers in Kentucky: "Our people here are very unfortunate in that they live in the meanest State in the Union; the last to let them go, and the last to do them justice in any case, when it is possible to do otherwise." As Embry's letter indicated, the post-emancipation order was not the same as under slavery. Yet Kentucky whites moved only as far from slavery as they had to, and an ex-Confederate Democratic party became the vehicle for their resistance.[10]

Kentucky's postwar Democratic politics was by no means monolithic. It was long divided between backward-looking, aristocratic, and unreconstructed "Bourbons" who lifted up the agrarian antebellum period as the pinnacle of the state's – and their own personal – history, and a more progressive branch that favored allegiances with New South boosters who looked toward industry and economic diversification for postwar vitality. This latter position, called the "New Departure," was first famously given voice in late 1866 by William C. P. Breckinridge, son of Robert J. Breckinridge, who, to his father's chagrin, rejected both formal ministry and the Union. W. C. P. had enlisted with Kentucky's Confederate cavalry, serving under the notorious raider, John Hunt Morgan. Yet after the war, as editor of the Lexington *Observer and Reporter* he pushed for economic diversification and a limited acceptance of civil rights – albeit not in "radical" ways sought by Republicans and only after changes in federal law had proved inevitable.[11]

9 Elijah P. Marrs, *Life and History of the Rev. Elijah P. Marrs, First Pastor of Beargrass Baptist Church and Author* (Louisville: Bradley & Gilbert, 1885), 78–90, quotes 79, 90; and George C. Wright, *Racial Violence in Kentucky, 1865–1940: Lynchings, Mob Rule, and "Legal Lynchings"* (Baton Rouge: Louisiana State University Press, 1990), 58–9. On the significance of armed black defense to civil and voting rights in Kentucky, see Astor, *Rebels on the Border*, 208–42.
10 J. C. Embry, "From Kentucky," *Christian Recorder*, June 8, 1867.
11 Tapp and Klotter, *Decades of Discord*, 29–36; James C. Klotter, *The Breckinridges of Kentucky* (Lexington: University Press of Kentucky, 1986), 144–9; Cooling, "After the Horror," 353–4.

After a failed political run for district attorney in 1867, W. C. P. Breckinridge sold the *Observer and Reporter* in 1868, but another significant newspaper editor and ex-Confederate, the Tennessee-born Henry Watterson, succeeded him as the primary mouthpiece of the New Departure. In 1868 Watterson began a fifty-year reign over the Louisville *Courier-Journal*, the state's most visible and widely read newspaper. Despite his military service and work during the war as a propagandist for the Confederacy, Watterson did not memorialize the lost cause. Like many white Kentuckians, including W. C. P. Breckinridge, Watterson's wartime support came late to the Confederacy. After the war, he also rejected the singularly agrarian past and called for a mixed economy and business-minded interests in banking, railroads, and factories that would help Kentucky compete economically with its northern neighbors. Watterson's version of the New Departure, in stark contrast to the Bourbons, argued that white Kentuckians needed to accept the legal changes that came with Reconstruction: the New Departure thus rejected backward-looking solutions to the contemporary problems of the postwar period. As an ex-Confederate and wartime apologist for the cause, like many conservatives before the war Watterson claimed the South had the constitutional right to hold slaves and defended secession on that ground. But by the late 1890s, Watterson would overtly condemn slavery for its legacy of economic lethargy, a position he was quietly honing as early as the 1860s and 1870s. Opposing the African American citizenship rights and voting rights that came with the Fourteenth and Fifteenth Amendments, he argued, simply stymied Kentucky's economic advancement and integration with the national economy.[12]

At face value, the New Departure might seem radically opposed to the values of proslavery religion. However, for two reasons that was not the case. First, the political disagreements between the New Departure and Bourbon Democrats, significant as they were at the level of state politics, counted for little when it came to national questions – whether the result of the war or expanding civil rights – that had already been decided. Theirs was still an anti-Republican, ex-Confederate, pro-southern version of Democracy. As was the case with redeemers elsewhere in the South, internal party divisions were sublimated in the name of ensuring white Democratic rule. Second, many of the New Departure's most visible spokesmen, such as Watterson, were essentially silent on the theology that lay behind slavery – even as they closely associated themselves with ministers who were not.[13]

[12] Paul M. Gaston, *The New South Creed: A Study in Southern Mythmaking* (New York: Knopf, 1970), 37–42, 52–3, 92–9, 127–36; Tapp and Klotter, *Decades of Discord*, 29–36; Anne E. Marshall, *Creating a Confederate Kentucky: The Lost Cause and Civil War Memory in a Border State* (Chapel Hill: University of North Carolina Press, 2010), 51–5; and Daniel S. Margolies, *Henry Watterson and the New South: The Politics of Empire, Free Trade, and Globalization* (Lexington: University Press of Kentucky, 2006), 23–4, 100–2.

[13] Marshall, *Creating a Confederate Kentucky*, 51–5; Cooling, "After the Horror," 351–3; and Margolies, *Henry Watterson*, 23.

In many ways, this silence was the genius of the proslavery argument that ensured its vitality into the postwar future. Because proslavery religion was never simply about slavery nor maintaining white supremacy, translating it to the postwar era required less intellectual slippage than later observers might imagine. Because their faith rested on a theological proposition – that a commonsensical, plain reading of the Bible revealed the Christian God's sanction for slavery – the military, political, and legal changes that came with emancipation did little to alter white southerners' patterns of belief.

Here was the purchase of the proslavery argument for the postslavery order: it was not necessary to hold slaves to be a faithful Christian. No conservative believer in the South had ever claimed as much. The point was that one could not say slavery was sinful. Although the context had changed significantly with emancipation, the argument – and the Bible – remained the same. In a United States without slaveholders, the biblical witness remained clear. In the antebellum era, it was possible to be a gradual emancipationist and remain part of the godly community. All the same in the postwar era, the issue was more about how one read the text than the slavery question itself. This religious principle stood outside human history. The laws of humanity might change, but the divine order was fixed – immutable.

By 1865 Kentucky thus found itself in lockstep with the rest of the white Christian South, institutionally securing solidarities of region and race. Much of the debate between white southern and northern believers in the Reconstruction era centered on the differences – or, for some, the potential for unity – between the sectional branches of the major Protestant denominations that had split over slavery before the war. Since the end of the Civil War, northern Methodists had implored their counterparts in the white South to let go of their past grievances and reunite the denomination that, before 1844, had been America's largest religious body. As northern Methodist bishops first claimed in June 1865, the end of the Civil War and American slavery meant that there was no reason to continue with two sectional churches: "The great cause which led to the separation from us ... has passed away, and we trust the day is not far distant when there shall be but one organization which shall embrace the whole Methodist family of the United States."[14]

But white southerners had no time for such overtures. In 1867 the *Christian Observer*, a Southern Methodist newspaper published in Catlettsburg, Kentucky – located at the confluence of the Ohio and Big Sandy rivers, the dividing line between Kentucky and West Virginia – condemned the idea of "Methodist Re-Union" because the northern church required extrabiblical standards of intersectional denominational fellowship: "loyalty to the general Government"

---

[14] *Formal Fraternity. Proceedings of the General Conference of the Methodist Episcopal Church and of the Methodist Episcopal Church, South, in 1872, 1874, and 1876, and of the Joint Commission of the Two Churches on Fraternal Relations, at Cape May, New Jersey, August 16–23, 1876* (New York: Nelson and Phillips, 1876), 9.

and "opposition to slavery." Such a basis for church union flew in the face of the Holy Writ's revealed truth. "Christ said, My kingdom is not of this world" and "also the Savior said to his disciples, ye are not of the world, but I have chosen you out of the world." Yet, according to the *Observer*, northern Methodist "Bishops make the Church not only of the world, but require its members to conform to the world, even to the most dangerous feature that the world presents." Sectional rapprochement between Methodists, the paper contended, would only happen "when we are willing to adopt their *political creed and receive the mark of the beast*." The northern church, in the words of these Kentucky Methodists, had made an illicit deal with the devil for their church's soul. It was a deal the white South wanted no part of.[15]

As far as these Methodists were concerned, northerners had never really understood the South's religious position. As S. C. Shaw of Parkersburg, West Virginia, wrote in the *Christian Observer* 1867, "[I]t was not slavery or abolitionism that caused the division of the Methodist Episcopal Church as it existed in 1844, but rather, it was disregard of a plighted faith on the part of the North."[16] Earlier in 1867, the *Christian Observer* editorialized that "Northern Methodist preachers in particular" insist on "the idea that in 1844 the M. E. Church was divided... because of the question of slavery." But that was simply not true. Rather, "[t]he separation was caused by the fact that the majority" of northern Methodists "claimed the right to interfere with the acts and doings of civil government on matters of a political character." Antislavery Yankees "did then interfere, and inflict disabilities upon a Bishop" – James O. Andrew of Georgia, the slaveholder whose case precipitated the antebellum Methodist Episcopal Church split – "and other ministers of the Church, not for *moral* wrongs or moral delinquencies, but for doing that which the laws of the State in which they lived allowed them to do in matters purely political." Northern adherents had long since abandoned any respect for the church's spiritual, nonpolitical character, and the Yankee "disposition as a Church to intermeddle in political affairs" had sickeningly "been growing more and more" in recent years.[17]

Kentucky's white Methodists, in attacking the North's ostensibly politicized religion, claimed their own position had little to do with the slavery question itself. It is difficult to imagine, however, the course of the postbellum debate without reference to slavery. Their language closely mirrored that of other Southern Methodists, especially those from border states, who rejected the emancipationist religion of the North. One of the earliest, and most influential, statements from Southern Methodists appeared in June 1865 from a meeting in Palmyra, Missouri. Missouri's Civil War religious landscape had been even more contentious than in Kentucky, with far more federal intervention into

---

[15] "Methodist Re-Union," *Christian Observer*, August 20, 1867.
[16] S. C. Shaw, "Fragments. Number Seven," *Christian Observer*, August 20, 1867.
[17] "What Was and Is the Difference," *Christian Observer*, July 7, 1867.

church life; numerous ostensibly disloyal preachers had been deposed from their churches by Union military force. In Palmyra, laity and clergy gathered to denounce the wartime efforts of northern Methodism to take over southern churches with military support and force denominational reunion without considering the white South's opinion. One day after the meeting began, MECS bishop and Kentuckian Hubbard H. Kavanaugh arrived with words of commendation, "imparting courage and inspiring hope" among these fellow religiously orthodox, proslavery border state believers.[18]

The slavery question loomed large in the document produced in Missouri, later called the "Palmyra Manifesto." "Those who publish to the world that all the difference between [the MEC and MECS] was swept away with the institution of slavery are either ignorant of the facts or are trying to mislead the public," it argued. "The question upon which the Church divided was not whether the institution of slavery was right or wrong, per se, but whether it was a legitimate subject for ecclesiastical legislation. The right or wrong of the institution, its existence or non-existence, could not affect this vital question." Their next words were significant: slavery was "now abolished by Federal and State legislation, which event we accept as a political measure which we have nothing to do as a Church." Read one way, the statement might be taken to mean that these Southern Methodists in Missouri accepted the death of American slavery. Perhaps they did. Yet read in the context of all other white southern Protestant writing on slavery in the period, it seems more obvious that they meant the political resolution to the slavery question had no bearing on church teaching on the subject.[19]

Within Kentucky, similar statements soon appeared. The official platform of the state's Democratic Party in 1866 acknowledged that slavery was a dead letter, "but earnestly assert[ed] that Kentucky has the right to regulate the political status of the negroes within her territory." Moreover, it argued, "The question of suffrage" – presumably meaning for ex-Confederates, but including freedpeople as well – "belongs exclusively to the states." Kentucky's Democrats argued in their deliberations that the "Freedman's Bureau" had been "illegally

---

[18] W. M. Leftwich, *Martyrdom in Missouri: A History of Religious Proscription, the Seizure of Churches, and the Persecution of Ministers of the Gospel, in the State of Missouri During the Late Civil War and under the "Test Oath" of the New Constitution*, 2 vols. (St. Louis: Southwestern Book and Publishing, 1870), 2:316 (quote); and Charles T. Thrift, "Rebuilding the Southern Church," in *The History of American Methodism*, ed. Emory Stevens Bucke, et al., 3 vols. (New York: Abingdon Press, 1964), 2:267–9. On churches and the Union military in Missouri more generally, see Dennis K. Boman, *Lincoln and Citizens' Rights in Civil War Missouri: Balancing Freedom and Security* (Baton Rouge: Louisiana State University Press, 2011), 158–70, 246–8; and Marcus J. McArthur, "'There Can Be No Neutral Ground': Samuel B. McPheeters and the Collision of Church and State in St. Louis, 1860–1864," *Journal of Presbyterian History* 89.1 (Spring/Summer 2011): 17–26.

[19] "Palmyra Manifesto," in *Sourcebook of American Methodism*, ed. Frederick A. Norwood (Nashville: Abingdon Press, 1982), 330–1. See also Thrift, "Rebuilding the Southern Church," 267–9.

established" in Kentucky and called for it to "be removed." The entire force of the Democratic platform rested on the notion of states' rights, and this in the face of the federal government, the only entity capable of enforcing the rights that seemed promised in the wake of emancipation. As white Kentuckians had long argued, Democrats "solemnly declared a warm attachment to the Union of the States," and by this term they meant supporting the "Constitution, by which the Union was effected." Their country, in other words, was the one that had existed with the rights of slaveholders intact, before the "convulsions of revolution" that came with the Civil War. They sought to restore "our Government to its ancient purity, and try to make it such as it was in the days of Washington, Jefferson, and Jackson. We wish to save both the Constitution and the Union as they came to us from the hands of our patriot fathers." Kentucky Democrats sought to "rescue the Government from the vandal grasp of that radical Congress" currently in Washington, who had passed "iniquitous and unconstitutional bills" sustaining the Freedmen's Bureau and civil rights. It was the political application of a widespread ex-Confederate religious doctrine.[20]

That explication was widespread in Kentucky's leading white denominations. In January 1866 Louisville's *Free Christian Commonwealth* – the Presbyterian newspaper that succeeded Stuart Robinson's *True Presbyterian* as the primary arbiter of Southern Presbyterianism in Kentucky – published an exceedingly favorable report on an 1865 "pastoral letter" by the Southern Presbyterian Church on the Civil War and slavery. The document so succinctly summarized the white Christian South's view of the stakes of the old religion-and-slavery dispute for the postslavery order that it merits lengthy quotation:

> While the existence of slavery may, in its civil aspects, be regarded as a settled question, an issue now gone... the lawfulness of the relation as a question of social morality, and of Scriptural truth, has lost nothing of its importance. When we solemnly declare to you brethren, that the [abolition] dogma which asserts the inherent sinfulness of this relation, is unscriptural and fanatical; that it is condemned not only by the word of God, but by the voice of the Church in all ages; that it is one of the most pernicious heresies of modern times; that its countenance by any Church is a just cause of separation from it, (1 Tim. 6:1–5.) we have surely said enough to warn you away from this insidious error, as from a fatal shore.[21]

That purposive language preceded the 1867 publication of the best-known defense of slavery after the Civil War, authored by the cantankerous Virginia Presbyterian Robert L. Dabney, former chaplain to the highly memorialized Confederate General Thomas J. "Stonewall" Jackson. Dabney opened his argument with a satirical question and answer: "Is not the slavery question

---

[20] *Official Proceedings of the Convention of the Democratic Party of Kentucky. Held in the city of Louisville, May 1st, 1866* (n.p., n.d. [1866]), 4–5, 6, 7, 8. See also Tapp and Klotter, *Decades of Discord*, 15.

[21] "The Platform of the Southern Church," *Free Christian Commonwealth*, January 25, 1866.

dead? . . . Would God it were dead!" For Dabney, the "slavery question" posed a moral dilemma only for those who resided outside the realm of southern religious orthodoxy. And he intended to show that abolitionists were such a people: "in the Church, abolitionism lives, and is more rampant and mischievous than ever, as infidelity."[22]

Such arguments resonated quite broadly in Kentucky. As religiously conservative whites in the Commonwealth had affirmed before 1865, the mixing of politics and religion was a grave religious error. The spiritual nature of the church was a rudimentary tenet of their faith. Yet there was no denying the fact that slavery proved the incendiary catalyst for a postbellum sectional conflagration among believers.

Just after Confederate surrender, in the summer of 1865, Kentucky Baptists found themselves embroiled in a controversy that would highlight their growing distance from northern believers. In May 1865 the northern American Baptist Home Mission Society met in St. Louis, Missouri. A substantial part of the meeting contained speeches suggesting how northern Baptists, like the Methodists before them, might contribute to the South's religious reconstruction. As one ABHMS speaker put it, thanks to emancipation and Union military victory, "Slavery has received its death-blow." Now northern Baptists found themselves faced with the task of providing "missionary care" for freedpeople. And, as slave soil, the mandate clearly applied to Kentucky.[23]

James M. Pendleton, the Kentucky native who rose to prominence in the antebellum era before leaving the South in the early 1860s because of his gradual emancipationist views and Unionism, made a special case for his home state. He argued that northern Baptists had avoided the Bluegrass State "[b]efore the war" because "it was under the general jurisdiction of the Southern Baptist Convention." However, because that denomination's "formation was owing to the existence of an *institution* which we may pronounce as abolished," there was little hope that the "Southern Baptist Convention" might "be revived" in Kentucky or anywhere else. Northern Baptists could thus reasonably treat former slave soil as fertile ground for missionary endeavor. Following Pendleton's speech, the ABHMS passed a resolution to that end.[24]

Before Pendleton's address, D. W. Phillips, a New Englander who had been working as a Baptist missionary in East Tennessee, expressed his hope that the ABHMS would be able to gain "the cooperation of the Baptists among whom they labor" and, specifically in the case of Kentucky, draw its missionaries from within the state. Of course, Phillips admitted, such local collaborators would have to prove their mettle as "suitable men." For Phillips that term meant Baptists "of unquestionable loyalty to the Government of the United

---

[22] Robert L. Dabney, *A Defence of Virginia, and Through Her, of the South* (New York: E. J. Hale & Son, 1867), 6.

[23] "St. Louis Anniversaries," *Western Recorder*, 10 June 1865.

[24] Ibid.

States, men who approve of the policy of the Government in slavery." Northern Baptists would not ally themselves with "pro-slavery ministers" of any kind nor with those "whose hearts throbbed for four sad years in favor of the rebellion of the South." To be sure, Phillips acknowledged his "fear" that such candidates would be hard to find in the Commonwealth, but he believed "many loyal preachers" existed "in Kentucky in the Baptist denomination" from which to cultivate a northern-aligned missionary base.[25]

Phillips' suspicion that most white Kentucky Baptists would treat northern overtures confrontationally proved exceedingly perceptive. Not only had they been marshaling resources against northern belief long before the war began but the war and emancipation had also brought those opinions to the fore. Kentucky's evangelical whites had signaled their disdain earlier, in 1863 and 1864, when religious reconstruction missionary work had began in earnest. Now in 1865, with Kentucky itself a primary focus of northern missionary endeavor, Bluegrass Baptists were predictably appalled.

The *Western Recorder*, which published the bulk of Pendleton's and Phillips' ABHMS speeches, printed a reactionary riposte from Henry McDonald. At the time, McDonald was serving as pastor of Waco Baptist Church in Madison County, Kentucky, and had developed a reputation as one of white Kentucky's most "popular preachers." Just a few years earlier, on the eve of the Civil War, McDonald had emerged as a mainstream political voice among Kentucky whites, when he argued for Unionist moderation. He was no rabid secessionist then, and he appreciated what a slaveholding Christian America had meant for the flourishing of his Baptist tradition.[26]

But that was before the war, before the unleashing of the forces of emancipation. In 1865, in his response to the meeting of the American Baptist Home Mission Society, McDonald's tone was very different. He spared no polemical language. McDonald had "watched" the churches of "the North, with 'continual sorrow in my heart' at the abundant evidence of terrible apostasy from the truth as it is in Jesus Christ." Long before the Civil War, northern "altars of the faith [had been] polluted by the blasphemous debaucheries of the Protestant carnivals." Now in the immediate aftermath of the war, "the fanaticism of a few clerical foplings, led on by some Mucklewrath, whose zeal is set on fire by his consuming patriotism," completely permeated Yankee pulpits. Northern churches had devolved into little more than stages for "[t]he most difficult questions of national policy, demanding rarest statesmanship." The clearly extrareligious matters of "the negro subject," "Confiscation of rebel property, and the just punishment of the rebels" received full-throated discussion. Yankee believers betrayed their true opinions with constant cries

---

[25] Ibid.

[26] See J. H. Spencer, *A History of Kentucky Baptists: From 1769 to 1885*, 2 vols. (Cincinnati: J. R. Baumes, 1885), 2:211; and George Braxton Taylor, *Virginia Baptist Ministers*, 5th ser., 1902–1914 (Lynchburg, Va.: J. P. Bell, 1915), 99–102.

of, "Negro suffrage, negro bravery, negro superiority." As McDonald saw it, northern Christians could make no claim to the title because, rather than having a pure faith, "They have determined to know nothing among the people but the negro and him crucified."[27]

According to McDonald's rant, the proposals heard by the ABHMS in St. Louis blatantly demonstrated how far "the mighty" northern church had "fallen" from "the cherished faith of an 'unsecularized Church.'" McDonald contended that he could not understand "[w]hy should it be requisite in a missionary to endorse the policy of the government *on slavery*" when missionaries did not have to signal agreement with other federal "policy" on matters such as "finances, agriculture, commerce, tariff, &c." Northern Baptists, the Kentuckian argued, elevated "*fealty* to a *party* above *fealty* to God." In so doing, they had proposed a "whole scheme" that was "destructive of Baptist principles, [and] subversive of the law of Christ." To condone religious policy such as that suggested by D. W. Phillips would fundamentally change church membership standards. Rather than the biblical test of church membership called for by the New Testament book of 1 Peter, "give a reason for the hope that is in you" – in other words, faith in Christ alone – prospective Baptists would be asked, "do you approve the policy of the government?" If the northern American Baptist Home Mission Society's "abolition evangelists" got their way, such a blatantly political "law of membership in the Churches" would receive direct sanction. Moreover, in the choosing of missionaries, the implication of the northern platform was plain: a potential missionary "must be a radical abolitionist. It is not enough that he is a good man, sound in faith, apt to teach, approved by his Church." Kentuckians wanted no part of such a program. In one sentence, McDonald summarized the opinion of most of his state's fellow white believers: "Kentucky Baptists have their own plans and can do their own work."[28]

The native Kentuckian James M. Pendleton attempted to prevent such a critique of northern Baptist efforts. Before the *Western Recorder* published McDonald's letter, Pendleton wrote to the newspaper's editors to contend that they had printed a flawed copy of his ABHMS address, one filled with "inaccuracies" and seemingly "mixed up in a sort of inextricable confusion with the [more hostilely political and abolition-minded] speech of Mr. Phillips." Furthermore, to show his distance from other northern Baptists, Pendleton assured his Kentucky readers that "two or three of Mr. P[hillips]'s statements did the South such injustice that I protested against them." In Pendleton's view, Phillips drew his views on the South's religiosity from "exaggerated accounts." Indeed, the Kentucky native maintained that he "was the only man who publicly complained" of such a false portrait of the South. In his

---

[27] Henry McDonald, "The Session of the Home Mission Society at St. Louis," *Western Recorder*, July 22, 1865.

[28] Ibid. The biblical reference is 1 Peter 3:15.

Western Recorder correspondence, Pendleton wrote that he did not "wish my old friends [in Kentucky] – the friends of my youth – to be under the erroneous impressions in regard to me." This son of the Bluegrass State did not mind being "held responsible only for what I believe," but he knew the South well and did not wish to be reflexively lumped in with more radicalized religious practitioners.[29]

There is no compelling reason to doubt Pendleton's sincerity, as he was a visible proponent for gradual emancipation in the antebellum era and a theological conservative. His ties with his home state continued to remain close. In coming decades, Pendleton regularly returned to Kentucky to lead various Baptist services and endeavors, before ultimately spending his last years in Bowling Green. Moreover, he remained uneasy with immediate abolition – as he claimed in 1891 at the end of his life – as well as with stereotypical denunciations of the white South.[30]

Nevertheless, in the immediate aftermath of the Civil War the fact that Pendleton appeared closely linked with an abolition-oriented faith, even if he denied it, proved enough to undermine much of his influence in Kentucky. As a direct target of much of Henry McDonald's venom, James M. Pendleton – currently in an Ohio pastorate and sympathetic to the aims of the northern American Baptist Home Mission Society's labors to religiously reconstruct Kentucky – seemed difficult to distinguish from more radicalized northerners. It was an intellectual move with which Pendleton himself was quite familiar. In the 1840s, leading up to the creation of the Southern Baptist Convention, Pendleton had painted all antislavery immediatists with a similarly broad stroke, making little religious distinction between evangelicals and more theologically speculative abolitionists. Now, in the wake of the Civil War and emancipation, as Pendleton favored a more flexible orthodoxy on the slavery question, he found himself on the receiving end of that sort of rigid religio-political typecasting. As McDonald interpreted the matter, "I did not know – however highly esteemed Elder J. M. Pendleton may be – that he was entitled to represent the Baptists of Kentucky." In the wake of emancipation, the religious bonds of sectional solidarity against abolitionism proved too strong for white Kentuckians to even attempt to break.[31]

In registering his antipathy for notions of African American civil rights, the North's ostensibly politicized religion, and the heretical legacy of abolitionist activism, Henry McDonald highlighted the main themes that persisted throughout white Kentucky into the 1870s and gave shape to the state's religious sense of unity with the former Confederacy. The 1865 Baptist debate

[29] J. M. Pendleton, "Elder J. M. Pendleton," *Western Recorder*, June 24, 1865.

[30] James M. Pendleton, *Reminiscences of a Long Life* (Louisville: Press Baptist Book Concern, 1891), 112–13, 195–6; and J. M. Pendleton, *The Condition of the Baptist Cause in Kentucky in 1837: An Address Delivered at the Jubilee of the General Association of Kentucky Baptists, in Walnut Street Baptist Church, Louisville, Oct. 20, 1887* (n.p., n.d.).

[31] McDonald, "The Session of the Home Mission Society at St. Louis."

over missionaries, however, was tame compared to the fights that occurred on a national denominational level among Methodists and Presbyterians. As had been the case in the 1845 creation of the Southern Baptist Convention, because of the Baptist commitment to congregational polity and the doctrine of "democratic exclusiveness" – which vested ecclesiastical authority in local churches and, contrasted with other Protestant denominations, downplayed the significance of broad Christian unity – nineteenth-century Baptists tended to deal with matters of political religion and slavery on a local, congregational level.[32] Kentucky Baptists, in other words, resolutely agreed with other white evangelicals in their state about the nature of slavery, abolition, and African American civil rights, but because the local congregation was the highest ruling body for matters of Baptist faith and practice, their ecclesiology allowed for a discourse that often avoided large-scale denominational confrontation.

Kentucky's Presbyterians, by contrast, fought tooth and nail for many years over who would control their denomination's religious future in the state. Because of the caustic and protracted nature of their national intersectional fights, the Presbyterians provide the most illustrative example of white religious Kentucky's postwar rejection of northern religiosity. As with the Baptists, the year 1865 proved particularly fractious. Every year since the start of the war, the Presbyterian Church USA's General Assembly – the denomination's overarching ruling body – had made nationalistic, pro-Union proclamations that border state Presbyterians found highly disconcerting. In 1865, however, the General Assembly went too far for border state taste.

Meeting less than a month after Confederate surrender, in May 1865 the General Assembly passed two major resolutions on the nation and slavery. Noting that there were some ministers who had sided with the Presbyterian Church in the Confederate States of America during the war who might seek to reapply for ordination in the northern Presbyterian Church, the General Assembly required two tests. First, ministers who had in "any way, directly or indirectly" been involved in "aiding or countenancing the rebellion and the war" were required to "confess and forsake" that action as sin. Second, ministers had to disavow the idea that "the system of negro slavery in the South is a Divine institution, and that it is 'the peculiar mission of the Southern Church to conserve the institution of slavery as there maintained.'" Any southern minister who refused to repent of these errors would not be allowed to preach in the Presbyterian Church USA.[33]

Those proclamations, although couched in the language of sectional reconciliation, only served to intensify the schism between northern and southern

---

[32] On Baptist "democractic exclusivism," see Gregory A. Wills, *Democratic Religion: Freedom, Authority, and Church Discipline in the Baptist South, 1785–1900* (New York: Oxford University Press, 1997), 88–90.

[33] Joseph M. Wilson, *Presbyterian Historical Almanac and Annual Remembrancer for the Church, for 1866* (Philadelphia: Joseph M. Wilson, 1866), 45.

Presbyterians. They embodied the Christian faith on Yankee terms.[34] For adherents in Kentucky, the actions of the 1865 General Assembly proved the beginning of the end of their fellowship with the northern branch of the denomination. Although many religious Kentuckians had never willingly taken arms against the United States, the idea that slavery was an inherently sinful institution proved too difficult to accept. Moreover, because the Emancipation Proclamation did not apply to Kentucky, slavery remained legal in the state at that time. To Kentuckians, the General Assembly was speaking to political affairs it had no business addressing.

In anticipation of such a pro-Union, pro-abolition ruling in the General Assembly, Kentucky's southern-sympathizing Presbyterian press marshaled much of the vitriol at its disposal to decry "political preaching." A late April 1865 article in the *Free Christian Commonwealth* reviewed the course of northern commingling of religion and politics in the Civil War. Relying on tropes well familiar to white evangelicals in the South, the essay argued, "Antislavery fanaticism is malignant and ferocious." Abolitionists had forced the Civil War because they "denounced the Federal Constitution as a 'covenant with hell and an agreement with death' because it recognized and protected slave property." There was more. "A preacher, closing a sermon on the war, and speaking of the Secessionists, exclaimed, 'Kill the devils! kill the devils!'" Yet another Yankee abolitionist "preacher declared," in the *Free Christian Commonwealth*'s telling, "The devil will never have his rights until he has the exquisite pleasure of roasting the leaders [of the rebellion] 'in hell!'" Stated succinctly, "The Abolition clergy hate Slavery, hate slave-holders, and hate and abuse all men who oppose their mad and destructive schemes." Throughout the antebellum era, Kentucky Presbyterians never doubted the resolve of abolitionists who hoped to spoil their true religion. The time for action against such a debased faith had come.[35]

In response to the actions of the 1865 General Assembly, the Presbytery of Louisville produced a monumental document principally authored by Samuel R. Wilson, but also with substantial contributions from Stuart Robinson. Wilson had made his ministerial mark as the pastor of Cincinnati's First Presbyterian Church before sympathizing publicly with the white South in November 1860. He moved to Kentucky in 1863 and became pastor of Louisville's First Presbyterian Church in 1865. Together Wilson and Robinson expressed much animus for the General Assembly's action. The treatise they produced presented a focused summary of the issues white Kentucky's conservative believers had debated – and come to answer in a collectively proslavery way – over the course of the Civil War era.[36]

[34] For an explication of broader northern religious attitudes toward the defeated South, see Daniel W. Stowell, *Rebuilding Zion: The Religious Reconstruction of the South, 1863–1877* (New York: Oxford University Press, 1998), 49–64.
[35] "The Clergy and Politics," *Free Christian Commonwealth*, April 20, 1865. Brackets in original.
[36] See Preston D. Graham Jr., *A Kingdom Not of this World: Stuart Robinson's Struggle to Distinguish the Sacred from the Secular during the Civil War* (Macon, GA: Mercer University Press, 2002), 150–1.

Titled *Declaration and Testimony against the Erroneous and Heretical Doctrines and Practices . . . Propagated in the Presbyterian Church, in the United States, during the Last Five Years*, the document represented a fundamental rejection of the political theology of northern Presbyterianism. It denounced fourteen "errors" in the Presbyterian Church USA, including the beliefs that the *"Courts of the Church"* had *"the right to decide questions of State Policy,"* that the church owed allegiance to any *"human Rulers or Governments,"* and that the church and state were in *"alliance"* toward a common goal. The *Declaration and Testimony* also denounced the General Assembly's rulings *"on the subject of slavery and emancipation."*[37]

Not only did the Presbyterian Church USA disregard the commonly held white opinion *"that immediate, indiscriminate emancipation of the negro slaves amongst us would be unjust and injurious* to both master and slave" but it had also "laid down a new doctrine" on slavery, "unknown to the apostolic and primitive church; a doctrine which has its origin in infidelity and fanaticism." Slavery, "an institution which has always existed in the Church uncondemned, and which was recognized by Christ and his apostles, is pronounced an *'evil and guilt,'* condemned as 'SIN' and affirmed to be the 'root of rebellion, war, and bloodshed, and the long list of horrors which follow in their train.'" By perpetuating such ideas, the "General Assembly," the *Declaration* argued, "has become the support[er] of heresy, the abettor of injustice and despotism, the fomentor of discord." The document ended on a somber tone: the signers of the *Declaration* would no longer recognize any religious authority for matters of church polity "other than the written Word of God," and until the Presbyterian Church USA's course was corrected, they would withhold all financial contributions from denominational boards.[38]

Just a month after the Louisville Presbytery endorsed the *Declaration and Testimony*, the Synod of Kentucky – which represented all the state's smaller presbyteries – met. There Robert J. Breckinridge, Stuart Robinson's long-time adversary, called for a flat condemnation of the document's signers. Because the treatise advocated "OPEN REBELLION AGAINST THE CHURCH, AND OPEN CONTEMPT AND DEFIANCE OF OUR SCRIPTURAL AUTHORITY," it made "EACH AND EVERY ONE OF THEM UNQALIFIED, UNFIT, AND INCOMPETENT TO SIT AND ACT AS A MEMBER OF THIS OR ANY OTHER PRESBYTERIAN CHURCH." Samuel R. Wilson, the chief author of the *Declaration and Testimony*, offered a spirited and lengthy response to Breckinridge, reasserting the main claims of the document.[39] Breckinridge, as an aged and distinguished theologian with a long record of service to the denomination, certainly maintained a position of

---

37 *Declaration and Testimony against the Erroneous and Heretical Doctrines and Practices Which Have Obtained and Been Propagated in the Presbyterian Church, in the United States, during the Last Five Years*, 2nd ed. (n.p., 1865), quotes 5, 6, 7, 8, 11, 21, 22, 24.

38 Ibid.

39 Samuel R. Wilson, *Reply to the Attack of Rev. R. J. Breckinridge, D.D., L.L.D., upon the Louisville Presbytery, and Defence of the "Declaration and Testimony," Made in the Synod of Kentucky, October 16, A. D., 1865* (Louisville: Hanna & Duncan, 1865), quote 4.

influence in the church's General Assembly, but the Unionist was losing authority in his home state. After much debate, the Synod of Kentucky ruled against
Breckinridge, though a sizable minority joined him in denouncing the *Declaration and Testimony*.[40]

Breckinridge's opinion did speak, however, to the dominant view in the Presbyterian Church USA. When the General Assembly reconvened the following
May, Stuart Robinson traveled to the meeting along with Samuel R. Wilson
and Presbyterian elder Charles A. Wickliffe (1788–1869), a former Kentucky
governor (1839–40), U.S. Postmaster General during the John Tyler administration (1841–5), and Unionist representative to Congress (1861–3) during
the Civil War. Wickliffe was also Kentucky's State Rights party candidate for
governor in 1863. Though losing in that effort, he shortly thereafter became a
Peace Democrat and was a major figure in creating the base of the state's postwar ex-Confederate Democracy. As elected representatives of the Louisville
Presbytery, the delegation hoped to take their seats, but the General Assembly
came down hard on the signers of the *Declaration and Testimony*. Robert L.
Stanton, the abolitionist and viscerally Unionist Danville Theological Seminary
professor who had condemned religious neutrality in 1864 – and also a close
friend of Breckinridge – was elected moderator and made it his mission to crush
the dissident Presbyterians. Robinson, Wilson, Wickliffe, and other signers of
the *Declaration and Testimony* were denied seats. Then the General Assembly
passed a motion that would dissolve any presbytery or synod that kept any
Declaration and Testimony signer on its membership rolls.[41]

The Louisville Presbytery responded by renouncing the General Assembly and declaring ecclesiastical independence. Although several leaders of the
Synod of Kentucky remained loyal to the national church, the vast majority
moved to create an "Independent Synod." In 1867 the northern Presbyterian
General Assembly essentially confirmed what had already taken place and dis-
solved the Synod of Kentucky, creating a new one to facilitate the activity of
loyal Presbyterians in the state. At the same time, Stuart Robinson began pressing the Independent Synod to look to the Southern Presbyterian Church. After
debate in 1867 and 1868, individual presbyteries under the Independent Synod
opted to send representatives to the 1869 General Assembly of the southern
church. At the meeting Stuart Robinson was elected moderator, and Kentucky
Presbyterians voted overwhelmingly to join a denomination founded in 1861
as the Presbyterian Church in the Confederate States of America, which rested
much of its postbellum identity in an embrace of southern sectionalism.[42]

---

[40] Louis B. Weeks, *Kentucky Presbyterians* (Atlanta: John Knox Press, 1983), 90–1.
[41] Ibid., 91–2; and Vander Velde, *Presbyterian Churches*, 218–79. For biographical information
on Wickliffe, see Lowell H. Harrison, "Wickliffe, Charles Anderson," in *The Kentucky Encyclopedia*, ed. John E. Kleber (Lexington: University Press of Kentucky, 1992), 950–1. See also
Astor, *Rebels on the Border*, 174–83.
[42] Weeks, *Kentucky Presbyterians*, 98–9. For a more extensive analysis of the move to the Southern
Presbyterian Church, see Harold M. Parker Jr., "The Synod of Kentucky: From Old School
Assembly to the Southern Church," *Journal of Presbyterian History* 41 (March 1963): 14–36.

Kentucky Presbyterians carried their denominational dispute into the 1870s, where it was most visibly manifested in a fight for institutional control over Centre College and Danville Theological Seminary, Kentucky's flagship institutions of the Presbyterian Church USA. The state's Southern Presbyterian majority tried assiduously to wrest control of the schools from the northern church but, after many protracted legal battles, realized by 1872 that Centre College was "lost to this Church." They would have to create their own distinctively southern institution of higher learning. The new college's name only slighty distinguished it from the old: in 1874, an "Alumni Association" of pro-southern Presbyterians founded "Central University" in Richmond.[43]

Central University's founders included long-time leading Kentucky Presbyterians Stuart Robinson and Robert L. Breck. Yet they also included some of New Departure Democracy's most visible exponents, among them Louisville *Courier-Journal* publisher Walter N. Haldeman, who had fled to Tennessee during the war, fearing arrest for his pro-Confederate views, as well as three former Confederate riders in John Hunt Morgan's cavalry raiders: W. C. P. Breckinridge, James McCreary, and prominent Louisville attorney Bennett H. Young (1843–1919). McCreary would soon become Kentucky's governor, handily defeating noted Republican John Marshall Harlan in 1875 by more than 35,000 votes (130,026 to 94,236) with a campaign demonizing the Grant administration and federal Reconstruction policy. Bennett Young was also Stuart Robinson's son-in-law, and he went on to serve as commander-in-chief of the United Confederate Veterans in 1913. In many ways, Central University's founders represented the brain trust of Kentucky's early neo-Confederate imagination. Through his various influential volumes on Kentucky's history, Young helped shape white Kentucky's understanding of its mythological Confederate past, whereas others worked through politics and the press to the same ends.[44]

Although most members of the Central University Alumni Association did not write on the slavery question or theology in the Reconstruction era, their

---

43 *Memorial of the Education Convention [Held at Lexington, Ky., May 7th and 8th, 1872.] To the Synod of Kentucky*, Central University Collection, Financial Series, Donation and Subscription lists 1874–1900 folder, RG 127, 84A2, Box 2, in Eastern Kentucky University Library, Special Collections and Archives, Richmond. On the founding of Central University, see also William E. Ellis, *A History of Eastern Kentucky University: A School of Opportunity* (Lexington: University Press of Kentucky, 2005), 1–19.

44 Alumni Association Minutes, 29 April 1873, Central University Collection, Alumni Association Series, Minutes of Meetings April 29, 1873–June 19, 1901 folder, RG 127, 84A2, Box 1, EKU; and Ellis, *Eastern Kentucky University*, 1–19. For biographical information, see Dennis Cusick, "Haldeman, Walter Newman"; Lowell H. Harrison, "McCreary, James Bennett"; and Sherrill Redmon, "Young, Bennett Henderson," all in *Kentucky Encyclopedia*, 398, 594, 972; and Nicholas C. Burckel, "James B. McCreary," in *Kentucky's Governors*, ed. Lowell H. Harrison, updated ed. (Lexington: University Press of Kentucky, 2004), 105–7. For Bennett H. Young's historical interpretations, see Young, *History and Texts of the Three Constitutions of Kentucky* (Louisville: Courier-Journal, 1890); and Young, *Confederate Wizards of the Saddle: Being Reminiscences and Observations of One Who Rode with Morgan* (1914; Nashville: J. S. Sanders, 1999).

figurehead – and the university's first chancellor – Stuart Robinson, did. The Kentucky Presbyterians' state-level fractures after the Civil War took place against the backdrop of ongoing northern overtures for denominational reunion. In 1869 the northern Old School and New School Presbyterian churches reunited. At the same time, northern Presbyterians sought to end division with their southern counterparts. In an attempt to move beyond the hostility that had marked the Civil War years, in 1868 the northern Presbyterian Church USA (PCUSA) General Assembly recognized the existence of the southern Presbyterian Church US (PCUS); then in 1869 the PCUSA wrote to the PCUS General Assembly with the hopes of establishing fraternal relations between the two bodies. However, Southern Presbyterians rebuffed these northern overtures in 1870, when its General Assembly – led by vocal defenders of slavery Benjamin M. Palmer of New Orleans, Robert L. Dabney of Virginia, and Stuart Robinson – overwhelmingly voted against them. The PCUS General Assembly then explained its position in a "pastoral letter" written by Palmer and sent to the northern Presbyterian denomination. Arguing that during the Civil War the northern church had abrogated its mission to keep the affairs of state separate from the church, the PCUS claimed the reason for the breech had not yet been resolved.[45]

In a widely circulated compendium that followed, Southern Presbyterians documented the history of their denomination since 1861 and clarified the reasons for the separate existence of their church. Among the denomination's "distinctives" in 1870, slavery played a central role. "The essential principle of slavery is submission or subjection to control by the will of another," the document argued. The necessity of submitting to unequal power relations "is an essential element in every form of civil government, also, and in the family relation itself." In this formulation slavery itself was "not an institution essential to the social state; and therefore is not of universal obligation." Thus the contrast was with what Southern Presbyterians argued were foundational aspects of their society: "civil government, as opposed to anarchy" and "marriage" rather than "concubinage, polygamy, and general licentiousness."[46]

Yet if slavery was a second-order institution, it was nonetheless "of divine appointment." Citing a series of biblical passages from both the Old and New

---

[45] For Robinson's appointment as first chancellor of Central University, see Minutes of the Boards of Curators and Trustees of Central University (1873–1901), Richmond, Kentucky, Organized May 28, 1873, bound unpublished manuscript, Central University Collection, Board of Curators Series, Minutes of Meetings 1873–1901 folder, RG 127, 84A2, Box 1, EKU. On the PCUS and the reunion question, see Stowell, *Rebuilding Zion*, 169–70; Ernest Trice Thompson, *Presbyterians in the South*, Vol. 2: *1861–1890* (Richmond: John Knox Press, 1973), 223–6; and *The Distinctive Principles of the Presbyterian Church in the United States, Commonly Called the Southern Presbyterian Church, as Set Forth in the Formal Declarations, and Illustrated by Extracts from Proceedings of the General Assembly, from 1861–70* (Richmond: Presbyterian Committee of Publication, [1871]), 91–107.

[46] *Distinctive Principles*, 131.

Testaments, these white southerners argued that "in certain conditions of society it has been expressly recognized by God, permitted and appointed." The point was not an abstract one. In this view, "the circumstances of [slavery] in this country made it right and best that such should be the relation, in general, of the negro to the white population." Many proslavery ministers had called for reform of slavery as it existed in America and saw the failure to do so as a key reason for Confederate defeat in the Civil War. Nevertheless, "the existence of wrong laws and usages connected with [slavery], no more disproves the lawfulness of the relation itself, than such things disprove the lawfulness of marriage or of civil government." Slavery might have needed reform – but slavery was righteous the same.[47]

For those who questioned this truth, Southern Presbyterians had strong words in 1870:

> The dogma which denies the lawfulness of this relation under any circumstances; which condemns it as always contrary to the Divine will; which asserts its inherent sinfulness, is completely contradicted by the plainest facts and teachings of the Old Testament and New; is a doctrine unknown to the Church until recent times; is a pernicious heresy, embracing a principle not only infidel and fanatical, but subversive of every relation of life, and every civil government on earth.[48]

This was not simply a backward-looking statement, pining for a bygone slave-holding era. In fact, these Southern Presbyterians expressly denied "that it was the duty of the Church to *perpetuate* the institution of slavery." Instead, they took issue with the approach of their northern counterparts to the theological stakes of the problem. They claimed they defended slavery not for slavery's sake, but because the Christian God had sanctioned it in Holy Scripture. And to take issue with that God was to take issue with the right order of things.[49]

As ever, much more than slavery was connected to that theology. The Kentucky Presbyterian realignment with the southern branch of the denomination had much to do with an understanding of the church's place in the civil society as a "nonsecular" institution, but that view was also closely connected to white supremacy. In the years to come, such opinions would closely align with those held by white religious conservatives farther South. In an 1870 essay justifying the course of the antebellum white South and the Confederate cause, South Carolina Presbyterian Arnold W. Miller (d. 1891/2) lashed out at the Fourteenth Amendment (1868). To Miller, the words of the South's most highly regarded antebellum politician, John C. Calhoun, had come true in the wake of emancipation: the South had experienced "degradation greater than has yet fallen the lot of a free and enlightened people." Miller, quoting

---

[47] Ibid. See also Eugene D. Genovese, *A Consuming Fire: The Fall of the Confederacy in the Mind of the White Christian South* (Athens: University of Georgia Press, 1998), 3–33.

[48] *Distinctive Principles*, 131–2.

[49] Ibid., 132–3.

Calhoun, argued that the result of such political action meant southern whites were "fleeing the homes of our ancestors and ... abandoning our country to our former slaves." The South was "to become the permanent abode of disorder, anarchy, poverty, misery, and wretchedness." Indeed, Kentucky's *Free Christian Commonwealth* had made a similar case against African American civil rights – a "New Negrophile Erastian Crusade" in the Presbyterian paper's terminology – not long after the war. Thus the idea of "making an inferior race predominant over a superior one" – or of giving African Americans citizenship rights and political power – in Miller's quote of a northern conservative, was abhorrent.[50]

Not all white religious Kentuckians were so taken with this racist vision. But any dissenters tended to come from the ranks of the minority abolitionist community that had persisted in Kentucky. In January 1866 John G. Fee's interracial, anti-caste, and nonsectarian experiment in higher education began on the Berea ridge, with the opening of the Berea Literary Institute. In March the school enrolled its first African American students, a decision that led to the departure of more than half of Berea's white students. As John A. R. Rogers wrote to the American Missionary Association, the result was that "the hearts of many were emboldened" to persist in trying to realize the founding mission, "and the truth that we are all one in Christ Jesus was exemplified anew." The Freedmen's Bureau provided some financial assistance for the school in 1867, and the Berea community began selling parcels of land to black families, many of whom came from Camp Nelson. Under the leadership of Rogers from 1866 to 1869, the school enrolled African American students in numbers equal to whites – a trend that persisted until the 1890s.[51]

In the decade of the 1890s, however, under the presidency of William G. Frost, Berea would shift from its interracial founding mission to emphasize its mandate to educate impoverished white "mountain people." The move was coincident with a larger trend in American culture toward segregation in the decade, and Frost argued that it was necessary so that the school could continue to raise funds from northern donors. Up until 1893, black student enrollments were either equal or more than those of whites at Berea College. Yet with Frost's new emphasis on white interests, white students soon came to outstrip blacks. The school remained interracial until 1904, when Kentucky's state legislature passed the Day Law banning interracial education in the

[50] Andrew W. Miller, "Southern Views and Principles Not 'Extinguished' by the War," *Southern Presbyterian Review* 21 (January 1870): 85; "Symptoms of a New Negrophile Erastian Crusade," *Free Christian Commonwealth*, October 19, 1865.

[51] Shannon H. Wilson, *Berea College: An Illustrated History* (Lexington: University Press of Kentucky, 2006), 21–3; [J. A. R. Rogers], "Report of the Berea Mission for 1866," *American Missionary* (December 1866): 279–80; John G. Fee, "Marked Progress," *American Missionary* (October 1867): 217–18. Both letters in typescript "Letters and Articles by and about Rev. John G. Fee, his life and work in the *American Missionary*," 156–8, RG 1.02, Series III, Box 5, Folder 7, Berea College Archives, Berea, KY.

Commonwealth – thereby forcing Berea's black students to leave – but by that date black students only comprised one-sixth of the student body.[52]

Still, for its first three decades, Berea's founding aspirations persisted in defining the college as an interracial oasis within a violently white supremacist state. But even abolitionist interracialism had its limits. At Berea, Fee specifically hoped to encourage racial amalgamation through interracial marriage among his students. In an 1866 pamphlet on its founding values, the college rejected anti-amalgamation arguments "as a mere appeal to popular prejudice." Bereans understood well the American South's long history of white masters raping black women and producing mixed-race offspring, and as these abolitionists argued, such arguments against interracialism were "often put by those who have no right to 'throw stones.'" If amalgamation came about because two people of different races loved one another, married, and produced mixed-race children – as Fee had long argued – that was a blessing and good for humanity as a whole. At the very least, it was a far cry from the hypocrisy that condemned "amalgamation" but sanctioned the American South's ubiquitous predatory, racialized sexual violence. As the college affirmed in its founding principles, taken from the language of the New Testament book of Acts, the Christian God "made the human family of one blood."[53]

Nonetheless, most members of Berea College's board of trustees did not support Fee's more radical position. At a July 1872 board meeting "a resolution [was] offered declaring amalgamation desirable," but it was defeated. The board instead affirmed that it was not "desirable in general for those of either race to cultivate the most intimate social relations with those of the other sex and a different race, especially when the difference in race is quite marked." The board's primary concern appeared to be the safety of their students and community because, as an openly anti-caste community, Berea had been the target of several incidents of Klan violence in recent years. The board did not think "persons of opposite races and sexes" needed to "be universally prohibited from attending each other to and from social gatherings and public lectures." Yet they argued, "if in our judgment" black and white students' "going together would expose them to violence, they should be prohibited" from doing so. And even if the trustees could not endorse interracial marriage and amalgamation as "desirable," they nonetheless agreed that "the mere fact that persons of different colors are engaged to be married, is not sufficient cause for removing them [from the school], providing they conduct themselves with appropriate discretion."[54]

---

[52] Wilson, *Berea College*, 75–101.

[53] *Origin and Principles of Berea Literary Institution* (n.p., [1866]), 6, 7, RG 1.01, Box 1, Folder 3, BCA. The biblical text is Acts 17:26.

[54] Board of Trustee Minutes, July 1, 1872, Vol. 1, 1858–1899, 81–2, RG 2, Box 8, BCA. See also Richard D. Sears, *"A Practical Recognition of the Brotherhood of Man": John G. Fee and the Camp Nelson Experience* (Berea, KY: Berea College Press, 1986), 66–8, 71–3.

Even if Fee's position on interracialism did not carry, what the Berea board did support was well beyond the pale of acceptability to most religious whites in Kentucky. As a *Free Christian Commonwealth* essay contended in 1865, abolitionists intended to destroy the human race as it presently existed by forcing race mixing through interracial sex. The paper's imagined (and stereotypical) abolitionist did not trust the Christian God, who had divinely ordered the races: rather the radical antislavery activist "exults, he blesses himself, and congratulates posterity, in view of the redeeming and elevating power of 'miscegenation!'" In the view of the article's Presbyterian author, the abolitionist "would mingle his blood with the blood of the African. He would take and wear somewhat of the dark hues of the African." The "Fanatic" abolitionist "would degrade and dishonor the whole white race to effect his purpose. Nay, he would degrade and dishonor himself" by "sink[ing] himself to the lowest depths of humanity, that the negro may seem to be exalted." There was nothing new about these white supremacist ideas, but they gained religious traction in the context of America's emerging postslavery society.[55]

This rejection of interracialism followed from a basic assumption of black dependency. In the proslavery mind, blacks were docile, infantile creatures, certainly not ready for the freedom provided by a federal government under the spell of heterodox abolitionists. In 1868 John Bailey Adger (1810–99), a South Carolina southern Presbyterian clergyman, joined with Presbyterian George James Atkinson Coulson of Maryland to claim that emancipation brought an important religious dilemma: how could devout southern whites continue to follow God's command and provide religious education for African Americans who, no doubt, were unable to produce mature religious reflection for themselves? As former slaves, "suddenly freed, suddenly invested with new and extraordinary privileges, and suddenly inspired with vague apprehensions of their own importance, with indefinite expectations of ease and affluence to be conferred upon them by governmental authority – are thrust upon the hearts and consciences of a Christian nation, the question assumes an aspect both perplexing and threatening." If southern whites forswore their prior duties as masters – to provide physical and spiritual care for their racial dependents – "[a] whole race" might "perish in the midst of us" and thereby bring "a lasting curse on the American name." The situation was dire, Adger and Coulson exclaimed: "The slave – may God pity him! Has no friend except his former master." Yet the former slaveholding class "has been legislated into a condition in which [the slaveholder] is utterly powerless to aid the servant born in his house, or even retard his doom."[56]

Adger and Coulson, like other proslavery southerners, believed former slaves incapable of governing themselves religiously because, as people with dark skin,

[55] "The Clergy and Politics," *Free Christian Commonwealth*, April 20, 1865.
[56] John Bailey Adger and G. J. A. Coulson, "The Future of the Freedmen," *Southern Presbyterian Review* 19 (April 1868): 281–3, 292.

African Americans could never acquire the same intellectual acumen as whites. Adger and Coulson, like proslavery divines in the antebellum era, did affirm the common ancestry of all humanity and did decry the scientific racism of polygenesis theory – "the pitiful work of [polygenetecists Josiah] Nott and [George] Gliddon" – because the Gospel message was given for all. But the "grave discussion of the relative capacities" of the races was a short one. The main point was clear to Adger and Coulson: "the elevation of the black people to a position of political and social equality with the whites, is simply an impossibility." The difference between the races was so plain, the Presbyterians argued, that obviously "God has so constituted the two races as to make their equality *forever* impossible." Every true believer knew that it was "[v]ain" to attempt "to resist the decrees of God," a fact that explained why "[i]t is not possible to take an infant from the banks of the Niger, and educate him up to the intellectual status of Newton, because God hath made them to differ." If that image did not resonate with their readers, Adger and Coulson pressed harder to show just how far the gap between black inferiority and white superiority really was: "if it were possible for the cultivated and Christianized races of the world to unite and devote all their energies to the elevation of the African race, giving each individual of this multitudinous family a separate and competent preceptor, the result of their labors would not be an intellectual equality, after long years of incessant application." For that reason, Adger and Coulson argued, blacks lived under the cruel delusion of so-called freedom. The former slaves had to now provide for their own physical and spiritual well-being, which freedpeople simply could not do without the help of good, Christian, paternalist masters.[57]

Kentucky's religious whites overwhelmingly agreed with this southern white evangelical portrait of African American limitations. An early 1868 editorial in the Methodist *Christian Observer* contended that African Americans had been so thoroughly disrupted by emancipation that the population would become "extinct" in short order.[58] That speculative article had been published to promote provocative conjecture among the paper's readers about the thoroughly debilitating nature of emancipation for African American life. But just a few months later, the Methodist paper went a step further and printed a report on the state of religious affairs in Catlettsburg, Kentucky, that showed even more unmistakably the white bias against the possibility of black self-determination. The article recorded the existence of "an African Church in town, with a pastor of their own color, and a new house of worship." In the estimation of the

57 Ibid., 269–70, 276, 279, 280. In denouncing Nott and Gliddon, Adger and Coulson were writing against the polygeneticists' work in the well-known multi-author volume, *Types of Mankind: Or, Ethnological Researches, Based upon the Ancient Monuments, Paintings, Sculptures, and Crania of Races, and upon their Natural, Geographical, Philological and Biblical History*, 2nd ed. (Philadelphia: Lippincott, Grambo, & Co., 1854).
58 "The Freedmen," *Christian Observer*, February 18, 1868.

Observer's white author, the black church was "doing, we suppose, as well as they can," but its members were "surrounded" by insurmountable "disabilities imposed upon them by the bondage of freedom."[59]

In the white religious mind of the Bluegrass State, along with the South in general, African Americans held only a limited capacity to assert independent religious agency. When such assertions occurred, they were easier for whites to understand by crediting the influence of abolitionists, "the influence of unscrupulous white emissaries" from the North. The *Free Christian Commonwealth* reflected much white opinion on the matter in October 1867, decrying "the persistent efforts of unprincipled political schemers to get the negro separated from the influence of their old masters."[60]

Indeed, in Kentucky, white evangelicals long seemed quite perplexed by the idea of independent African American religious agency. Although autonomous black churches had existed in Kentucky since the antebellum era, they were largely urban in nature. Civil War emancipation accelerated the establishment of free black churches in Kentucky and extended their reach to the countryside. In November 1864, on the heels of black military enlistment in Kentucky, the South Benson Baptist Church of Franklin County noted that, "As a church we lament that out Colored Brethren do not meet with us as they did in days past." The white church hoped to "obviate the difficulty in the way" and saw it "necessary to take some steps to bring back these our brethren to their place in the church of God." By the next year, however, South Benson's white members realized that those "who for some unknown cause have for some time absented themselves" were unlikely to return to fellowship. And, in July 1865, presumably after a number of overtures, the white Baptists decided to remove from their membership rolls those who had become blatant in their "non attendance + indifference towards the church." Similarly, the Forks of Otter Creek Baptist Church in Hardin County recorded in November 1866 that "all the colored members of the church" had "<u>gawn</u> off without <u>makeing</u> application for letters of dismission," following proper ecclesiastical standards, and were thus "excluded" from membership.[61]

For those black churches that were autonomous long before the Civil War, it did not take long for them to organize into more formal constellations of congregations. Although divisions over theology and ecclesiology permeated black Methodism after emancipation, the tradition nonetheless flourished in the Commonwealth. Northern white Methodists oversaw the establishment

---

[59] "Catlettsburg," *Christian Observer*, April 18, 1868.

[60] "Alarm of Christian Men in the South concerning the Religious prospects of the Negro," *Free Christian Commonwealth*, October 10, 1867.

[61] South Benson Baptist Church Records, October, November 1864; June, July 1865; Transcript, Forks of Otter Creek Baptist Church, Forks of Otter Creek Cemetery Association, November 18, 1866, p. 97. For another account of "colored members [who] absented themselves from the church," see Buck Run Baptist Church Records, August 1865. All located at the Kentucky Historical Society, Frankfort.

of a "Colored Mission District" in Kentucky in 1866, which placed African American ministers over black congregations throughout the state. That move led in 1869 to the creation of the Lexington Conference of the MEC, which retained its connection to the white denomination. Churches affiliated with the racially autonomous African Methodist Episcopal Church and the African Methodist Episcopal Zion Church (AMEZ) also made significant gains in members due to emancipation. Louisville's Quinn Chapel, which dated to the antebellum era and was known for its abolitionism, became a center of the city's black community and a pioneer in protesting Louisville streetcar segregation in 1870 and 1871, as well as calling for greater voting rights for Kentucky blacks.[62]

Henry Adams, the long-standing minister of Louisville's Fifth Street Baptist Church, helped to create the State Convention of Colored Baptists in August 1865. Beset by infighting among convention leaders for the first few years, the organization reemerged in 1869 with a new name, the General Association of Colored Baptists, claiming dozens of churches from every corner of the state and 12,260 members. Those numbers continued to swell over the next decade, and by 1880 the General Association recorded just fewer than 40,000 members.[63]

For many in the denomination, the causes of freedom and Christianity were inseparable from education. Kentucky's African American Baptists had long supported the establishment of local, church-based Sunday Schools for the training of children in the rudiments of Christian faith and social morality. Yet for many this education was not nearly enough to sustain their faith. Black Baptists such as Henry Adams; Paducah pastor George W. Dupee, who also edited the *Baptist Herald* when it launched in 1873; and lay leader Henry C. Marrs all pushed for the founding of an institution to train African American ministers. In 1879, the General Association approved plans for the establishment of the Baptist Normal and Theological Institute in Louisville for the training of clergy, which also received financial support from Kentucky's white Baptists. Henry C. Marrs convinced his brother – educator and minister Elijah P. Marrs – to help lead in the institution's founding. Within a year, the pastor of Lexington's historic black First Baptist Church, William J. Simmons agreed to preside over the college. Simmons was a former Union soldier, who had enlisted at age fifteen and had later been educated at Howard University. Although the school

[62] Wright, *Life behind a Veil*, 36–7, 129; Lucas, *History of Blacks in Kentucky*, 223–4; *Minutes of the Annual Conferences of the Methodist Episcopal Church for the Year 1866* (New York: Carlton & Porter, 1866), 9; Walter H. Riley, *Forty Years in the Lap of Methodism: History of the Lexington Conference of the Methodist Episcopal Church* (Louisville: Mayes Printing, 1915).

[63] Lucas, *History of Blacks in Kentucky*, 211–12; *Minutes of the First General Association of Colored Baptists in Kentucky, Held in the First Baptist Church, Lexington, Kentucky, August 3rd, 4th, 5th, 6th, and 7th, 1869* (Louisville: Louisville Anzeiger, 1869), 3; *Minutes of the General Association of Colored Baptists of Kentucky, Held with Fourth Street Baptist Church, Owensboro, Ky. August 11th, 12th, 13th, 14th, 15th, 1880* (Louisville: A. C. Caperton, 1880), 31.

was hampered by financial difficulties, Simmons steered it toward viability and an expanded curriculum in his ten years as president.[64]

The general post-emancipation trend in the religious life of black Kentuckians toward greater autonomy from whites, with the exception of receiving financial assistance, was widespread in the South. Although free black Christianity in Kentucky claimed a pre-emancipation history, elsewhere in the South more localized African American withdrawals from white congregations preceded a wider withdrawal of southern African Americans from white denominations. But autonomy did not always mean that Kentucky blacks overtly politicized their religion. Whereas the AME and AMEZ were famous for their civil rights advocacy, Baptists generally shied away from such approaches. Henry Adams in particular stressed the significance of hard work and thrift as the path to social respectability.[65]

But in some instances, the institutional ties between black and white Christians remained complicated. The December 1870 creation of the Colored Methodist Episcopal (CME) Church in Jackson, Tennessee, was a watershed moment in what historians have come to know as the mass African American exodus of southern blacks from white denominations after emancipation. Given the blessing of the Methodist Episcopal Church, South, for the creation of a separate black denomination, whites continued to financially support CME efforts. Where some historians have seen CME leadership as participants in a "new paternalism" that established the boundaries of the South's new racial order, many southern blacks were limited in their church options after the war – whether by rural location or a simple unwillingness to consider other churches for deeply held theological reasons.[66]

Kentucky black Methodist life after emancipation was particularly rife with these sorts of tensions. The African Methodist Episcopal Zion Church organized its Kentucky Conference in June 1866 at Center Street Church in Louisville – a church that withdrew from the MECS during the war. Within two years, however, the MECS won the legal right to reclaim the Center Street Church property because many African American members wanted to remain connected to it, a story that played out throughout the state.

---

[64] Lucas, *History of Blacks in Kentucky*, 212–19; Marrs, *Life and History of the Rev. Elijah P. Marrs*, 119–29. For one representative account of support for Sunday Schools, see "District S.S. Convention, Mayfield, Ky., Oct. 31, '73," *Baptist Herald*, January 1874.

[65] Wright, *Life behind a Veil*, 36–7; Lucas, *History of Blacks in Kentucky*, 222–3.

[66] Reginald F. Hildebrand, *The Times Were Strange and Stirring: Methodist Preachers and the Crisis of Emancipation* (Durham: Duke University Press, 1995), 3–27; Katherine L. Dvorak, *An African-American Exodus: The Segregation of the Southern Churches* (New York: Carlson, 1991), especially 132–8, 160–8, on the formation of the Colored Methodist Episcopal Church; and Stowell, *Rebuilding Zion*, 89. On the broad ecclesiastical negotiations that freedpeople faced, which were by no means straightforward, see Charles F. Irons, "'Two Divisions of the Same Great Army': Ecclesiastical Separation by Race and the Millennium," in *Apocalypse and the Millennium in the American Civil War Era*, eds. Ben Wright and Zachary W. Dresser (Baton Rouge: Louisiana State University Press, 2013), 194–215.

By the count of one AMEZ report, twelve black congregations in Kentucky were "lost" to what became the CME in the late 1860s. Yet if AMEZ critics may have disapproved of their actions, the CME in Kentucky still proved a center of black political mobilization and social relief, and later protest against segregation on railroad coaches. The ecclesiastical negotiations that emancipation required often meant agreeing to take white support to ensure keeping older church properties and allowing autonomy of religious practice in otherwise hostile countryside. But it did not mean an easy acquiescence to white demands.[67]

Yet however important the creation of the CME was for the flourishing of black religious life, that signal event gave southern white Methodists yet another chance to assume their own religio-racial superiority. In the report on the CME's founding, African American Methodists "gratefully acknowledge[d] the obligations we are under to the white brethren of the Methodist Episcopal Church, South, for what they have done for us, as a people." Moreover, in the *Christian Observer*, Kentucky whites pilloried a northern critique that called the creation of the CME "an abuse of denominationalism" because race, not "honest differences in evangelical belief or church politics," was the only reason for religious segregation.[68]

In many ways, this contention was quite accurate. Racial separation was a familiar and easily accessible solution to the unwanted problem of interracial interaction. Indeed, for more than fifty years, religiously conservative whites in the Commonwealth had been advocating racial segregation in the name of colonizationism. Although the historical scholarship on white support for African American expatriation after 1865 is considerably underdeveloped, there can be no question that it remained a popular idea in the white mind well into the late nineteenth century. The end of slavery did not obviate the need for black removal from white America. As a *Western Recorder* appeal put it in 1869, "colored missions" were required for the "preaching of the gospel to this unfortunate and needy race." Or, perhaps funds could be generated for "efforts to evangelize Africa" using "colored ministers" from the United States. In that proposed plan, African American believers would work for the Christianization of a heathen continent, and then it was hoped that "this same people in our own midst" would not "be left to retrograde into superstitious errors, and perhaps to barbarism."[69]

[67] Lucas, *History of Blacks in Kentucky*, 223–4; J. W. Hood, *One Hundred Years of the African Methodist Episcopal Zion Church; Or, The Centennial of African Methodism* (New York: A. M. E. Zion Book Concern, 1895), 327–36, quote 329.
[68] "Colored General Conference," *Christian Observer*, January 7, 1871; "Brief Editorials," *Christian Observer*, January 21, 1871.
[69] "Colored Missions – The Envelope Plan," *Western Recorder*, June 26, 1869; "The School for Colored Ministers," *Western Recorder*, November 20, 1869.

Despite the fact that the American Colonization Society did not dissolve until 1964 and operated in an exceedingly limited capacity after 1912, almost every major study of the white

To be sure, whites in the Commonwealth who endorsed colonization in the postslavery era did express concern for African American souls. However, as with antebellum arguments, such articulations always came in a racially paternalistic mode that assumed black inferiority. In April 1869 Thomas S. Malcolm of Philadelphia – who pastored Louisville's Second Baptist Church during the 1840s – appealed for "Emigration" in the name of the "missionary cause." Malcolm was a manager of the Pennsylvania Colonization Society, and as he saw it, there existed a divine "call upon pious freedmen to carry the gospel of Jesus Christ to the perishing millions of heathen in Africa." Just under a decade later, the *Western Recorder* published a succession of articles on "Our African Missions," detailing "the great amount of human happiness" among the "moral and religious" colonists in Liberia. The solution to America's race problem, which also produced the tangible benefit of Christianizing and civilizing a pagan continent, was colonization.[70]

As was the case in the antebellum era, because of colonizationism's overt emphasis on racial separatism – expressly due to white assumptions of black inferiority – advocates of the scheme shared fundamental aspects of the racial ideology of other white, more secular, political and racial conservatives. Indeed, it required only a small conceptual jump for Kentucky's white evangelicals to move from advocating racial separatism along religious lines to supporting rigid segregation in all other social and political arenas. In August 1869 the *Western Recorder* printed a letter from Thomas C. Teasdale, a noted Baptist minister with roots in Pennsylvania and New Jersey. Teasdale assessed the state of race relations around him by commenting, "How strange it seems that negro children should sit side by side with white children in our schools, and churches; that negroes should be elected to seats in the American Congress; that the judicial ermine should be enjoyed by black men." Teasdale, writing from New York City, contended that "even here in the North" there existed sustained, "strong repugnance" from whites to the idea of "social equality with the negroes." It was a sad day for America, Teasdale argued, when "the

colonization movement ends in 1865. See, for example, P. J. Staudenraus, *The African Colonization Movement, 1816–1865* (New York: Columbia University Press, 1961); and Eric Burin, *Slavery and the Peculiar Solution: A History of the American Colonization Society* (Gainesville: University Press of Florida, 2005). An exception is William Cohen, *At Freedom's Edge: Black Mobility and the White Quest for Racial Control, 1861–1915* (Baton Rouge: Louisiana State University Press, 1991), 138–67. Steven Hahn, *A Nation under Our Feet: Black Political Struggles in the Rural South from Slavery to the Great Migration* (Cambridge, MA: Belknap Press of Harvard University Press, 2003), 317–63, focuses on colonization in the context of black political aspirations after slavery, but all the same emphasizes the ACS's postwar white supremacist history.

70 Thomas S. Malcolm, "Emigration to Liberia," *Western Recorder*, April 24, 1869; "Pennsylvania Colonization Society," *African Repository* 49 (January 1873): 28; T. "Our African Missions. VI. – Liberia," *Western Recorder*, January 3, 1878.

colored man should be thus thrust into place and power, without much regard to qualifications" required for "these prominent positions."[71]

Similarly, an early 1871 *Christian Observer* editorial reported the "Considerable excitement" in "the District of Columbia" over a "a bill" proposed by noted Republican senator Charles Sumner – the prominent congressional abolitionist from Massachusetts and a favorite "radical" target of southern white derision – "compelling colored children to attend the white schools of [the] city." As whites throughout the South contended, the article's author "conceded that it will utterly ruin the public school system." As the white Methodist paper saw it, "The schools are now separate and are in a most flourishing condition.... Every right-minded man will condemn this action as unjust, humiliating, and intended to disgrace the white children who are too poor to attend select schools." School integration was nothing more than "a crime deserving the just indignation which it cannot but evoke from the friends of humanity everywhere." For Kentucky whites, their racial superiority was an unquestioned assumption. Thus the segregation of the races, already underway in the churches, extended for Kentucky's religious conservatives to every aspect of life.[72]

The racial separation of the churches – formalized among Southern Methodists but ubiquitous throughout the South after emancipation – became a critical component in the making of a distinctively white southern religion after the Civil War. Evangelical in tone, stridently anti-northern in geographical outlook, and constructed for whites only, this brand of Christianity made for a potent ideological amalgam that inspired a long-lasting white southern racist hegemony. For ex-Confederates, their convictions about the course of the war were inextricable from beliefs in the righteousness of slavery, anti-abolitionism, and white supremacy.[73]

That whites in Kentucky came to broad religious agreement with such a Confederate-minded religious outlook is ironic given the state's maintenance of a Union allegiance during the Civil War. But it is not surprising. During

---

[71] Thomas C. Teasdale, Letter from New York, July 26, 1869, *Western Recorder*, August 7, 1869.
[72] "Negroes in the Schools," *Christian Observer*, February 11, 1871. On Sumner and the proposed integration of Washington, DC, schools, as well as the significant moderate Republican opposition to the proposal for reasons of white supremacy, see Robert Harrison, "An Experimental Station for Lawmaking: Congress and the District of Columbia, 1862–1878," *Civil War History* 53 (March 2007): 47–50; and Kate Masur, *An Example for All the Land: Emancipation and the Struggle for Equality in Washington, D.C.* (Chapel Hill: University of North Carolina Press, 2010), 188–94. It is important to note that for different reasons, having to do with black aspirations for autonomy, many African Americans also did not support integrated schools.
[73] For a compelling synthetic survey that analyzes the formation of a distinctive variety of white southern religion, connected to evangelical theology and "nonpolitical" in outlook, see John B. Boles, *The Irony of Southern Religion* (New York: Peter Lang, 1994). See also Stowell, *Rebuilding Zion*, 33–48.

the Reconstruction era, white Kentuckians drew on long-standing theological arguments in defense of slavery and the racial ordering of society that they themselves had held for decades. For Kentucky – an antebellum border state with an antislavery legacy, and a slave state that remained with the Union during the Civil War – proslavery religion proved a critical ideological building block in the making of the Commonwealth's postwar Confederate identity. It was the source of their redemption, and that awakening aligned Kentucky politically with the ex-Confederate South's white Democratic hegemony.

Epilogue

The Antebellum Past for the Postwar Future

In the mid-1870s Louisville Presbyterian Stuart Robinson was the most politically and culturally influential white minister in Kentucky. For most of the
Civil War era, the staunchly Unionist Presbyterian Robert J. Breckinridge had
rivaled Robinson in the Commonwealth. When Robinson's most notable work,
his Christian defense of slavery, appeared in March 1865, the proslavery
Kentuckian was exiled in Toronto while Breckinridge courted favor with Union
military officers and Republican party leaders.

A decade later, Robinson had no challenger. Breckinridge died in his Danville
home in December 1871, but for nearly a decade earlier it had been clear that
the Bluegrass State's evangelical whites were more sympathetic to Robinson's
proslavery, pro-southern religious outlook. Like Breckinridge, the Louisville
minister had once openly opposed slavery. During the emancipation canvass of
the late 1840s, he cooperated with other religious whites in statewide efforts to
gradually end the institution in the Commonwealth. Yet Robinson never relin-
quished the idea that slavery, along with white supremacy, had been ordained
by God. Robinson never supported northern abolitionism and what he saw
as its heretical, radical agenda to immediately end slavery. With the escala-
tion of the sectional crisis to the Civil War and the death of American slavery
that followed, Robinson became a representative voice among the majority of
Kentucky's religious whites in defying what he saw as a heterodox, abolition-
driven federal agenda. Immediately after the war, the Louisville minister not
only led the vast majority of his fellow Kentucky Presbyterians to align with
the Southern Presbyterian Church but he also became the preeminent voice of
the proslavery, white southern cause in the postwar Commonwealth.

In his 1865 defense of slavery, Robinson had argued that "the whole orthodox biblical learning of the Church expounds the Scriptures on this subject
in one way – and that in the way it is understood in the Southern Church."
By contrast, abolitionism was a "perversion" of the Christian gospel, which

ignored the plain teaching of the Bible. With emancipation all but secured at the date of publication, Robinson lambasted the "dogmas of the noisy, cant-ing, infidel philanthropism whose prophets have seduced" the American public "to follow the pretended revelations of natural reason, 'spiritual insight,' and 'universal love,' instead of Jehovah's prophets whom their fathers followed." It was Robinson's hope that, after reading his book, true believers would give abolitionist ideas a "sober second thought," recognize how they contravened scriptural mandates, and understand the "relation of master and slave" as divinely sanctioned.[1]

Robinson saw that hope realized. Although slavery itself was dead by the end of 1865, old religious ideas about the righteousness of the institution con-tinued to live on – and indeed gained new life. Those ideas spanned the Civil War era and proved crucial to the forging of sectional identity in postbel-lum Kentucky, and not just among Robinson's own Presbyterians. Kentucky Methodists, already belonging to the southern sectional branch Methodist Episcopal Church, South, followed a similar pattern. Both the Louisville and Kentucky Conferences retained vocal minorities of Unionists, but like white believers throughout Kentucky after the Civil War, Methodists in the Com-monwealth found effective ways to keep northern sympathizers from positions of leadership and power.[2]

In July 1874 the *Central Methodist*, the weekly newspaper of the Kentucky Conference of the Methodist Episcopal Church, South, published a forceful article on antebellum slavery. Titled "Was Our Position on the Slavery Question Scriptural?" the essay answered the question it posed forthrightly: unapologet-ically, the answer was yes. For the last several years, the *Central Methodist*, like Methodist papers throughout the country, had offered opinion on whether or not the northern and southern branches of national Methodism should engage in "fraternal relations." Now in 1874, nearly a decade after the Civil War and the Thirteenth Amendment – and thirty years after the great Methodist slavery schism of 1844 that rent what had been America's largest religious group – some Methodists in both the North and South realized that denominational reunion would not be quick and easy. Instead of pursuing reunion outright, they held out hope that the sectional churches might agree to labor in Christian "fraternity," not hostility. Perhaps fraternal relations would then pave the way for reunion.[3]

The *Central Methodist*, however, could countenance no such reunion. "We don't ask our Northern brethren to come to our opinion. We cannot go to theirs," the essay contended. Speaking for their white Methodist readers in the Bluegrass State, the paper's editors argued, "If [northern Methodists] enter into

[1] Stuart Robinson, *Slavery, As Recognized in the Mosaic Civil Law, Recognized also, and Allowed, in the Abrahamic, Mosaic, and Christian Church* (Toronto: Rollo & Adam, 1865), quotes v, 11.
[2] See Roy Hunter Short, *Methodism in Kentucky* (Rutland, VT: Academy Books, 1979), 25–6.
[3] M., "Was Our Position on the Slavery Question Scriptural?," *Central Methodist*, July 18, 1874.

fraternal relations with us, they must do so with the distinct understanding that we occupy the same ground on this question that we have always occupied." The point was plain, and the decidedly unreconstructed *Central Methodist* wanted its readers to understand: "What we were in 1844 ... we still are."[4]

Just a few months earlier, the paper blamed the split of 1844 on "the unscriptural and radical abolition policy" that some northern Methodists had pursued. The *Central Methodist*'s editors would not pretend that their former enemies were now their allies. Although they had admitted elsewhere that the idea of "free and full" sectional rapprochement was attractive, they refused to endorse it "at the expense of principle." At the most basic level, that principle required the acknowledgment that the antebellum Southern Methodist defense of slavery was biblically correct. By attempting to circumvent the slavery question, supporters of fraternal relations ignored the key issues that led to denominational fracture in the first place. Leaders of "modern abolitionism" had agitated the question and spoken out against the plain teaching of the Bible in favor of slavery. Thus, by insisting on slavery's scriptural sanction nearly a decade after the death of legal slavery, the *Central Methodist* asserted that it remained a divinely approved institution, regardless of legal realities.[5]

Such an opinion had significant political implications, especially when it came to the matters of race so bound up in the postwar era. The *Central Methodist*, like white religious newspapers throughout the South, was a vociferous critic of civil rights for African Americans. Indeed, in the months leading up to the passage of the Civil Rights Act of 1875, the *Central Methodist* openly opposed the bill. In its view, the same "abolition partisans of the Northern and N. western states" who had co-opted national Methodism in the 1840s also brought the agitation that led to the Civil War. Those crimes were part of a long trajectory that had, in the wake of Confederate defeat, allowed for "the elevation of the lowest and worst citizens to offices of trust and power, and to bear rule in the allotment of our privileges and civil rights." Indeed, Northern Methodism was complicit in enabling the "worst features affecting society," because it had sent hundreds of "carpet-bag preachers" south. These, along with other representatives of "Northern Methodism," "[w]hile in the South ... prate lustily, are the champions of many of the most oppressive political measures, [and] are fierce and bitter politicians."[6]

One such example was abolitionist and Radical Republican Gilbert Haven (1821–80) who, in 1872, became the Northern Methodist Church's bishop in Atlanta. Haven cooperated extensively with the Freedmen's Bureau and

---

[4] Ibid.
[5] Ibid.; S. C. Shaw, "Western VA. Conference. Historical Sketches. Extra," *Central Methodist*, April 25, 1874; "Fraternity," *Central Methodist*, May 16, 1874.
[6] S. C. Shaw, "Western VA. Conference. Historical Sketches. Number Three," *Central Methodist*, May 2, 1874; "The Difference," *Central Methodist*, January 5, 1875; "How Do You Like It?," *Central Methodist*, July 26, 1873.

secured funding for what would become the historically black Clark College. After reprinting part of an article by Haven that championed the virtues of integrationism for the postslavery order, the *Central Methodist's* editors did not bother to interpret Haven's writing. They instead asked a question their readers presumably already knew the answer to: "The two ends which this 'Southern Bishop' labors for, chiefly, are the social equality of the races and an 'organic union' with our Church. How do you like the programme?" For Kentucky's white Methodists, the implication was explicit: their true religion was one to be practiced without northern white or African American influence or interference.[7]

As it turned out, fraternal relations came to white American Methodism just a few years later, but on terms southerners found wholly acceptable. After mutual exchanges between the General Conferences of northern and southern Methodism, a joint commission of the two denominations convened in Cape May, New Jersey, in August 1876. There, they agreed that both the northern and southern churches were "a legitimate Branch of Episcopal Methodism in the United States, having a common origin in the Methodist Episcopal Church organized in 1784." Moreover, the Methodist Episcopal Church, South, was affirmed as "an evangelical Church, reared on Scriptural foundations, and her ministers and members, with those of the Methodist Episcopal Church, have constituted one Methodist family, though in distinct ecclesiastical connections." The meaning of the Cape May declaration was plain for anyone paying attention: white Southern Methodism and all that was bound up in that identity – principally the biblical defense of slavery, which they did not apologize for nor did they concede – remained a legitimate form of Christian expression. It was distinct from northern belief, but a true faith all the same. Without compromising a single point, Southern Methodists had gotten exactly what they wanted.[8]

It took Presbyterians several more years to achieve their own version of fraternal relations. Significantly, it occurred only after the 1881 death of one of the southern church's most dogged opponents of such plans – Stuart Robinson. Yet when the PCUSA and PCUS reached an accord the following year, in 1882, the terms were broadly similar to the Methodist version: the tepid agreement required no concession of southern theological principles. Moreover, many of Robinson's old guard Southern Presbyterian compatriots, such as

---

[7] Ibid.

[8] *Formal Fraternity. Proceedings of the General Conference of the Methodist Episcopal Church and of the Methodist Episcopal Church, South, in 1872, 1874, and 1876, and of the Joint Commission of the Two Churches on Fraternal Relations, at Cape May, New Jersey, August 16–23, 1876* (New York: Nelson and Phillips, 1876), 67. On fraternal relations among Methodists, see also Daniel Stowell, *Rebuilding Zion: The Religious Reconstruction of the South, 1863–1877* (New York: Oxford University Press, 1998), 172–5; and Charles T. Thrift, "Rebuilding the Southern Church," in *The History of American Methodism*, ed. Emory Stevens Bucke, et al., 3 vols. (New York: Abingdon Press, 1964), 2:299–303.

Benjamin M. Palmer, ensured that the denomination remained on a southern sectional course for the future.[9]

Matters were plainer and less controversial among Kentucky's Baptists: fraternal relations were not even discussed. The Southern Baptist Convention was far less explicit in its use of historical disputes over slavery to justify ongoing ecclesiastical independence from the northern American Baptist Home Mission Society, but that was only because Baptist ecclesiology required no national polity. More than any other American Protestant tradition, Baptists maintained a rigid commitment to the autonomy of local congregations. Thus, Kentucky Baptists continued to overwhelmingly affirm a southern vision for their faith – a vision ultimately manifest in 1877 with the establishment of the Southern Baptist Theological Seminary in Louisville.[10]

What played out by the early 1880s in denominational ranks had profound ramifications for Kentucky's political order. The antebellum religious past was the key to unlocking its postwar future. It was not simply – or only – the political reality of emancipation that motivated white Kentuckians to identify with the Confederacy after the war. Emancipation's religious meaning factored prominently as well. White Kentuckians drew on long-standing theological proslavery arguments to invoke their religious solidarity with the rest of the white South after the Civil War. As evangelicalism proved central to the making of the antebellum Bible Belt, so it was also constitutive for the postwar Solid South. Thus, white evangelicalism cleared a path for the emergence of Kentucky's postwar political order. It sanctioned ex-Confederate Democratic domination, opposed African American civil rights, and challenged overtures from northern religious and political agents.

Although not all white Kentuckians were Confederates during the war, and certainly not all imagined themselves this way after the fact, to affirm a conservative theological vision was to affirm Confederate politics. At the dawn of emancipation, when most of the state's white Christians shared this belief, a political hegemony constituted by white evangelicalism was ensured. Conservative religion made Confederate Kentucky.

---

[9] See Stowell, *Rebuilding Zion*, 170–2; Ernest Trice Thompson, *Presbyterians in the South*, Vol. 2: *1861–1890* (Richmond: John Knox, 1973), 223–64.

[10] Stowell, *Rebuilding Zion*, 170–8; and Gregory A. Wills, *The Southern Baptist Theological Seminary, 1859–2009* (New York: Oxford University Press, 2009), 75–83.

Bibliography of Primary Sources

Periodicals

Abolition Intelligencer and Missionary Magazine, Shelbyville, KY
African Repository, Washington, DC
Baltimore Literary and Religious Magazine
Baptist Banner, Louisville
Baptist Herald, Paducah, KY
Biblical Repertory and Princeton Review, Princeton, NJ
Cincinnati *Gazette*
Central Methodist, Catlettsburg, KY
Christian Observer, Catlettsburg, KY
Christian Recorder, Philadelphia
Danville Quarterly Review, Danville, KY
The Examiner, Louisville
Free Christian Commonwealth, Louisville
Kentucky Messenger, Richmond
Lard's Quarterly, Georgetown, KY
The Liberator, Boston
Louisville *Bulletin*
Louisville *Journal*
Millennial Harbinger, Bethany, VA
National Anti-Slavery Standard, New York
New York Times
Southern Presbyterian Review, Columbia, SC
True Presbyterian, Louisville
Voice of the Fugitive, Sandwich, Canada West
Western Recorder, Louisville

Archival Sources

Berea College Founders and Founding Records. Berea College Library. Special Collections and Archives. Berea, KY.

Berea College Board of Trustees Records. Berea College Library. Special Collections and Archives. Berea, KY.

Breckinridge, Robert Jefferson (1800–71), Papers. The Filson Historical Society. Louisville.

Burbridge, Stephen Gano (1831–94), Papers. The Filson Historical Society. Louisville.

Buck Run Baptist Church Records. Kentucky Historical Society. Frankfort.

Central University Collection. Eastern Kentucky University Library. Special Collections and Archives. Richmond.

Forks of Otter Creek Baptist Church Records. Forks of Otter Creek Cemetery Association. Kentucky Historical Society. Frankfort.

McElroy, William Thomas (1829–1910), Papers. The Filson Historical Society. Louisville.

Pendleton, James M. (1811–91), Journal. Department of Library Special Collections, Manuscripts. Western Kentucky University. Bowling Green.

Robinson, Stuart (1814–81), Papers. The Filson Historical Society. Louisville.

South Benson Baptist Church Records. Kentucky Historical Society. Frankfort.

Published Sources

Acts Passed at the First Session of the Forty-Fourth General Assembly of the Commonwealth of Kentucky. Frankfort, KY: J. H. Holeman, 1836.

The Address of the Southern and Western Liberty Convention, to the People of the United States. Cincinnati: Gazette, 1845.

Baptist Home Missions in North America; Including a Full Report of the Proceedings and Addresses of the Jubilee Meeting, and a Historical Sketch of the American Baptist Home Mission Society, Historical Tables, Etc., 1832–1882. New York: Baptist Home Mission Books, 1883.

Barnes, Albert. *An Inquiry into the Scriptural Views of Slavery*. Philadelphia: Perkins and Purves, 1846.

Bascom, Henry B. *Methodism and Slavery: with Other Matters in Controversy between the North and the South; Being a Review of the Manifesto of the Majority, in Reply to the Protest of the Minority, of the Late General Conference of the Methodist E. Church, in the Case of Bishop Andrew*. Frankfort, KY: Hodges, Todd, and Pruett, 1845.

Beecher, Lyman. *A Plea for the West*. Cincinnati: Truman and Smith, 1835.

Berlin, Ira, et al., eds. *Freedom: A Documentary History of Emancipation, 1861–1867*. Ser. 1, Vol. 2. *The Wartime Genesis of Free Labor: The Upper South*. Cambridge: Cambridge University Press, 1993.

Bibb, Henry. *The Life and Adventures of Henry Bibb, an American Slave*. Introduction by Charles J. Heglar. Madison: University of Wisconsin Press, 2001.

Birney, James G. *The American Churches, The Bulwarks of American Slavery*. 3rd ed. Newburyport, MA: Charles Whipple, 1842.

———. *Letter on Colonization, Addressed to the Rev. Thornton J. Mills, Corresponding Secretary of the Kentucky Colonization Society*. New York: Anti-Slavery Reporter, 1834.

_____. *Letter to Ministers and Elders, on the Sin of Holding Slaves, and the Duty of Immediate Emancipation.* n.p., 1834.

Breck, Robert L. *The Habeas Corpus, and Martial Law.* Cincinnati: Richard H. Collins, 1862.

Breckinridge, Robert J. *The Black Race, Some Reflections on its Position and Destiny as Connected with Our American Dispensation.* Frankfort, KY: A. G. Hodges, 1851.

_____. *Discourse of Dr. Breckinridge Delivered on the Day of National Humiliation, January 4, 1861, at Lexington, KY.* Baltimore: John W. Woods, 1861.

_____. *Hints on Slavery.* Lexington: n.p., 1843.

_____. *The Knowledge of God, Objectively Considered: Being the First Part of Theology Considered as a Science of Positive Truth, Both Inductive and Deductive.* New York: Robert Carter, 1858.

_____. *The Knowledge of God, Subjectively Considered: Being the Second Part of Theology Considered as a Science of Positive Truth, Both Inductive and Deductive.* New York: Robert Carter, 1860.

_____. *The Question of Negro Slavery and the New Constitution of Kentucky.* Lexington: n.p., 1849.

_____. *Speech of Robert J. Breckinridge, Delivered on the Courthouse Yard at Lexington, KY. On the 12th day of October, 1840, in Reply to the Speech of Robert Wickliffe.* . . . Lexington: N. L. & J. W. Finnel, 1840.

_____. *The Third Defence of Robert J. Breckinridge Against the Calumnies of Robert Wickliffe.* . . . n.p., 1842.

Brown, Isaac V. *Biography of the Rev. Robert Finley,* 2nd ed. 1857. Reprint, New York: Arno Press, 1969.

Buck, William C. *The Slavery Question.* Louisville: Harney, Hughes and Hughes, 1849.

Clay, Henry. *An Address Delivered to the Colonization Society of Kentucky, at Frankfort, December 17, 1829.* Frankfort, KY: J. H. Holeman, 1830.

Colver, Nathaniel. *The Fugitive Slave Bill: Or, God's Laws Paramount to the Laws of Men. A Sermon, Preached on Sunday, October 20, 1850.* Boston: J. M. Hewes, 1850.

A Committee of the Synod of Kentucky. *An Address to the Presbyterians of Kentucky, Proposing a Plan for the Instruction and Emancipation of their Slaves.* Cincinnati: Taylor and Tracy, 1835.

A Committee of the Synod of Kentucky. *An Address to the Presbyterians of Kentucky, Proposing a Plan for the Instruction and Emancipation of their Slaves.* 1835. Reprint, Newburyport, MA: Charles Whipple, 1836.

Communication from Commissioners of the Kentucky Conference to the Legislature of Kentucky, in Reply to a Memorial from the Trustees of Augusta College. Lexington: Observer and Reporter, 1843.

Crothers, Samuel. *Strictures on African Slavery.* Rossville, OH: Taylor Webster, 1833.

Dabney, Robert L. *A Defence of Virginia, and Through Her, of the South.* New York: E. J. Hale & Son, 1867.

Debate at the Lane Seminary, Cincinnati. Boston: Garrison & Knapp, 1834.

Debate on "Modern Abolitionism," in the General Methodist Conference of the Episcopal Church. Held in Cincinnati, May, 1836. Cincinnati: Ohio Anti-Slavery Society, 1836.

Debate on Slavery: Held in the City of Cincinnati, on the First, Second, Third, and Sixth Days of October, 1845, upon the Question: Is Slave-holding in Itself Sinful, and the Relation between Master and Slave, a Sinful Relation? Cincinnati: William H. Moore, 1846.

Declaration and Testimony against the Erroneous and Heretical Doctrines and Practices Which Have Obtained and Been Propagated in the Presbyterian Church, in the United States, during the Last Five Years. 2ⁿᵈ ed. n.p., 1865.

Declaration of Sentiments and Constitution of the American Anti-Slavery Society. Philadelphia: Pennsylvania Anti-Slavery Society, 1861.

Discussion on American Slavery between George Thompson, Esq., and Rev. Robert J. Breckinridge, Holden in the Rev. Dr. Wardlaw's Chapel, Glasgow, Scotland. 2nd American ed. Annotated by William Lloyd Garrison. Boston: Isaac Knapp, 1836.

Discussion on American Slavery, in Dr. Wardlaw's Chapel, between Mr. George Thompson and the Rev. R. J. Breckinridge of Baltimore, United States, on the Evenings of the 13ᵗʰ, 14ᵗʰ, 15ᵗʰ, 16ᵗʰ, and 17ᵗʰ June, 1836, 2ⁿᵈ ed. Glasgow: George Gallie, 1836.

The Distinctive Principles of the Presbyterian Church in the United States, Commonly Called the Southern Presbyterian Church, as Set Forth in the Formal Declarations, and Illustrated by Extracts from Proceedings of the General Assembly, from 1861–70. Richmond: Presbyterian Committee of Publication [1871].

Dumond, Dwight L., ed. *The Letters of James Gillespie Birney, 1831–1857.* 2 vols. Gloucester, MA: Peter Smith, 1966.

Eaton, Clement, ed. "Minutes and Resolutions of an Emancipation Meeting in Kentucky in 1849." *Journal of Southern History* 14 (November 1948): 541–5.

Fast Day Sermons: Or the Pulpit on the State of the Country. New York: Rudd & Carelton, 1861.

Finney, Charles G. *Lectures on Revivals of Religion.* New York: Leavitt, Lord, and Co., 1835.

Fee, John G. *An Anti-Slavery Manual, Being an Examination in the Light of the Bible, and of Facts into the Moral and Social Wrongs of American Slavery, with a Remedy for the Evil.* 1848. Reprint, New York: Arno Press, 1969.

———. *An Anti-Slavery Manual or, The wrongs of American Slavery exposed by the Light of the Bible and of Facts, with a Remedy for the Evil.* 2ⁿᵈ ed. New York: William Harned, 1851.

———. *Autobiography of John G. Fee.* Chicago: National Christian Association, 1891.

———. "Circular No. 2. To the Citizens of Madison County, Kentucky." n.p., 1859. Printed circular. In Berea College Founders and Founding Records, Berea College Archives, Berea, KY.

———. *Colonization. The Present Scheme of Colonization Wrong, Delusive, and Retards Emancipation.* Cincinnati: American Reform Tract and Book Society, [1854].

———. *Non-Fellowship with Slaveholders the Duty of Christians.* New York: John A. Gray, 1851.

———. *The Sinfulness of Slaveholding as Shown by Appeals to Reason and Scripture.* New York: John A. Gray, 1851.

———. "To the Citizens of Madison County." n.p., 1859. Printed circular. In Berea College Founders and Founding Records, Berea College Archives, Berea, KY.

Formal Fraternity. Proceedings of the General Conference of the Methodist Episcopal Church and of the Methodist Episcopal Church, South, in 1872, 1874, and 1876, and of the Joint Commission of the Two Churches on Fraternal Relations, at Cape May, New Jersey, August 16–23, 1876. New York: Nelson and Phillips, 1876.

Fuller, Richard, and Francis Wayland. *Domestic Slavery Considered as a Scriptural Institution: In a Correspondence between the Rev. Richard Fuller of Beaufort, S. C., and the Rev. Francis Wayland, of Providence, R. I.* New York: Lewis Colby, 1845.

Garrison, William Lloyd. *Thoughts on African Colonization.* 1832. Reprint, New York: Arno Press, 1968.

Hardin, Mark. *Action of the General Assembly on Slavery.* Louisville: Hanna & Duncan, 1865.

Hay, Melba Porter, ed. *The Papers of Henry Clay.* Vol. 10: *Candidate, Compromiser, Elder Statesman, January 1, 1844–June 29, 1852.* Lexington: University Press of Kentucky, 1991.

Henson, Josiah. *The Life of Josiah Henson, Formerly a Slave, Now an Inhabitant of Canada, as Narrated by Himself.* Boston: Arthur D. Phelps, 1849.

History of the Organization of the Methodist Episcopal Church, South. Nashville: South-Western Christian Advocate, 1845.

Hood, J. W. *One Hundred Years of the African Methodist Episcopal Zion Church; Or, The Centennial of African Methodism.* New York: A. M. E. Zion Book Concern, 1895.

Humphrey, Edward P. *The Color Question. A Letter Written for the Sixtieth Annual Meeting of the American Colonization Society, Washington, D.C., January 16, 1877.* Washington, DC: Colonization Room, 1877.

Jones, Charles C. *The Religious Instruction of the Negroes.* Savannah: Thomas Purse, 1842.

Journals of the General Conference of the Methodist Episcopal Church. Vol. 2: *1840, 1844.* New York: Carlton and Phillips, 1856.

Leftwich, W. M. *Martyrdom in Missouri: A History of Religious Proscription, the Seizure of Churches, and the Persecution of Ministers of the Gospel, in the State of Missouri During the Late Civil War and under the "Test Oath" of the New Constitution.* 2 vols. St. Louis: Southwestern Book and Publishing, 1870.

Marrs, Elijah P. *Life and History of the Rev. Elijah P. Marrs, First Pastor of Beargrass Baptist Church and Author.* Louisville: Bradley & Gilbert, 1885.

Memorial of the Education Convention [Held at Lexington, Ky., May 7th and 8th, 1872.] To the Synod of Kentucky. n.p., [1872]. In Central University Collection. Eastern Kentucky University Special Collections and Archives. Richmond, KY.

Minutes of the Annual Conferences of the Methodist Episcopal Church, for the Years 1839–1845. Vol. 3. New York: T. Mason and G. Lane, 1840.

Minutes of the Annual Conferences of the Methodist Episcopal Church for the Year 1866. New York: Carlton & Porter, 1866.

The Minutes of the Christian Anti-Slavery Convention, Assembled April 17th–20th, 1850. Cincinnati, Ohio. [Cincinnati]: Franklin Book and Job Rooms, 1850.

Minutes of the First General Association of Colored Baptists in Kentucky, Held in the First Baptist Church, Lexington, Kentucky, August 3rd, 4th, 5th, 6th, and 7th, 1869. Louisville: Louisville Anzeiger, 1869.

Minutes of the General Association of Colored Baptists of Kentucky, Held with Fourth Street Baptist Church, Owensboro, Ky. August 11th, 12th, 13th, 14th, 15th, 1880. Louisville: A. C. Caperton, 1880.

Narrative of the Late Riotous Proceedings against the Liberty of the Press, in Cincinnati. Cincinnati: Ohio Anti-Slavery Society, 1836.

"Palmyra Manifesto." In *Sourcebook of American Methodism,* ed. Frederick A. Norwood, 330–2. Nashville: Abingdon Press, 1982.

Nott, Josiah C., George R. Gliddon, et al. *Types of Mankind: Or, Ethnological Researches, Based upon the Ancient Monuments, Paintings, Sculptures, and Crania of Races, and upon their Natural, Geographical, Philological and Biblical History,* 2nd ed. Philadelphia: Lippincott, Grambo, & Co., 1854.

Official Proceedings of the Convention of the Democratic Party of Kentucky. Held in the City of Louisville, May 1st, 1866. n.p., n.d. [1866].

Origin and Principles of Berea Literary Institution. n.p. [1866]. In Berea College Founders and Founding Records, Berea College Archives, Berea, KY.

"Our Idea." *The Presbyterial Critic and Monthly Review* 1:1 (January 1855). In *A Kingdom Not of This World: Stuart Robinson's Struggle to Distinguish the Sacred from the Secular during the Civil War,* ed. Preston D. Graham Jr., 193–9. Macon, GA: Mercer University Press, 2002.

Palmer, Benjamin M., ed. *The Life and Letters of James Henley Thornwell.* 1875. Reprint, Edinburgh: Banner of Truth, 1986.

Pendleton, James M. *The Condition of the Baptist Cause in Kentucky in 1837: An Address Delivered at the Jubilee of the General Association of Kentucky Baptists, in Walnut Street Baptist Church, Louisville, Oct. 20, 1887.* n.p., n.d.

_____. *Letters to Rev. W. C. Buck, In Review of His Articles on Slavery.* n.p., 1849.

_____. *An Old Landmark Re-Set.* Nashville: Graves & Marks, 1854.

_____. *Reminiscences of a Long Life.* Louisville: Press Baptist Book Concern, 1891.

A Presbyterian in the South. *A System of Prospective Emancipation, Advocated in Kentucky, By Robert J. Breckinridge, D.D., and Urged and Supported in the Princeton Review, in Article VI. – October, 1849.* Charleston: Walker & James, 1850.

Presidential Election, 1864. Proceedings of the National Union Convention Held in Baltimore, Md., June 7th and 8th, 1864. New York: Baker & Goodwin, 1864.

Proceedings of the Kentucky Anti-Slavery Society, Auxiliary to the American Antislavery Society at its First Meeting in Danville, Ky. March 19th, 1835. n.p., 1835.

Ralston, Thomas N., ed. *Posthumous Works of the Rev. Henry B. Bascom.* 4 vols. Nashville: E. Stevenson and F. A. Owen, 1855–1856.

Redford, A. H. *Life and Times of H. H. Kavanaugh, D.D., One of the Bishops of the Methodist Episcopal Church, South.* Nashville: n.p., 1884.

A Resident. *"Truth Is Stranger than Fiction": New Orleans as It Is.* Utica, NY: DeWitt C. Grove, 1849.

Rice, N. L. *The Old and New Schools: An Exhibit of the Most Important Differences in their Doctrines and Church Polity.* 2nd ed. Cincinnati: John D. Thorpe, 1853.

Ripley, C. Peter, et al., eds. *The Black Abolitionist Papers.* Vol. 2: *Canada, 1830–1865.* Chapel Hill: University of North Carolina Press, 1986.

Robinson, Stuart. *An Appeal to the Christian Public, and All with Whom Loyalty Is Not Madness.* Louisville: Hanna & Co., 1862.

_____. *The Church of God as an Essential Element of the Gospel, and the Idea, Structure, and Functions Thereof.* Philadelphia: Joseph M. Wilson, 1858.

_____. *The Relations of the Secular and Spiritual Power.* Louisville: Bradley & Gilbert, 1859.

_____. *Slavery, as Recognized in the Mosaic Civil Law, Recognized Also, and Allowed, in the Abrahamic, Mosaic, and Christian Church.* Toronto: Rollo & Adam, 1865.

Sears, Richard D. ed., *Camp Nelson, Kentucky: A Civil War History.* Lexington: University Press of Kentucky, 2002.

Stanton, Henry B. *Random Recollections.* 3rd ed. New York: Harper Brothers, 1887.

Stanton, Robert L. *The Church and the Rebellion: A Consideration of the Rebellion against the Government of the United States; and the Agency of the Church, North and South, in Relation Thereto.* New York: Derby & Miller, 1864.

Statement of the Reasons Which Induced the Students of Lane Seminary to Dissolve Their Connection with that Institution. Cincinnati: n.p., 1834.

Tappan, Lewis. *History of the American Missionary Association: Its Constitution and Principles.* New York: n.p., 1855.

Tarrant, Carter. *History of the Baptised Ministers and Churches in Kentucky, &c. Friends to Humanity.* Frankfort, KY: William Hunter, 1808.

Thornwell, James Henley. *The Collected Writings of James Henley Thornwell.* 4 vols. Edited by John B. Adger and John L. Girardeau. 1873. Reprint, Carlisle, PA: Banner of Truth, 1974.

Van Dyke, Henry Jackson. *The Character and Influence of Abolitionism! A Sermon Preached in the First Presbyterian Church, of Brooklyn, on Sunday Evening, December 9th, 1860,* 2nd ed. Baltimore: Henry Taylor, 1860.

Walker, David. *Appeal to the Colored Citizens of the World.* Edited by Peter P. Hinks. University Park: Pennsylvania State University Press, 2000.

The War of the Rebellion: A Compilation of the Official Records of the Union and Confederate Armies. 70 vols. Washington, DC: Government Printing Office, 1880–1901.

Wickliffe, Robert. *A Further Reply of Robert Wickliffe to the Billingsgate Abuse of Robert Judas Breckinridge, Otherwise Called Robert Jefferson Breckinridge.* Lexington: Kentucky Gazette, 1843.

_____. *Speech of Robert Wickliffe Delivered in the Court House, in Lexington, on Monday, the 10th day of August, 1840, Upon Resigning His Seat as Senator from the County of Fayette, More Especially in Reference to the "Negro Law."* Lexington: Observer & Reporter, 1840.

_____. *Speech of Robert Wickliffe, In Reply to the Rev. R. J. Breckinridge, Delivered in the Court House, in Lexington, on Monday, the 9th November, 1840.* Lexington: Observer & Reporter, 1840.

Wilson, Clyde N., ed. *The Papers of John C. Calhoun.* Vol. 22: *1845–1846.* Columbia: University of South Carolina Press, 1995.

Wilson, Joseph M. *The Presbyterian Historical Almanac, and Annual Remembrancer of the Church, for 1862.* Philadelphia: Joseph M. Wilson, 1862.

_____. *Presbyterian Historical Almanac and Annual Remembrancer of the Church, for 1863.* Philadelphia: Joseph M. Wilson, 1863.

_____. *Presbyterian Historical Almanac and Annual Remembrancer for the Church, for 1866.* Philadelphia: Joseph M. Wilson, 1866.

Wilson, Samuel R. *Causes and Remedies of Impending National Calamities.* Cincinnati: J. B. Elliot, 1860.

————. *Reply to the Attack of Rev. R. J. Breckinridge, D.D., L.L.D., upon the Louisville Presbytery, and Defence of the "Declaration and Testimony," Made in the Synod of Kentucky, October 16, A. D., 1865.* Louisville: Hanna & Duncan, 1865.

Young, Bennett H. *Confederate Wizards of the Saddle: Being Reminiscences and Observations of One Who Rode with Morgan.* 1914. Reprint, Nashville: J. S. Sanders, 1999.

————. *History and Texts of the Three Constitutions of Kentucky.* Louisville: Courier-Journal, 1890.

Index

Lightning Source UK Ltd.
Milton Keynes UK
UKOW01f0532240817
307878UK00001B/61/P